UNIX System Laboratories, Inc.

A Subsidiary of AT&T

UNIX® SYSTEM V RELEASE 4

User's Guide

Published by Prentice-Hall, Inc.
A Division of Simon & Schuster
Englewood Cliffs, New Jersey 07632

IMPORTANT NOTE TO USERS

While every effort has been made to ensure the accuracy of all information in this document, AT&T assumes no liability to any party for any loss or damage caused by errors or omissions or by statements of any kind in this document, its updates, supplements, or special editions, whether such errors are omissions or statements resulting from negligence, accident, or any other cause. AT&T further assumes no liability arising out of the application or use of any product or system described herein; nor any liability for incidental or consequential damages arising from the use of this document. AT&T disclaims all warranties regarding the information contained herein, whether expressed, implied or statutory, *including implied warranties of merchantability or fitness for a particular purpose.* AT&T makes no representation that the interconnection of products in the manner described herein will not infringe on existing or future patent rights, nor do the descriptions contained herein imply the granting or license to make, use or sell equipment constructed in accordance with this description.

AT&T reserves the right to make changes without further notice to any products herein to improve reliability, function, or design.

TRADEMARKS

DOCUMENTER'S WORKBENCH is a registered trademark of UNIX System Laboratories, Inc.
IBM is a registered trademark of International Business Machines.
Teletype is a registered trademark of AT&T.
UNIX is a registered trademark of UNIX System Laboratories, Inc.

10 9 8 7 6 5 4

ISBN 0-13-947052-2

P R E N T I C E   H A L L

ORDERING INFORMATION

UNIX® SYSTEM V, RELEASE 4 DOCUMENTATION

To order single copies of UNIX® SYSTEM V, Release 4 documentation, please call (201) 767-5937.

ATTENTION DOCUMENTATION MANAGERS AND TRAINING DIRECTORS:
For bulk purchases in excess of 30 copies please write to:
Corporate Sales
Prentice Hall
Englewood Cliffs, N.J. 07632.
Or call: (201) 592-2498.

ATTENTION GOVERNMENT CUSTOMERS: For GSA and other pricing information please call (201) 767-5994.

Prentice-Hall International (UK) Limited, *London*
Prentice-Hall of Australia Pty. Limited, *Sydney*
Prentice-Hall Canada Inc., *Toronto*
Prentice-Hall Hispanoamericana, S.A., *Mexico*
Prentice-Hall of India Private Limited, *New Delhi*
Prentice-Hall of Japan, Inc., *Tokyo*
Simon & Schuster Asia Pte. Ltd., *Singapore*
Editora Prentice-Hall do Brasil, Ltda., *Rio de Janeiro*

AT&T UNIX® System V Release 4

General Use and System Administration

UNIX® System V Release 4 Network User's and Administrator's Guide
UNIX® System V Release 4 Product Overview and Master Index
UNIX® System V Release 4 System Administrator's Guide
UNIX® System V Release 4 System Administrator's Reference Manual
UNIX® System V Release 4 User's Guide
UNIX® System V Release 4 User's Reference Manual

General Programmer's Series

UNIX® System V Release 4 Programmer's Guide: ANSI C and Programming Support Tools
UNIX® System V Release 4 Programmer's Guide: Character User Interface (FMLI and ETI)
UNIX® System V Release 4 Programmer's Guide: Networking Interfaces
UNIX® System V Release 4 Programmer's Guide: POSIX Conformance
UNIX® System V Release 4 Programmer's Guide: System Services and Application Packaging Tools
UNIX® System V Release 4 Programmer's Reference Manual

System Programmer's Series

UNIX® System V Release 4 ANSI C Transition Guide
UNIX® System V Release 4 BSD / XENIX® Compatibility Guide
UNIX® System V Release 4 Device Driver Interface / Driver–Kernel Interface (DDI / DKI) Reference Manual
UNIX® System V Release 4 Migration Guide
UNIX® System V Release 4 Programmer's Guide: STREAMS

Contents

5 Framed Access Command Environment Tutorial

6 Line Editor (ed) Tutorial

9 Shell Tutorial

10 awk Tutorial

11 Electronic Mail Tutorial

E Quick Reference to vi Commands

F Summary of Shell Command Language

G Setting up the Terminal

GL Glossary

I Index

Figures and Tables

PREFACE

Preface

Preface

The material in this guide is organized into two major parts: an overview of the UNIX operating system and a set of tutorials on the main tools available on the UNIX system. A brief description of each of these parts follows. The next section of this Preface contains information about the contents of the appendices to the *Guide* and the Glossary. In addition, the last section of this Preface, "Notation Conventions," describes the typographical notation to which all the chapters of this *Guide* conform. Because of its broad application across all chapters of the book, you may want to refer to this section from time to time as you read the *Guide*.

System Overview

The first part of the *Guide* consists of Chapters 1–3, which introduce you to the basic principles of the UNIX operating system. Each chapter builds on information presented in preceding chapters, so it is important to read them in sequence.

- Chapter 1, "What Is the UNIX System?", provides an overview of the operating system.
- Chapter 2, "Basics for UNIX System Users," discusses the general rules and guidelines for using the UNIX system. It covers topics related to using your terminal, obtaining a system account, and establishing contact with the UNIX system.
- Chapter 3, "Using the File System," offers a working perspective of the file system. It introduces commands for building your own directory structure, accessing and manipulating the subdirectories and files you organize within it, and examining the contents of other directories in the system for which you have access permission.

UNIX System Tutorials

The second part of the *Guide* consists of tutorials on the following topics: a new interface with the Unix system, the line and screen editors, the shell command language, the awk programming language, and electronic communication tools. For a thorough understanding of the material, we recommend that you work through the examples and exercises as you read each tutorial. The tutorials assume you understand the concepts introduced in Chapters 1–3.

- Chapter 4, "Overview of the Tutorials," introduces the eight chapters of tutorials that appear in the second half of the *Guide*. It highlights UNIX system capabilities -- such as command execution, text editing, electronic communication, programming, and aids to software development.
- Chapter 5, "Framed Access Command Environment (FACE) Tutorial," introduces a user-friendly interface to the UNIX system.
- Chapter 6, "Line Editor (ed) Tutorial," teaches you how to use the ed text editor to create and modify text on a video display terminal or paper printing terminal.
- Chapter 7, "Screen Editor (vi) Tutorial," teaches you how to use the visual text editor to create and modify text on a video display terminal.

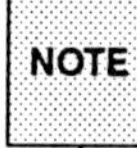

The visual editor, vi, is based on software developed by The University of California, Berkeley, California; Computer Science Division, Department of Electrical Engineering and Computer Science. This software is owned and licensed by the Regents of the University of California.

- Chapter 8, "LP Print Service Tutorial," teaches you how to print hard-copies of files by using the LP print service. It also provides instructions for other services made available by the print service, including enabling and disabling a printer, modifying the format mode of printed pages, and controlling the printing process.
- Chapter 9, "Shell Tutorial," teaches you how to use the shell, both as a command interpreter and as a programming language to create shell programs.

- Chapter 10, "awk Tutorial," explains the syntax, lexical units, and expressions of the language, as well as the use of these to process programs.
- Chapter 11, "Electronic Mail Tutorial," describes all aspects of electronic mail and how to use the commands associated with it.
- Chapter 12, "Communication Tutorial," teaches you how to send messages and files to users of both your UNIX system and other UNIX systems.

Reference Information

Seven appendices and a glossary of UNIX system terms are also provided for reference.

- Appendix A, "Summary of the File System," illustrates how information is stored in the UNIX operating system.
- Appendix B, "Summary of UNIX System Commands," describes, in alphabetical order, each UNIX system command discussed in the *Guide*.
- Appendix C, "Quick Reference to FACE," is a reference for the Framed Access Command Environment, discussed in Chapter 5.
- Appendix D, "Quick Reference to ed Commands," is a quick reference for the line editor, ed. (For details, see Chapter 6, "Line Editor (ed) Tutorial.") The commands are organized by topic, as they are covered in Chapter 6.
- Appendix E, "Quick Reference to vi Commands," is a reference for the full screen editor, vi, discussed in Chapter 7, "Screen Editor (vi) Tutorial." Commands are organized by topic, as covered in Chapter 7.
- Appendix F, "Summary of Shell Command Language," is a summary of the shell command language, notation, and programming constructs, as discussed in Chapter 9, "Shell Tutorial."
- Appendix G, "Setting Up the Terminal," explains how to configure your terminal for use with the UNIX system, and create multiple windows on the screens of terminals with windowing capability.
- The Glossary defines terms pertaining to the UNIX system used in this book.

Notation Conventions

The following notation conventions are used throughout this *Guide.*

`constant width`	User input, such as commands, options and arguments to commands, environment variable names, and the names of directories and files, appear in `constant width`. UNIX system output, such as prompt signs and responses to commands, also appear in `constant width`.
italic	Names of variables to which values must be assigned (such as *password*) and names of books appear in *italic*.
<>	Input that does not appear on the screen when typed, such as passwords, tabs, or RETURN, appear between angle brackets.
<^*char*>	Control characters are shown between angle brackets because they do not appear on the screen when typed. The circumflex (^) represents the control key (usually labeled CTRL). To type a control character, hold down the control key while you type the character specified by *char*. For example, the notation <^d> means to hold down the control key while pressing the D key; the letter D will not appear on the screen.
[ ]	Command options and arguments that are optional, such as `[-msCj]`, are enclosed in brackets.
|	The vertical bar separates optional arguments, from which you may choose one. For example, when a command line has the following format: *command* [*arg1* | *arg2*] You may use either *arg1* or *arg2* when you issue the *command*.

. . .	Ellipses after an argument mean that more than one argument may be used on a single command line.
↑	Arrows on the screen (shown in examples in Chapter 7, "Screen Editor (`vi`) Tutorial", represent the cursor.
command(number)	A command name followed by a number in parentheses refers to the part of a UNIX system reference manual that documents that command. (There are three reference manuals: the *User's Reference Manual, Programmer's Reference Manual,* and *System Administrator's Reference Manual.*) For example, the notation `cat(1)` refers to the page in section 1 (of the *User's Reference Manual*) that documents the `cat` command.

In sample commands, the `$` sign is used as the shell command prompt. This is not true for all systems. Whichever symbol your system uses, keep in mind that prompts are produced by the system; although a prompt is sometimes shown at the beginning of a command line as it would appear on your screen, you are not meant to type it. (The `$` sign is also used to reference the value of positional parameters and named variables; see Chapter 9, "Shell Tutorial", for details.)

In all chapters, full and partial screens are used to display examples of how your terminal screen will look when you interact with the UNIX system. These examples show how to use the UNIX system editors, write short programs, and execute commands. The input (characters typed by you) and output (characters printed by the UNIX system) are shown in these screens in accordance with the conventions listed above. All examples apply regardless of the type of terminal you use.

The commands discussed in each section of a chapter are reviewed at the end of that section. A summary of `vi` commands appears in Appendix E, where they are listed by topic. At the end of some sections, exercises are also provided so you can experiment with the commands. The answers to all the exercises in a chapter are at the end of that chapter.

The text in the *User's Guide* was prepared with the UNIX system text editors described in the *Guide* and formatted with the DOCUMENTER'S WORKBENCH Software.

1. WHAT IS THE UNIX SYSTEM?

1. WHAT IS THE UNIX SYSTEM?

1 What is the UNIX System?

What the UNIX System Does

The UNIX operating system, a set of programs (or software) that controls the computer, acts as the link between you and the computer and provides tools to help you do your work. Designed to provide an uncomplicated, efficient, and flexible computing environment, the UNIX system offers you several advantages:

- a general purpose system that performs a wide variety of jobs or applications
- an interactive environment that allows you to communicate directly with the computer and receive immediate responses to your requests and messages
- a multi-user environment that allows you to share the resources of the computer with other users without sacrificing productivity

  This technique is called timesharing. The UNIX system interacts with users on a rotating basis so quickly that it appears to be interacting with all users simultaneously.
- a multi-tasking environment that enables you to execute more than one program at the same time.

The UNIX system has four major components:

the kernel	The kernel is a program that constitutes the nucleus of the operating system; it coordinates the internal functions of the computer (such as allocating system resources). The kernel works invisibly; you are never aware of it while you are doing your work.
the shell	The shell is a program that acts as a liaison between you and the kernel by interpreting and executing your commands. Because it reads your input and sends you messages, it is described as interactive.
commands	Commands are the names of programs that you request the computer to execute. Packages of programs are called tools. The UNIX system provides tools for jobs such as creating and changing text,

writing programs, developing software tools, and exchanging information with others via the computer.

the file system	The file system is the collection of all the files available on your computer. It allows you to store and retrieve information easily.

How the UNIX System Works

Figure 1-1 is a model of the UNIX system. Each circle represents one of the main components of the UNIX system: the kernel, the shell, and the user programs or commands. The arrows suggest the shell's role as the medium through which you and the kernel communicate. The remainder of this chapter describes each of these components, along with another important feature of the UNIX system, the file system.

Figure 1-1: Model of the UNIX System

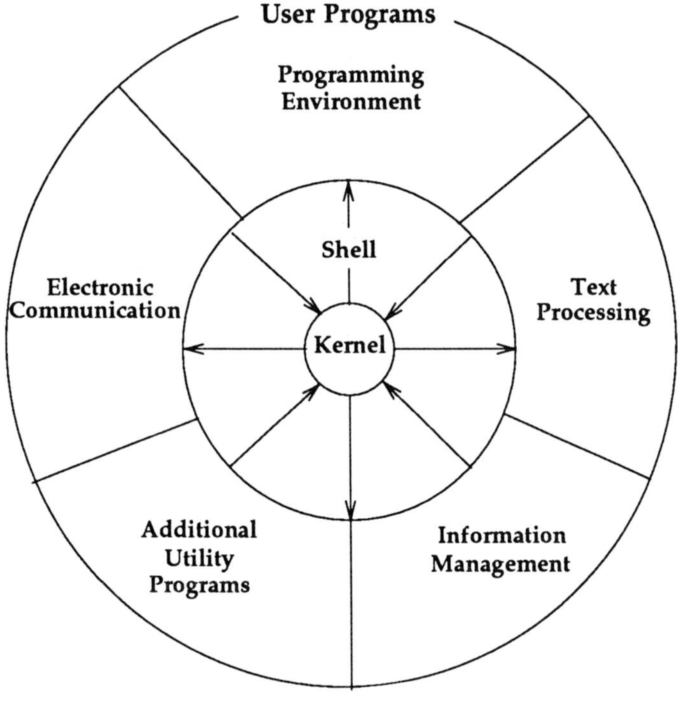

The Kernel

The nucleus of the UNIX system is called the kernel. The kernel controls access to the computer, manages computer memory, maintains the file system, and allocates computer resources among users. Figure 1-2 is a functional view of the kernel.

Figure 1-2: Functional View of the Kernel

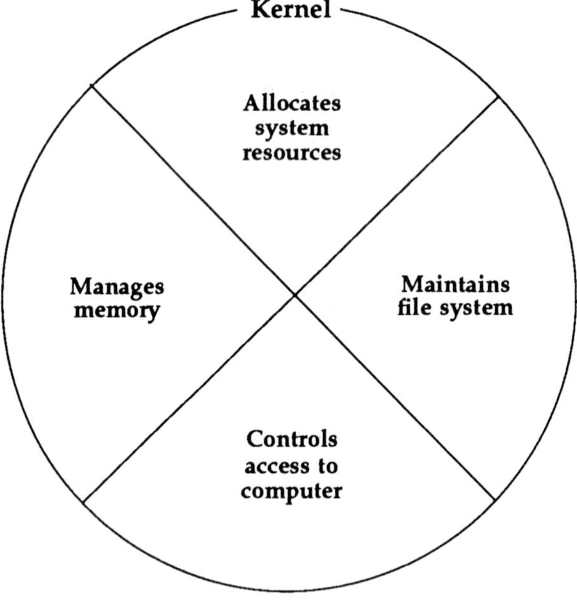

The Shell

The shell is a program that allows you to communicate with the operating system. The shell reads the commands you enter and interprets them as requests to execute other programs, access files, or provide output. The shell is also a powerful programming language, not unlike the C programming language, that provides conditional execution and control flow features. The model of the UNIX system in Figure 1-1 shows the two-way flow of communication between you and the kernel via the shell.

Chapter 4 describes the general capabilities of the shell. Chapter 9 is a tutorial that teaches you to write simple shell programs called shell scripts and tailor your environment to your needs.

Commands

A program is a set of instructions to the computer. Programs that can be executed by the computer without need for translation are called executable programs or commands. As a typical user of the UNIX system, you have many standard programs and tools available to you. If you use the UNIX system to write programs and develop software, you can also employ system calls, subroutines, and other tools. Of course, any programs you write yourself will be at your disposal, too.

This chapter introduces you to many of the UNIX system programs and tools that you will use regularly. If you need additional information on these or other standard programs, refer to the *User's Reference Manual*. For information on tools and routines related to programming and software development, consult the *Programmer's Reference Manual*. The *Documentation Roadmap* describes and explains how to order all UNIX system documents from AT&T.

The reference manuals may also be available online. (Online documents are stored in your computer's file system.) You can summon pages from the online manuals by executing the command `man` (short for manual page). For details on how to use the `man` command refer to the `man`(1) page in the *User's Reference Manual*.

What Commands Do

The outer circle of the UNIX system model in Figure 1-1 organizes the system programs and tools into functional categories. These functions include:

programming environment	Several UNIX system programs establish a friendly programming environment by providing interfaces between the UNIX system and programming languages and by supplying utility programs.
text processing	The system provides programs such as line and screen editors for creating and changing text, a spelling checker for locating spelling errors, and optional text formatters for producing high-quality, paper copies that are suitable for publication.
information management	The system provides many programs that allow you to create, organize, and remove files and directories.
additional utility programs	Other tools generate graphics and perform calculations.
electronic communication	Several programs, such as `mail`, enable you to transmit information to other users and to other UNIX systems.

How to Execute Commands

To make your requests comprehensible to the UNIX system, you must present each command in the correct format, or command line syntax. This syntax defines the order in which you enter the components of a command line. Just as you must put the subject of a sentence before the verb in an English sentence, so must you put the parts of a command line in the order required by the command line syntax. Otherwise, the UNIX system shell will not be able to interpret your request. Here is an example of the syntax of a UNIX system command line.

command *option(s)* *argument(s)*<CR>

On every UNIX system command line you must type at least two components: a command name and the `RETURN` key. (The notation <CR> is used as an instruction to press the `RETURN` key throughout this *Guide*.) A command line may also contain either options or arguments, or both. What are commands, options, and arguments?

- a *command* is the name of the program you want to run
- an *option* modifies how the command runs
- an *argument* specifies data that the command processes, usually the name of a directory or file

In command lines that include options and/or arguments, the component words are separated by at least one blank space. (You can insert a blank by pressing the space bar.) If an argument name contains a blank, enclose that name in double quotation marks. For example, if the argument to your command is `sample 1`, you must type it as follows: `"sample 1"`. If you forget the double quotation marks, the shell will interpret `sample` and `1` as two separate arguments.

Some commands allow you to specify multiple options and/or arguments on a command line. Consider the following command line:

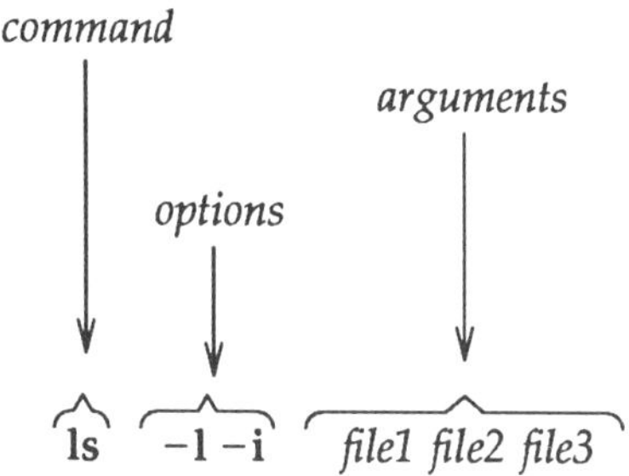

In this example, the `ls` command is used with two options, `-l` and `-i`, to list information about *file1*, *file2*, and *file3*. The `-l` option provides information in a long format, including such things as mode, owner, and size, while the `-i` option prints the inode number. (The UNIX system usually allows you to group options such as these to read `-li` if you prefer, and to enter them in any order.) In addition, three files (*file1*, *file2*, and *file3*) are specified as arguments. Although most options can be grouped together, arguments cannot.

The following examples show the proper sequence and spacing in command line syntax:

Incorrect	Correct
`ls`*file*	`ls` *file*
`ls-l`*file*	`ls -l` *file*
`ls -l i` *file*	`ls -li` *file* or `ls -l -i` *file*
`ls` *file1file2*	`ls` *file1* *file2*

Remember, regardless of the number of components, you must end every command line by pressing the RETURN key.

How Commands Are Executed

Figure 1-3 shows the flow of control when the UNIX system executes a command.

Figure 1-3: Execution of a UNIX System Command

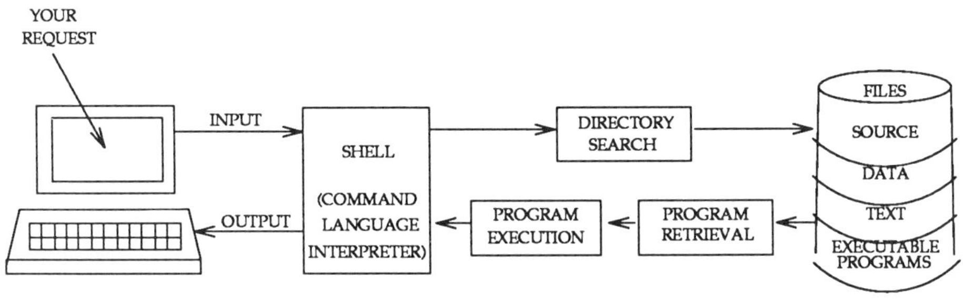

To execute a command, enter a command line when a prompt (such as a $ sign) appears on your screen. The shell considers your command as input, searches through one or more directories to retrieve the program you specified, and conveys your request, along with the program requested, to the kernel. The kernel then follows the instructions in the program and executes the command you requested. After the program has finished running, the shell signals that it is ready for your next command by printing another prompt.

The File System

The file system is the cornerstone of the UNIX operating system. It provides a logical method of organizing, retrieving, and managing information. The structure of the file system is hierarchical; if you could see it, it might look like an organization chart or an inverted tree (Figure 1-4).

Figure 1-4: The Hierarchical Structure of the File System

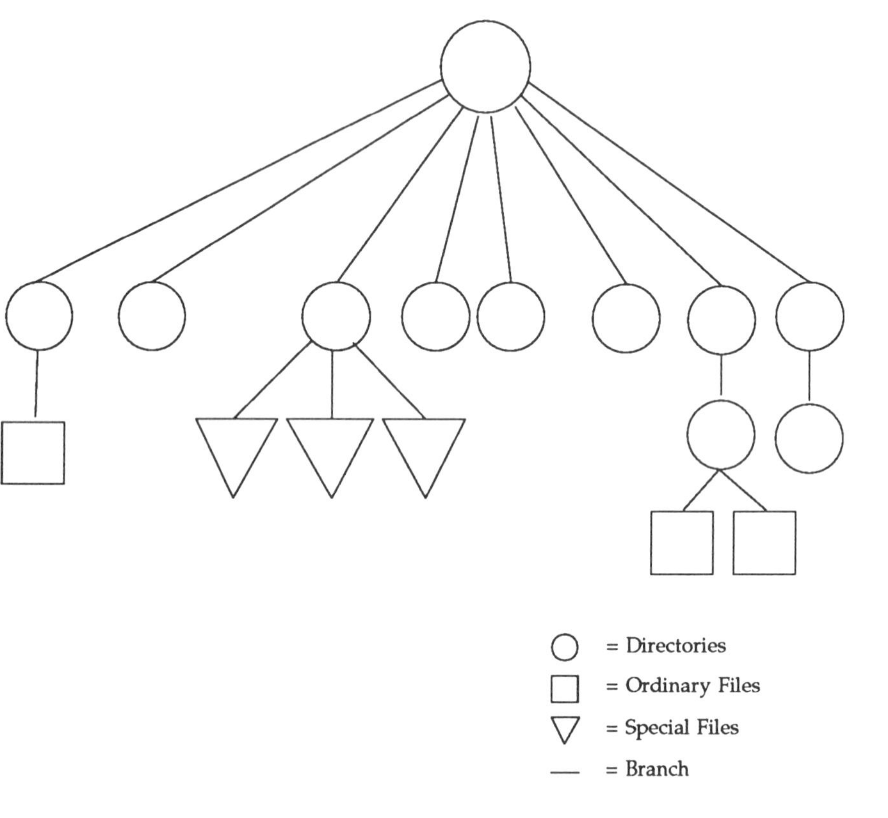

The file, which is the basic unit of the UNIX system, can be any of the following: an ordinary file, a directory, a special file, or a symbolic link. (See Chapter 3, "Using the File System.")

Ordinary Files

An ordinary file is a collection of characters that is treated as a unit by the system. Ordinary files are used to store any information you want to save. They may contain text for letters or reports, code for the programs you write, or commands to run your programs. Once you have created a file, you can add material to it, delete material from it, or remove it entirely when you no longer need it.

Directories

A directory is a super-file that may contain files and other directories. Usually the files it contains are related in some way. For example, a directory called `sales` may hold files containing monthly sales figures called `jan`, `feb`, `mar`, and so on. You can create directories, add or remove files from them, or remove directories themselves at any time.

All the directories that you create and own will be located in your home directory. This is a directory assigned to you by the system when you receive a recognized login. You have control over this directory; no one else except a privileged user can read or write files in it without your explicit permission, and you determine its structure.

The UNIX system also maintains several directories for its own use. The structure of these directories is much the same on all UNIX systems. These directories, which include several important system directories, are located directly under the root directory in the file hierarchy. The root directory (designated by /) is the source of the UNIX file structure; all directories and files are arranged hierarchically under it.

Special Files

Special files constitute the most unusual feature of the file system. A special file represents a physical device such as a terminal, disk drive, magnetic tape drive, or communication link. The system reads and writes to special files in the same way it does to ordinary files. However, the system read and write requests do not activate the normal file access mechanism; instead, they activate the device handler associated with the file, perhaps making the disk head move or the tape fast-forward.

Symbolic Links

Symbolic links are files that point to other files. For more information about them and their uses, see Chapter 6 of the *Application Programmer's Guide*.

System Layout

Some operating systems require you to define the type of file you have and to use it in a specified way. This requires you to consider how the files are stored, since they may be sequential, random-access, or binary files. To the UNIX system, however, all files are alike. This makes the UNIX system file structure easy to use. For example, you need not specify memory requirements for your files, since the system automatically does this for you. Or if you or a program you write needs to access a certain device, such as a printer, you specify the device just as you would another one of your files. In the UNIX system, there is only one interface for all input from you and output to you; this simplifies your interaction with the system.

Figure 1-4 shows an example of a typical file system. Notice that the root directory contains several important system directories.

Figure 1-5: Example of a File System

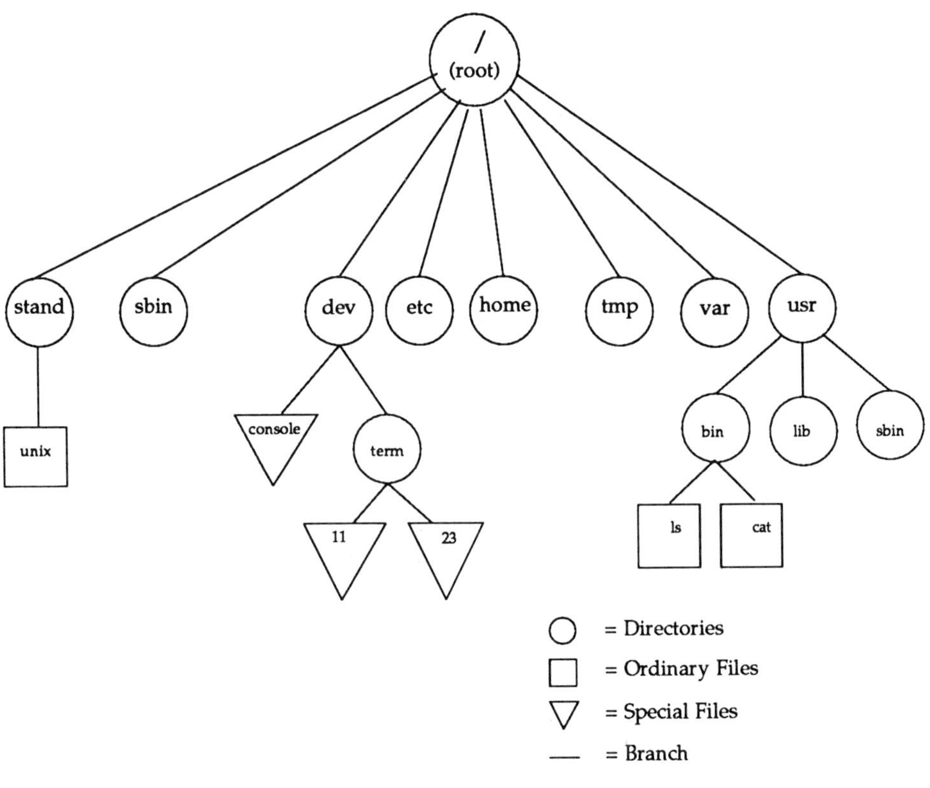

`/stand`	contains bootable programs and data files used in the booting process.
`/sbin`	contains essential executables used in the booting process and in manual system recovery.
`/dev`	contains special files that represent peripheral devices such as the console, the line printer, user terminals, and disks.

/etc	contains machine-specific administrative configuration files and system administration databases.
/home	the root of a subtree for user directories.
/tmp	contains temporary files.
/var	the root of a subtree for varying files such as log files.
/usr	contains other directories, including lib and bin.

In summary, the directories and files you create comprise the portion of the file system that is controlled by you. Other parts of the file system are provided and maintained by the operating system, such as /sbin, /dev, /etc, /tmp, and /usr, and have much the same structure on all UNIX systems.

You will learn more about the file system in other chapters. For example, Chapter 3 shows how to organize a file system directory structure, and access and manipulate files, and Chapters 5 and 6 are tutorials designed to teach you how to create and edit files.

This chapter has described some basic principles of the UNIX operating system. The following chapters will help you apply these principles.

2. BASICS FOR UNIX SYSTEM USERS

2. BASICS FOR UNIX SYSTEM USERS

2 Basics for UNIX System Users

Getting Started

This chapter tells you how to use the UNIX system. Specifically, it lists the required terminal settings, and explains how to use the keyboard, obtain a login, log on and off the system, and enter simple commands.

To establish contact with the UNIX system, you need:

- a terminal
- a login name that identifies you as an authorized user
- a password that verifies your identity
- instructions for dialing in and accessing the UNIX system if your terminal is not directly connected to the computer

This chapter follows the notation conventions used throughout this *Guide*. For a description of them, see the Preface.

The Terminal

A terminal is an input/output device: you use it to enter requests to the UNIX system, and the system uses it to send its responses to you. There are two basic types of terminals: video display terminals and printing terminals.

The video display terminal shows input and output on a display screen; the printing terminal, on continuously fed paper. In most respects, this difference has no effect on the user's actions or the system's responses. Instructions throughout this book that refer to the terminal screen apply in the same way to the paper in a printing terminal, unless noted otherwise.

Required Terminal Settings

Regardless of the type of terminal you use, you must configure it properly to communicate with the UNIX system. If you have not set terminal options before, you might feel more comfortable seeking help from someone who has.

How you configure a terminal depends on the type of terminal you are using. Some terminals are configured with switches; others are configured directly from the keyboard by using a set of function keys. To determine how to configure your terminal, consult the owner's manual provided by the manufacturer.

The following is a list of configuration checks you should perform on any terminal before trying to log in on the UNIX system.

1. Turn on the power.
2. Set the terminal to on-line or remote operation. This setting ensures the terminal is under the direct control of the computer.
3. Set the terminal to full duplex mode. The UNIX system operates in full duplex. Full duplex is a communication protocol in which both sides send and receive simultaneously, usually by using different signal frequencies. A full duplex connection allows you to send information to the UNIX system even while it is sending to you. (In half duplex communication, one side must be in receive mode while the other is in send mode.)
4. If your terminal is not directly connected to the computer, make sure the modem you are using is set to the full duplex mode.

5. Set character generation to lower case.
6. Set the terminal to no parity. Parity is used by some systems to do error checking. The UNIX system does not use parity.
7. Set the baud rate. This is the speed at which the computer communicates with the terminal, measured in characters per second. (For example, a terminal set at a baud rate of 4800 sends and receives 480 characters per second.) Depending on the computer and the terminal, baud rates between 300 and 19200 are available. Some computers may be capable of processing characters at higher speeds.

Keyboard Characteristics

There is no standard layout for terminal keyboards. However, all terminal keyboards share a standard set of 128 characters called the ASCII character set. (ASCII is an acronym for American Standard Code for Information Interchange.) While the keys are labeled with characters that are meaningful to you (such as the letters of the alphabet), each one is also associated with an ASCII code that is meaningful to the computer.

The keyboard of a typical ASCII terminal is similar to that of a typewriter, but contains a few additional keys for functions such as interrupting programs. The keys may be divided into the following groups:

- the letters of the English alphabet (both upper case and lower case)
- the numerals (0 through 9)
- a variety of symbols (including ! @ # $ % ^ & ( ) _ − + = ~ ' { } [ ] \ : ; " ' < > , ? /)
- specially defined words (such as <RETURN> and <BREAK>), and abbreviations (such as <DEL> for delete, <CTRL> for control, and <ESC> for escape)

While terminal and typewriter keyboards both have alphanumeric keys, terminal keyboards also have keys designed for use with a computer. These keys are labeled with characters or symbols that remind the user of their functions. However, their placement may vary from terminal to terminal because there is no standard keyboard layout.

Typing Conventions

To interact with the UNIX system, you must be familiar with its typing conventions. The UNIX system requires that you enter commands in lower case letters (unless the command includes an upper case letter). Other conventions enable you to perform tasks, such as erasing letters or deleting lines, by pressing one or two keys. Figure 2-1 lists these conventions. Note that the key(s) associated with each function are default values; in most cases different keys could be chosen to perform the same function. Detailed explanations of several of the keys are provided on the next few pages.

Figure 2-1: UNIX System Typing Conventions

Key(s)*	Function
$	System's command prompt (your cue to issue a command)
<BACKSPACE> or <^h>	Erase a character
@	Erase an entire line
<BREAK>	Stop execution of a program or command
<DEL>	Delete the current command line
<ESC>	When used with another character, performs a specific function (called an escape sequence)
	When used in an editing session with the `vi` editor, ends the text input mode and returns you to the command mode
<CR>	The <RETURN> key. This ends a line of typing and puts the cursor on a new line.
<^d>†	Stop input to the system or log off
<^h>	Backspace for terminals without a backspace key
<^i>	Horizontal tab for terminals without a tab key
<^s>	Temporarily stops output from printing on the screen
<^q>	Makes the output resume printing on the screen after it has been stopped by the <^s> keys

* Nonprinting characters are shown in angle brackets (< >).

† Characters preceded by a circumflex (^) are called control characters and are pronounced control-*letter*. To type a control character, hold down the control key and press the specified letter.

The Command Prompt

The standard UNIX system command prompt is the dollar sign ($). When the prompt appears on your terminal screen, the UNIX system is waiting for instructions from you. The appropriate response to the prompt is to issue a command and press the <RETURN> key.

The dollar sign ($) is the default value for the command prompt. Chapter 7 explains how to change it if you want a different character or a character string as your command prompt.

Correcting Typing Errors

There are several methods of deleting text so that you can correct typing errors. The @ (at) sign erases the current line, and the <BACKSPACE> key and <^h> both erase the last character typed. All these signs and keys are defaults; the functions they provide may be reassigned to other keys. (For instructions, see "Reassigning the Delete Functions" later in this section and "Setting Terminal Options" in Chapter 7.)

Deleting the Current Line: the @ Sign

The @ sign deletes the current line. When you press it, an @ sign is added to the end of the line, and the cursor moves to the next line. The line containing the error is not erased from the screen but is ignored.

The @ sign works only on the current line; be sure to press it before you press the <RETURN> key if you want to delete a line. In the following example, a misspelled command is typed on a command line; the command is cancelled with the @ sign:

```
whooo@
who<CR>
```

Deleting the Last Characters Typed: <^h> and <BACKSPACE>

The <BACKSPACE> key and <^h> both delete the character(s) last typed on the current line. When you type either, the cursor backs up over the last character and lets you retype it, thus effectively erasing it. This is an easy way to correct a typing error.

You can delete as many characters as you like as long as you type a corresponding number of <BACKSPACE> keys or <^h> characters. For example, in the following command line, two characters are deleted by typing two <BACKSPACE> keys.

```
dattw<BACKSPACE><BACKSPACE>e<CR>
```

The UNIX system interprets this as the `date` command, typed correctly.

Reassigning the Delete Functions

As stated earlier, you can change the keys that kill lines and erase characters. If you want to change these keys for a single working session, you can issue a command to the shell to reassign them; the delete functions will revert to the default keys as soon as you log off. If you want to use other keys regularly, you must specify the reassignment in a file called `.profile`. Instructions for making both temporary and permanent key reassignments, along with a description of the `.profile`, are given in Chapter 7.

There are three points to keep in mind if you reassign the delete functions to non-default keys. First, when you reassign a function to a non-default key, you also take that function away from the default key. For example, if you reassign the erase function from the <BACKSPACE> key to the # sign, you will no longer be able to use the <BACKSPACE> key to erase characters. Neither will you have two keys that perform the same function.

Secondly, such reassignments are inherited by any other UNIX system program that allows you to perform the function you have reassigned. For example, the interactive text editor called ed (described in Chapter 5) allows you to delete text with the same key you use to correct errors on a shell command line (as described in this section). Therefore, if you reassign the erase function to the # sign, you will have to use the # sign to erase characters while working in the ed editor, as well. The <BACKSPACE> key will no longer work.

Finally, keep in mind that any reassignments you have specified in your `.profile` do not become effective until after you log in. Therefore, if you make an error while typing your login name or password, you must use the <BACKSPACE> key to correct it.

Whichever keys you use, remember that they work only on the current line. Be sure to correct your errors before pressing the <RETURN> key at the end of a line.

Using Special Characters as Literal Characters

What happens if you want to use the literal meaning of a special character? Since the UNIX system's default behavior is to interpret special characters as commands, you must tell the system to ignore or escape from a character's special meaning whenever you want to use it as a literal character. The backslash (\) enables you to do this. Type a \ before any special character that you want to have treated as it appears. By doing this you essentially tell the system to ignore this character's special meaning and treat it as a literal unit of text.

For example, suppose you want to add the following sentence to a file:

He bought three pounds @ $.05 cents each.

To prevent the UNIX system from interpreting the `@` sign as a request to delete a character, enter a \ in front of the `@` sign. If you do not, the system will erase all the words before the `@` sign and print your sentence as follows:

```
$.05 cents each.
```

To avoid this, type your sentence as follows:

```
He bought three pounds \@ $.05 cents each.
```

Typing Speed

After the prompt appears on your terminal screen, you can type as fast as you want, even when the UNIX system is executing a command or responding to one. Since your input and the system's output appear on the screen simultaneously, the printout on your screen will appear garbled. However, while this may be inconvenient for you, it does not interfere with the UNIX system's work because the UNIX system has read-ahead capability. (It communicates in full duplex mode.) This capability allows the system to handle input and output separately. The system takes and stores input (your next request(s)) while it sends output (its response to your last request) to the screen.

Stopping a Command

To stop the execution of most commands, simply press the <BREAK> or <DELETE> key. The UNIX system will stop the program and print a prompt on the screen. This is its signal that it has stopped the last command from running and is ready for your next command.

Using Control Characters

Locate the control key on your terminal keyboard. It may be labeled CONTROL or CTRL and is probably to the left of the A key or below the Z key. The control key is used in combination with other characters to perform physical controlling actions on lines of typing. Commands entered in this way are called control characters. Some control characters perform mundane tasks such as backspacing and tabbing. Others define commands that are specific to the UNIX system. For example, one control character (control-s by default) temporarily halts output that is being printed on a terminal screen.

To type a control character, hold down the control key while pressing the appropriate alphabetic key. Since most control characters do not appear on the screen when typed, they are shown between angle brackets in this text. (See "Notation Conventions" in the Preface.) The control key is represented by a circumflex (^) before the letter. Thus, for example, <^s> designates the control-s character.

The two functions for which control characters are most often used are to control the printing of output on the screen and to log off the system. To prevent information from rolling off the screen on a video display terminal, type <^s>; the printing will stop. When you are ready to read more output, type <^q> and the printing will resume.

To log off the UNIX system, type <^d>. (See "Logging Off" later in this chapter for a detailed description of this procedure.)

In addition, the UNIX system uses control characters to provide capabilities that some terminals fail to make available through function specific keys. If your keyboard does not have a backspace key, you can use the <^h> key instead. You can also insert a tab without a tab key by typing <^i>. (Refer to the section entitled "Possible Problems When Logging In" for information on how to set the tab key.)

Now that you have configured the terminal and inspected the keyboard, one step remains before you can establish communication with the UNIX system: you must obtain a login name.

Obtaining a Login Name

A login name is the name by which the UNIX system verifies that you are an authorized user of the system when you request access to it. It is so called because you must enter it every time you want to log in. (The expression logging in is derived from the fact that each time a user logs in the system records the date and time of the log in.)

To obtain a login name, set up a UNIX system account through your local system administrator. There are few rules governing your choice of a login name. Typically, it is three to eight characters long. It can consist of uppercase and lowercase letters, numbers, and the underscore character (_), but it cannot start with a number.

However, your login name will probably be determined by local practices. The users of your system may all use their initials, last names, or nicknames as their login names. Here are a few examples of legal login names: `starship`, `mary2`, and `jmrs`.

Communicating with the UNIX System

This section assumes that you will be using a terminal that is wired directly to a computer or that communicates with a computer over a telephone line. Although it describes a typical procedure for logging in, the instructions it gives may not apply to your system since there are many ways to log in to a UNIX system over a telephone line. For example, security precautions on your system may require that you use a special telephone number or other security code. For instructions on logging in to your UNIX system from outside your computer installation site, consult your system administrator.

Turn on your terminal. If it is directly connected, the `login:` prompt will immediately appear in the upper lefthand corner of the screen.

If you are going to communicate with the computer over a telephone line, you must establish a connection. The following procedure is an example of a method you might use to do this.

1. Enter the telephone number that connects you to the UNIX system. You will see one of the following on your screen:

    1. `BUSY` This means that the circuits are busy. Try dialing again.
    2. `NO ANSWER` This usually means that the system is inoperable because of mechanical failure or electronic problems. Check the connections between your terminal, modem, and phone line and try dialing again.
    3. `ONLINE` This means that the system is accessible.

2. Press the <RETURN> key. The `login:` prompt will appear.

3. A series of meaningless characters may appear on your screen. This means that the telephone number you called serves more than one baud rate; the UNIX system is trying to communicate with your terminal, but is using the wrong speed. Press the <BREAK> or <RETURN> key; this signals the system to try another speed. If the UNIX system does not display the `login:` prompt within a few seconds, press the <BREAK> or <RETURN> key again.

Login Procedure

When the `login:` prompt appears, type your login name and press the <RETURN> key. For example, if your login name is `starship`, your login line will look like this:

```
login: starship<CR>
```

If you make a mistake while typing in your login name, you may correct it using the editing characters discussed earlier, i.e. the <BACKSPACE> and @ characters.

Remember to type in lower case letters. If you use upper case when you log in, the UNIX system will expect to receive and will send only upper case letters for as long as you are logged in.

Password

Next, the system prompts you for your password. Type your password and press the <RETURN> key. If you make a mistake while typing in your password, you may correct it using the editing characters discussed earlier, i.e. the <BACKSPACE> and @ characters. For security reasons, the UNIX system does not print (or echo) your password on the screen.

If both your login name and password are acceptable to the UNIX system, the system may print the message of the day and/or current news items and then the default command prompt ($). (The message of the day might include a schedule for system maintenance, and news items might include an announcement of a new system tool.) When you have logged in, your screen will look similar to this:

```
login:  starship<CR>
password:
UNIX system news
$
```

If you make a typing mistake when logging in, the UNIX system prints the message `login incorrect` on your screen. Then it gives you a second chance to log in by printing another `login:` prompt.

```
login: starship<CR>
password:
login incorrect
login:
```

If you have never logged in on the UNIX system, your login procedure may differ from the one just described. This is because some system administrators follow the optional security procedure of assigning temporary passwords to new users when they set up their accounts. If you have a temporary password the system will force you to choose a new password before it allows you to log in.

By forcing you to choose a password for your exclusive use, this extra step helps to ensure a system's security. Protection of system resources and your personal files depends on your keeping your password private.

The actual procedure you follow will be determined by the administrative procedures at your computer installation site. However, it will probably be similar to the following example of a first-time login procedure.

1. You establish contact; the UNIX system displays the `login:` prompt. Type your login name and press the <RETURN> key.
2. The UNIX system prints the password prompt. Type your temporary password and press the <RETURN> key.
3. The system tells you your temporary password has expired and you must select a new one.
4. The system asks you to type your old password again. Type your temporary password.
5. The system prompts you to type your new password. Type the password you have chosen.

   Passwords should be constructed to meet the following requirements:

- Each password must have at least six characters. Only the first eight characters are significant.
- Each password must contain at least two alphabetic characters and at least one numeric or special character. Alphabetic characters can be upper case or lower case letters.
- Each password must differ from your login name and any reverse or circular shift of that login name. For comparison purposes, an upper case letter and its corresponding lower case letter are equivalent.
- A new password must differ from the old by at least three characters. For comparison purposes, an upper case letter and its corresponding lower case letter are equivalent.

Examples of valid passwords are: `mar84ch`, `JonathOn`, and `BRAV3S`.

The UNIX system you are using may have different requirements to consider when choosing a password. Ask your system administrator for details.

6. For verification, the system asks you to reenter your new password. Type your new password again.
7. If you do not reenter the new password exactly as typed the first time, the system tells you the passwords do not match and asks you to try the procedure again. On some systems, however, the communication link may be dropped if you do not reenter the password exactly as typed the first time. If this happens, you must return to step 1 and begin the login procedure again. When the passwords match, the system displays the prompt.

The following screen summarizes this procedure (steps 1 through 6) for first-time UNIX system users.

```
login: starship  <CR>
password: <CR>
Your password has expired.
Choose a new one.
Old password: <CR>
New password: <CR>
Re-enter new password: <CR>
$
```

Possible Problems when Logging In

A terminal usually behaves predictably when you have configured it properly. Sometimes, however, it may act peculiarly. For example, the carriage return may not work properly.

Some problems can be corrected simply by logging off the system and logging in again. If logging in a second time does not remedy the problem, you should first check the following and then try logging in again:

the keyboard	Keys labeled `CAPS`, `LOCAL`, `BLOCK`, and so on should not be enabled (put into the locked position). You can usually disable these keys simply by pressing them.
the modem	If your terminal is connected to the computer via telephone lines, verify that the baud rate and duplex settings are correctly specified.
the switches	Some terminals have several switches that must be set to be compatible with the UNIX system. If this is the case with the terminal you are using, make sure they are set properly.

Refer to the section "Required Terminal Settings" in this chapter if you need information to verify the terminal configuration. If you need additional information about the keyboard, terminal, or modem, check the owner's manuals for the appropriate equipment.

Figure 2-2 presents a list of procedures you can follow to detect, diagnose, and correct some problems you may experience when logging in. If you need further help, contact your system administrator.

Figure 2-2: Troubleshooting Problems When Logging In*

Problem †	Possible Cause	Action/Remedy
Meaningless characters	UNIX system at wrong speed	Press <RETURN> or <BREAK> key
Input/output appears in UPPERCASE letters	Terminal configuration includes UPPER CASE setting	Log off and set character generation to lower case
Input appears in UPPER CASE, output in lower case	Key labeled CAPS (or CAPS LOCK) is enabled	Press CAPS or CAPS LOCK) key to disable setting
Input is printed twice	Terminal is set to HALF DUPLEX mode	Change setting to FULL DUPLEX mode
Tab key does not work properly	Tabs are not set correctly	Type `stty -tabs`‡
Communication link cannot be established although high pitched tone is heard when dialing in	Terminal is set to LOCAL or OFF-LINE mode	Set terminal to ON-LINE mode and try logging in again
Communication link (connection to UNIX system) is repeatedly dropped	Bad telephone line or bad communications port	Call system administrator

* Numerous problems can occur if your terminal is not configured properly. To eliminate these possibilities before attempting to log in, perform the configuration checks listed under "Required Terminal Settings."

† Some problems may be specific to your terminal or modem. Check the owner's manual for the appropriate equipment if suggested actions do not remedy the problem.

‡ Typing `stty -tabs` corrects the tab setting only for your current computing session. To ensure a correct tab setting for all sessions, add the line `stty -tabs` to your `.profile` (see Chapter 7).

Simple Commands

When the prompt appears on your screen, the UNIX system has recognized you as an authorized user and is waiting for you to request a program by entering a command.

For example, try running the `date` command. After the prompt, type the command and press the <RETURN> key. The UNIX system accesses a program called `date`, executes it, and prints its results on the screen, as shown below.

```
$ date<CR>
Tues Jul 18 14:49:07 EDT 1989
$
```

As you can see, the `date` command prints the date and time, using the 24-hour clock.

Now type the `who` command and press the <RETURN> key. Your screen will look something like this:

```
$ who<CR>
starship        term/00     Jul 18      8:53
mlf             term/02 Jul 188:56
jro             term/05     Jul 18      8:54
ral             term/06     Jul 18      8:56
$
```

The `who` command lists the login names of everyone currently working on your system. The tty designations refer to the special files that correspond to each user's terminal. The date and time at which each user logged in are also shown.

Logging Off

When you have completed a session with the UNIX system, type <^d> after the prompt. (Remember that control characters such as <^d> are typed by holding down the control key and pressing the appropriate alphabetic key. Because they are nonprinting characters, they do not appear on your screen.) After several seconds, the UNIX system may display the `login:` prompt again.

```
$ <^d>
login:
```

This shows that you have logged off successfully and the system is ready for someone else to log in.

Always log off the UNIX system by typing <^d> before you turn off the terminal or hang up the telephone. If you do not, you may not really be logged off the system.

3. USING THE FILE SYSTEM

3. USING THE FILE SYSTEM

3 Using the File System

Introduction

To use the UNIX file system effectively you must be familiar with its structure, know something about your relationship to this structure, and understand how the relationship changes as you move around within it. This chapter prepares you to use this file system.

The first two sections ("How the File System is Structured" and "Your Place in the File System") offer a working perspective of the file system. The rest of the chapter introduces UNIX system commands that allow you to build your own directory structure, access and manipulate the subdirectories and files you organize within it, and examine the contents of other directories in the system for which you have access permission.

Each command is discussed in a separate subsection. Tables at the end of these subsections summarize the features of each command so that you can later review a command's syntax and capabilities quickly. Many of the commands presented in this section have additional, sophisticated uses. These, however, are left for more experienced users and are described in other UNIX system documentation. All the commands presented here are basic to using the file system efficiently and easily. Try using each command as you read about it.

How the File System is Structured

The file system is made up of a set of ordinary files, special files, symbolic links, and directories. These components provide a way to organize, retrieve, and manage information electronically. Chapter 1 introduced the properties of directories and files; this section will review them briefly before discussing how to use them.

- An ordinary file is a collection of characters stored on a disk. It may contain text for a report or code for a program.
- A special file represents a physical device, such as a terminal or disk.
- A symbolic link is a file that points to another file.
- A directory is a collection of files and other directories (sometimes called subdirectories). Use directories to group files together on the basis of any criteria you choose. For example, you might create a directory for each product that your company sells or for each of your student's records.

The set of all the directories and files is organized into a tree shaped structure. Figure 3-1 shows a sample file structure with a directory called root (/) as its source. By moving down the branches extending from root, you can reach several other major system directories. By branching down from these, you can, in turn, reach all the directories and files in the file system.

In this hierarchy, files and directories that are subordinate to a directory have what is called a parent/child relationship. This type of relationship is possible for many layers of files and directories. In fact, there is no limit to the number of files and directories you may create in any directory that you own. Neither is there a limit to the number of layers of directories that you may create. Thus you have the capability to organize your files in a variety of ways, as shown in Figure 3-1.

Figure 3-1: A Sample File System

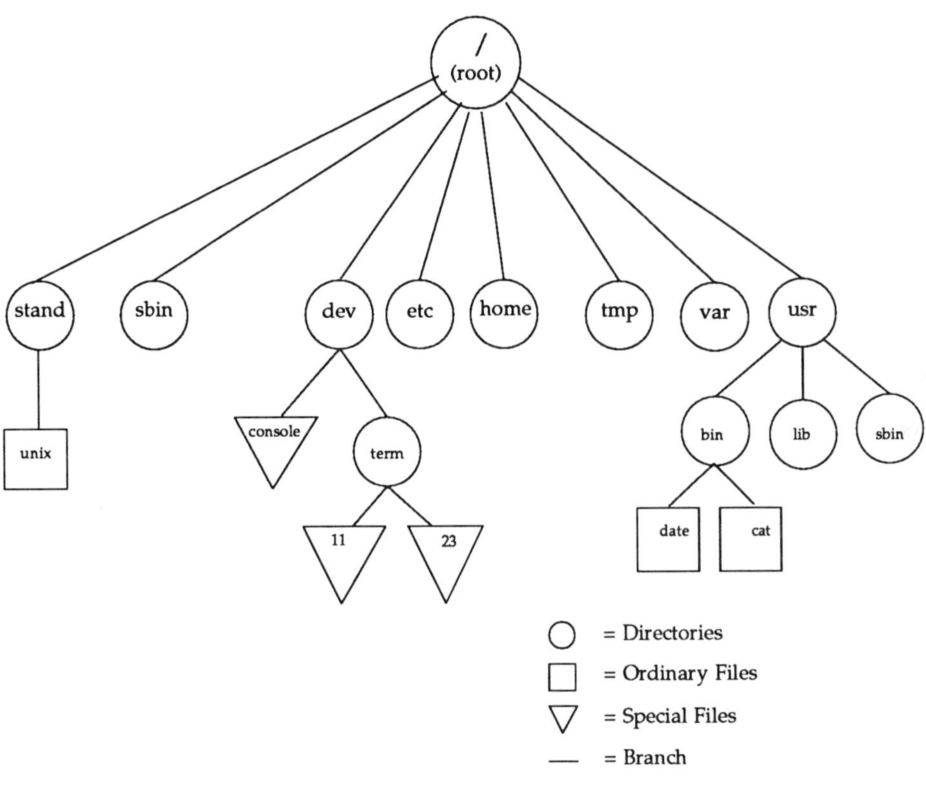

Your Place in the File System

Whenever you interact with the UNIX system, you do so from a location in its file system structure. The UNIX system automatically places you at a specific point in its file system every time you log in. From that point, you can move through the hierarchy to work in any of your directories and files and to access those belonging to others that you have permission to use.

The following sections describe your position in the file system structure and how this position changes as you move through the file system.

Your Home Directory

When you successfully complete the login procedure, the UNIX system places you at a specific point in its file system structure called your login or home directory. The login name assigned to you when your UNIX system account was set up is usually the name of this home directory. Every user with an authorized login name has a unique home directory in the file system.

The UNIX system is able to keep track of all these home directories by maintaining one or more system directories that organize them. For example, the home directories of the login names `starship`, `mary2`, and `jmrs` are contained in a system directory called `home`. Figure 3-2 shows the position of a system directory such as `home` in relation to the other important UNIX system directories discussed in Chapter 1.

Figure 3-2: Directory of Home Directories

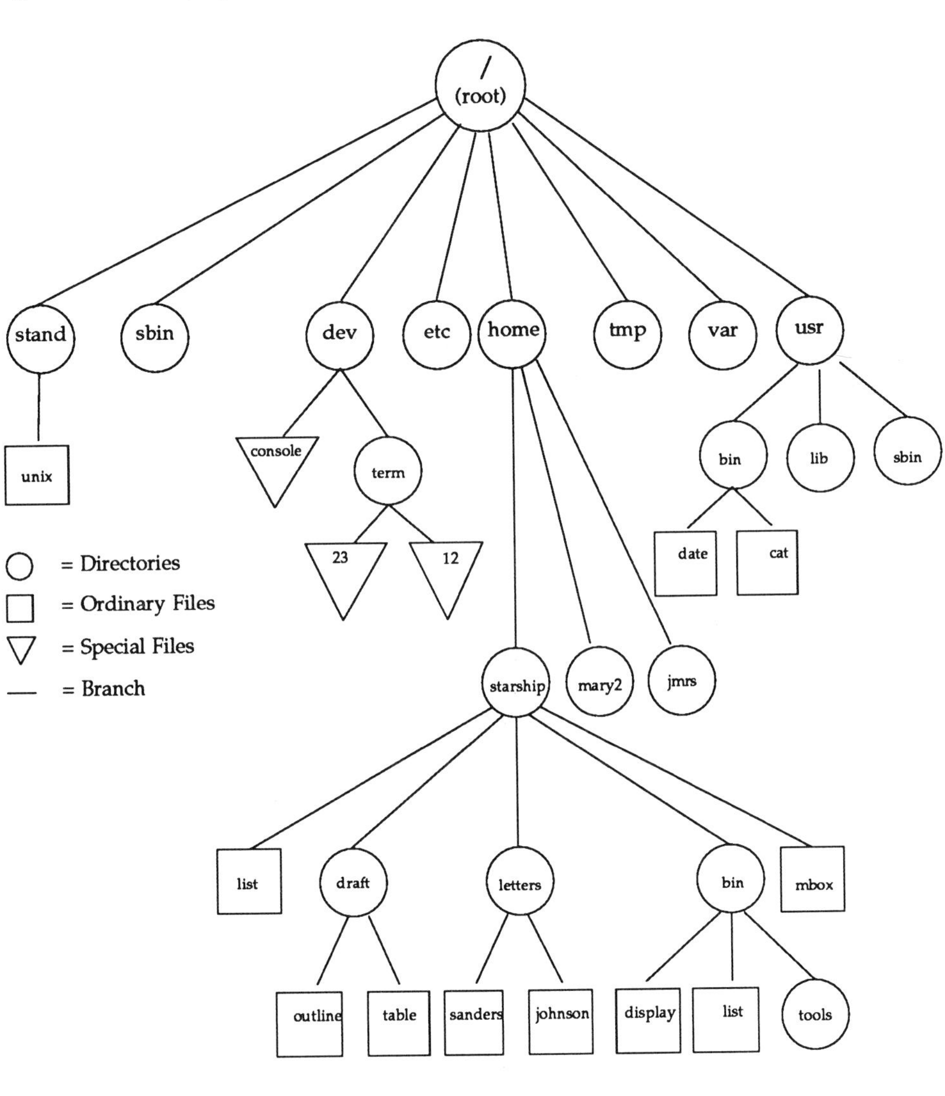

Within your home directory, you can create files and additional directories (sometimes called subdirectories) in which to group them. You can move and delete your files and directories, and you can control access to them. You have full responsibility for everything you create in your home directory because you own it. Your home directory is a vantage point from which to view all the files and directories it holds, and the rest of the file system, all the way up to root.

Your Current Directory

As long as you continue to work in your home directory, it is considered your current working directory. If you move to another directory, that directory becomes your new current directory.

The UNIX system command pwd (short for print working directory) prints the name of the directory in which you are now working. For example, if your login name is starship and you execute the pwd command in response to the first prompt after logging in, the UNIX system will respond as follows:

```
$pwd<CR>
/home/starship
$
```

The system response gives you both the name of the directory in which you are working (starship) and the location of that directory in the file system. The path name /home/starship tells you that the root directory (shown by the leading / in the line) contains the directory home which, in turn, contains the directory starship. (All other slashes in the path name other than root are used to separate the names of directories and files, and to show the position of each directory relative to root.) A directory name that shows the directory's location in this way is called a full or complete directory name or path name. In the next few pages we will analyze and trace this path name so you can start to move around in the file system.

Remember, you can determine your position in the file system at any time simply by issuing a pwd command. This is especially helpful if you want to read or copy a file and the UNIX system tells you the file you are trying to access does not exist. You may be surprised to find you are in a different directory than you thought.

Figure 3-3 provides a summary of the syntax and capabilities of the `pwd` command.

Figure 3-3: Summary of the `pwd` Command

Command Recap		
`pwd` – print full name of working directory		
command	*options*	*arguments*
`pwd`	none	none
`Description:`	`pwd` prints the full path name of the directory in which you are currently working.	

Path Names

Every file and directory in the UNIX system is identified by a unique path name. The path name shows the location of the file or directory, and provides directions for reaching it. Knowing how to follow the directions given by a path name is your key to moving around the file system successfully. The first step in learning about these directions is to learn about the two types of path names: full and relative.

Full Path Names

A full path name (sometimes called an absolute path name) gives directions that start in the root directory and lead you down through a unique sequence of directories to a particular directory or file. You can use a full path name to reach any file or directory in the UNIX system in which you are working.

Because a full path name always starts at the root of the file system, its leading character is always a / (slash). The final name in a full path name can be either a file name or a directory name. All other names in the path must be directories.

To understand how a full path name is constructed and how it directs you, consider the following example. Suppose you are working in the `starship` directory, located in `/home`. You issue the `pwd` command and the system responds by printing the full path name of your working directory: `/home/starship`. Analyze the elements of this path name using the following diagram and key.

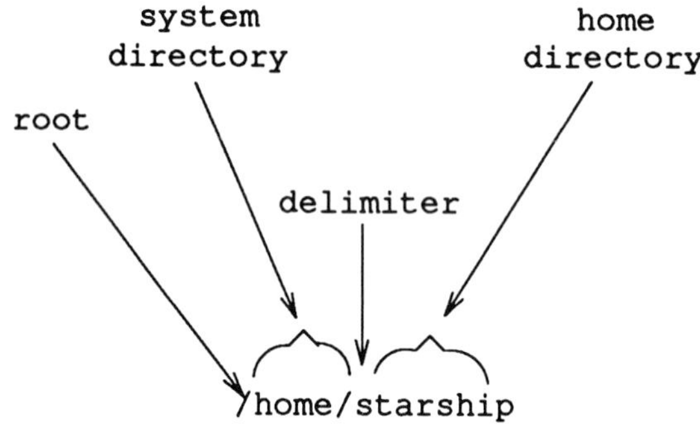

/ (leading)	= the slash that appears as the first character in the path name is the root of the file system
home	= system directory one level below root in the hierarchy to which root points or branches
/ (subsequent)	= the next slash separates or delimits the directory names home and `starship`
`starship`	= current working directory

Now follow the dashed lines in Figure 3-4 to trace the full path to `/home/starship`.

Figure 3-4: Full Path Name of the `/home/starship` Directory

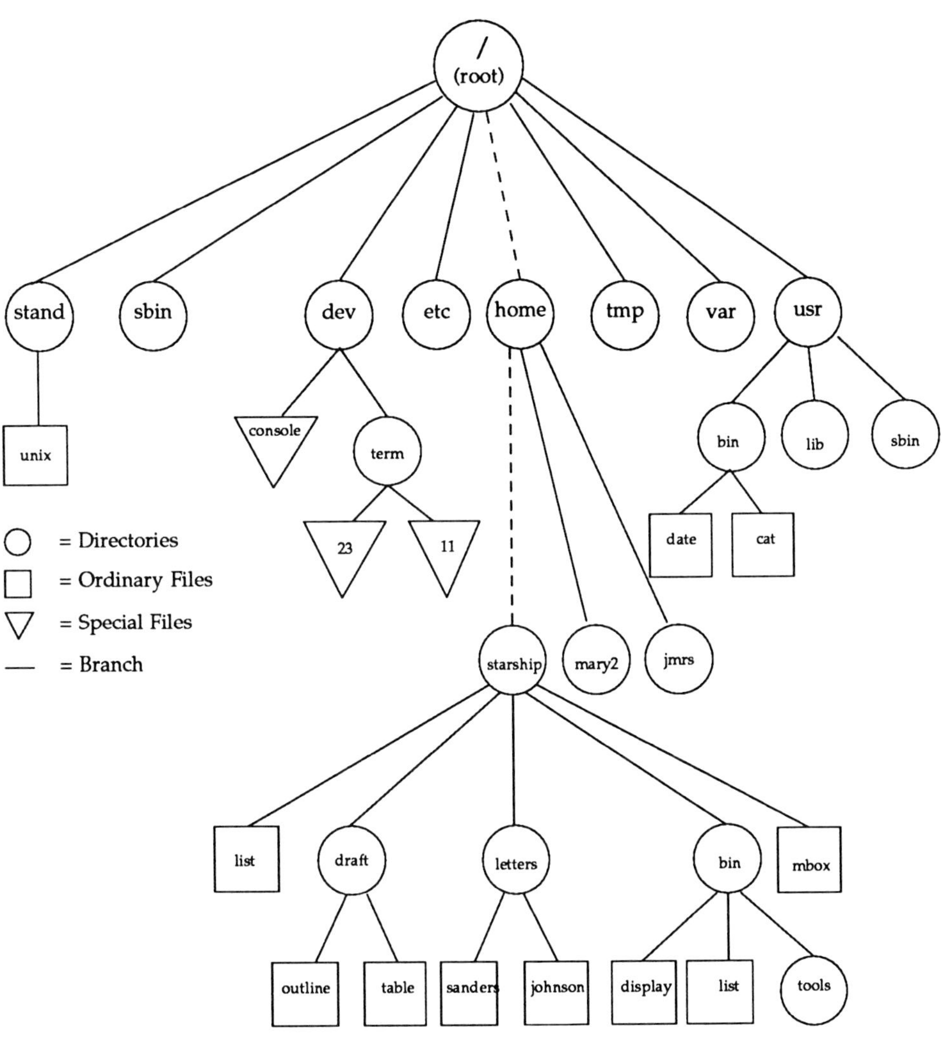

Relative Path Names

A relative path name gives directions that start in your current working directory and lead you up or down through a series of directories to a particular file or directory. By moving down from your current directory, you can access files and directories you own. By moving up from your current directory, you pass through layers of parent directories to the grandparent of all system directories, root. From there you can move anywhere in the file system.

A relative path name begins with one of the following: a directory or file name; a `.` (pronounced dot), which is a shorthand notation for your current directory; or a `..` (pronounced dot dot), which is a shorthand notation for the directory immediately above your current directory in the file system hierarchy. The directory represented by `..` (dot dot) is called the parent directory of `.` (your current directory).

For example, suppose you are in the directory `starship` in the sample system and `starship` contains directories named `draft`, `letters`, and `bin` and a file named `mbox`. The relative path name to any of these is simply its name, such as `draft` or `mbox`. Figure 3-5 traces the relative path from `starship` to `draft`.

Figure 3-5: Relative Path Name of the `draft` Directory

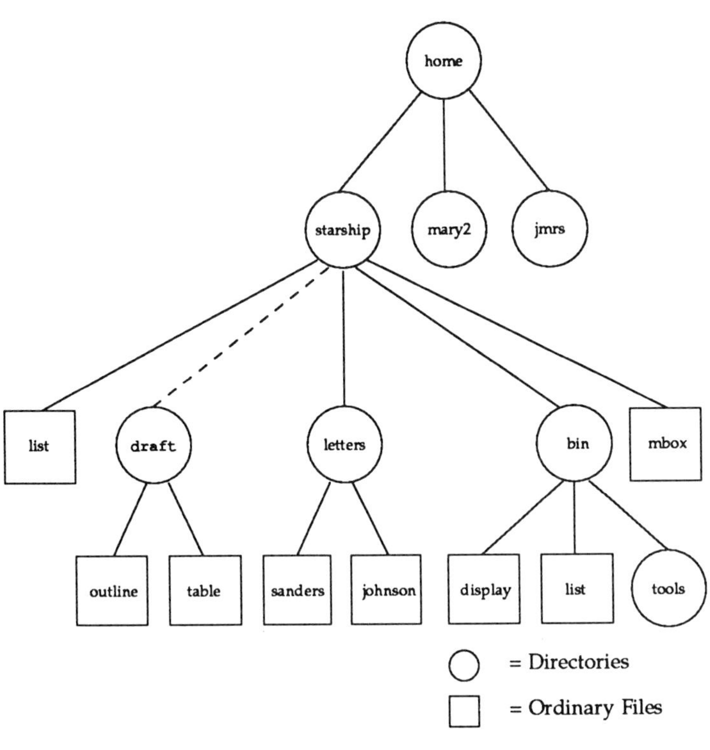

The `draft` directory belonging to `starship` contains the files `outline` and `table`. The relative path name from `starship` to the file `outline` is `draft/outline`.

Figure 3-6 traces this relative path. Notice that the slash in this path name separates the directory named `draft` from the file named `outline`. Here, the slash is a delimiter showing that `outline` is subordinate to `draft`; that is, `outline` is a child of its parent, `draft`.

Figure 3-6: Relative Path Name from `starship` to `outline`

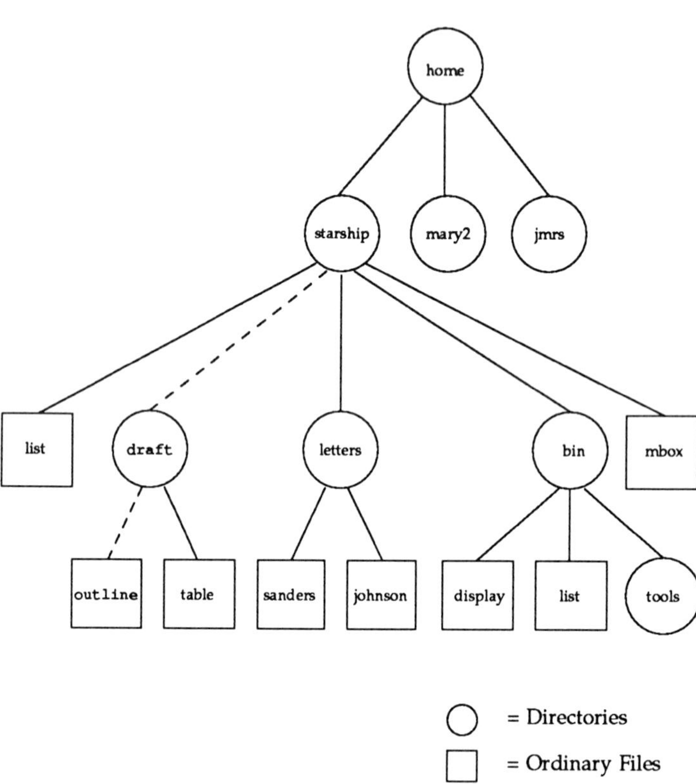

So far, the discussion of relative path names has covered how to specify names of files and directories that belong to, or are children of, your current directory. You now know how to move down the system hierarchy level by level until you reach your destination. You can also, however, ascend the levels in the system structure or ascend and subsequently descend into other files and directories.

To ascend to the parent of your current directory, you can use the `..` notation. This means that if you are in the directory named `draft` in the sample file system, `..` is the path name to `starship`, and `../..` is the path name to `starship`'s parent directory, `home`.

From draft, you can also trace a path to the file sanders by using the path name ../letters/sanders. The .. brings you up to starship. Then the names letters and sanders take you down through the letters directory to the sanders file.

Keep in mind that you can always use a full path name in place of a relative one.

Figure 3-7 shows some examples of full and relative path names.

Figure 3-7: Example Path Names

Path Name	Meaning
/	full path name of the root directory
/usr/bin	full path name of the bin directory that belongs to the usr directory that belongs to root (contains most executable programs and utilities)
/home/starship/bin/tools	full path name of the tools directory belonging to the bin directory that belongs to the starship directory belonging to home that belongs to root
bin/tools	relative path name to the file or directory tools in the directory bin If the current directory is /, then the UNIX system searches for /usr/bin/tools. However, if the current directory is starship, then the system searches the full path /home/starship/bin/tools.
tools	relative path name of a file or directory tools in the current directory.

You may need some practice before you can use path names such as these to move around the file system with confidence. However, this is to be expected when learning a new concept.

Naming Directories and Files

You can give your directories and files any names you want, as long as you observe the following rules:

- All characters other than / are legal.
- Some characters are best avoided, such as a space, tab, backspace, and the following:

  ```
  ? @ # $ ^ & * ( ) ` [ ] \ | ; ' " < >
  ```

  If you use a blank or tab in a directory or file name, you must enclose the name in quotation marks on the command line.
- Avoid using a `+`, `-` or `.` as the first character in a file name.
- Upper case and lower case characters are distinct to the UNIX system. For example, the system considers a directory (or file) named `draft` to be different from one named `DRAFT`.

The following are examples of legal directory or file names:

```
memo      MEMO       section2    ref:list
file.d    chap3+4    item1-10    outline
```

The rest of this chapter introduces UNIX system commands that enable you to examine the file system.

Organizing a Directory

This section introduces four UNIX system commands that enable you to organize and use a directory structure: `mkdir`, `ls`, `cd`, and `rmdir`.

`mkdir`	enables you to make new directories and subdirectories within your current directory
`ls`	lists the names of all the subdirectories and files in a directory
`cd`	enables you to change your location in the file system from one directory to another
`rmdir`	enables you to remove an empty directory

These commands can be used with either full or relative path names. Two of the commands, `ls` and `cd`, can also be used without a path name. Each command is described more fully in the four sections that follow.

Creating Directories: the `mkdir` Command

It is recommended that you create subdirectories in your home directory according to a logical and meaningful scheme that will facilitate the retrieval of information from your files. If you put all files pertaining to one subject together in a directory, you will know where to find them later.

To create a directory, use the command `mkdir` (short for make directory). Simply enter the command name, followed by the name you are giving your new directory or file. For example, in the sample file system, the owner of the `draft` subdirectory created `draft` by issuing the following command from the home directory (`/home/starship`):

```
$ mkdir draft <CR>
$
```

The second prompt shows that the command has succeeded; the subdirectory `draft` has been created.

Still in the home directory, this user created other subdirectories, such as `letters` and `bin`, in the same way.

```
$ mkdir letters<CR>
$ mkdir bin<CR>
$
```

The user could have created all three subdirectories (`draft`, `letters`, and `bin`) simultaneously by listing them all on a single command line.

```
$ mkdir draft letters bin<CR>
$
```

You can also move to a subdirectory you created and build additional subdirectories within it. When you build directories or create files, you can name them anything you want as long as you follow the guidelines listed earlier under "Naming Directories and Files."

Figure 3-8 summarizes the syntax and capabilities of the `mkdir` command.

Figure 3-8: Summary of the `mkdir` Command

Command Recap `mkdir` – make a new directory		
command	*options*	*arguments*
`mkdir`	available	*directoryname(s)*
`Description:`	`mkdir` creates a new directory (subdirectory).	
`Remarks:`	The system returns a prompt (`$` by default) if the directory is successfully created.	

Listing the Contents of a Directory: the `ls` Command

All directories in the file system have information about the files and directories they contain, such as name, size, and the date last modified. You can obtain this information about the contents of your current directory and other system directories by executing the command `ls` (short for list).

The `ls` command lists the names of all files and subdirectories in a specified directory. If you do not specify a directory, `ls` lists the names of files and directories in your current directory. To understand how the `ls` command works, consider the file system in Figure 3-2 once again.

Suppose you are logged in to the UNIX system as `starship` and you run the `pwd` command. The system will respond with the path name `/home/starship`. To display the names of files and directories in this current directory, you then type `ls` and press the RETURN key. After this sequence, your terminal will read:

```
$ pwd<CR>
/home/starship
$ ls<CR>
bin
draft
letters
list
mbox
$
```

As you can see, the system responds by listing, in alphabetical order, the names of files and directories in the current directory `starship`. (If the first character of any of the file or directory names had been a number or an upper case letter, it would have been printed first.)

To print the names of files and subdirectories in a directory other than your current directory without moving from your current directory, you must specify the name of that directory as follows:

`ls` *pathname*<CR>

The directory name can be either the full or relative path name of the desired directory. For example, you can list the contents of `draft` while you are working in `starship` by entering `ls draft` and pressing the RETURN key. Your screen will look like this:

```
$ ls draft<CR>
outline
table
$
```

Here, `draft` is a relative path name from a parent (`starship`) to a child (`draft`) directory.

You can also use a relative path name to print the contents of a parent directory when you are located in a child directory. The `..` (dot dot) notation provides an easy way to do this. For example, the following command line specifies the relative path name from `starship` to `home`:

```
$ ls ..<CR>
jmrs
mary2
starship
$
```

You can get the same results by using the full path name from root to `home`.

If you type `ls /home` and press the RETURN key, the system will respond by printing the same list.

Similarly, you can list the contents of any system directory that you have permission to access by executing the `ls` command with a full or relative path name.

The `ls` command is useful if you have a long list of files and you are trying to determine whether one of them exists in your current directory. For example, if you are in the directory `draft` and you want to determine if the files named `outline` and `notes` are there, use the `ls` command as follows:

```
$ ls outline notes<CR>
outline
notes: No such file or directory
$
```

The system acknowledges the existence of `outline` by printing its name, and indiates that the file `notes` is not found.

The `ls` command does not print the contents of a file. If you want to see what a file contains, use the `cat`, `pg`, or `pr` command. These commands are described in "Accessing and Manipulating Files," later in this chapter.

Frequently Used `ls` Options

The `ls` command also accepts options that cause specific attributes of a file or subdirectory to be listed. There are more than a dozen available options for the `ls` commands. Of these, the `-a` and `-l` will probably be most valuable in your basic use of the UNIX system. Refer to the `ls`(1) page in the *User's Reference Manual* for details about other options.

Listing All Files in a Directory

Some important file names in your home directory, such as `.profile` (pronounced "dot-profile"), begin with a period. (As you can see from this example, when a period is used as the first character of a file name it is pronounced dot.) When a file name begins with a dot, it is not included in the list of files reported by the `ls` command. If you want the `ls` to include these files, use the `-a` option on the command line.

For example, to list all the files in your current directory (`starship`), including those that begin with a `.` (dot), type `ls -a` and press the RETURN key.

```
$ ls -a<CR>
.
..
.profile
bin
draft
letters
list
mbox
$
```

Listing Contents in Short Format

The -C and -F options for the ls command are frequently used. Together, these options list a directory's subdirectories and files in columns, and identify executable files (with an *), directories (with a /), and symbolic links (with an @). Thus, you can list all files in your working directory starship by executing the command line shown here:

```
$ ls -CF<CR>
bin/                letters/             mbox
draft/              list*
$
```

Listing Contents in Long Format

Probably the most informative ls option is -l, which displays the contents of a directory in long format, giving mode, number of links, owner, group, size in bytes, and time of last modification for each file. For example, suppose you run the ls -l command while in the starship directory.

```
$ ls -l<CR>
total 30
drwxr-xr-x   3 starship    project       96  Oct 27  08:16  bin
drwxr-xr-x   2 starship    project       64  Nov  1  14:19  draft
drwxr-xr-x   2 starship    project       80  Nov  8  08:41  letters
-rwx------   2 starship    project    12301  Nov  2  10:15  list
-rw-------   1 starship    project       40  Oct 27  10:00  mbox
$
```

The first line of output (`total 30`) shows the amount of disk space used, measured in blocks. Each of the rest of the lines comprises a report on a directory or file in `starship`. The first character in each line (`d`, `-`, `l`, `b`, or `c`) tells you the type of file.

`d` = directory

`-` = ordinary disk file

`l` = symbolic link file

`b` = block special file

`c` = character special file

Using this key to interpret the previous screen, you can see that the `starship` directory contains three directories and two ordinary disk files.

The next several characters, which are either letters or hyphens, identify who has permission to read and use the file or directory. (Permissions are discussed in the description of the `chmod` command under "Accessing and Manipulating Files" later in this chapter.)

The following number is the link count. For a file, this equals the number of users linked to that file. For a directory, this number shows the number of directories immediately under it plus two (for the directory itself and its parent directory).

Next, the login name of the file's owner appears (here it is `starship`), followed by the group name of the file or directory (`project`).

The following number shows the length of the file or directory entry measured in units of information (or memory) called bytes. The month, day, and time that the file was last modified is given next. Finally, the last column shows the name of the directory or file.

Figure 3-9 identifies each column in the rows of output from the `ls -l` command.

Figure 3-9: Description of Output Produced by the `ls -l` Command

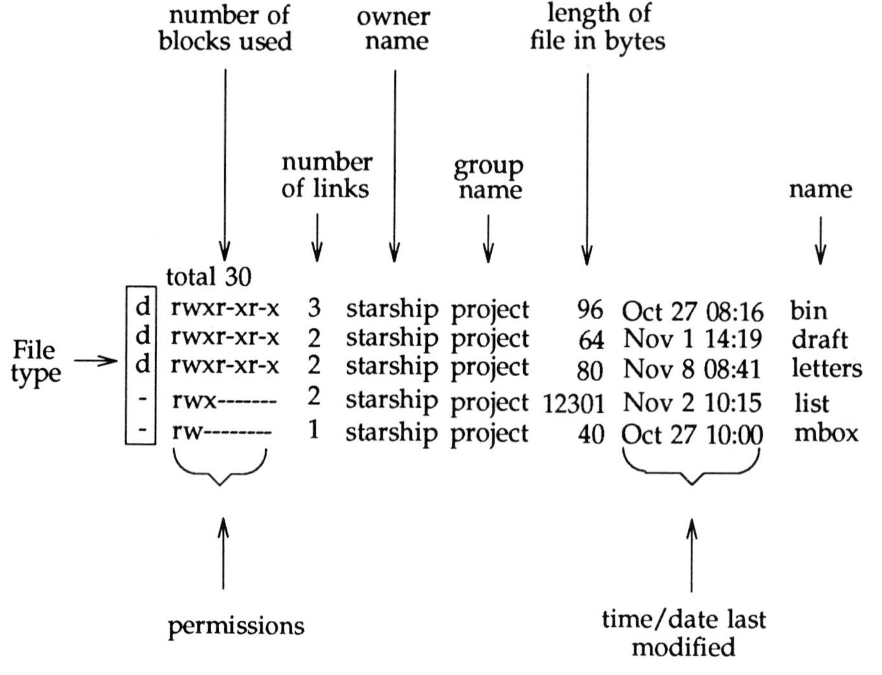

Figure 3-10 summarizes the syntax and capabilities of the `ls` command and two available options.

Figure 3-10: Summary of the `ls` Command

Command Recap `ls` – list contents of a directory		
command	*options*	*arguments*
`ls`	`-a`, `-l`, and others*	*directoryname(s)*

`Description:`	`ls` lists the names of the files and subdirectories in the specified directories. If no directory name is given as an argument, the contents of your working directory are listed.
`Options:`	`-a` Lists all entries, including those beginning with . (dot). `-l` Lists contents of a directory in long format furnishing mode, permissions, size in bytes, and time of last modification.
`Remarks:`	If you want to read the contents of a file, use the `cat` command.

* See the `ls`(1) page in the *User's Reference Manual* for all available options and an explanation of their capabilities.

Changing Your Current Directory: the cd Command

When you first log in on the UNIX system, you are placed in your home directory. As long as you do work in it, it is also your current working directory. However, by using the command cd (short for change directory), you can work in other directories as well. To use this command, enter cd, followed by a path name to the directory to which you want to move.

cd *pathname_of_newdirectory*<CR>

Any valid path name (full or relative) can be used as an argument to the cd command. If you do not specify a path name, the command will move you to your home directory. Once you have moved to a new directory, it becomes your current directory.

For example, to move from the starship directory to its child directory draft (in the sample file system), type cd draft and press the RETURN key. (Here draft is the relative path name to the desired directory.) When you get a prompt, you can verify your new location by typing pwd and pressing the RETURN key. Your terminal screen will look like this:

```
$ cd draft<CR>
$ pwd<CR>
/home/starship/draft
$
```

Now that you are in the draft directory you can create subdirectories in it by using the mkdir command, and new files, by using the ed and vi editors. (See Chapters 6 and 7 for tutorials on the ed and vi commands, respectively.)

It is not necessary to be in the draft directory to access files within it. You can access a file in any directory by specifying a full or relative path name for it. For example, to cat the sanders file in the letters directory (/home/starship/letters) while you are in the draft directory (/home/starship/draft), specify the full path name of sanders on the command line.

```
cat /home/starship/letters/sanders<CR>
```

You may also use full path names with the `cd` command. For example, to move to the `letters` directory from the `draft` directory, specify `/home/starship/letters` on the command line, as follows:

```
cd /home/starship/letters<CR>
```

Also, because `letters` and `draft` are both children of `starship`, you can use the relative path name `../letters` with the `cd` command. The `..` notation moves you to the directory `starship`, and the rest of the path name moves you to `letters`.

Figure 3-11 summarizes the syntax and capabilities of the `cd` command.

Figure 3-11: Summary of the `cd` Command

Command Recap `cd` – change your working directory		
command	*options*	*arguments*
`cd`	none	*directoryname*
`Description:`	`cd` changes your position in the file system from the current directory to the directory specified. If no directory name is given as an argument, the `cd` command places you in your home directory.	
`Remarks:`	When the shell places you in the directory specified, the prompt (`$` by default) is returned to you. To access a directory that is not in your working directory, you must use the full or relative path name in place of a simple directory name.	

Removing Directories: the `rmdir` Command

If you no longer need a directory, you can remove it with the command `rmdir` (short for remove a directory). The standard syntax for this command is:

`rmdir` *directoryname(s)*<CR>

You can specify more than one directory name on the command line.

The `rmdir` command will not remove a directory if you are not the owner of it or if the directory is not empty. If you want to remove a file in another user's directory, the owner must give you write permission for the parent directory of the file you want to remove.

If you try to remove a directory that still contains subdirectories and files (that is, is not empty), the `rmdir` command prints the message *directoryname* `not empty`. You must remove all subdirectories and files; only then will the command succeed.

For example, suppose you have a directory called `memos` that contains one subdirectory, `tech`, and two files, `june.30` and `july.31`. (Create this directory in your home directory now so you can see how the `rmdir` command works.) If you try to remove the directory `memos` (by issuing the `rmdir` command from your home directory), the command responds as follows:

```
$ rmdir memos<CR>
rmdir:  memos not empty
$
```

To remove the directory `memos`, you must first remove its contents: the subdirectory `tech`, and the files `june.30` and `july.31`. You can remove the `tech` subdirectory by executing the `rmdir` command. For instructions on removing files, see "Accessing and Manipulating Files" later in this chapter.

Once you have removed the contents of the `memos` directory, `memos` itself can be removed. First, however, you must move to its parent directory (your home directory). The `rmdir` command will not work if you are still in the directory you want to remove. From your home directory, type:

`rmdir memos<CR>`

If `memos` is empty, the command will remove it and return a prompt.

Figure 3-12 summarizes the syntax and capabilities of the `rmdir` command.

Figure 3-12: Summary of the `rmdir` Command

Command Recap `rmdir` – remove a directory		
command	*options*	*arguments*
`rmdir`	available	*directoryname(s)*
`Description:`	`rmdir` removes specified directories if they do not contain files and/or subdirectories.	
`Remarks:`	If the directory is empty, it is removed and the system returns a prompt. If the directory contains files or subdirectories, the command returns the message, `rmdir:` *directoryname* `not empty`.	

Accessing and Manipulating Files

This section introduces several UNIX system commands that access and manipulate files in the file system structure. Information in this section is organized into two parts; basic and advanced. The part devoted to basic commands is fundamental to using the file system; the advanced commands offer more sophisticated information processing techniques for working with files.

Basic Commands

This section discusses UNIX system commands that are necessary for accessing and using the files in the directory structure. Figure 3-13 lists these commands.

Figure 3-13: Basic Commands for Using Files

Command	Function
`cat`	prints the contents of a specified file on a terminal
`pg`	prints the contents of a specified file on a terminal in chunks or pages
`pr`	prints a partially formatted version of a specified file on the terminal
`cp`	makes a duplicate copy of an existing file
`mv`	moves and renames a file
`rm`	removes a file
`wc`	reports the number of lines, words, and characters in a file
`chmod`	changes permission modes for a file (or a directory)

Each command is discussed in detail and summarized in a table that you can easily reference later. These tables will allow you to review the syntax and capabilities of these commands at a glance.

Displaying a File's Contents: the `cat`, `pg`, and `pr` Commands

The UNIX system provides three commands for displaying and printing the contents of a file or files: `cat`, `pg`, and `pr`. The `cat` command (short for concatenate) outputs the contents of the file(s) specified. This output is displayed on your terminal screen unless you tell `cat` to direct it to another file or a new command.

The `pg` command is particularly useful when you want to read the contents of a long file because it displays the text of a file in pages a screenful at a time. The `pr` command formats specified files and displays them on your terminal or, if you so request, directs the formatted output to a printer (see the `lp` command in Chapter 8, "LP Print Service Tutorial").

The following sections describe how to use the `cat`, `pg`, and `pr` commands.

Concatenating and Printing the Contents of a File: the `cat` Command

The `cat` command displays the contents of a file or files. For example, suppose you are located in the directory `letters` (in the sample file system) and you want to display the contents of the file `johnson`. Type the command line shown on the screen and you will receive the following output:

```
$ cat johnson<CR>
March 5, 1986

Mr. Ron Johnson
Layton Printing
52 Hudson Street
New York, N.Y.

Dear Mr. Johnson:

I enjoyed speaking with you this morning
about your company's plans to automate
your business.
Enclosed please find
the material you requested
about AB&C's line of computers
and office automation software.

If I can be of further assistance to you,
please don't hesitate to call.

Yours truly,

John Howe
$
```

To display the contents of two (or more) files, simply type the names of the files you want to see on the command line. For example, to display the contents of the files `johnson` and `sanders`, type:

```
$ cat johnson sanders<CR>
```

The `cat` command reads `johnson` and `sanders` and displays their contents in that order on your terminal.

```
$ cat johnson sanders<CR>
March 5, 1986

Mr. Ron Johnson
Layton Printing
52 Hudson Street
New York, N.Y.

Dear Mr. Johnson:

I enjoyed speaking with you this morning
.
.

Yours truly,

John Howe

March 5, 1986

Mrs. D.L. Sanders
Sanders Research, Inc.
43 Nassau Street
Princeton, N.J.

Dear Mrs. Sanders:

My colleagues and I have been following, with great interest,
.
.

Sincerely,

John Howe
$
```

To direct the output of the cat command to another file or to a new command, see the sections in Chapter 9 that discuss input and output redirection.

Figure 3-14 summarizes the syntax and capabilities of the cat command.

Figure 3-14: Summary of the cat Command

Command Recap cat – concatenate and print a file's contents		
command	*options*	*arguments*
cat	available*	*filename(s)*
Description:	The cat command reads the name of each file specified on the command line and displays its contents.	
Remarks:	If a specified file exists and is readable, its contents are displayed on the terminal screen; otherwise, the message cat: cannot open *filename* appears on the screen. To display the contents of a directory, use the ls command.	

* See the cat(1) page in the *User's Reference Manual* for all available options and an explanation of their capabilities.

Paging Through the Contents of a File: the pg Command

The command pg (short for page) allows you to examine the contents of a file or files, page by page, on a terminal. The pg command displays the text of a file in pages (chunks) followed by a colon prompt (:), a signal that the program is waiting for your instructions. Possible instructions you can then issue include requests for the command to continue displaying the file's contents a page at a time, and a request that the command search through the file(s) to locate a specific character pattern. Figure 3-15 summarizes some of the available instructions.

Figure 3-15: Summary of Commands to Use with pg

Command*	Function
h	help; display list of available pg† commands
q or Q	quit pg perusal mode
<CR>	display next page of text
l	display next line of text
d or ^d	display additional half page of text
. or ^l	redisplay current page of text
f	skip next page of text and display following one
n	begin displaying next file you specified on command line
p	display previous file specified on command line
$	display last page of text in file currently displayed
/*pattern*	search forward in file for specified character pattern
?*pattern*	search backward in file for specified character pattern

* Most commands can be typed with a number preceding them. For example, +1 <CR>(display next page), −1 <CR>(display previous page), or 1 <CR>(display first page of text).

† See the *User's Reference Manual* for a detailed explanation of all available pg commands.

The pg command is useful when you want to read a long file or a series of files because the program pauses after displaying each page, allowing time to examine it. The size of the page displayed depends on the terminal. For example, on a terminal capable of displaying twenty-four lines, one page is defined as twenty-three lines of text and a line containing a colon. However, if a file is less than twenty-three lines long, its page size will be the number of lines in the file plus one (for the colon).

To look at the contents of a file with pg, use the following command line format:

pg *filename(s)*<CR>

For example, to display the contents of the file `outline` from the directory `draft` in the sample file system, type:

```
pg outline<CR>
```

The first page of the file will appear on the screen. Because the file has more lines in it than can be displayed on one page, a colon appears at the bottom of the screen. This is a reminder to you that there is more of the file to be seen. When you are ready to read more, press the RETURN key and pg will print the next page of the file.

The following screen summarizes our discussion of the pg command this far.

```
$ pg outline<CR>
After you analyze the subject for your
report, you must consider organizing and
arranging the material you want to use in
writing it.
       .
       .
       .
An outline is an effective method of
organizing the material.  The outline
is a type of blueprint or skeleton,
a framework for you the builder-writer
of the report; in a sense it is a recipe
:<CR>
```

After you press the RETURN key, pg will resume printing the file's contents on the screen.

```
that contains the names of the
ingredients and the order in which
to use them.
     .
     .
     .
Your outline need not be elaborate or
overly detailed; it is simply a guide you
may consult as you write, to be varied,
if need be, when additional important
ideas are suggested in the actual writing.
(EOF):
```

Notice the line at the bottom of the screen containing the string `(EOF):`. This expression `(EOF)` means you have reached the end of the file. The colon prompt is a cue for you to issue another command.

When you have finished examining the file, press the RETURN key; a prompt will appear on your terminal. (Typing `q` or `Q` and pressing the RETURN key also gives you a prompt.) Or you can use one of the other available commands, depending on your needs. In addition, there are a number of options that can be specified on the `pg` command line (see the `pg`(1) page in the *User's Reference Manual*).

Proper execution of the `pg` command depends on specifying the type of terminal you are using. This is because the `pg` program was designed to be flexible enough to run on many different terminals; how it is executed differs from terminal to terminal. By specifying one type, you are telling this command:

- how many lines to print
- how many columns to print
- how to clear the screen
- how to highlight prompt signs or other words
- how to erase the current line

To specify a terminal type, assign the code for your terminal to the `TERM` variable in your `.profile` file. (For more information about `TERM` and `.profile`, see Chapter 9; for instructions on setting the `TERM` variable, see Appendix F.)

Figure 3-16 summarizes the syntax and capabilities of the `pg` command.

Figure 3-16: Summary of the `pg` Command

Command Recap `pg` – display a file's contents in chunks or pages		
command	*options*	*arguments*
`pg`	available*	*filename(s)*
`Description:`	The `pg` command displays the contents of the specified file(s) in pages.	
`Remarks:`	After displaying a page of text, the `pg` command awaits instructions from you to do one of the following: continue to display text, search for a pattern of characters, or exit the `pg` perusal mode. In addition, a number of options are available. For example, you can display a section of a file beginning at a specific line or at a line containing a certain sequence or pattern. You can also opt to go back and review text that has already been displayed.	

* See the **pg**(1) page in the *User's Reference Manual* for all available options and an explanation of their capabilities.

Printing Files: the `pr` Command

The `pr` command is used to format and print the contents of a file. It supplies titles and headings, paginates, and prints a file on your terminal screen in any of various page lengths and widths.

You have the option of requesting that the command print its output on another device, such as a line printer (read the discussion of the `lp` command in Chapter 8, "LP Print Service Tutorial"). You can also direct the output of `pr` to a different file (see the sections on input and output redirection in Chapter 9).

If you choose not to specify any of the available options, the `pr` command produces output in a single column that contains sixty-six lines per page and is preceded by a short heading. The heading consists of five lines: two blank lines; a line containing the date, time, file name, and page number; and two more blank lines. The formatted file is followed by five blank lines. (Complete sets of text formatting tools are available on UNIX systems equipped with the DOCUMENTER'S WORKBENCH Software. Check with your system administrator to see if this software is available to you.)

The `pr` command is often used together with the `lp` command to provide a paper copy of text as it was entered into a file. However, you can also use the `pr` command to format and print the contents of a file on your terminal. For example, to review the contents of the file `johnson` in the sample file system, type:

```
$ pr johnson<CR>
```

The following screen gives an example of output from this command.

```
$ pr johnson<CR>


Mar  5 15:43 1986 johnson Page 1


March 5, 1986

Mr. Ron Johnson
Layton Printing
52 Hudson Street
New York, N.Y.


Dear Mr. Johnson:

I enjoyed speaking with you this morning
about your company's plans to automate
your business.
Enclosed please find
the material you requested
about AB&C's line of computers
and office automation software.

If I can be of further assistance to you,
please don't hesitate to call.

Yours truly,

John Howe




$
```

The blank lines after the last line in the file represent the remaining lines (all blank in this case) that `pr` adds to the output so that each page contains a total of sixty-six lines. If you are working on a video display terminal, which allows you to view twenty-four lines at a time, the entire sixty-six lines of the formatted file will be printed rapidly without pause. This means that the first forty-two lines will roll off the top of your screen, making it impossible for you to read them unless you have the ability to roll back a screen or two. However, if the file you are examining is particularly long, even this ability may not be sufficient to allow you to read the file.

In such cases, type <^s> (control–s) to interrupt the flow of printing on your screen. When you are ready to continue, type <^q> (control–q) to resume printing.

Figure 3-17 summarizes the syntax and capabilities of the `pr` command.

Figure 3-17: Summary of the `pr` Command

Command Recap		
`pr` – print formatted contents of a file		
command	*options*	*arguments*
`pr`	available*	*filename(s)*

`Description:`	The `pr` command produces a formatted copy of a file(s) on your terminal screen unless you specify otherwise. It prints the text of the file(s) on sixty-six line pages, and places five blank lines at the bottom of each page and a five-line heading at the top of each page. The heading includes: two blank lines; a line containing the date, time, file name, and page number; and two additional blank lines.
`Remarks:`	If a specified file exists, its contents are formatted and displayed; if not, the message `pr: can't open` *filename* is printed. The `pr` command is often used with the `lp` command to produce a paper copy of a file. It can also be used to review a file on a video display terminal. To stop and restart the printing of a file on a terminal, type <^s> and <^q>, respectively.

* See the `pr`(1) page in the *User's Reference Manual* for all available options and an explanation of their capabilities.

Making a Duplicate Copy of a File: the cp Command

When using the UNIX system, you may want to make a copy of a file. For example, you might want to revise a file while leaving the original version intact. The command cp (short for copy) copies the complete contents of one file into another. The cp command also allows you to copy one or more files from one directory into another while leaving the original file or files in place.

To copy the file named `outline` to a file named `new.outline` in the `draft` directory, simply type `cp outline new.outline` and press the **RETURN** key. The system returns the prompt when the copy is made. To verify the existence of the new file, you can type `ls` and press the **RETURN** key. This command lists the names of all files and directories in the current directory, in this case `draft`. The following screen summarizes these activities.

```
$ cp outline new.outline<CR>
$ ls<CR>
new.outline
outline
table
$
```

The UNIX system does not allow you to have two files with the same name in a directory. In this case, because there was no file called `new.outline` when the cp command was issued, the system created a new file with that name. However, if a file called `new.outline` had already existed, it would have been replaced by a copy of the file `outline`; the previous version of `new.outline` would have been deleted.

If you had tried to copy the file `outline` to another file named `outline` in the same directory, the system would have told you the file names were identical and returned the prompt to you. If you had then listed the contents of the directory to determine exactly how many copies of `outline` existed, you would have received the following output on your screen:

```
$ cp outline outline<CR>
cp: outline and outline are identical
$ ls<CR>
outline
table
$
```

The UNIX system does allow you to have two files with the same name as long as they are in different directories. For example, the system would let you copy the file `outline` from the `draft` directory to another file named `outline` in the `letters` directory. If you were in the `draft` directory, you could use any one of four command lines. In the first two command lines, you specify the name of the new file you are creating by making a copy.

- `cp outline /home/starship/letters/outline<CR>` (full path name specified)
- `cp outline ../letters/outline<CR>` (relative path name specified)

However, the `cp` command does not require that you specify the name of the new file. If you do not include a name for it on the command line, `cp` gives your new file the same name as the original one, by default. Therefore you could also use either of these command lines:

- `cp outline /home/starship/letters<CR>` (full path name specified)
- `cp outline ../letters<CR>` (relative path name specified)

In any of these four cases, `cp` will make a copy of the `outline` file in the `letters` directory and call it `outline`, too.

Of course, if you want to give your new file a different name, you must specify it. For example, to copy the file `outline` in the `draft` directory to a file named `outline.vers2` in the `letters` directory, you can use either of the following command lines:

- `cp outline /home/starship/letters/outline.vers2<CR>` (full path name)
- `cp outline ../letters/outline.vers2<CR>` (relative path name)

When assigning new names, keep in mind the conventions for naming directories and files described in "Naming Directories and Files" in this chapter.

Figure 3-18 summarizes the syntax and capabilities of the `cp` command.

Figure 3-18: Summary of the `cp` Command

Command Recap cp – make a copy of a file		
command	*options*	*arguments*
`cp`	available	*file1 file2* *file(s) directory*

`Description:` cp allows you to make a copy of *file1* and call it *file2* leaving *file1* intact or to copy one or more files into a different directory.

`Remarks:` When you are copying *file1* to *file2* and a file called *file2* already exists, the cp command overwrites the first version of *file2* with a copy of *file1* and calls it *file2*. The first version of *file2* is deleted.

If the arguments to cp are *file(s)* and *directory*, cp copies the *file(s)* into *directory*.

You cannot copy directories with the cp command.

Moving and Renaming a File: the mv Command

The command mv (short for move) allows you to rename a file in the same directory or to move a file from one directory to another. If you move a file to a different directory, the file can be renamed or it can retain its original name.

To rename a file within one directory, follow this format:

mv *file1* *file2*<CR>

The mv command changes a file's name from *file1* to *file2* and deletes *file1*. Remember that the names *file1* and *file2* can be any valid names, including path names.

For example, if you are in the directory `draft` in the sample file system and you would like to rename the file `table` to `new.table`, simply type `mv table new.table` and press the RETURN key. If the command executes successfully, you will receive a prompt. To verify that the file `new.table` exists, you can list the contents of the directory by typing `ls` and pressing the RETURN key. The screen shows your input and the system's output as follows:

```
$ mv table new.table<CR>
$ ls<CR>
new.table
outline
$
```

You can also move a file from one directory to another, keeping the same name or changing it to a different one. To move the file without changing its name, use the following command line:

mv *file(s) directory*<CR>

The file and directory names can be any valid names, including path names.

For example, suppose you want to move the file `table` from the current directory named `draft` (whose full path name is `/home/starship/draft`) to a file with the same name in the directory `letters` (whose relative path name from `draft` is `../letters` and whose full path name is `/home/starship/letters`), you can use any one of several command lines, including the following:

```
mv table /home/starship/letters<CR>

mv table /home/starship/letters/table<CR>

mv table ../letters<CR>

mv table ../letters/table<CR>

mv /home/starship/draft/table /home/starship/letters/table<CR>
```

Now suppose you want to rename the file `table` as `table2` when moving it to the directory `letters`. Use any of these command lines:

```
mv table /home/starship/letters/table2<CR>

mv table ../letters/table2<CR>

mv /home/starship/draft/table2 /home/starship/letters/table2<CR>
```

You can verify that the command worked by using the `ls` command to list the contents of the directory.

Figure 3-19 summarizes the syntax and capabilities of the mv command.

Figure 3-19: Summary of the `mv` Command

Command Recap `mv` – move or rename files		
command	*options*	*arguments*
`mv`	available	*file1 file2* *file(s) directory*
`Description:`	`mv` allows you to change the name of a file or to move a file(s) into another directory.	
`Remarks:`	When you are moving *file1* to *file2*, if a file called *file2* already exists, the `mv` command overwrites the first version of *file2* with *file1* and renames it *file2*. The first version of *file2* is deleted. If the arguments to the command are *file(s)* and *directory*, `mv` moves *file(s)* to *directory*.	

Removing a File: the `rm` Command

When you no longer need a file, you can remove it from your directory by executing the command `rm` (short for remove). The basic format for this command is:

`rm` *file(s)*<CR>

You can remove more than one file at a time by specifying those files you want to delete on the command line with a space separating each filename:

`rm` *file1 file2 file3*<CR>

The system does not save a copy of a file it removes; once you have executed this command, your file is removed permanently.

After you have issued the rm command, you can verify its successful execution by running the ls command. Because ls lists the files in your directory, you'll immediately be able to see whether or not rm has executed successfully.

For example, suppose you have a directory that contains two files, outline and table. You can remove both files by issuing the rm command once. If rm is executed successfully, your directory will be empty. Verify this by running the ls command.

```
$ rm outline table <CR>
$ ls
$
```

The prompt shows that outline and table were removed.

Figure 3-20 summarizes the syntax and capabilities of the rm command.

Figure 3-20: Summary of the rm Command

Command Recap rm – remove a file		
command	*options*	*arguments*
rm	available*	*file(s)*
Description:	rm allows you to remove one or more files.	
Remarks:	Files specified as arguments to the rm command are removed permanently.	

* See the rm(1) page in the *User's Reference Manual* for all available options and an explanation of their capabilities.

Counting Lines, Words, and Characters in a File: the `wc` Command

The command `wc` (short for word count) reports the number of lines, words, and characters there are in the file(s) named on the command line. If you name more than one file, the `wc` program counts the number of lines, words, and characters in each specified file and then totals the counts. In addition, you can direct the `wc` program to give you only a line, a word, or a character count by using the `-l`, `-w`, or `-c` options, respectively.

To determine the number of lines, words, and characters in a file, use the following format on the command line:

```
wc file1<CR>
```

The system responds with a line in the following format:

l *w* *c* *file1*

where

- *l* represents the number of lines in *file1*
- *w* represents the number of words in *file1*
- *c* represents the number of characters in *file1*

For example, to count the lines, words, and characters in the file `johnson` (located in the current directory, `letters`), type the following command line:

```
$ wc johnson<CR>
24      66      406 johnson
$
```

The system response means that the file `johnson` has twenty-four lines, sixty-six words, and 406 characters.

To count the lines, words, and characters in more than one file, use this format:

`wc` *file1* *file2*`<CR>`

The system responds in the following format:

l	*w*	*c*	*file1*
l	*w*	*c*	*file2*
l	*w*	*c*	`total`

Line, word, and character counts for *file1* and *file2* are displayed on separate lines and the combined counts appear on the last line beside the word `total`.

For example, ask the `wc` program to count the lines, words, and characters in the files `johnson` and `sanders` in the current directory.

```
$ wc johnson sanders<CR>
    24      66      406 johnson
    28      92      559 sanders
    52     158      965 total
$
```

The first line reports that the `johnson` file has twenty-four lines, sixty-six words, and 406 characters. The second line reports twenty-eight lines, ninety-two words, and 559 characters in the `sanders` file. The last line shows that these two files together have a total of fifty-two lines, 158 words, and 965 characters.

To get only a line, a word, or a character count, select the appropriate command line format from the following lines:

`wc`	`-l`	*file1*`<CR>`	(line count)
`wc`	`-w`	*file1*`<CR>`	(word count)
`wc`	`-c`	*file1*`<CR>`	(character count)

For example, if you use the `-l` option, the system reports only the number of lines in `sanders`.

```
$ wc -l sanders<CR>
      28 sanders
$
```

If the -w or -c option had been specified instead, the command would have reported the number of words or characters, respectively, in the file.

Figure 3-21 summarizes the syntax and capabilities of the wc command.

Figure 3-21: Summary of the wc Command

Command Recap		
wc – count lines, words, and characters in a file		
command	*options*	*arguments*
wc	-l, -w, -c	*file(s)*
Description:	wc counts lines, words, and characters in the specified file(s), keeping a total count of all tallies when more than one file is specified.	
Options	-l counts the number of lines in the specified file(s) -w counts the number of words in the specified file(s) -c counts the number of characters in the specified file(s)	
Remarks:	When a file name is specified in the command line, it is printed with the count(s) requested.	

Protecting Your Files: the chmod Command

The command chmod (short for change mode) allows you to decide who can read, write, and use your files and who cannot. Because the UNIX operating system is a multi-user system, you usually do not work alone in the file system. System users can follow path names to various directories and read and use files belonging to one another, as long as they have permission to do so.

If you own a file, you can decide who has the right to read it, write in it (make changes to it), or, if it is a program, to execute it. You can also restrict permissions for directories with the `chmod` command. When you grant execute permission for a directory, you allow the specified users to `cd` to it and list its contents with the `ls` command.

To assign these types of permissions, use the following three symbols:

`r`	allows system users to read a file or to copy its contents
`w`	allows system users to write changes into a file (or a copy of it)
`x`	allows system users to run an executable file

To specify the users to whom you are granting (or denying) these types of permission, use these three symbols:

`u`	you, the owner of your files and directories (`u` is short for user)
`g`	members of the group to which you belong (the group could consist of team members working on a project, members of a department, or a group arbitrarily designated by the person who set up your UNIX system account)
`o`	all other system users

When you create a file or a directory, the system automatically grants or denies permission to you, members of your group, and other system users. You can alter this automatic action by modifying your environment (see Chapter 9 for details). Moreover, regardless of how the permissions are granted when a file is created, as the owner of the file or directory you always have the option of changing them. For example, you may want to keep certain files private and reserve them for your exclusive use. You may want to grant permission to read and write changes into a file to members of your group and all other system users as well. Or you may share a program with members of your group by granting them permission to execute it.

How to Determine Existing Permissions

You can determine what permissions are currently in effect on a file or a directory by using the command that produces a long listing of a directory's contents: `ls -l`. For example, typing `ls -l` and pressing the `RETURN` key while in the directory named `starship/bin` in the sample file system produces the following output:

```
$ ls -l<CR>
total 35
-rwxr-xr-x   1 starship     project      9346  Nov 1  08:06  display
-rw-r--r--   1 starship     project      6428  Dec 2  10:24  list
drwx--x--x   2 starship     project        32  Nov 8  15:32  tools
$
```

Permissions for the `display` and `list` files and the `tools` directory are shown on the left of the screen under the line `total 35`, and appear in this format:

`-rwxr-xr-x` (for the `display` file)
`-rw-r--r--` (for the `list` file))
`drwx--x--x` (for the `tools` directory)

After the initial character, which describes the file type (for example, a – (dash) symbolizes a regular file and a `d` a directory), the other nine characters that set the permissions comprise three sets of three characters. The first set refers to permissions for the owner, the second set to permissions for group members, and the last set to permissions for all other system users. Within each set of characters, the `r`, `w`, and `x` show the permissions currently granted to each category. If a dash appears instead of an `r`, `w`, or `x`, permission to read, write, or execute is denied.

The following diagram summarizes this breakdown for the file named `display`.

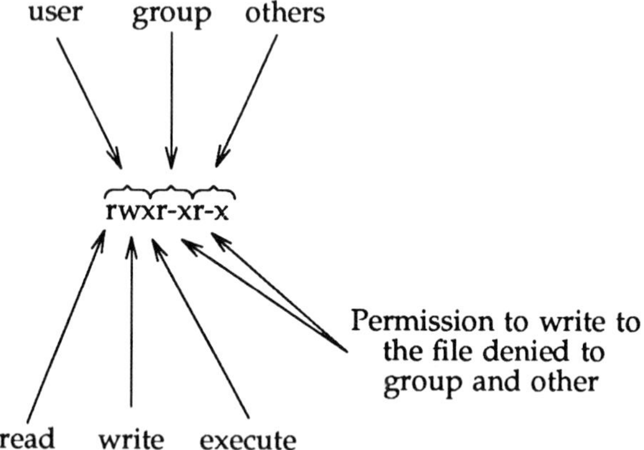

As you can see, the owner has `r`, `w`, and `x` permissions and members of the group and other system users have `r` and `x` permissions.

There are two exceptions to this notation system. Occasionally the letter `s` or the letter `l` may appear in the permissions line, instead of an `r`, `w` or `x`. The letter `s` (short for set user ID or set group ID) represents a special type of permission to execute a file. It appears where you normally see an `x` (or –) for the user or group (the first and second sets of permissions). From a user's point of view it is equivalent to an `x` in the same position; it implies that execute permission exists. It is significant only for programmers and system administrators. (See the *System Administrator's Guide* for details about setting the user or group ID.) The letter `l` indicates that locking will occur when the file is accessed. It does not mean that the file has been locked.

How to Change Existing Permissions

After you have determined what permissions are in effect, you can change them by executing the `chmod` command in the following format:

> `chmod` *who+permission file(s)*<CR>

or

> `chmod` *who=permission file(s)*<CR>

The following list defines each component of this command line.

chmod	name of the program
who	one of three user groups (u, g, or o) u = user g = group o = others
+ or –	instruction that grants (+) or denies (–) permission
permission	any combination of three authorizations (r, w, and x) r = read w = write x = execute
file(s)	file (or directory) name(s) listed; assumed to be branches from your current directory, unless you use full pathnames.

The chmod command will not work if you type a space(s) between *who*, the instruction that gives (+) or denies (–) permission, and the *permission*.

The following examples show a few possible ways to use the chmod command. As the owner of display, you can read, write, and run this executable file. You can protect the file against being accidentally changed by denying yourself write (w) permission. To do this, type the command line:

```
chmod u-w display<CR>
```

After receiving the prompt, type ls -l and press the RETURN key to verify that this permission has been changed, as shown in the following screen.

```
$ chmod u-w display<CR>
$ ls -l<CR>
total 35
-r-xr-xr-x   1 starship      project        9346  Nov 1   08:06  display
rw-r--r--    1 starship      project        6428  Dec 2   10:24  list
drwx--x--x   2 starship      project          32  Nov 8   15:32  tools
$
```

As you can see, you no longer have permission to write changes into the file. You will not be able to change this file until you restore write permission for yourself.

Now consider another example. Notice that permission to write into the file `display` has been denied to members of your group and other system users. However, they do have read permission. This means they can copy the file into their own directories and then make changes to it. To prevent all system users from copying this file, you can deny them read permission by typing:

```
chmod go-r display<CR>
```

The `g` and `o` stand for group members and all other system users, respectively, and the `-r` denies them permission to read or copy the file. Check the results with the `ls -l` command.

```
$ chmod go-r display<CR>
$ ls -l<CR>
total 35
-rwx--x--x   1 starship      project        9346  Nov 1   08:06  display
rw-r--r--    1 starship      project        6428  Dec 2   10:24  list
drwx--x--x   2 starship      project          32  Nov 8   15:32  tools
$
```

A Note on Permissions and Directories

You can use the `chmod` command to grant or deny permission for directories as well as files. Simply specify a directory name instead of a file name on the command line.

However, consider the impact on various system users of changing permissions for directories. For example, suppose you grant read permission for a directory to yourself (u), members of your group (g), and other system users (o). Every user who has access to the system will be able to read the names of the files contained in that directory by running the `ls -l` command. Similarly, granting write permission allows the designated users to create new files in the directory and remove existing ones. Granting permission to execute the directory allows designated users to move to that directory (and make it their current directory) by using the `cd` command.

An Alternative Method

There are two methods by which the `chmod` command can be executed. The method described above, in which symbols such as `r`, `w`, and `x` are used to specify permissions, is called the symbolic method.

An alternative method is the octal method. Its format requires you to specify permissions using three octal numbers, ranging from 0 to 7. (The octal number system is different from the decimal system that we typically use on a day-to-day basis.) To learn how to use the octal method, see the chmod(1) entry in the *User's Reference Manual*.

Figure 3-22 summarizes the syntax and capabilities of the `chmod` command.

Figure 3-22: Summary of the chmod Command

Command Recap		
chmod – change permission modes for files (and directories)		
command	*instruction*	*arguments*
chmod	who + – permission	*filename(s)* *directoryname(s)*
Description:	chmod gives (+) or removes (–) permission to read, write, and execute files for three categories of system users: user (you), group (members of your group), and other (all other users able to access the system on which you are working).	
Remarks:	The instruction set can be represented in either octal or symbolic terms.	

Advanced Commands

Use of the commands already introduced will increase your familiarity with the file system.

Here are three commands you may need when manipulating your files: chown, id, and groups. If you are the owner of a file, your login name is located in the *owner* category. The chown command allows you, the owner of a file, to change your owner ID to someone else's ID for that file. For example, if you type:

```
ls -l display <CR>
```

the following information will appear on the screen:

```
-r-xr-xr-x  1 owner  group   9346  Nov 1  08:06  display
```

In order to change the owner ID from yours to, for example, Sara's, whose login name is sara, you would type:

```
chown sara display
```

If you type:

```
ls -l display <CR>
```

the message on the screen will read:

```
-r-xr-xr-x  1 sara   group   9346 Nov 1   08:06 display
```

If you use the chown command and an error message is displayed across the screen, this would indicate that your system administrator has restricted this option when the system was initially set up. If you type:

```
id <CR>
```

the system will display the user's ID (uid) and your effective group ID (gid). Depending on the initial setup of the system, you may belong to more than one group. In order to find out which groups you are a member of type:

```
groups <CR>
```

A list of all groups to which you have membership will appear on the screen. You have access to files whose group ID matches one from your supplementary group list.

As you become familiar with these commands, your need for more sophisticated information processing techniques when working with files may increase. This section introduces three more commands that begin providing just that.

`diff`	finds differences between two files
`grep`	searches for a pattern in a file
`sort`	sorts and merges files

For additional information about these commands refer to the *User's Reference Manual*.

Identifying Differences Between Files: the `diff` Command

The `diff` command locates and reports all differences between two files and tells you how to change the first file so that it is a duplicate of the second. The basic format for the command is:

`diff` *file1 file2*<CR>

If *file1* and *file2* are identical, the system returns a prompt to you. If they are not, the `diff` command instructs you on how to change the first file so it matches the second by using `ed` (line editor) commands. (See Chapter 6 for details about the line editor.) The UNIX system flags lines in *file1* (to be changed) with the < (less than) symbol, and lines in *file2* (the model text) with the > (greater than) symbol.

For example, suppose you execute the `diff` command to identify the differences between the files `johnson` and `mcdonough`. The `mcdonough` file contains the same letter that is in the `johnson` file, with appropriate changes for a different recipient. The `diff` command will identify those changes as follows:

```
3,6c3,6
< Mr. Ron Johnson
< Layton Printing
< 52 Hudson Street
< New York, N.Y.
---
> Mr. J.J. McDonough
> Ubu Press
> 37 Chico Place
> Springfield, N.J.
9c9
< Dear Mr. Johnson:
---
> Dear Mr. McDonough:
```

The first line of output from `diff` is :

`3,6c3,6`

This means that if you want `johnson` to match `mcdonough`, you must change (c) lines 3 through 6 in `johnson` to lines 3 through 6 in `mcdonough`. The `diff` command then displays both sets of lines.

If you make these changes (using a text editor such as `ed` or `vi`), the `johnson` file will be identical to the `sanders` file. Remember, the `diff` command identifies differences between specified files. If you want to make an identical copy of a file, use the `cp` command.

Figure 3-23 summarizes the syntax and capabilities of the `diff` command.

Figure 3-23: Summary of the `diff` Command

Command Recap		
`diff` – finds differences between two files		
command	*options*	*arguments*
`diff`	available*	*file1 file2*
`Description:`	The `diff` command reports what lines are different in two files and what you must do to make the first file identical to the second.	
`Remarks:`	Instructions on how to change a file to bring it into agreement with another file are line editor (`ed`) commands: `a` (append), `c` (change), and `d` (delete). Numbers given with `a`, `c`, or `d` show the lines to be modified. Also used are the symbols < (showing a line from the first file) and > (showing a line from the second file).	

* See the `diff`(1) page in the *User's Reference Manual* for all available options and an explanation of their capabilities.

Searching a File for a Pattern: the `grep` Command

You can instruct the UNIX system to search through a file for a specific word, phrase, or group of characters by executing the command `grep` (short for globally search for a regular expression and print). Put simply, a regular expression is any pattern of characters (be it a word, a phrase, or an equation) that you specify.

The basic format for the command line is:

```
grep pattern file(s)<CR>
```

For example, to locate any lines that contain the word automation in the file `johnson`, type:

```
grep automation johnson<CR>
```

The system responds:

```
$ grep automation johnson<CR>
and office automation software.
$
```

The output consists of all the lines in the file `johnson` that contain the pattern for which you were searching (automation).

If the pattern contains multiple words or any character that conveys special meaning to the UNIX system, (such as `$`, `|`, `*`, ?, and so on), the entire pattern must be enclosed in single quotes. (For an explanation of the special meaning for these and other characters see "Metacharacters" in Chapter 9.) For example, suppose you want to locate the lines containing the pattern `office automation`. Your command line and the system's response will read:

```
$ grep 'office automation' johnson<CR>
and office automation software.
$
```

But what if you cannot recall which letter contained a reference to office automation; your letter to Mr. Johnson or the one to Mrs. Sanders? Type the following command line to find out:

```
$ grep 'office automation' johnson sanders<CR>
johnson:and office automation software.
$
```

The output tells you that the pattern `office automation` is found once in the `johnson` file.

In addition to the `grep` command, the UNIX system provides variations of it called `egrep` and `fgrep`, along with several options that enhance the searching powers of the command. See the `grep`(1), `egrep`(1), and `fgrep`(1) pages in the *User's Reference Manual* for further information about these commands.

Figure 3-24 summarizes the syntax and capabilities of the `grep` command.

Figure 3-24: Summary of the `grep` Command

Command Recap `grep` – searches a file for a pattern		
command	*options*	*arguments*
`grep`	available*	*pattern file(s)*
`Description:`	The `grep` command searches through specified file(s) for lines containing a pattern and then prints the lines on which it finds the pattern. If you specify more than one file, the name of the file in which the pattern is found is also reported.	
`Remarks:`	If the pattern you give contains multiple words or special characters, enclose the pattern in single quotes on the command line.	

* See the **grep**(1) page in the *User's Reference Manual* for all available options and an explanation of their capabilities.

Sorting and Merging Files: the `sort` Command

The UNIX system provides an efficient tool called `sort` for sorting and merging files. The format for the command line is:

`sort` *file(s)*`<CR>`

This command causes lines in the specified files to be sorted and merged in the following order.

- Lines beginning with numbers are sorted by digit and listed before lines beginning with letters.
- Lines beginning with upper case letters are listed before lines beginning with lower case letters.
- Lines beginning with symbols such as `*`, `%`, or `@`, are sorted on the basis of the symbol's ASCII representation.

For example, suppose you have two files, `group1` and `group2`, each containing a list of names. You want to sort each list alphabetically and then interleave the two lists into one. First, display the contents of the files by executing the `cat` command on each.

```
$ cat group1<CR>
Smith, Allyn
Jones, Barbara
Cook, Karen
Moore, Peter
Wolf, Robert
$ cat group2<CR>
Frank, M. Jay
Nelson, James
West, Donna
Hill, Charles
Morgan, Kristine
$
```

(Instead of printing these two files individually, you could have requested both files on the same command line. If you had typed `cat group1 group2` and pressed the `RETURN` key, the output would have been the same.)

Now sort and merge the contents of the two files by executing the `sort` command. The output of the `sort` program will be printed on the terminal screen unless you specify otherwise.

```
$ sort group1 group2<CR>
Cook, Karen
Frank, M. Jay
Hill, Charles
Jones, Barbara
Moore, Peter
Morgan, Kristine
Nelson, James
Smith, Allyn
West, Donna
Wolf, Robert
$
```

In addition to combining simple lists as in the example, the `sort` command can rearrange lines and parts of lines (called fields) according to a number of other specifications you designate on the command line. The possible specifications are complex and beyond the scope of this text. Refer to the *User's Reference Manual* for a full description of available options.

Figure 3-25 summarizes the syntax and capabilities of the `sort` command.

Figure 3-25: Summary of the `sort` Command

Command Recap `sort` – sorts and merges files		
command	*options*	*arguments*
`sort`	available*	*file(s)*
`Description:`	The `sort` command sorts and merges lines from a file or files you specify and displays its output on your terminal screen.	
`Remarks:`	If no options are specified on the command line, lines are sorted and merged in the order defined by the ASCII representations of the characters in the lines.	

* See the `sort`(1) page in the *User's Reference Manual* for all available options and an explanation of their capabilities.

4. OVERVIEW OF THE TUTORIALS

4. OVERVIEW OF THE TUTORIALS

4 Overview of the Tutorials

Introduction

This chapter serves as a transition between the overview that comprises the first three chapters and the tutorials that constitute the following seven chapters. Specifically, this chapter provides a brief description of the subjects covered in these tutorials: using a new system interface to perform conventional office tasks; text editing; working in the shell; using an efficient programming language for data processing and information retrieval; and communicating electronically.

The "Framed Access Command Environment (FACE) Tutorial," Chapter 5, covers a new feature of the UNIX system. Text editing spans Chapter 6, "Line Editor Tutorial (`ed`)," and Chapter 7, "Screen Editor Tutorial (`vi`)." Chapter 8, "`lp` Print Service Tutorial," explains how to print copies of files and how to perform other tasks associated with print services. How to work and program in the shell is the subject of Chapter 9, "Shell Tutorial." An efficient and powerful programming language, `awk`, is explained in detail in Chapter 10, "`awk` Tutorial," which also summarizes the `awk` commands. The broad spectrum of electronic communication is taught in Chapter 11, "Electronic Mail Tutorial," and Chapter 12, "Communication Tutorial."

Managing the System Office

Your UNIX system "office," like your business office, consists of files, records, copies, cabinets to hold these data, and the means of storing, moving, reproducing or discarding such data. The Framed Access Command Environment (FACE) enables you to organize your "office" for efficiency and ease of use. With FACE you cannot only manipulate your own files but you can also access the files of other users. Just as you would make environmental choices in your business office, FACE offers you numerous choices in the form of menus. The menus, the frames in which they appear, and the keys you would use to establish your selections are detailed and summarized in the FACE tutorial.

Editing Text

Using the file system is a way of life in a UNIX system environment. This section will teach you how to create and modify files with a software tool called a text editor. The section begins by explaining what a text editor is and how it works. Then it introduces two types of text editors supported on the UNIX system: the line editor, `ed`, and the screen editor, `vi` (short for visual editor). A comparison of the two editors is also included. For detailed information about `ed` and `vi`, see Chapters 6 and 7, respectively.

What is a Text Editor?

Whenever you revise a letter, memo, or report, you must perform one or more of the following tasks: insert new or additional material, delete unneeded material, transpose material (sometimes called cutting and pasting), and, finally, prepare a clean, corrected copy. Text editors perform these tasks at your direction, making writing and revising text much easier and quicker than if done by hand.

The UNIX system text editors, like the UNIX system shell, are interactive programs; they accept your commands and then perform the requested functions. To the shell, the editors are executable programs.

A major difference between a text editor and the shell, however, is the set of commands that each recognizes. All the commands introduced up to this point belong to the set of shell commands. A text editor has its own distinct set of commands that allow you to create, move, add, and delete text in files, as well as acquire text from other files.

How Does a Text Editor Work?

To understand how a text editor works, you need to understand the environment created when you use an editing program and the modes of operation understood by a text editor.

Text Editing Buffers

When you use a text editor to create a new file or modify an existing one, you first ask the shell to put the editor in control of your computing session. As soon as the editor takes over, it allocates a temporary work space called the editing buffer; any information that you enter while editing a file is stored in this buffer where you can modify it.

Because the buffer is a temporary work space, any text you enter and any changes you make to it are also temporary. The buffer and its contents will exist only as long as you are editing. If you want to save the file, you must tell the text editor to write the contents of the buffer into a file. The file is then stored in computer memory. If you do not, the contents of the buffer will disappear when you leave the editing program. To prevent this from happening, the text editors send you a reminder to write your file if you attempt to end an editing session without doing so.

If you have made a critical mistake or are unhappy with the edited version, you can choose to leave the editor without writing the file. By doing so, you leave the original file intact; the edited copy disappears.

Regardless of whether you are creating a new file or updating an existing one, the text in the buffer is organized into lines. A line of text is simply a series of characters that appears horizontally across the screen and is ended when you press the RETURN key. Occasionally, files may contain a line of text that is too long to fit on the terminal screen. Some terminals automatically display the continuation of the line on the next row of the screen; others do not.

Modes of Operation

Text editors are capable of understanding two modes of operation: command mode and text input mode. When you begin an editing session, you will be placed automatically in command mode. In this mode you can move around in a file, search for patterns in it, or change existing text. However, you cannot create text while you are in command mode. To do this, you must be in text input mode. While you are in this mode, any characters you type are placed in the buffer as part of your text file. When you have finished entering text and want to run editing commands again, you must return to command mode.

Because a typical editing session involves moving back and forth between these two modes, you may sometimes forget which mode you are working in. You may try to enter text while in command mode or to enter a command while in input mode. This is something even experienced users do from time to time. It will not take long to recognize your mistake and determine the solution after you complete the tutorials in Chapters 6 and 7.

Line Editor

The line editor, accessed by the `ed` command, is a fast, versatile program for preparing text files. It is called a line editor because it manipulates text on a line-by-line basis. This means you must specify, by line number, the line containing the text you want to change. Then `ed` prints the line on the screen where you can modify it.

This text editor provides commands with which you can change lines, print lines, read and write files, and enter text. In addition, you can invoke the line editor from a shell program; something you cannot do with the screen editor. (See Chapter 9, "Shell Tutorial," for information on basic shell programming techniques.)

The line editor (`ed`) works well on video display terminals and paper printing terminals. It will also accommodate you if you are using a slow-speed telephone line. (The visual editor, `vi`, can be used only on video display terminals.) Refer to Chapter 6, "Line Editor (`ed`) Tutorial," for instructions on how to use this editing tool. Also see Appendix D for a summary of line editor commands.

Screen Editor

The screen editor, accessed by the `vi` command, is a display-oriented, interactive software tool. It allows you to view the file you are editing a page at a time. This editor works most efficiently when used on a video display terminal operating at 1200 or higher baud.

For the most part, you modify a file (by adding, deleting, or changing text) by positioning the cursor at the point on the screen where the modification is to be made and then making the change. The screen editor immediately displays the results of your editing; you can see the change you made in the context of the surrounding text. Because of this feature, the screen editor is considered more sophisticated than the line editor.

Furthermore, the screen editor offers a choice of commands. For example, a number of screen editor commands allow you to move the cursor around a file. Other commands scroll the file up or down on the screen. Still other commands allow you to change existing text or to create new text. In addition to its own set of commands, the screen editor can access line editor commands.

The trade-off for the screen editor's speed, visual appeal, efficiency, and power is the heavy demand it places on computer processing time. Every time you make a change, no matter how simple, `vi` must update the screen. Refer to Chapter 7, "Screen Editor Tutorial," for instructions on how to use this editor. Appendix E contains a summary of screen editor commands, and Table 4-1 compares the features of the line editor (`ed`) and the screen editor (`vi`).

Table 4-1: Comparison of Line and Screen Editors (ed and vi)

Feature	Line Editor (ed)	Screen Editor (vi)
Recommended terminal type	Video display or paper-printing	Video display
Speed	Accommodates high- and low-speed data transmission lines.	Works best via high-speed data transmission lines (1200+ baud).
Versatility	Can be specified to run from shell scripts as well as used during editing sessions.	Must be used interactively during editing sessions.
Sophistication	Changes text quickly. Uses comparatively small amounts of processing time.	Changes text easily. However, can make heavy demands on computer resources.
Power	Provides a full set of editing commands. Standard UNIX system text editor.	Provides its own editing commands and recognizes line editor commands as well.
Advantages	There are fewer commands you must learn to use ed.	vi allows you to see the effects of your editing in the context of a page of text, immediately. (When you use the ed editor, making changes and viewing the results are separate steps.)

Using the Shell

Every time you log into the UNIX system you start communicating with the shell, and you continue to do so until you log off the system. However, while you are using a text editor, your interaction with the shell is suspended; it resumes as soon as you stop using the editor.

The shell is much like other programs, except that instead of performing one job, as `cat` or `ls` does, it is central to your interactions with the UNIX system. The primary function of the shell is to act as a command interpreter between you and the computer system. As an interpreter, the shell translates your requests into language the computer understands, calls requested programs into memory, and executes them.

To Apply System Features

Various methods of using the shell enhance your ability to use system features. Besides using it to run a single program, you can also use the shell to:

- interpret the abbreviated name of a file or a directory
- redirect the flow of input and output of the programs you run
- execute multiple programs simultaneously or in a pipeline format
- tailor your computing environment to meet your individual needs

In addition to being the command language interpreter, the shell is a programming language. For detailed information on how to use the shell as a command interpreter and a programming language, see Chapter 9, "Shell Tutorial."

To Customize Your Computing Environment

The shell can be used to control your environment. When you log into the UNIX system, the shell automatically sets up a computing environment for you. The default environment set up by the shell includes these variables:

`HOME`	your login directory
`LOGNAME`	your login name

`PATH`	route the shell takes to search for executable files or commands (typically `PATH=:/usr/bin:/usr/usr/bin`)

The `PATH` variable tells the shell where to look for the executable program invoked by a command. Therefore it is used every time you issue a command. If you have executable programs in more than one directory, you will want all of them to be searched by the shell to make sure every command can be found.

You can use the default environment supplied by your system or you can tailor an environment to meet your needs. If you choose to modify any part of your environment, you can use either of two methods to do so. If you want to change a part of your environment only for the duration of your current computing session, specify your changes in a command line. However, if you want to use a different environment (not the default environment) regularly, you can specify your changes in a file that will set up the desired environment for you automatically every time you log in. This file must be called `.profile` and must be located in your home directory.

The `.profile` typically performs some or all of the following tasks: checks for mail; sets data parameters, terminal settings, and tab stops; assigns a character or character string as your login prompt; and assigns the erase and kill functions to keys. You can define as few or as many tasks as you want in your `.profile`. You can also change parts of it at any time. For instructions on modifying a `.profile`, see the section titled "Modifying Your Login Environment" in Chapter 9.

Now check to see whether or not you have a `.profile`. If you are not already in your home directory, use the cd command to get there. Then examine your `.profile` by issuing this command:

```
cat .profile
```

If you have a `.profile`, its contents will appear on your screen. If you do not have a `.profile` you can create one with a text editor, such as ed or `vi`. (See the section titled "Modifying Your Login Environment" in Chapter 9 for instructions.)

Programming in the Shell

The shell is not only the command language interpreter; it is also a command level programming language. This means that instead of always using the shell strictly as a liaison between you and the computer, you can also program it to repeat sequences of instructions automatically. To do this, you must create executable files containing lists of commands. These files are called shell procedures or shell scripts. Once you have a shell script for a particular task, you can simply request that the shell read and execute the contents of the script whenever you want to perform that task.

Like other programming languages, the shell provides such features as variables, control structures, subroutines, and parameter passing. These features enable you to create your own tools by linking together system commands.

For example, you can combine three UNIX system programs (the `date`, `who`, and `wc` commands) into a simple shell script called `users` that tells you the current date and time, and how many users are working on your system. If you use the `vi` editor (described in Chapter 7) to create your script, you can follow this procedure. First, create the file `users` with the editor by typing:

```
vi users<CR>
```

The editor will draw a blank page on your screen and wait for you to enter text after you type "i" to insert or "a" to append.

```
cursor
~
~
~
~
~
~
~
~
~
"users" [New file]
```

Enter the three UNIX system commands on one line:

```
date; who | wc -l
```

Then press the ESCAPE key and write and quit the file by typing:

```
:wq
```

Make users executable by adding execute permission with the chmod command.

```
chmod ug+x users<CR>
```

Now try running your new command. The following screen shows the kind of output you will get.

```
$ users<CR>
Sat Mar 11 16:40:12 EST 1989
     4
$
```

The output tells you that four users were logged in on the system when you typed the command at 16:40 on Saturday, March 11, 1989.

For step-by-step instructions on writing shell scripts and information about more sophisticated shell programming techniques, see Chapter 9, "Shell Tutorial."

Programming with awk

Both an efficient programming language and a sophisticated tool you can use to execute shell scripts, awk lets you handle data processing and information retrieval tasks easily. Chapter 10, "awk Tutorial" explains the concepts of the language, and the structure of an awk program.

A typical awk program consists of a single pattern-action statement. In general, an awk program matches each line of input against each of the patterns in turn. For each pattern that matches, the associated action is executed. The process continues until all the inut has been read.

Because of the wide range of usage and the conceptual nature of the discussion of awk, you may want to skip the detailed discussion of awk until you have gained more experience with the shell and all its capabilities. Until such time, the summary at the end of Chapter 10 may be informative and guide you toward specific aspects of the awk language.

Communicating Electronically

As a UNIX system user, you can send messages or transmit information stored in files to other users who work on your system or another UNIX system. Specifically, you can send and receive messages, exchange files, and form networks with other UNIX systems. To do so, you must be logged in on a UNIX system that is capable of communicating with the UNIX system to which you want to send information. The command you use to send information depends on what you are sending. This guide introduces you to these communication programs and the commands that you must use. Chapter 11, "Electronic Mail Tutorial," and Chapter 12, "Communication Tutorial," cover these subjects with exercises for each command and summaries of the commands you must know to handle communication under the UNIX system.

Programming in the UNIX System

The UNIX system provides a powerful and convenient environment for programming and software development. In addition to the various languages you can use, the UNIX system provides some sophisticated tools designed to make software development easier and to provide a systematic approach to programming.

For information on available UNIX system programming languages, see the *Product Overview* or *Documentation Roadmap*.

For information on the general topic of programming in the UNIX system environment, see the *Programmer's Guide*. Besides supplementing texts on programming languages, the *Programmer's Guide* provides tutorials on several software development tools.

5. FRAMED ACCESS COMMAND ENVIRONMENT TUTORIAL

5. FRAMED ACCESS COMMAND ENVIRONMENT TUTORIAL

5 Framed Access Command Environment Tutorial

What is FACE?

FACE (Framed Access Command Environment) is a user-friendly interface to the UNIX System that displays an electronic "office" from which you can easily select commands that complete many conventional office tasks, such as organizing your file cabinet, collaborating on projects, and working on several tasks at once. It also gives you access to printer operations, installed programs, System Administration, and the UNIX system.

Organization of This Chapter

The material in this chapter is organized as follows:

- This preface, "What is FACE", gives an introduction to AT&T FACE and tells how this chapter is organized.
- The section "Getting Started", introduces you to your FACE Office. Logging in, logging out, named keys and their alternate keystrokes, navigating in and between menu, form, and text frames, moving and reshaping frames, the Command menu, and getting help are discussed.
- The section "Using Your FACE Office", discusses files, file folders, and the FACE commands most often used to manipulate them. This section also explains how to customize your AT&T FACE office, how to increase security on your files, and how to use the Wastebasket feature.
- The section "Using Other Features of FACE", tells how to use Printer Operations and the `print` command, describes how to administer FACE when you select System Administration, how to use the Programs feature (including Mail Services and Spell Checker), how to use the Programs Administration feature, how to access the UNIX system directly, how to globally administer other programs in FACE, how to use executable files and run UNIX system shell scripts while in FACE, and how to suspend files.

In addition to this chapter, Appendix C, *Quick Reference to FACE*, summarizes the tasks you can do using FACE, and the commands to do them.

Getting Started

This section explains the basics of using your AT&T FACE environment. You will learn how to log in, what menus, forms, and text frames are and how to use them, how to move frames around on the screen, how to get help, and how to log out.

You will learn how to navigate from frame to frame and from file folder to file folder within a frame. You will also learn how to access FACE commands: with the function keys (or their alternate keystrokes), from the Command menu, and from the command line.

Logging In

Before you can begin to use FACE, you must log into your computer. Logging in is equivalent to having a lock on your office door. Just as other people cannot get into your office without the key to the door, unauthorized users cannot log into your computer without the key to your login ID: your password.

It is never a good idea to share your login ID with another person. Besides making your Office less secure, if two people are using one login ID at the same time, your FACE screen can deteriorate severely (frames may be distorted and you may not be able to navigate properly).

You will need to know the following things before you can log into FACE. Some of them are dependent on the type of computer, and the type of terminal you will be using.

- how to turn on your terminal
- how to request connection to the computer
- your login ID (often referred to as just "login")
- your password
- your terminal type

When you have this information, you are ready to start.

1. If your terminal is off, turn it on.

2. If it is necessary for you to request a connection to a particular computer, do so.

3. When you receive the `Login:` prompt, type your login ID, and press **ENTER**.

   If you make a mistake while typing your login ID, the computer will start over, presenting you with the `Login:` prompt again.

   When you receive the `Password:` prompt, type your password, and press **ENTER**. Notice, as you type your password, that it is not displayed on the screen as you type it. This is to help keep the password secret.

4. If you are prompted for your terminal type, type in that information and press **ENTER**.

   If you are using an AT&T terminal and you don't know your terminal type, just pressing **ENTER** will result in FACE attempting to determine your terminal type.

Not all terminal types are automatically determined by FACE. If FACE cannot determine the terminal type, you will be prompted with `TERM=` again, and will have to supply the terminal information.

That's all there is to logging in. But before you begin using the AT&T FACE Office you should understand the way the parts of the FACE screen work.

If FACE is not invoked automatically at login, you may access it by typing `face` at the UNIX System prompt. (For complete information see `face`(1), in the *User's Reference Manual*.

Structure of the FACE Screen

The FACE screen has a logical structure behind it. Figure 5-1 is a diagram of the five functional areas of the FACE screen. As you read the explanations of these five areas, which follow the diagram, compare the FACE screen that you see on your terminal to this structure.

Figure 5-1: The Logical Structure of the FACE Screen

Title

Work Area

Message Line

Command Line

F1	F2	F3	F4	F5	F6	F7	F8

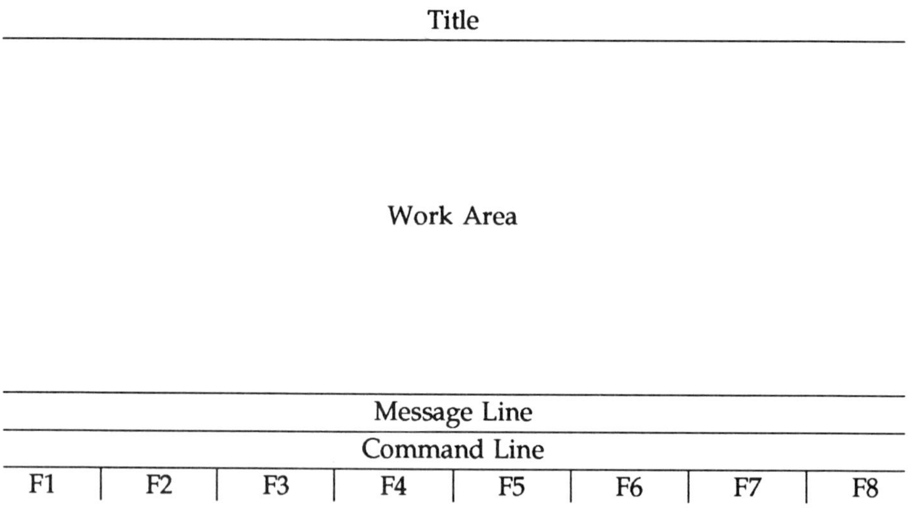

Title

The title line displays information about the status of the system. The words `AT&T FACE`, the day, and the date always appear in the center of this line. If electronic mail is available on your system, the word `MAIL` is displayed at the far left of this line when you have mail to read. When FACE is busy, the word `working ...` will be displayed at the far right on this line. When this message is displayed, you cannot do anything else in your FACE Office until FACE removes the message.

To read your mail, select `Programs` from the FACE menu and then select `Mail Services` . This invokes the `mailx` command. (See the section "Programs", for more information on how to read your mail.)

Work Area

The work area is the central portion of your screen. It is here that the forms, menus, files, and file folders you will work with are displayed in frames. The AT&T FACE menu that appears in this area immediately after you log into FACE is an example of a frame. Frames that you have opened (selected) always appear in the work area. A frame or part of a frame may be temporarily written over by another frame if several are open at the same time.

Message Line

The message line is the second line above the screen labels for the function keys. It is where feedback and error messages are displayed during or after the action you are performing. It is also where you are prompted for more information, when more information is required by the action you are performing. When you first log in, this line shows the message `Move to an item with arrow keys and press the ENTER key to select the item.`

Command Line

The command line displays commands as you type them. It is accessed by pressing either [CTRL-j] or [CTRL-f] [c]. (The command line will probably be blank when you first log in.) You will learn how to use the command line in the section "Navigating Between Frames".

Screen Labels for Function Keys

Eight screen labels for the function keys occupy the last line on your FACE screen. They are designated as areas F1 through F8 in Figure 5-1. If your keyboard has function keys, these labels correspond to the function keys [F1] through [F8] on your keyboard. For example, on your FACE screen right now, the label that corresponds to function key [F4] is [PREV-FRM].

The functions assigned to the function keys change, depending on what type of frame is currently active. When the functions change, the labels on your screen change. For example, a menu frame has a different set of functions than a form frame because you do different things in menus.

If your terminal does not have function keys, or if they don't work properly, you may access the functions named on these labels by using the alternate keystrokes listed in Figure 5-3.

Whether or not the function keys work can depend on what terminal type you entered at the `TERM=` prompt during the logging in procedure.

What You See After You Log In

Now that you have logged in successfully, the screen will clear and the first frame (the AT&T FACE menu) appears. This frame is always open and displayed on the screen. Open frames can be either active or inactive, but as long as a frame is open, it is accessible to you in the work area. Even if other frames are opened, the AT&T FACE menu is always identified by the number 1 at the left of the title, and the title is always AT&T FACE. It serves as a base from which you can access all parts of FACE. The AT&T FACE menu is shown in Figure 5-2.

Figure 5-2: The AT&T FACE Menu

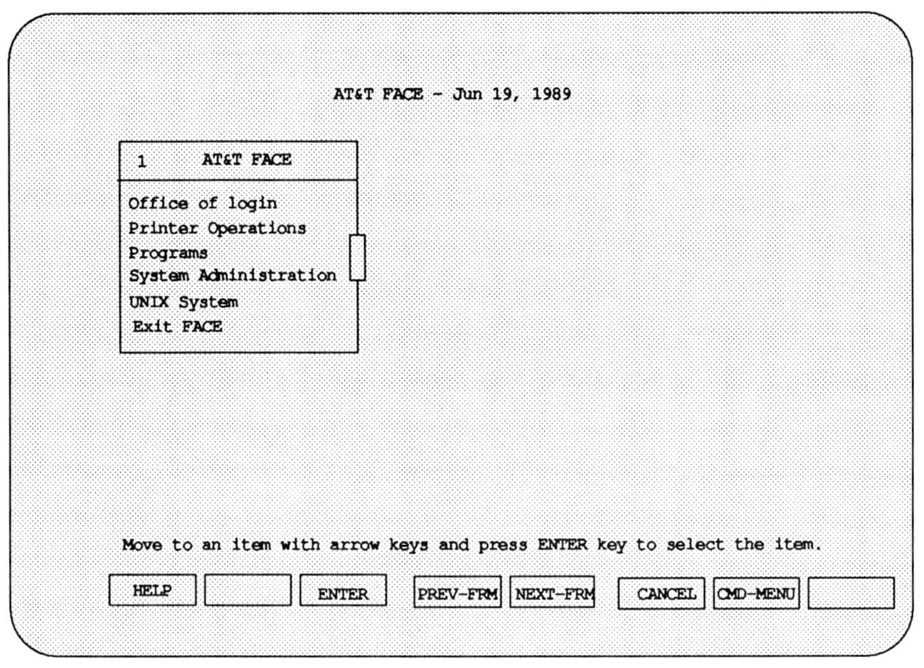

What you see on your screen should look similar to Figure 5-2. The prominent feature in the FACE screen is the AT&T FACE menu. Items in the FACE menu are as follows:

`Office of login` — When you select this item, a new frame titled `Office of login` opens in the work area, displaying a menu of other office functions you can perform. This item identifies *your* FACE Office. For example, if your login ID is `tom`, when you log in, this item will read `Office of tom`. For ease of reference, we'll use the term `Office of login` whenever this menu item is discussed. Just remember that your own login ID will replace `login` when you are using AT&T FACE.

`Printer Operations` This item gives you information about printers that are connected to your computer and allows you to customize the print command to suit your needs. Refer to "Printer Operations" for more information.

`Programs` This item presents a menu listing all the programs installed on the computer that you can access. By selecting a program name, you can run that program. If there are no programs installed for use in FACE, this item will not appear in your AT&T FACE menu. (The section "Using Other Features of FACE" covers the use of this item in detail.)

`System Administration`
This item gives a person who has administration privileges the ability to administer FACE, add logins, install software programs, add printers or modems, display user information, get a report of system configurations, copy floppies, and perform many other administration tasks. If you have not been given system administration privileges you will not see this item in your AT&T FACE menu. Refer to "System Administration" for more information.

`UNIX System` This item allows you to access the UNIX System directly. If you have not been given UNIX system privileges you will not see this item in your AT&T FACE menu. Refer to "Using Other Features of FACE" for more information.

`Exit FACE` This entry logs you out of FACE. Refer to "Logging Out", in this section, for more information.

Other frames of information may appear on the FACE screen if you have previously designated them to appear. Ignore them for now, and continue reading.

After the AT&T FACE menu and possibly other frames open, a prompt may appear on the message line telling you that files or file folders in your wastebasket are scheduled to be removed. A menu of the files or file folders scheduled for removal is also displayed. You can use MARK to mark specific files or file folders to save, then delete the rest by pressing ENTER. Or, you may choose not to delete any files or file folders by pressing CANCEL or the alternate keystroke CTRL-f 6. (Complete information on navigating in menu frames is covered in section "How to Use a Menu"). For now, if this menu appears, press CANCEL.

The section "Using your FACE Office" covers the Wastebasket feature in detail.

Alternate Keystrokes

It is unlikely that any keyboard has all the named keys referred to in this guide. For example, many keyboards do not have a BACKTAB key or the function keys F1 through F8. If your keyboard does not have all the keys referred to in this guide (or if your keyboard has them, but they do not work properly), you can use alternate keystrokes instead.

Figure 5-3 shows sequences of alternate keystrokes (two or three keys that, when typed, are equivalent to pressing the named key). In these sequences, CTRL represents the control key. The control key is used the same way you hold down the shift key when you want to type a capital letter. For example, the sequence of alternate keystrokes to type if you can't use function key F1 is CTRL-f 1. To type this sequence, hold the control key down while you type the first character that follows the dash (here "`f`"), but release it before you type the second character (here "`1`"). Or, if you are instructed to "`...press` →," and your keyboard doesn't have a key with a picture of an arrow pointing right on it (or if it doesn't function), you would type this sequence: CTRL-r.

Figure 5-3: Named Keys and Their Alternate Keystrokes

Named Key	Alternate Keystroke	Named Key	Alternate Keystroke
BACKSPACE	CTRL-h	INSERT-CHAR	CTRL-a
BACKTAB	CTRL-t	INSERT-LINE	CTRL-o
BEG	CTRL-b	←	CTRL-l
CLEAR	CTRL-y	NEXT	CTRL-n
CLEAR-EOL or CLEAR-LINE	CTRL-f y	NEXTPAGE or PAGE-DOWN	CTRL-w
CMD LINE	CTRL-j or CTRL-f c	PAGE-UP or PREVPAGE	CTRL-v
DEL or DEL-CHAR	CTRL-x	PREV	CTRL-p
DEL-LINE	CTRL-k	↑	CTRL-u
↓	CTRL-d	RESET	CTRL-f r
END	CTRL-e	→	CTRL-r
ENTER	CTRL-m	SCROLL-DOWN	CTRL-f d
F1 thru F8	CTRL-f 1 thru CTRL-f 8	SCROLL-UP	CTRL-f u
HOME	CTRL-f b	SPACEBAR	none
HOME-DOWN	CTRL-f e	TAB	CTRL-i

NOTE

Depending on your keyboard, the carriage return key may be called ENTER or RETURN. Throughout this chapter the ENTER key is used to represent the carriage return key. ENTER may also be assigned to screen-labeled function key F3. However, if your keyboard only has a RETURN key, use it or CTRL-m instead.

How to Use a Menu

Function Key Labels in Menus

The set of screen labels that appears across the bottom line of the FACE screen corresponds to the eight function keys on your keyboard, F1 through F8. When the currently active frame is a menu, as is the case now, the first level of function keys shown in Figure 5-4 appears at the bottom of the screen. When the currently active frame is a file folder, however, the label for F8 changes from blank to CHG-KEYS, and you have access to the second level of function keys (also shown in Figure 5-4). (You'll see examples of this later in the section "Using Your FACE Office".)

If you are using the AT&T 5620 or AT&T 630 series terminal running layers, the functions assigned to the function keys do not get downloaded and alternate keystrokes must be used (see "Alternate Keystrokes" in this section). Some terminals have programmable function keys, which you may be able to program to execute FACE commands. See the manual for your terminal for instructions.

Figure 5-4: Function Keys Available in a Menu

First Level		Second Level	
F1	HELP	F1	HELP
F2	blank	F2	COPY
F3	ENTER	F3	MOVE
F4	PREV-FRM	F4	DELETE
F5	NEXT-FRM	F5	RENAME
F6	CANCEL	F6	CREATE
F7	CMD-MENU	F7	SECURITY
F8	blank*	F8	blank*

* Function key F8 is labeled CHG-KEYS when a menu displays the contents of a file folder.

Navigating in a Menu

FACE uses two methods to show the item that you are currently positioned on in a menu. The first is an icon to the left of the menu item. (An icon is a graphic symbol used to represent visually some aspect of your computer's functionality.) On some terminals the icon indicating position is a right-angle bracket (>), on others it is an underscore (_). On still other terminals it may be something different.

The second method can be seen only if your terminal supports inverse video. Inverse video is a feature that enables two-color display terminals to display parts of the screen in the opposite combination of colors (for example, instead of white characters on a black background, parts of the screen are displayed as black characters on a white background). If your terminal has this feature, the item on which you are currently positioned is highlighted in inverse video.

Check your AT&T FACE menu now and take note of what method is used to mark your current position on your terminal screen. (This mark is also called the "highlight bar" or "cursor," and all these terms refer to the visible symbol that indicates your current location on the screen.) In this guide the right-angle bracket (>) is used to show the position of the cursor in figures showing terminal output.

All FACE menus use the same keys for moving around (navigating) inside the frame.

If your function keys and named keys do not work as described, use the alternate keystrokes instead.

Figure 5-5: Keys Used to Navigate in a Menu

Named Key	Alternate Keystroke	What It Does in a Menu
↓	CTRL-d	moves the cursor down one item, wrapping to the top of the next column when it reaches the bottom. If there is only one column, or if the cursor is on the last column, it wraps to the top of the first column.
↑	CTRL-u	moves the cursor up one item, wrapping to the bottom of the previous column when it reaches the top of the current one. When the cursor is on the first menu item, it wraps to the last item in the last column.
→ or SPACEBAR	CTRL-r	moves the cursor down one item on a single column menu, right one item on a multicolumn menu. It does not wrap in multicolumn menus.
← or BACKSPACE	CTRL-l	moves the cursor up one item on a single column menu, left one item on a multicolumn menu. It does not wrap in multicolumn menus.
NEXT	CTRL-n	the same as →, but wraps to the first item in its row or column when it reaches the last item.

Named Key	Alternate Keystroke	What It Does in a Menu
PREV	CTRL-p	the same as ←, but wraps to the last item in its row or column when it reaches the first item.
HOME	CTRL-f b	moves the cursor to the first item currently visible on the menu.
HOME-DOWN	CTRL-f e	moves the cursor to the last item of the first column, or the first page, in the menu.

If a menu contains too many items to display at once, the frame is scrollable. A scrollable frame is identified in the scroll bar on the right hand border of the screen. Scroll icons in the bar indicate which way the frame may be scrolled.

Not all terminals use the same graphic symbols for scroll icons. Some use ^ to show a frame can be scrolled up, and v to show a frame can be scrolled down.

If a menu is scrollable, the following named keys will also work.

Figure 5-6: Additional Keys Used to Navigate in a Scrollable Menu

Named Key	Alternate Keystroke	What It Does in a Menu
PAGE-DOWN	CTRL-w	moves the cursor to the first item on the next page full of items and displays that page, if there is another full page of menu items.
PAGE-UP	CTRL-v	moves the cursor to the first item in the previous page full of items and displays that page, if there is a previous full page of menu items.
BEG	CTRL-b	moves the cursor to the first item in the menu whether it is currently visible or not, and displays the first page.
END	CTRL-e	moves the cursor to the last item in the menu whether it is currently visible or not, and displays the last page.
SCROLL-DOWN	CTRL-f d	rolls the contents of the menu down one line.
SCROLL-UP	CTRL-f u	rolls the contents of the menu up one line.

Since the AT&T FACE menu only has one column of items, many of these keys cannot be demonstrated now, but you can try the various arrow keys (or alternate keystrokes) to move through the list of items.

Selecting an Item from a Menu

The following brief exercises show you two methods of selecting an item from a menu. Try both, then you can continue to use whichever one you like best throughout these exercises, and whenever you are working in FACE.

Navigate to the Item and Press ENTER

A menu item can be selected simply by navigating to it and pressing ENTER.

1. Continue to press ↓ (or CTRL-d) until the cursor is positioned on the menu item `Office of login` . (`login` will be whatever your login ID is)
2. Press ENTER to select (open) this item. The Office of login frame displays

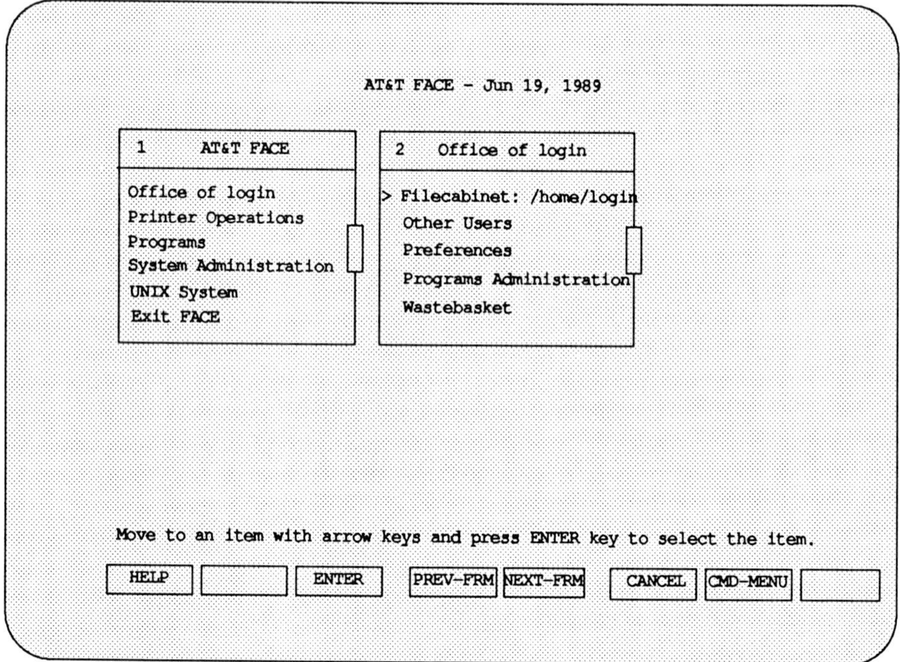

The name /home may be something different if your system administrator has changed the default location for user logins.

3. Continue to press [↓] (or [CTRL-d]) until the cursor is positioned on `Filecabinet`, then press [ENTER] to select (open) it.

   Once `Filecabinet` has been selected, the /home/login frame will appear in the work area.

4. Press [CANCEL] (or [CTRL-f] [6]) to close the /home/login frame.

   It disappears and you are back in the Office of login menu again.

Type the First Letters of the Menu Item

The second way to select an item from a menu is by simply typing its name.

1. Type the letter `o`. (The case of letters is ignored.)

   Notice that the cursor moves immediately to the item `Other Users`.

2. Now type the letter `w`.

   The cursor does not move to `Wastebasket`. FACE doesn't know that you changed your mind about what you were looking for. It still remembers the `o` that you typed, and tries to find a menu item that begins with the letters `ow`. When it can't find it, it lets you know, on the message line.

3. Press [↓] (or [CTRL-d]), or use any of the other navigation keys to clear the letters you typed.

   When you make a typing error or change your mind about what you want to select, you must press a navigation key to clear out the letters you have typed so far, before you can use this method again to select another menu item.

4. Type `o` again and press [ENTER]. This time you have selected `Other Users` from the Office menu, and the Other Users menu appears and is the active frame. The Other Users menu lists the login IDs of other people also authorized to work on your computer system.

5. Press CANCEL to close the Other Users menu.

For the rest of this guide, when you are asked to "select an item," use the method that is easiest for you.

How to Use a Form

A second type of frame in FACE, is a form. A form looks like a fill-in-the-blanks questionnaire. Figure 5-7 shows how one of the forms in FACE, the Display Frames form, looks.

Figure 5-7: The Display Frames Form

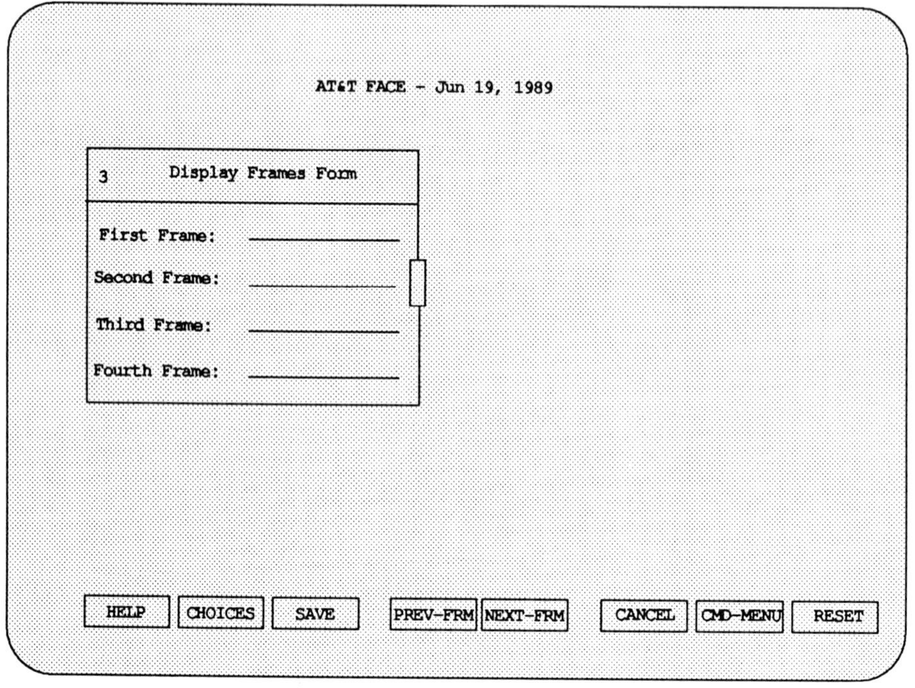

The information you enter in the fields of a form is used by FACE to change the way your FACE Office looks, or to change what a FACE command does. In the example in Figure 5-7, the fields you can enter information into are `First`

`Frame`, `Second Frame`, `Third Frame`, and `Fourth Frame`. (How to fill in this form is covered in the section "Changing Other Office Preferences".)

The only other thing to remember is that forms often appear with default values already in most of the fields. (A default value is one that is automatically assigned to the field by FACE, and which will remain the value for that field unless *you* change it.)

Function Key Labels in Forms

Forms have a different set of function keys from menus. These are shown in Figure 5-8. Notice that since there are only eight functions available in forms, there is no need for FACE to reserve F8 to act as a toggle between levels, as happens in menus. You'll see the function key labels change when you practice navigating and editing a form later in this section.

Figure 5-8: Function Keys Available in a Form

	Function Key
F1	HELP
F2	CHOICES
F3	SAVE
F4	PREV-FRM
F5	NEXT-FRM
F6	CANCEL
F7	CMD-MENU
F8	RESET

The three function keys that are different than in menus are CHOICES, SAVE, and RESET. The CHOICES function key will display the valid choices for the current field. (If the message `No choices available` is displayed on the message line, it means you must type in a valid entry for the field.) The RESET function key restores the value of the current field to whatever it was before you changed it. The SAVE function key saves the values you have entered in all the fields and closes the form.

Navigating in and Editing a Form

Because you type new information in a form or change information that is already there, as well as move around in it, you need an editing capability as well as a navigation capability. To allow you to edit a form as well as move around in it, some of the named keys act differently when they are used in a form than they act when they are used in a menu. The keys used inside forms are shown in Figure 5-9.

Remember that if your keyboard does not have some of these named keys (or if they don't work), you can use alternate keystrokes.

Figure 5-9: Navigation Keys Used in a Form

Named Key	Alternate Keystrokes	What It Does in a Form
↓	CTRL-d	moves the cursor down to the next field. If you are on the last field, the cursor wraps around to the top field.
↑	CTRL-u	moves the cursor up to the previous field. If you are on the top field, the cursor wraps around to the bottom field.
→	CTRL-r	non-destructively moves the cursor right one character within a field. It does not wrap to the next field.
←	CTRL-l	non-destructively moves the cursor left one character within a field. It does not wrap to the previous field.
TAB	CTRL-i	moves the cursor to the next field in the form. The wrap-around feature works as it does with ↓.
BACKTAB	CTRL-t	moves the cursor to the previous frame. It wraps the same way as ↑.

Figure 5-10: Navigation Keys Used in a Form (continued)

Named Key	Alternate Keystrokes	What It Does in a Form
HOME BEG	CTRL-f b CTRL-b	moves the cursor to the first character of the current field.
HOME-DOWN END	CTRL-f e CTRL-e	moves the cursor to the last character of the current field.
BACKSPACE	CTRL-h	moves the cursor to the left, deleting the character there.
SPACEBAR	none	replaces the current character with a space and moves the cursor one character to the right.
DEL or DELETE-CHAR	CTRL-x	deletes the character under the cursor and closes the gap.
DELETE-LINE	CTRL-k	deletes the current line of a field and closes the gap. In a single line field, it acts the same as CLEAR-LINE.
RESET	CTRL-f r	resets a field to its previous value.
CLEAR-EOL	CTRL-f y	clears the line from the current cursor position to the end of the line.
CLEAR CLEAR-LINE	CTRL-y	clears the current line of the current field.

In the following exercise, you will learn how to navigate to the Office Functions form and practice changing its field values. Remember that in FACE, "select" means navigate to an item in a menu and press ENTER.

If your cursor icon is an underscore (_), you may have difficulty seeing it when you are using a form, because fields are underlined by default.

If you decide to type in a new value in a field, the first character you type will clear the entire field. If the first character you type is a space, it will look like the field is empty, but it isn't. The space character is at the beginning of the line and your cursor is actually positioned on the second character of this line. If you forget to remove that first space, your entry will look okay, but probably will not work correctly.

1. Select `Preferences` from the Office of login menu.

   The Preferences menu appears and has four items in it. (The use of these item will be discussed in detail later.)

2. Select `Office Functions` from the Preferences menu.

   The Office Functions form appears on the screen. This form has seven fields and the cursor is positioned on the first field, `Delete objects in my Wastebasket after (# of days)`. The default value for this field is `1`.

   Notice that the function key labels at the bottom of the screen have changed. The message line tells you the valid entries you can make in this field.

3. Type `32` in this field and press (ENTER).

   Notice that `Input is not valid` is displayed on the message line, and that the cursor did not move to the next field. If FACE can determine that the new value you are trying to enter in a field is not valid (here `32`), you will not be able to leave the field until it contains a valid value.

   You can use this field to try some of the form editing keys listed in Figure 5-10, such as (BACKSPACE), or (DELETE-CHAR).

4. Press (RESET) (or (CTRL-f) (8)) to restore the previous value for this field.

   (RESET) only affects the current field.

5. Navigate to the `Prompt before deleting ...` field (it displays the default value `yes`) and press CHOICES (or CTRL-f 2). The value in the field will change to `no`.
6. Press CHOICES again, and the value of the field changes back to `yes`.
7. Press ↓ to navigate to the `Folder Display Format:` field. It displays the default value `Name only`.
9. Press CHOICES (or CTRL-f 2) again.

   This time a Choices menu appears on the screen. CHOICES (or CTRL-f 2) will show the valid choices for a field by Toggling through them in the field itself when there are fewer than four choices. When there are four or more valid choices, they are shown in a Choices menu.

   A Choices menu is different from other menus in several ways. First, only two function keys are available: ENTER, and CANCEL. Second, selecting an item from a Choices menu doesn't open anything. The item you select is simply entered into the form field.
10. Press the function key labeled ENTER (or CTRL-f 3), to select any item from the Choices menu. (You can also press RETURN or CTRL-m to select items from a Choices menu.)

    The Choices menu disappears and the selected item is entered in the `Folder Display Format:` field.
11. Press CANCEL (or CTRL-f 6), which "cancels" any changes you may have made in *all* the fields in the Office Fucntions form and closes it, returning you to the Preferences menu.
12. Press CTRL-j, to access the command line, type `cancel` and then press ENTER.

    This closes the Preferences menu and puts you back in the Office menu.

    When you type `cancel` on the command line, FACE does the same thing that it would have done if you had pressed the CANCEL function key (or CTRL-f 6). In fact, when you press CANCEL, FACE simply executes the `cancel` command for you. That is, it closes the frame you are in, and removes it from the work area.

13. Press CANCEL (or CTRL-f 6) to close the Office frame and return to the AT&T FACE menu.

Navigating Between Frames

The term navigate, until now, has only been applied to movement inside a frame. You may also navigate between frames. You have already used two methods to do this.

- Selecting (opening) an item will always cause navigation to the frame that item is displayed in (except when in a Choices menu).
- Canceling (closing) a frame will cause navigation to the previously active frame (except when in a Choices menu).

To practice four ways of navigating between frames without closing the currently active one, you will need to have several frames open on your FACE screen. The following instructions will open the Office of login, /home/login, and Wastebasket frames. After opening the frames, you will practice navigating between them without canceling (closing) them.

1. Select `Office of login` from the AT&T FACE menu.
2. Select `Filecabinet` from the Office of login menu.
3. Select `WASTEBASKET` from the /home/login menu.

Of course, there are valid reasons for wanting to navigate to a different frame without closing the currently active frame. At this point in a work session, you might want to look at the Other Users menu to find out who owns a login ID. To open the Other Users menu you have to go back to the Office menu, but perhaps you don't want to close the WASTEBASKET frame.

Navigating Between Frames from the Command Line

This method of navigating between frames makes use of the frame numbers that appear to the left of the title of each open frame. Notice that each open frame has a unique number, starting with the AT&T FACE menu, which is numbered `1`.

1. Press CTRL-j to access the command line.
2. Type the number 2 and press ENTER to navigate back to frame 2, the Office menu.
3. Select `Other Users`.

   The Other Users menu opens, and you can look through the list of other users, perhaps to find a login ID you need. The Other Users menu also has a unique number to the left of the frame title.
4. When you are finished with the Other Users menu, press CTRL-j, type `cancel`, and then press ENTER to close it.

   The cursor is now in the previously active frame, the Office of login menu.

The command `goto` can also be used to move to a frame by referencing its frame ID number. (See Appendix C for details on its use.)

Navigating Between Frames with Function Keys

Most frames that appear on the FACE screen have PREV-FRM and NEXT-FRM assigned to function keys F4 and F5. These function keys cause the cursor to jump from frame to frame. The frame jumped to becomes active, and the frame jumped from becomes inactive.

Right now, the Office of login menu should be the active frame.

1. Press PREV-FRM (or CTRL-f 4) to jump to the frame that was active before you opened the Office of login menu.

   The cursor jumps to the AT&T FACE menu.
2. Press NEXT-FRM (or CTRL-f 5) to jump back to the Office of login menu.
3. Press CANCEL (or CTRL-f 6) to close the Office of login menu.

   The AT&T FACE menu should again be the active frame.

Navigating Between Frames with the `frm-mgmt` Command

Although the Command Menu is explained fully in the next section, one of the commands available from it is explained here because it enables you to navigate between frames without closing the currently active frame. For now, follow the exercise exactly.

1. Select `Office of login` from the AT&T FACE menu.
2. Press CMD-MENU (or CTRL-f 7) to access the Command Menu.

   You can select items from the Command Menu as you can in any other menu. In the Command Menu however, the items are neither menus nor forms, but FACE commands. A command for navigating between frames is `frm-mgmt`.
3. Select `frm-mgmt` from the Command Menu.

   The Command Menu disappears and the Frame Management menu appears, listing the item `list`.
4. Select `list`. The Open Frames menu appears, listing all open frames on your screen.
5. Select `Office of login`.

   The Open Frames menu disappears and the Office of login frame becomes active.
6. Press CANCEL (or CTRL-f 6) to close the Office of login frame.

   The AT&T FACE menu is again the active frame.

By now, you have probably noticed an important difference between closing a frame with CANCEL, and navigating from frame to frame in the ways described here. When you close a frame with CANCEL, it disappears, and the cursor automatically moves back to the frame you were in before. You no longer have access to the frame you canceled, except by repeating the selection process that opened it in the first place. But when you navigate out of an open frame in one of the ways just discussed, the frame does not disappear, it merely becomes inactive. You can still re-activate it and continue to use it.

Managing the Appearance of Your Office

Each time you open a frame, FACE automatically determines its shape and location on the screen. FACE positions frames so that they do not overlap unless it is necessary. FACE also sizes each frame to fit the files and file folders listed.

The `frm-mgmt` command enables you to change the position and size of an open frame. As you just learned, it can also be used to list all open frames and activate any one of them. (See "Navigating Between Frames with the `frm-mgmt` Command.")

If you reshape a menu or text frame, the change remains in effect *as long as the frame's contents do not change.* Once you close a moved, updated, or reshaped frame, or log out, FACE will automatically reposition and reshape the frame the next time it is opened. It will try to return the frame to its original position unless other frames have been opened in the meantime that make that impractical.

Moving a Frame

Some people want frames in specific locations, such as the /home/login frame in the upper right of the work area. Others may want frames to be narrow so that more frames can be seen at one time.

In the following exercise, you will use `frm-mgmt` from the Command menu to move the /home/login frame to a new location in your work area.

1. Select `Office of login` from the AT&T FACE menu.
2. Select `Filecabinet` from the Office menu.

   The frame to be moved, here the /home/login frame, must be the active frame *before* you execute `frm-mgmt`.
3. Press [CMD-MENU] (or [CTRL-f] [7]) to display the Command menu.
4. Select `frm-mgmt`.
5. Select `move` from the Frame Management menu.

   Notice that the cursor is on the top-left corner of the /home/login frame, the other three corners are blinking, and the message line instructs you to position the corner where you want it to be moved.

6. Use the arrow keys to position the top-left corner marker: when it is where you want that corner to be, press ENTER.

   The /home/login frame has been relocated on your screen.

7. Navigate back to the Office menu, but do not close /home/login (use PREV-FRM or CTRL-f 4).

   Notice that the /home/login frame stays in its new location.

8. Navigate back to the /home/login frame with NEXT-FRM (or CTRL-f 5), then press CANCEL (or CTRL-f 6) to close it.

9. Select `Filecabinet` from the Office menu again.

   The /home/login frame is back in its original location. Remember, if you move a frame with `frm-mgmt`, and then close it, it may revert to its original position when it is re-opened.

Reshaping a Frame

In this exercise you will reshape the /home/login frame using `frm-mgmt` from the command line.

1. You should still be in the /home/login frame, but if you aren't, navigate to it.

2. Press CTRL-j to access the command line, then type `frm-mgmt` and press ENTER.

3. Select `Reshape` from the Frame Management menu.

4. When the prompt instructs you to position the top-left corner, use the arrow keys to position it where you want it.

5. Press ENTER.

   The prompt now instructs you to position the bottom-right corner where you want it to be.

6. Use arrow keys to make the frame larger, and press ENTER.

   Remember, after you close a frame you have reshaped, or exit from FACE, it will revert to the location FACE assigns to it automatically. If the frame contains a file folder menu, any command that causes the menu to be updated, such as creating a new file, will also cause it to revert to its original shape and location.

Only menus and text frames can be reshaped. Forms cannot be reshaped.

The Command Menu

The Command Menu, shown in Figure 5-11, is a complete list of FACE commands from which you can select commands, just as you select items from other FACE menus. It is displayed by pressing CMD-MENU (or CTRL-f 7). (All these commands can also be executed directly from the command line by typing CTRL-j, typing the command name, and then pressing ENTER. The Command Menu is actually provided as a type of help.)

Figure 5-11: The Command Menu

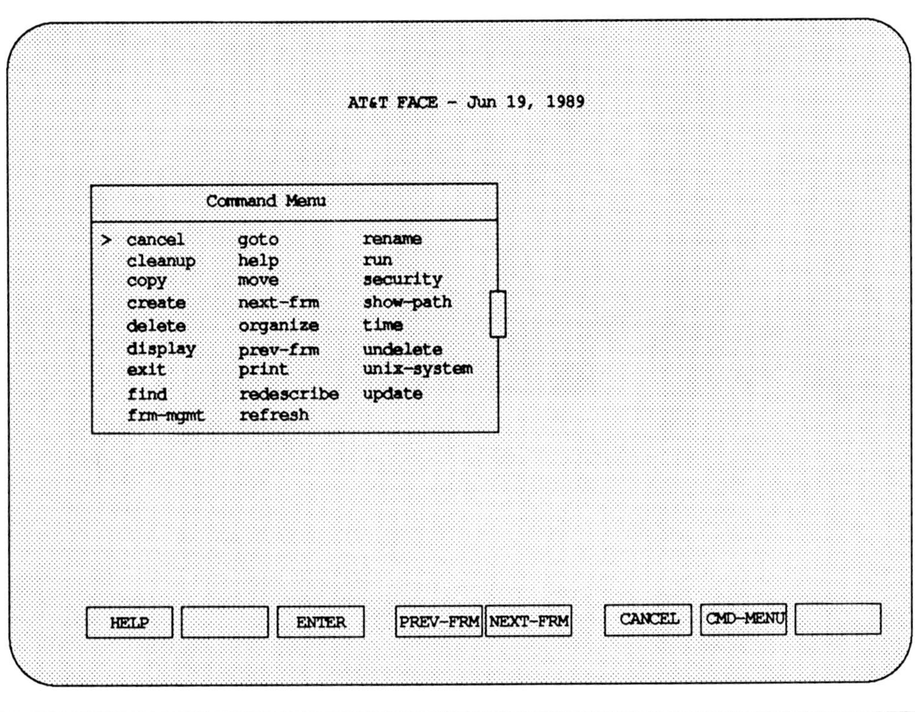

In this exercise, you will use only a couple of commands from the Command Menu. However, the specific use of every command in the Command Menu is described in Appendix C. There is also on-screen help available for each command, and access to that help is covered in section "Getting Help".

1. Select `Office of login` from the FACE menu.
2. Press [CMD-MENU] (or [CTRL-f] [7]) to open the Command Menu.

   At this point, you may want to try some of the menu navigation keys that work in menus that have more than one column. Notice that keys like [→] (or [CTRL-r]) and [←] (or [CTRL-l]) work differently when there are more than one column in a menu.

You already know that you can select a command by navigating to it and pressing ENTER. If the command you select requires more information from you, you will be prompted for it.

You are also familiar with pressing CTRL-j to access the command line. If you press it when you are in the Command Menu, the item on which the cursor is currently positioned will appear on the command line after the prompt.

3. Navigate to the `time` command and type CTRL-j. Notice that it now appears on the command line, after the --> prompt. The Command Menu disappears, and the function key labels now display only CANCEL, and HELP. These are the function keys that apply to the command line.
4. Press CANCEL (or CTRL-f 6). The command line prompt disappears because CANCEL currently applies to the command line. In effect, you have canceled the `time` command, and the frame that was most recently active, the Office menu, becomes active again.
5. Press CMD-MENU (or CTRL-f 7) again, navigate to `cancel` and press CTRL-j to access the command line.

   The Command menu disappears (closes), and `cancel` is displayed on the command line.
6. Press ENTER. By pressing it you have run the `cancel` command. This time, `cancel` operated on the currently active frame, the Office of login menu. The Office of login menu disappears and the AT&T FACE menu becomes the active frame.

Getting Help

The Help Facility is a built-in user's aid, offering help on all aspects of using FACE. The following section discusses how to get help on specific commands, menus, and form fields. The section following that discusses how to get help on FACE in general.

Getting Help on FACE Commands, Menus, and Form Fields

Help on the currently active command, menu, or form field is easy to get because the `help` command is always assigned to function key F1 (or CTRL-f 1) if there is help available.

- When the active frame is the Command Menu, pressing HELP presents you with a frame of information about how to use the command on which you are currently positioned.
- When the active frame is a menu, pressing HELP will present you with a frame of information describing each item in that menu.
- When the active frame is a form, pressing HELP presents you with a frame of information on how to fill out the field you are currently positioned on.
- When you are on the command line, pressing HELP presents you with menu of the commands, and gives help on the command you select.

The next exercise shows how to get specific help on a FACE command. Later, you can try the same procedure and navigation techniques when you want help on a specific menu or form field. The Help Facility gives you help on the currently active FACE command or frame. This exercise explains how to get help on the use of a specific command.

1. Navigate to the Office of login frame.
2. Press CMD-MENU or CTRL-f 7 to open the Command Menu. The cursor is positioned on the command `cancel`. Suppose you want to refresh your memory about what this command does before you use it.
3. Press HELP (or CTRL-f 1) to open the Help Facility frame for the `cancel` command.

   The Command Menu disappears and a new frame, Help on cancel, displays a brief summary of what the `cancel` command does, and how to use it.

   Function keys F2 and F3, now labeled PREVPAGE and NEXTPAGE, show you the previous and next frame full of text in a Help frame. The scroll bar in the right border of the frame shows the v icon, indicating that there are more pages of text following this one.

4. Press NEXTPAGE (or CTRL-f 3).

   A second icon, ^, appears in the scroll bar, and means that there is a page preceding this one that you can access with PREVPAGE (or CTRL-f 2).
   (For an additional list of navigation keys that are used in Help and other text frames, see Figure 5-13.)

5. Press CANCEL (or CTRL-f 6) to close the Help on cancel frame.

Getting Help on FACE in General

Help on FACE in general is available after you have pressed HELP. It is available from the Overview of Contents menu, and this menu is accessed by pressing the CONTENTS (or CTRL-f 8 function key, which is only displayed while a Help frame is open on the screen. General help is not available from the first level of function keys because it is used less frequently than specific help on commands or frames.

You can begin this exercise from whatever frame is currently active on your screen (if you just completed the previous section, "Getting Help on FACE Commands," the Office of login menu will be active).

1. Press HELP (or CTRL-f 1) and a frame of information will display help text about the currently active frame.

   Notice that the screen label for function key F8 now reads CONTENTS.

2. Press CONTENTS (or CTRL-f 8).

   Function key F8 always displays this screen label when you are in a Help frame. The Contents menu that appears now lists topics on the mechanics of using FACE.

3. Select `Frames and Function Keys` from the Contents menu.

   A frame titled Help Facility: Frames and Function Keys opens. The scroll icon in the scroll bar shows that there are more pages of text following this one.

4. Press NEXTPAGE (or CTRL-f 3). A second scroll icon shows that there is a page preceding this one. The PREVPAGE key (or CTRL-f 2) will show you the preceding page.

   (For an additional list of navigation keys that are used in Help and other text frames, see Figure 5-13, which follows this exercise.)

5. Press CMD-MENU (or CTRL-f 7), and select the `cleanup` command.

   The `cleanup` command closes the current frame, as well as all other frames except the AT&T FACE frame. (You can also use the CANCEL command to exit from a Help frame.)

While in a Help or other text frames, the following keys allow you to navigate through the text. These keys supplement PREVPAGE and NEXTPAGE. Remember that if your keyboard does not have some of these named keys (or if they don't work), you can use the alternate keystrokes.

Figure 5-12: Navigation Keys That Work in Help or Other Text Frames

Named Key	Alternate Keystroke	What It Does in Text Frame
↑	CTRL-u	moves the cursor up one line.
↓	CTRL-d	moves the cursor down one line.
SCROLL-DOWN	CTRL-f d	rolls the text down one line.
SCROLL-UP	CTRL-f u	rolls the text up one line.
PAGE-DOWN	CTRL-w	presents the next frame full of text, preserving two lines from the current frame.
PAGE-UP	CTRL-v	presents the previous frame full of text, preserving two lines from the current frame.
BEG	CTRL-b	presents the first frame full of text.
END	CTRL-e	presents the last frame full of text.

Exiting from FACE

You have completed a beginner's tour of FACE. If you want to exit from FACE, use the `Exit FACE` item in the AT&T FACE menu. Here's how:

1. It is not necessary to close all open frames to exit from FACE. Navigate to the AT&T FACE menu by any method you like.
2. Select `Exit FACE`.

   To make sure that you really want to exit, the following message appears.

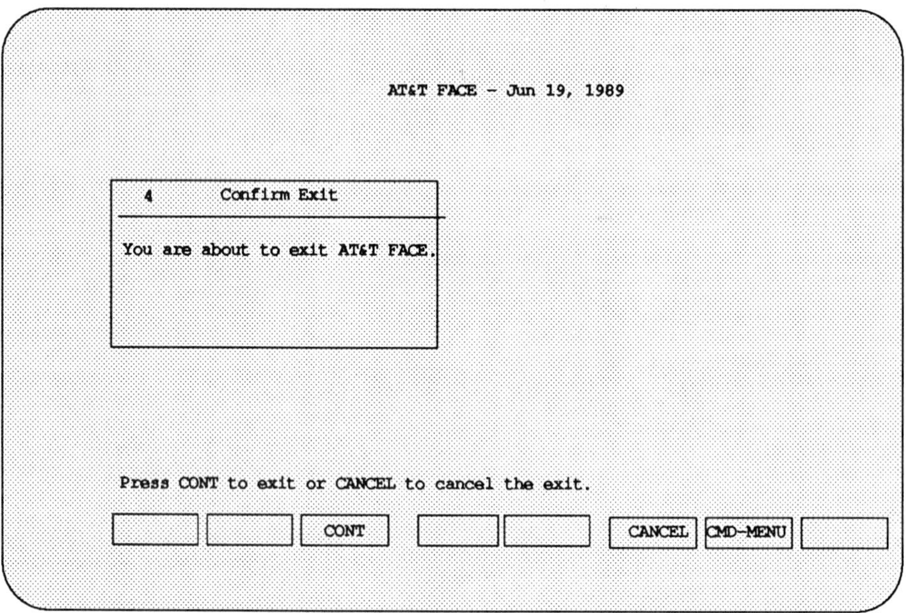
AT&T FACE - Jun 19, 1989
4 Confirm Exit
You are about to exit AT&T FACE.
Press CONT to exit or CANCEL to cancel the exit.
CONT
CANCEL
CMD-MENU

3. Press CONT to confirm that you want to exit, or press CANCEL to cancel the exit procedure if you change your mind and want to stay in AT&T FACE.

If FACE was invoked automatically when you logged in, you will be logged off the computer. If it was not invoked automatically, you will be returned to the UNIX System prompt. You can change this behavior through `Office Functions` on the `Preferences` menu.

Always remember to exit from FACE and log off your computer before you leave your terminal. This protects both your files and your entire computer system.

Using Your FACE Office

Your Filecabinet

What are Files and File Folders?

Files and file folders are used to store information in your FACE Office. Usually you will create and keep them in your filecabinet.

File — A file is the lowest-level entry that can contain information in your FACE Office. That is, you cannot store other files or file folders in a file. You can compare a file to a flat piece of paper: words, pictures, and other information can be "stored" in it, but not another piece of paper or a file folder. A file can be a standard file (one that you type text or data into), a data file (one whose contents are in binary format), an executable program, or a foreign file (one created on some other computer operating system). Files are always stored in file folders. For example, a file folder called `NEW-PRODUCTS`, can be stored in your filecabinet, and a file called `gizmo` containing a memo about a new product, can be stored in `NEW-PRODUCTS`.

File Folder — A file folder is an entry that contains files or other file folders. Within the /home/login frame, which is a file folder itself, your work is contained in other files and file folders. Usually, the items in a file folder are related in some way. For example, a file folder called `BUDGET` could contain 12 other file folders called `JAN`, `FEB`, etc., and each of those 12 file folders could contain files called `food`, `transportation`, `entertainment`, etc.

The standard way that FACE lists file folders and files is alphabetically by name. Figure 5-14 shows how the file `gizmo` and the file folder `BUDGET`, would be displayed in your filecabinet in the standard way. Note that in alphabetical sequencing, upper-case names are listed before lower-case names.

Figure 5-13: The Standard Form of Menu Display for Files and File Folders

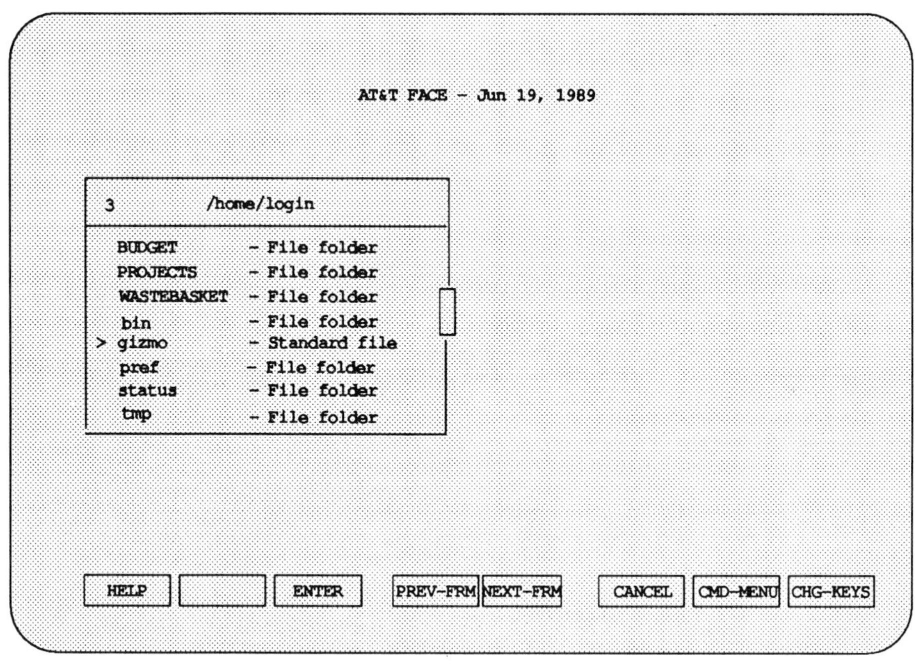

There are other ways in which you can list them, such as in chronological order of creation or change. (You will learn how to change the standard order in which files are listed in your filecabinet in the section "Organizing the Contents of a Single File Folder".)

Guidelines for Naming Files and File Folders

Files and file folders can have up to 4 separate identifiers when they are listed in a menu: a name, a description, a type, and the date and time the file or file folder was last modified. You provide the names for all files and file folders you create in your filecabinet. FACE adds a default description, based on the type of file or file folder you are creating. In Figure 5-14, for example, the description for each item listed in the sample /home/login frame is either File Folder or Standard File, depending on what the user defined it to be when it was created.

Follow these naming guidelines when creating or renaming a file folder or file.

- Length: A file or file folder created or renamed in your FACE Office can be from 1 to 14 characters long if you are using the UNIX System V Release 4.0 file system.

If you are using some other, supported, file system, file or file folder names can be up to 255 characters long. On some file systems, however, problems can occur if you use the `vi` editor on a file whose full pathname exceeds 128 characters: a file gets created whose name is the first 128 characters only, and a message will display telling you that the actual file you named has not been created.

- Letters/characters: You can use any combination of numerals and letters.
- Beginning character restrictions: A file or file folder name cannot begin with a period (.) or control characters (e.g., CTRL or ESC).
- Some characters cannot be used anywhere in a file or file folder name: space, tab, nonprinting characters (such as ESC or CTRL) or any of the following: & ! | < >

The importance of avoiding these characters when you are naming or renaming a file or file folder cannot be overstressed, because they have special meanings to the UNIX System and to FACE. If a file or file folder name contains any of these characters, you may not be able to open or use it.

- Two files, or a file folder and a file, can have the same name, as long as they are not in the same file folder. For example, you can have a file called `status` in your Filecabinet (/home/login), and another file called `status` in a file folder called `PROJECTS` in your Filecabinet (/home/login/PROJECTS). You cannot have a file and a file folder, both called `status`, in the same file folder.

  FACE will issue an error message and prevent you from creating a new file or file folder with the same name as an existing one in the file folder.

Using Pathnames in FACE Commands

When you refer to a file folder or file in a FACE command, you must tell FACE the route (pathname) to it. If the file folder or file is in the same file folder you are currently in, you only need to specify its actual name. But, if the file folder or file is in a different file folder than the one you are in, you need to specify the path to the file folder. For example, if there is a file folder named `BUDGET` listed in the /home/login menu, the pathname of that file folder is `/home/login/BUDGET`.

Every user with a login ID on the computer has a unique /home/login, or `$HOME`. `$HOME` is "computer shorthand" for the place you are when you first log in. By default, the UNIX System calls this place `/home/`*login*, where *login* is your login ID, and that's where you were when you first logged in to FACE. Both the UNIX System and FACE know what you're referring to when you use the shorthand `$HOME`. For a complete explanation of `$HOME`, full pathnames, and relative pathnames, see "Your Place in the UNIX System" in Chapter 1 of this guide.

The first name in your `$HOME` may be different from `/home` if the default setting has been changed on your system.

As long as the current pathname of a file folder is 255 or fewer characters long (1023 characters long in BSD file systems), you can create a new file or file folder whose name can be up to 14 characters long. Problems can occur, however, if you use the `vi` editor on a file whose full pathname exceeds 128 characters: a file whose name is truncated at 128 characters will be created, and a message will display, telling you that the actual file has not been created. (The length of a path name includes the slashes (/) that separate each name in the path.) FACE will not allow you to create, copy or move a new file or file folder to a file folder if by creating, copying, or moving it there you will exceed the pathname limit, and will print an error message to that effect.

When you refer to a file by its full pathname in a FACE command, you must type every part of it. But FACE might shorten it to fit on the screen when it displays the pathname as feedback from a command. (Parts of the pathname will be replaced with dots.)

Remember, however, that you can use the **showpath** command to display the entire pathname of the file or file folder.

For example, a person who has a login ID of `det` could create a file called `footnotes` whose full pathname is:

```
/home/det/work/newbook/src_text/chapter1/footnotes
```

When FACE needs to display this pathname in a frame, it may shorten it in the following way:

```
/home/det/.../chapter1/footnotes
```

Creating Files and File Folders

The following exercises give you some practice creating files and file folders. You'll be supplied with the file and file folder names to use. However, when you are choosing your own file names be sure not to use any of the special characters listed in the section "Guidelines for Naming Files and File Folders".

Creating a File Folder

In this exercise, you will create two file folders, named `alpha` and `beta`, in the /home/login frame.

1. Select `Filecabinet` from the Office menu.
2. Press [CHG-KEYS] (or [CTRL-f] [8]) to display the second level of function keys for menus.

   Most of the second level of function keys in a menu relate to file and file folder manipulation. Notice that the function key [F6] is now labeled [CREATE]. That means the FACE command `create` is now assigned to function key [F6].
3. Press [CREATE] (or [CTRL-f] [6]) to execute `create`.

   A prompt, `Enter the new object name:`, will appear on the command line.

4. Type `alpha` and press ENTER to name the new file folder.

   At this point, FACE knows what you want to call the new file folder, but it doesn't know that you want it to be a file folder. A menu titled `Create alpha` appears and displays at least two entries to choose from: `File Folder` and `Standard File`.

5. Select `File Folder` from the Choices menu.

   The `alpha` folder is now listed in the /home/login frame. If the type is also displayed, the /home/login frame should look like this:

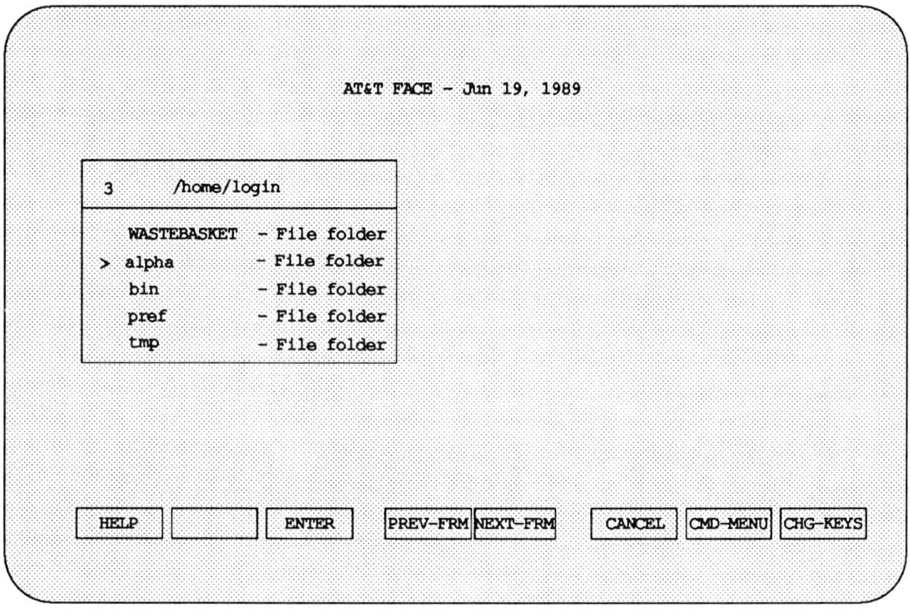

The message line also displays the name and location of the new file folder.

6. Create another file folder, named `beta`, in the /home/login frame.

Nested File Folders A file folder that is created in another file folder is known as a "nested file folder." You may be familiar with the "nesting blocks" that children play with: one hollow block contains a smaller hollow block, and that one contains a smaller one, and so on. Like nested blocks, one file folder can contain another file folder, and that one can contain yet another one. (File folders don't necessarily get smaller as they are nested in other file folders, and a file folder can contain more than one other file folder, but the nesting principle is the same.) In this exercise, you will create a file folder in the `alpha` file folder.

1. Select `alpha` from the /home/login frame.

   Notice that a new frame, titled alpha, is displayed in your work area and becomes the active frame.

2. Create a file folder named `alpha2` in the alpha frame.

Creating a File

In this exercise, you will create two files using the same method that you used to create file folders.

1. Press [PREV-FRM] (or [CTRL-f] [4]) to return to the /home/login frame.
2. Press [CHG-KEYS] (or [CTRL-f] [8]) and then press [CREATE] (or [CTRL-f] [6]).

   A prompt, `Enter the new object name:`, will appear on the command line.

3. Type the name of the new file, `file1`, and press [ENTER] to name the new file.
4. Select `Standard File` from the Choices menu.

   When you select `Standard File`, `create` opens a new file, the entire FACE screen will clear, and you will be in an editor program automatically (the default editor in FACE is the UNIX System editor `vi`), with which you can add information to the file. A line at the bottom of the screen tells you the full path name of your new file.

If this doesn't happen when the file opens, your default editor may not be `vi`. Therefore, ignore the directions in this exercise on the use of `vi`. Use of the `ed` editor is discussed in Chapter 6 of this guide.

5. For more information about `vi`, see chapter 7 in this guide, "vi Tutorial". For now, follow this exercise exactly.
6. Press `i` to enter the `vi` insert mode.

7. Type a few lines of text.
8. Press ESC, to get out of (EScape) vi's insert mode (that is, to stop adding text to the file).
9. Type :wq and press ENTER.

   The colon, : puts you in vi command mode, w writes (and thus saves) the file, and q quits the vi editor, returning you to your FACE Office. file1 is now listed in the /home/login menu.

Only 18 items appear in a file folder menu at any one time. If you already have 18 or more items in your /home/login file folder, you may have to scroll the menu up or down to see file1.

In the next part of this exercise, you will create one more file. This time you'll put it in the file folder alpha.

1. Select alpha from the /home/login menu.

   alpha is now the active frame, and anything you create will now be created here.

2. Press CHG-KEYS (or CTRL-f 8) and then press CREATE (or CTRL-f 6).
3. At the command line prompt, type file2 and press ENTER.
4. Select Standard File from the Choices menu.
5. Once again, a new file is opened. Enter some text with your editor.
6. Write and quit file2 and your work area will again display the Office menu and the other open frames.

   Notice that file2 is now listed in the alpha frame and is identified as a Standard file.

Copying and Moving Files and File Folders

As your work progresses, you may need to change the way you have stored files or file folders in your Filecabinet. That may involve copying or moving a file or file folder from one location to another. There are many reasons for using the copy and move commands:

- as insurance against losing or corrupting important information
- when you want to use parts of one file as the foundation for a second file, or when you want to provide another user with a copy of a file

If you copy a file or file folder from the UNIX System to your FACE Office, it will retain the permissions that were set for it by the UNIX System. These permissions may be different from those you have set for files and file folders you create in FACE and you may need to change them before you can edit or use a copied file. (See "Setting the Security of an Existing File.")

The steps you follow for move and copy are identical, but remember the important difference in their results:

- After you copy file or file folder, it exists in two places: the original location and the new location.
- After you move a file or file folder, it exists in one place: the new location.

In the following exercise, you will copy a file. You won't practice moving anything now, but remember the procedure for copying and moving files and file folders are the same.

Copying a File

In the previous section, you created `file1` in the /home/login frame. Suppose that now you want a second copy of `file1` in the /home/login frame.

1. Navigate to the /home/login frame if you aren't already there.
2. Position the cursor on `file1`.
3. Press [CHG-KEYS] (or [CTRL-f] [8]) to display the second level of function keys, and then press [COPY] (or [CTRL-f] [2]).

   The function key labels have changed again, and [F8] is now labeled [SELECT]. A message line prompt instructs you to open (navigate to) the destination file folder, and press [SELECT]. The destination file folder is the file folder you want to copy the file to.

4. Here the /home/login file folder is the destination file folder. Since you're already in it, just press SELECT (or CTRL-f 8).
5. The message line now tells you that there is already a file named `file1` in the /home/login file folder, so you will have to give this copy a new name.

   Type `file2` and press ENTER.

   The menu of items in the /home/login frame is immediately updated to include `file2`. The message line also reports where the copy was made, and that it was named `file2`.

When you want to copy or move a file folder, the same method is used.

An important thing to remember when organizing your file folders and files is that when you copy or move a file folder, all the file folders and files contained in it are also copied or moved.

Renaming a File or File Folder

Use the `rename` command whenever you need to change the name of a file or file folder. For example, a file folder called `newwork` could be renamed `old-work` when it is no longer current.

You'll be supplied with the file name to use in this exercise. However, when you are choosing your own file names be sure you do not use any of the special characters listed in the section "Guidelines for Naming Files and File Folders".

Suppose that `file2`, which you created earlier in the /home/login file folder, is a memo to your boss about your upcoming work plans. Now that you're beginning to have more than a few files in your filecabinet, you might want to rename `file2` to more closely reflect what it contains.

1. Navigate to the /home/login frame.
2. Position the cursor on the menu item `file2` in the /home/login menu.
3. Press CHG-KEYS (or CTRL-f 8), then press RENAME (or CTRL-f 5).

4. When prompted for a new name for the file, type `workplans` and press (ENTER).

   The /home/login frame now lists `workplans` as a menu item instead of `file2`. The contents of the file are the same as before, only its name has changed.

Redescribing a File or File Folder

When you create a new file or file folder, a description of it can be displayed along with its name. (FACE displays descriptions of items in a menu if you have used the Preferences feature or the `organize` command to request it. You will learn how to use Preferences and `organize` later.) When you create a new file or file folder, its description is identical to its type, by default. That is, FACE uses the item's type (File folder or Standard file, in most cases), as the description that gets displayed. Since FACE always remembers the type of file or file folder, there is nothing keeping you from changing the description to something more significant to you. You can add to, or change, the description part of a menu item with the `redescribe` command, but you cannot change the type.

It is important that you understand the difference between the description of a file and the type of file. FACE only knows about a few types of files and file folders, and can search for them based on their type. The types of files or file folders that FACE knows about are: Standard file, File folder, Foreign file, Data file, Executable file, Text file, Form, and Menu. However, the description of a file or file folder can be anything you decide to make it. FACE does nothing with the description except show it to you, and let you change what it says if you wish.

The four identifier fields that can appear when a file or file folder is listed in a menu are the name, description, type, and date/time the file or file folder was created or last modified. All four identifiers will appear only when the following two conditions are met: if the `Folder Display Format` field in the Office Functions form is set to the value `long form`, and if you have redescribed one or more of the files or file folders listed in the menu.

As you create more files and file folders in your filecabinet, you will find it helpful to customize the description field so that you can more easily distinguish one file from another. In the exercise that follows, you will learn how to change the description of a file or file folder with the `redescribe` command.

Description Guidelines

Follow these guidelines when redescribing a file folder or file.

- Length: A description may contain 23 or fewer characters. (Note that only 19 characters will be displayed when you list files in the long form.)
- Letters/characters: You can use any combination of numerals, letters, and spaces.
- Special characters that cannot be used: You cannot use a pipe character (|) or nonprinting characters such as ESC or CTRL.

In the following exercise, you will use the file `workplans` to practice the `redescribe` command.

1. Position the cursor on `workplans` in the /home/login frame.
2. Press CMD-MENU (or CTRL-f 7), and select `redescribe`.

   (Note that the `redescribe` command is not assigned to one of your function keys.)
3. At the command line prompt, type a new description and press ENTER.

   Use any description that will clearly identify the contents of the file, such as "plans for 1990." Be sure to follow the guidelines presented in "Description Guidelines" at the beginning of this exercise.

   FACE will not accept a null description (a zero-length response), so if you simply press ENTER at this point, it will prompt you again for a description. You must type something in response.

   Notice that the description field of the `workplans` menu item now displays the new description.

The `redescribe` command can be used in exactly the same way to change the description of a file folder.

Organizing the Contents of a Single File Folder

You can choose how many identifier fields are displayed for each item listed in a file folder, and/or change the order in which the items are listed. When you use `organize`, only the files and file folders contained within that file folder will be affected.

In the following exercise, you will use `organize` to change the order in which files and file folders in the `alpha` file folder are listed, and to change how many identifier fields will be displayed.

1. Select the file folder `alpha` from the /home/login menu.
2. Press CMD-MENU (or CTRL-f 7) and select `organize`.

   A form titled `Organize alpha` appears, and contains three input fields.

   The `Default Oganization` field displays the default value `no`. Since you want to organize this folder in a particular way, leave this field set to `no`.

   If you were to change the value in this field to `yes`, and save this form, the behavior of this folder would revert to the defaults as set in the Preferences form. (Changing preferences for your entire FACE Office is discussed in "Changing Office Preferences" later in this chapter.)
3. Navigate to the `Folder Display Format:` field.

   It controls how much identifier information is displayed for each file in the file folder. These are the available choices for this field:

   `long form` — this value in the field causes the name, description, file type, and date/time created to be displayed, in that order.

   `name and description` — the default value for this field. Each item listed in the folder shows the file name and the description (either the default description, which is the same as the file's type, or one that you supply using the `redescribe` command).

   `name and marks` — this value causes the file name to be displayed followed by a symbol indicating its type: an asterisk (*) if it is an executable file, a slash (/) if

	it is a file folder, and no mark if it is a standard file.
`name only`	this value causes only the file name to be displayed.

When the file folder you are organizing is your WASTEBASKET, an additional choice, **`wastebasket`**, is available, which is equivalent to **`name and description`** plus the path to the original location of the objects currently in the WASTEBASKET folder.

The value in this field should currently read `name and description`. What this means is that until now, all the files and file folders in the alpha folder have been displayed showing their name followed by a brief description.

4. Press CHOICES (or CTRL-f 2).

   A Choices menu displays the four values described above.

5. Navigate to `long form.` and press ENTER (or CTRL-f 3) to enter this new field value in the `Folder Display Format` field.

6. Press SAVE (or CTRL-f 3), to save this new value.

   Notice what has happened to the display of the menu items in the alpha file folder. The name and the description of each item are still displayed, but the date and time that the item was created or last modified is also displayed.

The **`organize`** and **`redescribe`** commands do not affect the date and time, because they do not change the file or file folder. They simply change how much descriptive information is displayed.

Between the name of a file listed in a menu and the date/time identifier, there may be either one or two other identifiers. If you have not used `redescribe` to change the description of an item, then the description FACE assigned it when it was created (the default) is displayed following the name. Since this default description is identical to the file's type (see "Creating Files and File Folders"), FACE does not also display the type. But if you have redescribed a file, your description will follow the name, and the type will follow your description. The date/time identifier always comes last in the long form.

You may want to redescribe an item in the `alpha` file folder to see how this works.

The `Folder Display Order` field controls the order in which files and file folders are listed. These are the available choices:

`alphabetical` Files and file folders are listed alphabetically in the following order:

- Names beginning with numbers
- Names beginning with upper-case letters
- Names beginning with lower-case letters

`alphabetical by description`
Files and file folders are alphabetized by the description, and then by name when more than one file of a particular type exists.

`least recent first`
Files and file folders are ordered from the least- to the most-recently created or modified.

`most recent first`
Files and file folders are ordered from the most- to the least-recently created or modified.

The `Folder Display Order` field is set to `alphabetical` by default. The following exercise shows you how to change this setting.

1. The file folder alpha should already be open and the active frame in your work area, so execute the `organize` command to bring up the `Organize alpha` form again.
2. Navigate to the `Folder Display Order` field.
3. Press [CHOICES] (or [CTRL-f] [2]) and a new frame labeled Choices opens.
4. Select `most recent first` from the Choices menu.

   The Choices menu closes and the Organize alpha frame becomes active again. The value `most recent first` now appears in the `Folder Display Order` field.

5. Press SAVE (or CTRL-f 3) to record these values.

   The form disappears, and immediately, the alpha file folder is organized to show the most recently created or modified file first.

An `Organize` form will not appear if you don't have either write permission on, or ownership of, the current file folder. This might be the case if you are working in another user's filecabinet. (Permissions are explained in "Setting the Security of an Existing File.")

Deleting a File or File Folder

You should delete file folders and files when they are no longer needed. When you delete a file or file folder, FACE puts it into your wastebasket. It will be held there for the number of days specified in your Office Functions form and then permanently removed from the system.

You cannot delete a file or file folder if one with that name already exists in your wastebasket. For example, if this morning you deleted a file from the /home/login frame that was named `memo1`, and this afternoon you created a new `memo1` file and then decided you didn't need that either, you will be prompted to rename the second `memo1` before it will be deleted. After you rename it, the file will be removed from your file folder and held in the wastebasket under its new name.

You cannot delete a file folder if it, or any file or file folder in it, is open. Remember, if you delete a file folder, all the files and file folders it contains are also deleted.

Since you don't need the alpha file folder, use it in the following exercise to practice using the `delete` command.

1. Make sure the `alpha` file folder is closed (use CANCEL or CTRL-f 6).
2. Position the cursor on the menu item `alpha` in the /home/login menu.
3. Press CHG-KEYS (or CTRL-f 8).
4. Press DELETE (or CTRL-f 4) to execute the `delete` command.

   The message line warns you that file folder `alpha` is not empty.

5. A command line prompt instructs you to press ENTER to delete `alpha`.

   After you do that, a message appears saying that `alpha` has been moved to the /home/login/WASTEBASKET file folder.

   On your screen, the /home/login menu no longer lists `alpha` as a menu item.

Now, you can check the /home/login/WASTEBASKET file folder to confirm that the `alpha` file folder is being held there, awaiting permanent removal. (If your /home/login/WASTEBASKET folder has been organized so that the `Folder Display Format:` field is set to `wastebasket`, items in the /home/login/WASTEBASKET frame will show the path to the original location of each item in addition to their names and descriptions.)

1. Navigate to the Office of login frame and select `Wastebasket`.

   A new frame, titled /home/login/WASTEBASKET, appears on your screen. It should list the `alpha` file folder.

2. Select the menu item `alpha` from the /home/login/WASTEBASKET menu. Notice what's inside! When you delete a file folder, all its contents are also thrown out.

3. Close the /home/login/WASTEBASKET/alpha frame.

If you're absolutely sure you want to delete a file or file folder, you can use the `delete` command to remove items from the wastebasket itself. You may delete all files or file folders being held there, or a specific file folder or file. For example, typing `delete wastebasket` on the command line will permanently remove all files or file folders currently being held in your wastebasket (after prompting you to confirm that that is what you want to do).

Undeleting a File or File Folder

The default amount of time that FACE will hold files or file folders in your wastebasket is one day. As an added safeguard against your accidental deletion of a file or file folder you should have saved, FACE will give you a chance to cancel the final deletion. This "second chance" is the default behavior of the wastebasket feature. (Changing the default behavior of the wastebasket feature is covered in "Changing Other Office Preferences".)

As long as a file or file folder is being held in your wastebasket you can retrieve it. (See "Changing Office Preferences" for more information on specifying the length of time a file or file folder is held in your wastebasket.) You might want to use `undelete` if you realize you've deleted something you should have held on to. In this exercise, you will undelete the `alpha` file folder.

When you closed the /home/login/WASTEBASKET/alpha frame in the previous exercise, you returned to the /home/login/WASTEBASKET menu.

1. Position the cursor on `alpha` in the /home/login/WASTEBASKET menu.

   Note that the full pathname of the `alpha` folder is displayed in addition to its name and description. This additional information serves as a reminder to you of where the file or file folder will be returned to when you undelete it.

2. Press CMD-MENU (or CTRL-f 7), and select `undelete`.

   The `undelete` command is not assigned to a function key, which is why you must access it from the command line, or from the Command menu, as you are doing here.

   Watch the contents of the /home/login/WASTEBASKET menu. The `alpha` file folder is returned to the /home/login menu and the /home/login/WASTEBASKET menu displays the message `Empty Folder`.

3. Close the /home/login/WASTEBASKET frame.

It is not unusual to want to retrieve files or file folders that you have thrown out. When you use `undelete`, the files or file folders will automatically be returned to their original file folders. If you are undeleting a file folder, all the items in the file folder will also be returned. (If you want to return files or file folders to a file folder other than the original, use the `copy` or `move` commands instead of the `undelete` command.)

If FACE prompts you that it cannot open a file folder or access an item you are trying to undelete, you may have deleted or renamed the file folder that formerly contained the item. In that case, you must use the `move` or `copy` command to retrieve the item from your wastebasket.

Finding a File or File Folder

One function of computers is to save time. In FACE, you can quickly locate and act on files or file folders anywhere in your filecabinet by using the `find` command. The `find` command will prove useful when you have file folders nested several levels deep, or if you cannot remember where you stored a file.

When you use `find`, a Find form will open in your work area, allowing you to specify search criteria in any of four fields. Figure 5-15 is an example of a Find form, opened when the /home/login frame was active. It shows the four fields in which you can specify your search criteria: `Name`, `Type`, `Owner`, and `Age`.

Figure 5-14: The Find Form

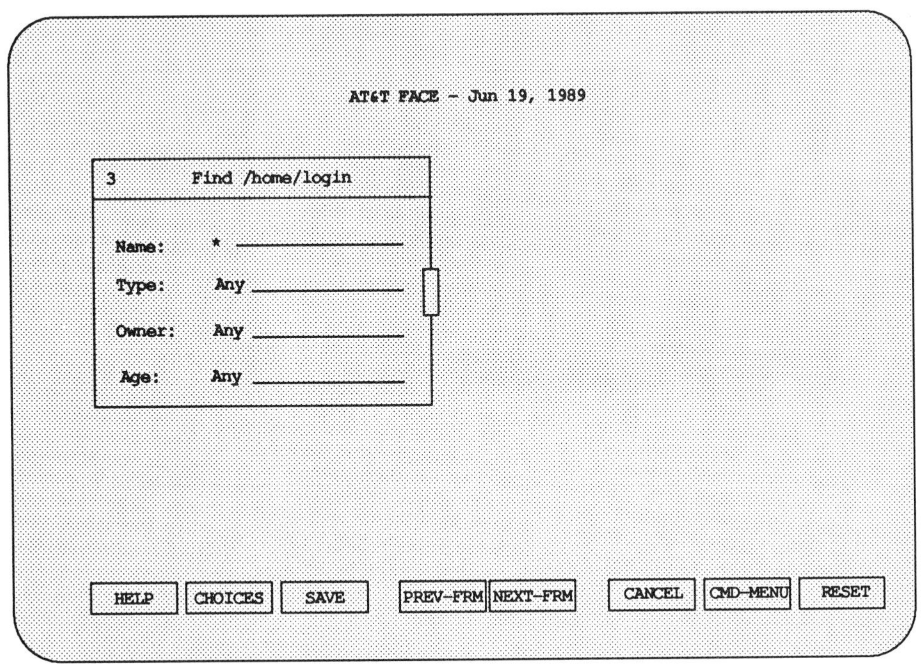

Unlike most forms, which close automatically when you press SAVE, this form remains open until *you* close it. It remains open so that if an item is not found, you can check your criteria for correctness, or enter different criteria. The four fields, and valid search criteria you can enter in them, are listed here for reference.

`Name:` The `Name` field contains the name of the item you want to find; the name can be complete or partial, and it can include special characters. (In the exercise that follows, you will use HELP to obtain an explanation of special characters and how you can use them in this field.)

`Type:` The `Type` field contains the item's type, such as `File folder` or `Standard file`. You can use CHOICES (or CTRL-f 2) in this field to display a complete list of types available in your FACE Office. Note that FACE can distinguish between a file and a file folder.

`Owner:` The `Owner` field contains the login ID of the owner of the file or file folder. You can use CHOICES (or CTRL-f 2) in this field to display a list of all system logins. The `find` command will search for files owned by this login ID that exist *under* the file folder you are currently in.

`Age:` The `Age` field can contain a numerical value that stipulates the number of days since the file or file folder was created or changed. You can use CHOICES (or CTRL-f 2) in this field to see a brief message explaining acceptable values. Remember that renaming or redescribing a file does not affect its age.

By default, `find` will start a search in your /home/login file folder, if you are not in a file folder when you execute it (for example, if you execute `find` from a form or text frame).

When `find` locates files or file folders that meet your criteria, it displays them in an Objects Found frame. Actions you do on items in the Objects Found frame (for example, `copy`, `move`, `delete`) affect the items just as they would if you executed them from the file folder in which the item is actually located.

The Objects Found menu is not updated automatically, so you must execute the `update` command from the Command menu, or from the command line, after performing any of the actions listed above. If you do not, the menu will not show any changes your action may have caused.

Suppose you've forgotten where you stored `file2`, which you created in an earlier exercise.

1. Navigate to the /home/login menu. The `find` command searches through all file folders, whether open or closed, from the active frame down. By beginning the search from the /home/login menu, `find` will search your entire filecabinet, but not your wastebasket.

2. Press CMD-MENU (or CTRL-f 7), and select `find`.

   A Find form will appear. Notice that this form is titled Find /home/login. The title in a Find form always tells you the point at which the search will start.

3. Type `file2` into the `Name` field, and press SAVE (or CTRL-f 3).

   When you use `find` on other occasions, you can stop after entering the file name as a search criteria, as we are doing here, or you can enter information in the other fields, if you want to specify more precise criteria.

4. An Objects Found in /home/login frame displays the pathname to the file or file folder, `alpha/file2`. This tells you that `file2` is stored in the alpha file folder. Since alpha is the only file folder in this pathname, you also know that alpha is stored right under the /home/login file folder.

You can select `alpha/file2` from the Objects Found in /home/login frame and do any filing tasks that you want to do, just as if you were in the alpha file folder itself. The next exercise introduces you to the `display` command, and you'll use it from the Objects Found in /home/login frame you just opened, to display the contents of `file2`.

Displaying a File

Now that you've found `file2`, this exercise shows you how to use the command to see what's in it without opening it up for editing. You can simply view the contents of a file in a frame, by using `display`.

1. Position the cursor on `alpha/file2` in the Objects Found in /home/login frame.

2. Press CMD-MENU (or CTRL-f 7), and select `display`.

   A new frame, titled "`file2 - Standard file`" opens in the work area.

   You may use the following navigation keys to scroll this text frame up or down.

   ↑ (or CTRL-u)
   ↓ (or CTRL-d)
   SCROLL-UP (or CTRL-f u)
   SCROLL-DOWN (or CTRL-f d)
   BEG (or CTRL-b)
   END (or CTRL-e)

3. When you are finished reading, press the CANCEL (or CTRL-f 6) key.

When you use `display`, what you are seeing is only a temporary image of `file2`. It follows that you cannot make any changes to a file while viewing it with `display`.

Use this procedure with text files only. File folders are not viewable items.

Setting the Security of an Existing File

The `security` command defines how much access other users have to your individual files and file folders. While some files and file folders might require confidentiality, others might need to be accessed by co-workers, supervisors, or editors. You can give different amounts of access permission to yourself, your group, and all other users, to Read (look at or copy), Write (edit, move, delete), or Run/Search (open file folders, list the contents of file folders, run executable files or shell scripts) a file or file folder. Here are two ways you can use `security` to do this:

- You can protect a master copy of a file by setting its access permissions so that no one, including you, can change it. When it is time to update the master, you can change the permissions level so you can edit the file (write permission). Later, you can re-institute the higher level of protection.
- You may normally have a high level of protection on all files or file folders in your filecabinet, so no one else can read your files. But you may want to allow your group to read a specific document, such as a staff memo. Conversely, you may have a fairly open filecabinet, but want to protect one file, perhaps a salary report. You can change its access permissions so no one else can read or write (make changes) to it.

If you want to use the `security` command on a file in another user's filecabinet, you must first select the appropriate user from the Other Users menu and open his or her /home/login file folder.

It is important to keep in mind the access permission levels of file folders above the file folder or file you want to change. The permissions on a file or file folder also depend on the access permissions of the file folders in which it is contained. For example, if you give your group permission to write to a file, that file should be in a file folder that has the same permissions. If the group can't access the file folder, they won't be able to add information to the file.

Suppose a member of your work group needs to edit a file in your filecabinet. Before your co-worker can do that, you must change the permissions on that file. The following steps describe how to change permissions on the file `workplans`, which you created earlier in the /home/login file folder.

1. Navigate to the /home/login file folder and position the cursor on `workplans`.
2. Press CHG-KEYS (or CTRL-f 8) and then press SECURITY (or CTRL-f 7).

   The Security form is displayed. Notice the title of this form—it tells you that you are looking at the current security settings of the `workplans` file. The title of the Security form always tells you what file or file folder your changes will affect.

   There are ten fields in this form. They show the default settings of permissions in your /home/login. Look them over to get an idea of how the same three permissions are set differently for you (the owner), for the members of your group, and for all other users on your computer. The ten fields are divided into four sections.

   `Owner:`
   The current owner's login is displayed. If you are the owner, you can change the permissions. If you are not the owner, you can only look at the permissions. (Note that if you change the owner of a file to another user, you cannot change the ownership back to yourself.)

   `Owner's Permissions:`
   Files and file folders in your filecabinet are usually owned by you. You will probably want Read (permission to look at the contents of a file), Write (permission to change the contents of a file), and Run/Search (permission to run an executable file or list the contents of a file folder) set to `yes` for you.

File folders, and some files created by executable files, are not meant to be read or written to with an editor. You may not want to give yourself Read or Write permission for these, but you will need to give yourself Run/Search permission. Only under rare circumstances should the owner's Run/Search permission be set to `no`.

`Group's Permissions:`
These apply to users assigned to your group on the computer. They define what your group members can do with a file or file folder.

`All Others' Permissions:`
These apply to any other person who might be logged on to your computer. They define what other users can do with a file or file folder (usually Read, or Run/Search, but not Write).

3. In this example, you want to allow a member of your group to be able to edit `workplans`, so you will need to change the `Group Write Permissions` from `no` to `yes`.

   Position the cursor on the `Group Write Permissions` field.

4. Press CHOICES (or CTRL-f 2) and notice what happens. The entry in this field changes from `no` to `yes`.

5. Press SAVE (or CTRL-f 3) to record the new value for this field.

   The Security form disappears, and `workplans` in your /home/login file folder is now available to other members of your group to edit, move, or delete.

Accessing Other Users' Filecabinets

One of the items in your Office of login menu, `Other Users`, provides you with a path to the filecabinets of people who have login IDs on your system.

When you select `Other Users`, a list of login IDs displays. By selecting a login, you then have access to that user's Filecabinet (UNIX System home directory `$HOME`). Typically, you will have permission to view some of the file folders and files in that user's filecabinet. On occasion, you may have permission to write or change a file folder or file that is stored in someone else's filecabinet. To see what access permissions another user has given you for one of his or her files or file folders, use the `security` command (explained in the section "Setting the Security of an Existing File").

You can try `Other Users` on your own, now if you have time, or when needed. Use some of the FACE commands you have learned so far. Some may work, and some may not, depending on the access permissions the other user has set for you.

Setting Your Office Preferences

When you are a new FACE user, you do not have to worry about setting up your office because FACE has a standard default set-up, which you have been working in. As you become more familiar with FACE, you may decide that you want to change certain features in your office.

You've already learned how you can organize the way individual files and file folders are displayed in your filecabinet. You've also learned how you can limit or expand the access that other people have to individual files and file folders in your filecabinet.

In this section you'll learn how to organize your entire filecabinet, change the access permissions for your entire filecabinet, customize the wastebasket feature, specify other frames to be open when you log in, change your password, and choose the editor you want to use when you are editing files.

In FACE, these things are known as preferences. The ones that you may customize are listed in the Preferences menu, shown in Figure 5-16.

Figure 5-15: Contents of the Preferences Menu

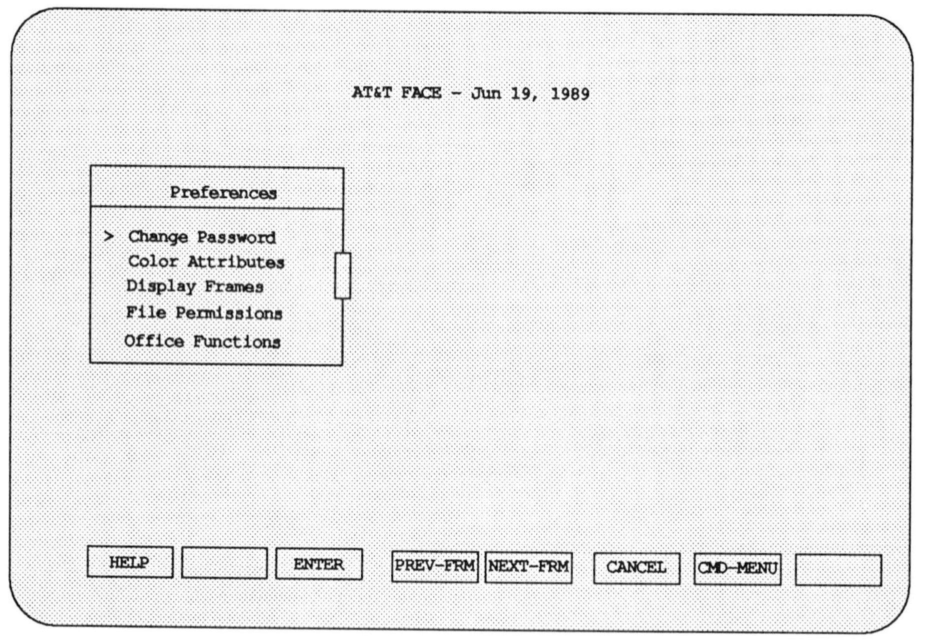

Here is an overview of the Preferences menu items:

`Change Password` Enables you to change the password to your login.

`Color Attributes` Allows you to customize your FACE Office colors. This item will only appear in the Preferences menu if you are running FACE on a terminal with color capabilities.

`Display Frames` Allows you to automatically display more menus when you log in.

`File Permissions` Enables you to set file folder and file permissions, not just for one existing file folder or file, but for all file folders and files you will create in the future. Permissions may be set to Read, Write, or Search/Run for You (the Owner), your Group, or All Others.

`Office Functions` Enables you to set the number of days before FACE deletes a file or file folder from your wastebasket, choose whether to be prompted before it is actually deleted, select a default editor, specify file folder display format and order, and specify whether to invoke FACE when you log in.

Change Password

Using a password when you log into your computer is like having a key to your office door; changing your password periodically helps maintain security in your FACE Office.

If you don't have a password, or if you've had the same one for a long time, or if other users on your computer have learned what it is, you can change it using the `Change Password` selection from the Preferences menu. The following steps show how to access this feature. Once you've accessed `Change Password` supply the information you are asked for. For more information about UNIX system passwords and how to assign one to your login, refer to "Password" in chapter 1, "Basics for UNIX System Users".

1. Select `Office of login` from the AT&T FACE menu.
2. Select `Preferences` from the Office of login menu.
3. Select `Change Password` from the Preferences menu.

Color Attributes

You must have a color monitor to display frame colors. If you don't, this menu item will not appear.

The Color Attributes entry allows you to change the default colors of your FACE frames. You can change the colors of the following screen attributes:

Screen Attribute	Default Color
Title:	cyan
Frame Text:	cyan
Active Frame Border:	red
Active Frame Title Bar:	red
Active Frame Title Text:	cyan
Inactive Frame Border:	blue
Inactive Frame Title Bar:	blue
Inactive Frame Title Text:	cyan
Highlighted Bar:	blue
Screen Label Key Bar:	white

FACE will validate each color you select to ensure that you do not choose the same color for an attribute and the background.

1. Select `Preferences` from the Office menu.
2. Select `Color Attributes` from the Preferences menu.
3. Use arrows keys to navigate from field to field and CHOICES to select the colors you want.
4. Press SAVE when you are finished.

   A confirmation message is displayed, `The Color Attributes have been updated.`

   The colors you select will display as soon as you press SAVE. If you don't like the way they look you the form remains open so you can change them.
5. Press CANCEL to close the Color Attribute form.

How to Display More Menu Frames When You Log In

The Display Frames entry allows you to specify up to four menus to be displayed automatically after you log in. You can enter the full pathname of any menu in your FACE Office, including ones you have created. For your convenience, however, some often-used FACE menus are can be easily entered in this form via the CHOICES function key:

- Filecabinet
- Mail Services
- Office of login
- Preferences
- Printer Operations*
- Programs**

  * The Printer Operations menu will not be listed as a choice unless the `lp` command has been installed in the UNIX system.

  ** The Programs menu will not be listed as a choice unless at least one program has been installed for use in FACE.

1. Select `Preferences` from the Office menu.
2. Select `Display Frames` from the Preferences menu.
3. Use the arrow keys to navigate from field to field and [CHOICES] (or [CTRL-f] [2]), and [ENTER] function keys to select the menus to be displayed. Or you can type in the full pathname of any menu frame in your Office.
4. Press [SAVE] when you are finished. FACE will display a help message if you have typed in an invalid pathname or named the same menu more than once.

   A confirmation message will be displayed on the message line.

The next time you log in the menus you have specified will be displayed.

File Permissions

When you select `File Permissions` from the Preferences menu, you can change the default access permissions for all new file folders and files (the permissions they will have when you create them). The permission levels you set in the File Permissions form do not affect previously created file folders and files.

Typically, you have complete access permissions to your own file folders and files, while the members of your UNIX System-defined working group and all others can view but not change or delete your work. In fact, it's especially important that your own Run/Search permissions be set to `yes`. If they are set to no, you will be unable to view the contents of file folders, or create new files and file folders, or run programs.

The default permission levels have been set by FACE, and you may choose not to reset them. However, you can access the File Permissions form by following these two steps:

1. Select `Preferences` from your Office menu.
2. Select `File Permissions` from the Preferences menu.

From this point, refer to the procedure for changing permission levels in "Setting Security on a Single File or File Folder" in this chapter. The difference is that the permissions you set here will apply to files and file folders you create in the future.

Recall that you can change the permission levels for any existing single file or file folder with the `security` command.

Office Functions

The `Office Functions` form should look somewhat familiar to you. It includes the two fields you edited when you used the `organize` command to change the description and order of presentation for the `alpha` file folder earlier. And there are several other fields in the Office Functions form that customize the way your office works.

By now you are probably familiar with the processes of navigating in a form, and changing fields in a form, so you might want to explore the other preferences listed in the Office Functions form on your own. Here's how to get to it:

1. Select `Preferences` from your Office of login menu.
2. Select `Office Functions`.

An explanation of each field in the Office Function form is given below, and you can change those you want to change. Remember, you can also press (HELP) to get help on the field you are on.

`Delete objects from my Wastebasket after (# of days):`

This field specifies the number of days that each file or file folder in your wastebasket is kept before being permanently removed. Any number of days, from 1 to 30, is an acceptable value in this field.

`Prompt before deleting objects from my Wastebasket (yes or no):`

If this field is set to `yes`, you will be notified, when you log in, if there are files or file folders in your wastebasket that are scheduled for permanent removal that day. This gives you an opportunity to review the items and decide whether they should be removed or saved.

If this field is set to `no`, you will not be notified when you log in that there are files or file folders scheduled for permanent removal. FACE will automatically remove them without telling you.

Files and file folders are not deleted if you do not log in to your computer, even if they are scheduled for deletion that day. Also, if you cancel a deletion but do not move the files out of the /home/login/WASTEBASKET file folder, those files are then scheduled for deletion every time you log in thereafter.

`Default Editor:`

This field specifies which editor FACE will invoke when you open a standard file. You can only specify an editor available on your system. The value in the `Default Editor` field is set to `vi` initially if it has been installed on your computer. Otherwise, it defaults to `ed`. You can change the default editor to any editor package that has been installed on your computer system.

`Folder Display Format:`

Specifies the information that will be displayed about the items listed in a file folder. New file folders and file folders that currently exist (except those you have specifically reorganized with the `organize` command) will be display information according to the value you enter in this field. The value you enter into this field now will apply to all files and file folders in your FACE Office (except those that you organize individually with organize). Refer to "Organizing the Contents of a Single File Folder" for more information.

Folder Display Order:

Specifies how items will be ordered in a file folder (alphabetically, etc.). New file folders and file folders that currently exist
(except those you have specifically reorganized with the organize command) will be ordered according to the value you enter in this field. Refer to "Organizing the Contents of a Single File Folder" for more information.

Confirm at Exit:

Specifies whether you will see a confirmation frame when you select Exit FACE from the AT&T FACE menu, or select exit from the Command menu or type it on the command line. If this field is set to no you will exit immediately, with no second chance to remain in your FACE Office.

Invoke FACE at login:

Specifies whether to invoke FACE automatically when you log in. This field will not appear in this form if access to the UNIX system has been denied for your login.

If FACE is not invoked automatically at login, you may access it by typing face at the UNIX System prompt.

Programs Administration

The Programs Administration item in the Office of login menu allows you to list, add, modify, and remove personal programs on your Programs menu. This feature of your FACE Office is covered in the next section, following a discussion of how to run programs (applications) from your FACE Office.

(This menu item does not apply to global programs. See "System Administration" for information on administering global programs.)

Wastebasket

When you select `Wastebasket` from the `Office of login` menu, a new frame will open in the work area, titled `/home/login/WASTEBASKET`. The items listed in it are the files and file folders you have deleted, copied, or moved here to await permanent removal from the system. The files and file folders in it are like any others in your FACE Office and you can do any action you can normally do to a file or file folder. Keep in mind, though, that simply by being in the `/home/login/WASTEBASKET` frame, these files and file folders are scheduled for permanent removal from the system by FACE.

Refer to the earlier sections in this chapter; "Deleting a File or File Folder", and "Undeleting a File or File Folder", to learn how to add and remove items from the wastebasket. Refer to "Changing Other Office Preferences", to learn how to change the length of time items are held in your wastebasket, and how to request FACE to remind you when items are about to be removed. Also refer to "Organizing the Contents of a Single File Folder" to learn how to change the amount of information displayed for each item being held in your WASTEBASKET.

You can also use the Help Facility to learn more about the wastebasket.

1. Select `WASTEBASKET` from the Office of login menu.
2. Press HELP (or CTRL-f 1) to view `Help on Wastebasket`.

Files and file folders are not deleted if you do not log in to your computer, even if they are scheduled for deletion that day. Also, if you cancel a deletion but do not move the files out of the `WASTEBASKET` file folder, those files are then scheduled for deletion every time you log in thereafter.

Using Other Features of FACE

Printer Operations

Although every so often someone in the computer software industry announces that the age of the "Paperless Office" has arrived, anyone who works in a real office knows that time is not here quite yet.

When you require paper printouts of your files use the FACE `Printer Operations` feature and the `print` command. `Printer Operations` customizes your system's printing command to suit your needs, and the `print` command prints a file on paper. In FACE `print` defaults to the UNIX System `lp` command.

Before beginning these procedures, check with your system administrator to make sure that `lp` is the print command installed on your computer. If it is not, you will have to get information on the print command that is installed.

Printer Status

Before you can print a file on paper, you need to know the name of the printer you want to use and whether it is currently working. The `Printer Status` item in the Printer Operations menu gives you that information. The following procedure tells how to use it:

1. Select `Printer Operations` from the AT&T FACE menu.
2. Select `Printer Status` from the Printer Operations menu.
3. A frame is displayed, showing you the available printers

   If no printers have been defined, or if `lp` has not been installed on your computer, a frame titled `Warning` will display a message to that effect. In this case, see your system administrator.

The output from `Printer Status` lets you know which printers are currently available for your use.

If there are no printers accepting requests or no printers at all, you will not be able to print files until that situation is corrected by your system administrator. An error message is generated if you try to send a file to be printed.

If there is an operating printer, but your printouts don't appear at the printer, talk to your system administrator.

Print Options

The next exercise explains how you can add or change options and arguments to the `lp` command, such as the option that tells `lp` to send your file to a particular printer. This procedure can be followed when you want to change `Print Command #2` and `Print Command #3` as well.

Change Print Options for Login You can change the options to the `lp` command with the `Print Options` item in the Printer Operations menu.

1. Select `Printer Operations` from the AT&T FACE menu.
2. Select `Print Options` from the Printer Operations menu.
3. A form titled `Change Print Options for login` is displayed. It has three fields, corresponding to the first three items in the menu that appears when you run the `print` command.

   Once you start typing in this field, the value that was there will disappear. Make sure you remember, or write down, the command that was there, so you can re-enter any options that you want to preserve.

4. Type the additions or changes you want to make to `Print Command #1:`

   Since FACE has no way of knowing what options or arguments to `lp` you might need to use when you send files to your printer, you must determine which `lp` options (if any) you need to add or change. Refer to Chapter 8, "Line Printer Tutorial" in this guide, and the `lp` manual page in section "Commands (1)," in the *UNIX System V User's Reference Manual* for complete information on `lp`.

Do not include the name of the file to be printed in the `Print Command #1:` field.

5. Press SAVE (or CTRL-f 3) to save the new value in the `Print Command #1:` field. Or press CANCEL to leave this form without making any changes to it.

   You will return to the Printer Operations menu.

You can display a list of requests queued to the printer(s) by using the following procedure. You might want to use `Printer Queue` to determine which of several available printers is least busy. Or, you can use it as a way to estimate how long it will take before your job will be printed.

1. Select `Printer Operations` from the AT&T FACE menu.
2. Select `Printer Queue` from the Printer Operations menu.

   When the Printer Queue mark menu is displayed, follow the instructions on the screen and use HELP (or CTRL-f 1) for additional information.

If no print requests have been queued, a warning will be displayed.

Only 30 print requests can be displayed at one time.

Printing a File on Paper

1. Navigate to the file folder containing the file you want to print.
2. Position the cursor on the file you want to print.
3. Select `print` from the Command menu or type `print` and press ENTER on the command line.

4. Select one of the three print commands that will appear in a Print menu.

   The screen will clear, and a message will give you the id number of your printing job.

5. Press ENTER to get back to your FACE Office.

The last item in the Print menu is `Print Options`. Selecting this allows you to access the `Change Print Options for login` form discussed in the section "Print Options." It is included in this menu as well, for your convenience.

Programs

A program is an executable file (also called an application), that can be as simple as a one line shell script that you write (see Chapter 9 for information on how to write a shell script), or an existing command from the UNIX System (see the *UNIX System V User's Reference Manual* for complete descriptions of UNIX commands.) or it can be as complicated as a spreadsheet with many features. The specific applications available vary from one computer system to another.

The Programs menu allows you to access other applications that have been installed on your computer system without having to leave your FACE Office. The Programs menu will include Spell Checker and Mail Services when FACE is first installed. (Others may also be listed, if your system administrator has installed them for general use.) You can run any program in the Programs menu by simply selecting it.

Mail Services

One of the programs you can run from the Programs menu is `Mail Services`. `Mail Services` enables you to send and receive mail. `Mail Services` invokes the UNIX system `mailx` command. The following information briefly describes how you can read and send mail using `Mail Services`. For information on the complete range of functions available to you through `mailx`, see Chapter 11, "Electronic Mail Tutorial", in this guide, or the `mailx`(1) manual page in the *UNIX System V User's Reference Manual*. The following brief summary describes basic use of the two items on the Mail Services menu:

`New Mail` This menu item lists the messages that other users send you and allows you to read them. When you select this item, the screen clears and your mail messages are listed in chronological order. If you have no mail, a message on the message line will tell you so. If you have mail, type the number of the message you want to read. Type `?` to get help. Type `q` to quit and return to the FACE interface.

`Send Mail` This menu item enables you to send mail to users on this system and other systems. A form is displayed in which you can enter the login ID of the recipient. After you press SAVE, the screen clears, and then you can type your message. Type `~?` for help. Type `~.` to end the message, send it to the recipient, and return to the FACE interface. Or, type `~x` to exit from `mailx` without sending the message.

To send mail to a user on a different system the login ID must be in the form `system_name!login_ID`.

For example, entering `merc!dlt` in this field would send the mail to the person with the login ID `dlt` on the system named `merc`. The system name must be a name of a system that was set up through the Mail Setup feature on the Administration menu.

After you press SAVE, the screen will clear and `mailx` prompts you for the subject of the mail, after which you can type your message. You can get help by typing `~?`. Type `~.` to send your message to the recipient and return to the interface. Or, type `~x` to exit from `mailx` without sending the message.

Spell Checker

The `Spell Checker` menu item in the Programs menu invokes the UNIX system `spell` program, which checks for spelling errors in the files you create. The procedure for using it is as follows:

1. Select `Spell Checker` from the Programs menu.

   A form titled `Spell Checker` appears in which you can enter the name of the file to be checked for spelling errors.

2. Type the path name of the file you want to check.

   You must use the full pathname (path from `root`) or relative path name (path from the current folder) of the file you want to check. A file name by itself is acceptable only when the file is located in the file folder you were in *before* you navigated to the Programs menu. (Press [CHOICES] to see a list of such files.)

3. Press [SAVE].

   A new frame will open in the work area, listing possible misspellings in the file.

4. Press [CANCEL] to close the frame.

After you have reviewed the list you can edit the file and correct the misspelled words using your editor.

Using Other Programs

Follow this procedure to use any program listed in the Programs menu.

Some programs display instructions for creating or working with existing files. Be sure to obtain information on how to use the program you selected, how to save your work, and how to exit from the program, before you use it.

1. Select `Programs` from the Office menu.

2. Select the program you want to use from the Programs menu.

   The program will start to run.

3. If the program requires command line arguments to run, you will see the prompt `Enter arguments for program:`. Type the arguments and press the [ENTER] key.

   You can name files using their full pathname (path from `root`) or their relative pathname (path from the current folder).

4. The program will continue.

5. Once you have exited from a program, a prompt instructs you to press the ENTER key.

   Do so, and the FACE screen reappears.

Programs Administration

Programs can be global or personal. Global programs are added to FACE and maintained by the FACE system administrator, or any person who has FACE system administration privileges (see "FACE Administration" for information on adding global programs). Personal programs are added to FACE by individual users, and are maintained by them. Both personal and global programs are listed in the Programs menu; however, global programs appear in every user's Programs menu, while your personal programs appear only in *your* Programs menu, not in anyone else's.

Personal Programs

You can add personal programs to your Programs menu using the `Programs Administration` feature from the Office menu.

Since the procedure to select a program is the same whether it is a global or personal program, no distinction is made between them in the Programs menu.

The Programs menu is automatically updated to show the addition, modification, or removal of a program the next time you open it. If the Programs menu is currently open on your screen you can update it immediately by navigating to it and executing the `update` command.

Adding a Program

It is important for you to understand that most programs will be added to your Programs menu by your system administrator. However, if you do create or obtain a program that not everyone else on the computer needs to use, you can add it to your own Programs menu.

This exercise explains how to add a personal program to your Programs menu.

1. Select `Office of login` from the AT&T FACE menu.
2. Select `Programs Administration` from the Office menu.
3. Select `Add Programs` from the Programs Administration menu.

   A form, titled `Add Programs` will appear. This form displays four fields that define the program to be added to the Programs menu.

   Notice that some of the fields in the form already contain default values.
4. The first field is the `Program Menu Name:` field.

   Type the name of the program as you would like it to appear in the Programs menu, and press (ENTER).

   In general, you can type any name that is from 1 to 42 characters long and that will help you remember what the program does.
5. The second field is the `Name of Command:` field.

   Type the full pathname of the program (or just the name of the program if your PATH includes the location of the program), and press (ENTER).

   If you don't know the full pathname of the program (that is, where it is stored on the computer), you may be able to find it in documents about the program: otherwise ask your system administrator.
6. The third field is the `Working Directory:` field. Notice that it contains a default value, which is the current working directory. For most users, the value in the `Working Directory:` field will be `/home/login` (the full pathname of their `$HOME` folder), but in some cases it can be a different value.

   The `Working Directory:` field defines the folder you want to be in while the application is running, and where files created by the application will be placed. If the program doesn't create files, or if you want to stay in the current folder, you can just type a dot (`.`). (The dot (`.`) is computer shorthand for "current folder.")

   FACE will automatically put you into the folder that is named in this field when this program is selected from the Programs menu. When you finish using the program, you will automatically return to the Programs menu.

   Type a dot (.) or the full pathname of a folder, and press (ENTER).

7. The fourth field is the `Prompt for arguments:` field.

   If you want the user of this program to be able to supply arguments, such as a filename, or an option to the program, then this field should be set to the value `yes`. If a user will never need to supply arguments to this command, set this field to the value `no`.

8. Press SAVE (or CTRL-f 3) to save the values you have just entered in the Add Programs form.

The next time you select `Programs` from the Office menu, the program you have added will be listed. When you select it, it will be executed.

Listing Personal Programs

You can display a list of just the personal programs you have added by selecting the item `List Programs` from the Programs Administration menu.

1. Select `List Programs` from the Programs Administration menu.

   The List Personal Programs menu appears: notice that global programs are not listed. You can select programs from this menu, just as you can from the Programs menu.

   If you have not added any personal programs to your Programs menu, the message `No Programs Installed` will display on the message line.

2. Press CANCEL (or CTRL-f 6) to return to the Programs Administration menu.

Modifying a Personal Program

You are not allowed to modify a global program (listed in your Programs menu), but any of your personal programs can be modified whenever you wish. Use the following procedure to modify an existing personal program.

1. Select `Modify Programs` from the Programs Administration menu.

   The Modify Personal Programs menu appears and lists all personal programs you have added.

2. Select the program you want to modify from the Modify Personal Programs menu.

3. The Modify Programs form appears, showing the values you entered in the fields when you added this program to your Programs menu. You can edit this form using any of the navigation and editing keys that work in forms (see "How to Use a Form" in "Getting Started").

4. Press SAVE (or CTRL-f 3) to save the modifications you have made.

   You will return to the Programs Administration menu.

Removing a Personal Program

You are not allowed to remove a global program from your Programs menu, but any of your personal programs can be removed whenever you wish. Use this procedure to remove a personal program.

1. Select `Remove Programs` from the Programs Administration menu.

   The Remove Personal Programs menu appears, and lists all the personal programs you have added.

2. Select the program you want to remove.

3. The `Confirm Delete of Program` frame will appear and displays the message `You are about to delete program.`

   - If you decide you do not want to remove this program, press CANCEL (or CTRL-f 6).

   - If you want to remove the program press CONT (or CTRL-f 3).

     You will be returned to the Programs Administration menu.

FACE Administration

System administrators who have installed FACE should use the Operations, Administration, and Maintenance program to add themselves as a FACE user (see the section "Adding a New User to FACE") before doing any of these procedures.

FACE users will not be able to use these procedures unless they have been given system administration privileges, and know the system administration password. If you need such privileges, see your system administrator.

FACE is easy to administer for two reasons: first, administration is done through the UNIX system Operations, Administration, and Maintenance (OA&M) system, which is an easy-to-use, menu-based program that guides you through most of the tasks required to administer the computer; second, only four categories of tasks need to be performed by the FACE system administrator—FACE user administration, FACE Global Programs administration, Mail Services administration, and Spell Checker administration.

FACE User management consists of four tasks: adding users as FACE users (setting up the FACE environment for their login IDs) modifying the FACE environment for users, removing FACE users (removing permission for a user to use FACE), and listing FACE users.

FACE Global Programs management consists of four tasks: adding, removing, modifying, or listing global programs to be available for all FACE users.

Mail Services and Spell Checker administration each consist of two tasks—adding and removing the service.

FACE User Administration

Adding a New FACE User

A user must have a UNIX System login ID before you can set up a FACE environment for that user:

1. Select `System Administration` from the AT&T FACE menu.

   The screen will clear, and you will be prompted to supply the system administration password. If you enter the wrong password you will be returned to your FACE Office. If you enter the correct password, you will be put into the UNIX System V Administration menu interface. This inteface operates similarly to FACE, and you can use many of the same navigation keys to navigate and select menu items, to edit forms, and to execute commands.

2. Select `applications` from the UNIX System V Administration menu.
3. Select `FACE` from the Administration for Available Applications menu.
4. Select `users` from the FACE Administration menu.
5. Select `add` from the FACE User Administration menu.

   A menu titled `Add a FACE Environment for a UNIX System User` appears.
6. Fill in, or change, the four fields in this form.

   When you navigate to a field, the message line displays an explanation of how to fill it in.

If you enter `yes` in the `Show System Administration in FACE menu:` field, `System Administration` will appear in the user's AT&T FACE menu, and the user will need to know the UNIX system administration password before he or she can use the `System Administration` menu item. This password is best communicated by word-of-mouth.

If you enter `yes` in the `Provide UNIX System Access:` field, `UNIX System` will appear in the user's AT&T FACE menu, and the user will be able to access a full-screen UNIX sub-shell by selecting it.

7. Press **SAVE** when you are done.

   A confirmation message will summarize what's been done to enable the user to use FACE.
8. Press **CANCEL** to return to the Add a FACE Environment for a UNIX System User form.
9. If you have no more users to add, press **CMD-MENU** and select `exit` to exit from UNIX System V Administration. You will be prompted to press **ENTER** to return to your FACE Office.

The new user will be given a complete FACE environment including a `.profile` file (pronounced "dot-profile") in his or her `$HOME` folder that automatically invokes FACE upon logging in, if you have entered `yes` in the `Invoke FACE at Login:` field. The following folders are created under the new user's `$HOME` folder if they don't already exist:

`WASTEBASKET` — `$HOME/WASTEBASKET` is where deleted files and folders are held, awaiting permanent removal from the computer.

`bin` — `$HOME/bin` will contain the shell scripts that run applications that the user has added as personal programs. If the `$HOME/bin` directory has been removed for some reason, FACE will create it when a user adds a personal program, and display a message to that effect.

`pref` — `$HOME/pref` contains environment variables used by FACE, and may contain files with additional FMLI scripts for the user's Office menu and the Programs menus. FMLI is a programming language and interpreter that programmers can use to create a form and menu interface like FACE or to customize FACE itself. To find out more about FMLI scripts, see the FMLI section of the *Character User Interface Programmer's Guide.*

`tmp` — `$HOME/tmp` is used for temporary storage. It must exist for FACE to run.

Once users start creating files and folders in AT&T FACE, `$HOME`, `$HOME/WASTEBASKET`, and any other folders they create will also contain a file named `.ott` (pronounced "dot-ott"). A `.ott` file contains an object type table, which describes the contents of the folder to FACE. Typically, users will never see the `.ott` files, but if they do, and accidentally delete one, FACE will re-create it automatically.

Users should be warned not to edit the contents of a `.ott` file.

An empty `.ott` file in a folder will cause that folder to appear empty when a user opens that folder in the FACE Office, even though files and folders exist there. If a user accidentally creates an empty `.ott` file, they should remove the empty file, FACE will re-create a new one, and the files in that folder will then be listed normally in the frame (as long as the pathname of the folder does not exceed the length limitations on pathnames, discussed in "Using Pathnames in FACE Commands," in Chapter 2).

The formats of `.ott` files and some other files used by FACE are described in FACE manual pages in the section "File Formats (4)," of your *System Administrator's Reference Manual.*

Modifying a FACE User's Environment

You can modify a FACE user's environment by selecting `modify` from the FACE User Administration menu. When you select `modify` the same form appears as when you add a new user. Enter the login ID of the user you want to modify and the rest of the fields will then display the current values for that user. You can change the values in any field using form navigation and editing keys. A confirmation message will be displayed when you are done.

Removing a FACE User

You can remove a user as a FACE user. If you do so, the user will still have his or her login ID, but will not be able to use FACE.

1. Select `remove` from the FACE User Administration menu.

   The Remove FACE Environment for a FACE User form will display the `User's Login ID:` field.

2. Enter the login ID of the user you want to remove.

   You can press **CHOICES** to see a pop-up menu listing all FACE users on the computer.

3. Press **SAVE** and the user will be removed. Or, press **CANCEL** to return to the FACE User Administration menu without removing the user.

   If you press **SAVE** a frame showing the results of the remove procedure is displayed as verification.

4. Navigate to the UNIX System V Administration menu you want to use next, or press CMD-MENU and select `exit` to exit from System Administration.

Listing FACE Users

You can see a list of all FACE users on the computer by selecting `list` from the FACE User Administration menu. When you select `list` a frame titled `FACE Users on This System` appears and displays the login ID of all users who have been set up to use FACE. You might want to use this item to check current FACE login IDs before you select the `add`, `modify`, or `remove` menu items.

Global Program Administration

A global program is a program that is available to every FACE user on the computer, and whose name appears in all FACE users' Programs menus. Only a system administrator, or a user who has been given system administration privileges can add, remove, or modify, a global program

A global program is one that you add, modify, or delete through the UNIX System V Administration menu interface. The tasks done in Global Program Administration are the same tasks that an individual FACE user can do through Programs Administration for his or her personal programs. The difference is that when you use the UNIX System V administration menu interface to do these tasks, all Programs menus for all FACE users on your computer will be affected.

All the global programs administration tasks are accessed from the FACE Administration menu in the UNIX System V Administration menu interface. These steps will get you there:

1. Select `System Administration` from the AT&T FACE menu.

   The screen will clear, and you will be prompted to supply the system administration password. If you enter the wrong password you will be returned to your FACE Office. If you enter the correct password, you will be put into the UNIX System V Administration menu interface. This inteface operates similarly to FACE, and you can use many of the same navigation keys to navigate and select menu items, to edit forms, and to execute commands.

2. Select `applications` from the UNIX System V Administration menu
3. Select `FACE` from the Administration for Available Applications menu.
4. Select `programs` from the FACE Administration menu.

   You will be presented with a menu of four operations:

   ```
   add
   list
   modify
   remove
   ```

Adding a Global Program

When you select `add` the Add Global Programs form will be displayed, in which you can define a program that will appear in the Programs menu for all FACE users on the system.

This exercise explains how to add a global program to the FACE Programs menu.

1. Select `add` from the Global Programs Administration menu.
2. The Add Global Programs form appears with four fields.
3. Fill in the four fields in the form.

   When you navigate to a field, the message line displays an explanation of how to fill in the field. You can also press **HELP** for additional information.
4. Press **SAVE** to save your definition of the new global program.

   You will then be returned to the Global Program Administration menu.
5. If you have no other tasks to complete, press **CANCEL** to return to the FACE Administration menu. Or, press **CMD-MENU** and select `exit` to exit from the UNIX System V Administration menu interface.
6. At the prompt, press **ENTER** to return to FACE.
7. Select the new global program from the Programs menu, to check that everything works.

Once you have added a new global program, don't forget to inform the other FACE users on your computer that it is available.

When you are back in FACE, and are no longer acting in your capacity of system administrator, neither you (nor any other FACE user) can remove, modify, or list this global program by selecting `Programs Administration` from the Office of Login menu. (Remember, only personal programs can be administered from `Programs Administration`.)

Listing, Modifying, and Removing a Global Program

The steps you take to access `list`, `modify`, and `remove` in the Global Program Administration menu are the same as the steps you took to access `add`. (Refer to "Adding a Global Program" if you need a reminder.)

After you access the Global Program Administration menu in the UNIX System V Administration menu interface, you will again see the list of four tasks you can choose from:

```
add
list
modify
remove
```

The `list` operation is the simplest of the Global Program Administration operations. It merely displays a current list of the global programs added to FACE, returning you to the Global Programs Administration menu when you cancel the frame.

You can select a global program from the List Global Programs menu and it will be executed.

When you select `modify` you the Modify Global Programs menu is displayed. This menu lists the global programs that have been added to FACE. Notice that it does not list global programs that were supplied with FACE by AT&T (`Mail Services` or `Spell Checker`). When you select the program you want to modify from this menu, the `Modify Global Programs` form is displayed, and has the same fields as the `Add Global Programs` form. You can edit each field in the same way. When you have modified the fields you want to modify, press **SAVE** to save the new values and return to the Global Programs Administration menu. Once again, you can exit from UNIX System V Administration by pressing **CMD-MENU** and selecting `exit`. When you see the prompt `Press ENTER to continue`, do so to return to FACE.

When you select `remove`, a menu titled `Remove Global Programs` lists global programs that have been added to FACE. When you select a program from this menu, a Confirmation frame displays the name of the program you are about to remove. You can press CONT to remove it, or CANCEL to exit from this procedure without removing the program. In either case, you will be returned to the Global Programs Administration menu. Again, you can exit from UNIX System V Administration by pressing CMD-MENU and selecting `exit`. When you see the prompt `Press ENTER to continue`, do so to return to your FACE Office.

Mail Services and Spell Checker Administration

Two global programs, `Mail Services` and `Spell Checker` are provided with FACE. Notice that the administration of these two programs is not included in the Global Program Administration menu item. This is because they were supplied with FACE as "built-in" features. As such, they are not modifiable or removable through the `programs` menu item in the FACE Administation menu. To administer these built-in features, you must select `mail_services`, and `spell_checker`, from the FACE Administration menu.

Mail Services Administration

1. Select `mail_services` from the FACE Administration menu.

   A frame titled `Mail Services Administration` will appear.

2. From this menu you can select `add`, if you want to add the Mail Services menu item to users' Programs menus, or `remove`, if you want to remove Mail Services from users' Programs menus.

3. Once you have selected the procedure you want to perform, check the message line for confirmation that the task is complete.

Spell Checker Administration

1. Select `spell_checker` from the FACE Administration menu.

   A frame titled `Spell Checker Administration` will appear.

2. From this menu you can select `add`, if you want to add the Spell Checker menu item to users' Programs menus, or `remove`, if you want to remove Spell Checker from users' Programs menus.

3. Once you have selected the procedure you want to perform, check the message line for confirmation that the task is complete.

Always remember to inform FACE users when a global program has been added, modified, or deleted.

UNIX System

If you have not been given access to the UNIX system through FACE, `UNIX System` will not appear in your AT&T FACE menu, and you will not be able to perform the activities described in this section.

Selecting `UNIX System` from the AT&T FACE menu is another way of accessing the UNIX System shell. This creates a subshell that takes up the entire screen. At the top of the screen the name of the current directory is displayed, along with the following directions:

```
To return, type 'exit' or control-d
```

The prompt for the subshell is `UNIX:`. This unique prompt lets you know you are in a UNIX System subshell.

To return to AT&T FACE, type `exit` and press ENTER or press CTRL-d.

You can run a program or execute commands in the subshell, but when you return to AT&T FACE, the subshell is terminated as well as all processes running within the subshell. More about the UNIX System shell is described in Chapters 1, 2, 3, and 9, in this guide.

Using UNIX System Commands from Your FACE Office

It is not necessary to select `UNIX System` from the AT&T FACE menu to use UNIX System commands. They can be executed from the FACE command line by preceding them with an exclamation mark `!`).

Although a complete discussion of all UNIX System commands is not within the scope of this tutorial, you will learn the basic use of two UNIX System commands, `news`, and `pg`, in the following exercises because they are useful commands that will enhance your ability to work in your FACE Office. See section

"Commands (1)" in the *UNIX System V User's Reference Manual* for complete discussions of these and other UNIX System commands.

If you have not been given UNIX system privileges, you will not be able to use `!` to execute UNIX system commands from the command line.

The `news` Command

When you log into your computer, you may notice a line that tells you that there are news items. The message may even list them. This UNIX System news may be read by all users of the computer, and is like an electronic newspaper. This exercise explains how to read this electronic newspaper, and submit news items to it.

1. Press CTRL-j to access the command line, type `!news` and press ENTER.

   The screen will clear and start to print out the news items (if there are any). When you are using a UNIX System command, you can temporarily stop printing the output by typing CTRL-s and start printing it again by typing CTRL-q.

2. When all the news is printed (or if there are no news items to print), a message will instruct you to press ENTER to return to FACE. Do so, and you will return to the same frame you were in when you accessed the command line.

To put a news item in this electronic newspaper, create a file containing the story, ad, or whatever, and then copy or move it to the UNIX System directory `/home/news`. If you need help doing this, contact your system administrator.

The `pg` Command and Piping

The UNIX System `pg` command displays its input one screenful at a time. It's helpful when you want to control the rate at which the output of a command is displayed. It waits for you to press ENTER before scrolling to the next screenful.

The `pg` command can be used two ways. You may give it a file name as an argument, or you may redirect the output of another program to it through the pipe (which will be explained later in this exercise).

1. Press CTRL-j to access the command line, type `!pg facetest2` and then press ENTER.

   The file `facetest2` will be displayed, one screenful at a time, pausing when the screen is full to display the : prompt.

   1. To continue to the next screen of text, simply press ENTER.
   2. To move back a screen, type a minus (–) and press ENTER.
   3. To skip to the end of the file, type a dollar sign ($) and press ENTER.

2. When you are at the end of the file, the prompt will change to `(EOF) :` (for "end of file"). Press ENTER to exit from the pg command.
3. When you are prompted to do so, press ENTER to return to FACE.

This paging capability is useful for reading the sometimes lengthy output from `news`, but the output of `news` is not a file. However, the UNIX System will let you run a command and, instead of sending its output to the screen, you can redirect the output to the pg command, which will handle it as if it were a file. This is called "piping" and you use the pipe symbol (|) to tell the UNIX System that this is what you want to do.

1. Press CTRL-j to access the command line, type `!news | pg` and press ENTER.
2. The screen will clear, and the electronic news will start to print. But since the output of `news` is being piped to pg, if it is longer than one screenful, you can move back and forth in it as described above. Try moving forward, backward, or skipping to the end of the output.
3. Exit from the pg command and return to FACE.

Remember to precede this and all UNIX System commands with an exclamation mark (!) when executing them from the FACE command line.

Using an Executable File

There are many files on your computer that are executable. An executable file (also called a "binary" file) contains instructions to the computer that are neither readable by, nor meant to be read by humans. It is possible to copy an executable file into one of your file folders. If you do so, the description of the file is `Executable`.

Because the description `Executable`, supplied automatically by FACE, is the only way you can tell which of your files contain executable programs if you do not display files in the long form in a menu, it is not advised that you redescribe such files.

If you do choose to redescribe an executable file, the only way you can then identify it as Executable in a menu is to set the value of the `Display Type` field in the Office Functions form to `long form` so that its type will also be displayed.

Once you have copied an executable file to your filecabinet, you can use it by selecting it. This exercise shows you how to copy and use an executable file.

1. Type CTRL-j to access the command line and then type

   ```
   copy /usr/bin/news $HOME
   ```

   and press ENTER.

2. Now open the `/home/login` file folder and you will see the file `news` listed and described as `Executable`.

   Files copied to your FACE Office from the UNIX system may not have the same permissions you have defined as your defaults via the Preferences form. You may want to check the `news` file permissions (use `security`) to make sure the read, write, and execute permissions for you (the owner) are set to `yes`.

3. To run `news`, position the cursor on the file name and press ENTER. The `news` command takes over the entire screen, and if there is news from other users on your computer, it is displayed.

It is not a good idea to make copies of the UNIX System executables in your own filecabinet, because system executables such as `news` are usually stored in well-known places (such as the /usr/bin directory) and can be easily added as personal programs in your Programs menu.

This capability is probably most useful when someone gives you a copy of a program he or she wrote that is not a part of the UNIX System.

Running a Shell Script

There is another type of file that your computer can run. When a standard file is used in this way, it is called a "shell script." To understand what a shell script is, you first need to understand what a shell is. Briefly, the UNIX System shell is a command interpreter program that reads a command you type and tells the UNIX System what to do.

When you enter the UNIX System a prompt saying `UNIX:` is displayed. This is put there by the UNIX System shell. It means the shell is waiting for you to type a command. A shell script is a file that contains one or more lines of text, each of which is a command that the shell can interpret. Once the file is created, permissions need to be changed on it to give it run/search capability. Even when the permissions are changed, FACE will continue to think that this is a Standard file, not an Executable file.

The description `Executable`, supplied automatically by FACE, is the only way you can tell which of your files contain executable programs (ones you don't have to use `run` to execute). It is not advised that you redescribe shell scripts as `Executable`, even though in one sense they are.

If you do choose to redescribe a shell script as `Executable`, the only way you can identify files whose type is `Executable` is to set the value of the `File Folder Display Type` field in the Office Functions form to `long form` so that its type as well as its description will be displayed.

In the following exercise, you will create a simple shell script and change its permissions to include run/search capability and use `run` to execute it.

1. In your `/home/login` file folder, create a standard file called `test.sh` and enter these lines into it.

```
echo What is your name?
read name
echo Hello $name.
echo I\'m a shell script and now I am finished.
```

2. Write and quit the file.

   Notice that `test.sh` is now listed in your `/home/login` menu as a Standard File.

3. Position the cursor on `test.sh` in the `/home/login` menu.

4. Execute the `security` command and give yourself run/search permission for this file. When you return to the `/home/login` file folder, you will notice no change in the description.

5. Now select `test.sh`.

   Instead of running the file, as it ran the executable in the previous exercise, FACE seems to think you want to edit it. You don't, so quit the editor without making any changes.

6. With the cursor still positioned on `test.sh`, press CMD-MENU (or CTRL-f 7), and select `run`.

   The screen will clear, and the shell script, `test.sh` will run.

7. In response to the prompt `What is your name?`, type your name and press ENTER.

8. When the shell script is finished, press ENTER to return to FACE.

When you store a shell script in your FACE Office or filecabinet in the way just described, you must use the `run` command to run it.

Suspending and Returning to Files

Suppose you were editing a file, and you wanted to get some information from another file. You might think you would have to mark your place, write and quit your file, return to FACE, open the other file and read it, return to the file you were editing, find your place, delete the marker, and then continue editing. Suppose you wanted to refer to several other files while you were editing the first file?

It's easy to see that this is not an efficient use of your time. Fortunately, you can use the `facesuspend` command to suspend up to five `vi` sessions and then use `frm-mgmt` to choose which one to return to.

The `facesuspend` can only be used in programs that have a built-in method to escape to the UNIX shell, as `vi` does. If you try using it in a program that does not have such a built-in method, `facesuspend` will be ignored.

Suspending Files

In this exercise you will practice suspending a few files while you are editing them with `vi`.

1. Navigate to the /home/login folder and create three new files called `facetest3`, `facetest4`, and `facetest5`.

   As you create each one you will be put into `vi`. Insert enough text into each file to make it recognizable, then write it and quit, using `:wq`). When you are finished, the three new files will be listed in your /home/login folder.

2. Select `facetest3`.

   Now suppose you need information from the file `facetest4`. Instead of typing `:wq` to write `facetest3` and quit the `vi` editor, type `:!facesuspend`, then press ENTER.

   Recall that while in the `vi` command mode, typing `!command` is how you can execute a UNIX System command without exiting `vi`. The command you are executing here is `facesuspend`, which is supplied with FACE. The `facesuspend` command leaves the current process (here `vi`), running but returns you to the FACE screen.

3. Repeat step 2 to open and suspend `facetest4`.
4. Now suppose you discover you need information from the file `facetest5` as well.

   Open and suspend `facetest5`.

There are now three files opened and suspended in your work area, although none is visible on your screen at this point. You are back in your FACE Office, and the /home/login frame is the active frame.

Returning to Suspended Files

Using the three short files you just created, it might not be obvious how much of your time the `facesuspend` command can save, but they serve to teach the process.

In this exercise you will learn how to use the `frm-mgmt` command to list your suspended files and choose which one you want to return to.

1. Execute `frm-mgmt` from the Command menu or the command line.

   This opens the Frame Management menu.
2. Select `list` from the Frame Management menu.

   You will be presented with a menu of open frames. Notice that your suspended files are listed even though they are not visible on the screen.
3. Select `facetest3`.

   You will return to `facetest3`, and it will be in exactly the state it was in when you suspended it. You can continue to edit the file, and eventually write it and quit the editor, or you can suspend it again.
4. For the purposes of this exercise, to leave `facetest3`, just suspend it again!
5. Repeat steps 1 through 4 for `facetest4` and `facetest5`.

   After you suspend `facetest5` a second time, you will be back in the /home/login frame.

6. Press CTRL-J, type `exit`, and press ENTER to exit from FACE.

   Ordinarily you would be allowed to exit from FACE at this point, even though the /home/login frame, and other frames, are open. But instead, you are returned to the first suspended item in the Open Frames list. An additional message tells you that this item must be closed before you can exit from FACE.

7. Using `:q` or `:wq`, and then pressing ENTER, close each `vi` session as it is presented to you. When the last suspended file is closed, FACE will finish executing the `exit` command, and you will be logged out of your FACE Office.

NOTE

Suspended files that were accessed through `UNIX System` in the Office menu are listed by their name in the `frm-mgmt` list. Suspended files that were accessed through the Programs menu or a command line shell command (`!unix_command`) are listed by their full pathname in the `frm-mgmt` list.

6. LINE EDITOR (ed) TUTORIAL

6. LINE EDITOR (ed) TUTORIAL

6 Line Editor (ed) Tutorial

Introducing the Line Editor

This chapter is a tutorial on the line editor, ed. ed is versatile and is relatively fast. It can be used on any type of terminal. The examples of command lines and system responses described in this chapter will apply to your terminal, whether it is a video display terminal or a paper printing terminal. The ed commands can be typed in at your terminal or they can be used in a shell program (see Chapter 9, "Shell Tutorial").

ed is a line editor. During editing sessions, it is always pointing to a single line in the file called the current line. When you access an existing file, ed makes the last line the current line so you can start appending text easily. Unless you specify the number of a different line or a range of lines, ed will perform each command you issue on the current line. In addition to letting you change, delete, or add text on one or more lines, ed allows you to add text from another file to the buffer.

During an editing session with ed, you are altering the contents of a file in a temporary buffer where you work until you have finished creating or correcting your text. When you edit an existing file, a copy of that file is placed in the buffer and your changes are made to this copy. The changes have no effect on the original file until you instruct ed, by using the write command, to move the contents of the buffer into the file.

After you have read this tutorial and tried the examples and exercises, you will have a good working knowledge of ed. The following basic operations are included in the chapter:

- entering the line editor ed, creating text, writing the text to a file, and quitting ed
- addressing particular lines of the file and displaying lines of text
- deleting text
- substituting new text for old text
- using special characters in search and substitute patterns
- moving text around in the file, as well as other useful operating commands and information

Suggestions for Using this Tutorial

The commands discussed in each section are reviewed at the end of that section. A summary of all ed commands introduced in this chapter is found in Appendix D, where the commands are listed by topic.

At the end of some sections, exercises are given so you can experiment with the commands. The answers to all exercises are at the end of this chapter.

The notation conventions used in this chapter are those used throughout this *Guide*. They are described in the Preface.

Getting Started

The best way to learn ed is to log in to the UNIX system and try the examples as you read this tutorial. Do the exercises; do not be afraid to experiment. As you experiment and try out ed commands, you will learn a fast and versatile method of text editing.

In this section you will learn the commands used to:

- enter ed
- append text
- move up or down in the file to display a line of text
- delete a line of text
- write the buffer to a file
- quit ed

How to Enter ed

To enter the line editor, type ed and a file name:

ed *filename*<CR>

Choose a name that reflects the contents of the file. If you are creating a new file, the system responds with a question mark and the filename:

```
$ ed new-file<CR>
?new-file
```

If you are going to edit an existing file, ed responds with the number of bytes in the file:

```
$ ed old-file<CR>
235
```

How to Create Text

The editor receives two types of input, editing commands and text, from your terminal. To avoid confusing them, ed recognizes two modes of editing work: command mode and text input mode. When you work in command mode, any characters you type are interpreted as commands. In input mode, any characters you type are interpreted as text to be added to a file.

Whenever you enter ed you are put into command mode. To create text in your file, change to input mode by typing a (for append), on a line by itself, ana pressing the RETURN key:

```
a<CR>
```

Now you are in input mode; any characters you type from this point wil be added to your file as text. Be sure to type a on a line by itself; if you do not, the editor will not execute your command.

After you have finished entering text, type a period on a line by itself. This takes you out of the text input mode and returns you to the command mode. Now you can give ed other commands.

The following example shows how to enter ed, create text in a new file called try-me, and quit text input mode with a period.

```
$ ed try-me<CR>
?try-me
a<CR>
This is the first line of text.<CR>
This is the second line,<CR>
and this is the third line.<CR>
.<CR>
```

Notice that ed does not give a response to the period; it just waits for a new command. If ed does not respond to a command, you may have forgotten to type a period after entering text and may still be in text input mode. Type a period and press the RETURN key at the beginning of a line to return to command mode. Now you can execute editing commands. For example, if you have added some unwanted characters or lines to your text, you can delete them once you have returned to command mode.

How to Display Text

To display a line of a file, type p (for print) on a line by itself. The p command prints the current line, that is, the last line on which you worked. Continue with the previous example. You have just typed a period to exit input mode. Now type the p command to see the current line.

```
$ ed try-me<CR>
?try-me
a<CR>
This is the first line of text.<CR>
This is the second line,<CR>
and this is the third line.<CR>
.<CR>
p<CR>
and this is the third line.
```

You can print any line of text by specifying its line number (also known as the address of the line). The address of the first line is 1; of the second, 2; and so on. For example, to print the second line in the file try-me, type:

```
2p<CR>
This is the second line,
```

You can also use line addresses to print a span of lines by specifying the addresses separated by a comma, of the first and last lines of the section you want to see. For example, to print the first three lines of a file, type:

```
1,3p<CR>
```

You can even print the whole file this way. For example, you can display a 20-line file by typing 1,20p. If you do not know the address of the last line in your file, you can substitute a $ sign, ed symbol for the address of the last line. (These conventions are discussed in detail in the section titled "Line Addressing.")

```
1,$p<CR>
This is the first line of text.
This is a second line,
and this is the third line.
```

If you forget to quit text input mode with a period, you will add text that you do not want. Try to make this mistake. Add another line of text to your `try-me` file and then use the `p` command without quitting text input mode. Then quit text input mode and print the entire file.

```
p<CR>
and this is the third line.
a<CR>
This is the fourth line.<CR>
p<CR>
.<CR>
1,$p<CR>
This is the first line of text.
This is the second line,
and this is the third line.
This is the fourth line.
p
```

What did you get? The next section explains how to delete the unwanted line.

How to Delete a Line of Text

To delete text, you must be in the command mode of `ed`. Typing `d` deletes the current line; typing `d` and the line number deletes the specified line. Try this command on the last example to remove the unwanted line containing `p`. Display the current line (`p` command), delete it (`d` command), and display the remaining lines in the file (`p` command). Your screen should look like this:

```
p<CR>
p
d<CR>
1,$p<CR>
This is the first line of text.
This is a second line,
and this is the third line.
This is the fourth line.
```

ed does not send you any messages to confirm that you have deleted text. The only way you can verify that the d command has succeeded is by printing the contents of your file with the p command. To receive verification of your deletion, you can put the d and p together on one command line. If you repeat the previous example with this command, your screen should look like this:

```
p<CR>
p
dp<CR>
This is the fourth line.
```

How to Move Up or Down in the File

To display the line below the current line, press the RETURN key while in command mode. If there is no line below the current line, ed responds with a ? and continues to treat the last line of the file as the current line. To display the line above the current line, press the minus key (–).

The following screen provides examples of how both of these commands are used:

```
p<CR>
This is the fourth line.
-<CR>
and this is the third line.
-<CR>
This is the second line,
-<CR>
This is the first line of text.
<CR>
This is the second line,
<CR>
and this is the third line.
```

Notice that by typing -<CR> or <CR>, you can display a line of text without typing the p command. These commands are also line addresses. Whenever you type a line address and do not follow it with a command, ed assumes that you want to see the line you have specified. Experiment with these commands; create some text, delete a line, and display your file.

How to Save the Buffer Contents in a File

As we discussed earlier, during an editing session, the system holds your text in a temporary storage area called a buffer. When you have finished editing, you can save your work by writing it from the temporary buffer to a permanent file in secondary memory. By writing to a file, you are simply putting a copy of the contents of the buffer into the file. The text in the buffer is not disturbed, and you can make further changes to it.

It is a good idea to write the buffer text into your file frequently. If an interrupt occurs (such as an accidental loss of power to your terminal), you may lose the material in the buffer, but you will not lose the copy written to your file.

To write your text to a file, enter the w command. You do not have to specify a file name; first type w and press the RETURN key. If you have just created new text, ed creates a file for it with the name you specified when you entered the editor. If you have edited an existing file, the w command writes the contents of the buffer to that file by default.

If you prefer, you can specify a new name for your file as an argument on the w command line. Be careful not to use the name of a file that already exists unless you want to replace its contents with the contents of the current buffer. ed will not warn you about an existing file; it will simply overwrite that file with your buffer contents.

For example, if you decide you would prefer the try-me file to be called stuff, you can rename it:

```
w stuff <CR>
110
```

Notice the last line of the screen. This is the number of characters in your text. When the editor reports the number of characters in this way, the write command has succeeded.

How to Quit the Editor

When you have completed editing try-me, write it from the buffer into a file with the w command. Then leave the editor and return to the shell by typing q (for quit).

```
w<CR>
110
q<CR>
$
```

The system responds with a shell prompt. At this point the editing buffer is discarded. If you have not executed the write command, your text in the buffer has also vanished. If you did not make any changes to the text during your editing session, no harm is done. However, if you did make changes, you could lose your work in this way. Therefore, if you type q after changing the file without writing it, ed warns you with a ?. You then have a chance to write and quit.

```
q<CR>
?
w<CR>
110
q<CR>
$
```

If, instead of writing, you type q a second time, ed assumes you do not want to write the contents of the buffer to your file and returns you to the shell. Your file is left unchanged and the contents of the buffer are wiped out.

You now know the basic commands needed to create and edit a file using ed.

Table 6-1 summarizes these commands.

Table 6-1: Summary of ed Editor Commands

Command	Function
ed *file*	enter ed to edit *file*
a	append text after the current line
.	quit text input mode and return to ed command mode.
p	print text on your terminal
d	delete text
<CR>	display the next line in the buffer (literally, carriage return)
–	display the previous line in the buffer
w	write the contents of the buffer to the file
q	quit ed and return to the shell

Exercise 1

Answers for all the exercises in this chapter are found at the end of the chapter. However, they are not necessarily the only possible correct answers. Any method that enables you to perform a task specified in an exercise is correct, even if it does not match the answer given.

1-1. Enter `ed` with a file named `junk`. Create a line of text containing `Hello World`, write it to the file and quit `ed`.

Now use `ed` to create a file called `stuff`. Create a line of text containing two words, `Goodbye world`; write this text to the file, and quit `ed`.

1-2. Enter `ed` again with the file named `junk`. What was the program response? Was the character count for it the same as the character count reported by the `w` command in Exercise 1-1?

Display the contents of the file. Is that your file `junk`?

How can you return to the shell? Try `q` without writing the file. Why do you think the editor allowed you to quit without writing to the buffer?

1-3. Enter `ed` with the file `junk`. Add a line:

```
Wendy's horse came through the window.
```

Since you did not specify a line address, where do you think the line was added to the buffer? Display the contents of the buffer. Try quitting the buffer without writing to the file. Try writing the buffer to a different file called `stuff`. Notice that `ed` does not warn you that a file called `stuff` already exists. You have erased the contents of `stuff` and replaced them with new text.

Now type `q` to quit. Notice that `ed` does *not* give the `?` warning, even though you typed `q` without writing the changes to `junk`. The reason for this is that, once you write the buffer to *any* file, `ed` no longer considers the buffer modified.

General Format of ed Commands

ed commands have a simple and regular format:

[*address1*[,*address2*]]*command*[*argument*]<CR>

The brackets around *address1*, *address2*, and *argument* show that these are optional. The brackets are not part of the command line.

address1,address2	The addresses give the position of lines in the buffer. *Address1* through *address2* gives you a range of lines that will be affected by the *command*. If *address2* is omitted, the command will affect only the line specified by *address1*.
command	The *command* is one character and tells the editor what task to perform.
argument	The *arguments* to a *command* are those parts of the text that will be modified, or a filename, or another line address.

This format will become clearer to you when you begin to experiment with the ed commands.

Line Addressing

A line address is a character or group of characters that identifies a line of text. Before `ed` can execute commands that add, delete, move, or change text, it must know the line address of the affected text. Type the line address before the command:

[*address1*],[*address2*]*command*<CR>

Both *address1* and *address2* are optional. Specify *address1* alone to request action on a single line of text; specify both *address1* and *address2* to request a span of lines. If you do not specify any *address*, `ed` assumes that the line address is the current line.

The most common ways to specify a line address in `ed` are:

- by entering line numbers (assuming that the lines of the files are consecutively numbered from 1 to *n*, beginning with the first line of the file)
- by entering special symbols for the current line, last line, or a span of lines
- by adding or subtracting lines from the current line
- by searching for a character string or word on the desired line

You can access one line or a span of lines, or make a global search for all lines containing a specified character string. (A character string is a set of successive characters, such as a word.)

Numerical Address

`ed` gives a numerical address to each line in the buffer. The first line of the buffer is 1, the second line is 2, and so on, for each line in the buffer. Any line can be accessed by `ed` with its line address number. To see how line numbers address a line, enter `ed` with the file `try-me` and type a number.

```
$ ed try-me<CR>
110
1<CR>
This is the first line of text.
3<CR>
and this is the third line.
```

Remember that p is the default command for a line address specified without a command. Because you gave a line address, ed assumes you want that line displayed on your terminal.

Numerical line addresses frequently change in the course of an editing session. Later in this chapter you will create lines, delete lines, or move lines to different positions. This will change the line address numbers of some lines. The number of a specific line is always the current position of that line in the editing buffer. For example, if you add five lines of text between lines 5 and 6, line 6 becomes line 11. If you delete line 5, line 6 becomes line 5.

Symbolic Address

Symbolic Address of the Current Line

The current line is the line most recently acted on by any ed command. If you have just entered ed with an existing file, the current line is the last line of the buffer. The symbol for the address of the current line is a period. Therefore you can display the current line by typing a period (.) and pressing the RETURN key.

Use this command in the file try-me:

```
$ ed try-me<CR>
110
.<CR>
This is the fourth line.
```

The . is the address. Because a command is not specified after the period, ed executes the default command p and displays the line found at this address.

To get the line number of the current line, type the following command:

```
.=<CR>
```

ed responds with the line number. For example, in the try-me file, the current line is 4.

```
.<CR>
This is the fourth line.
.=<CR>
4
```

Symbolic Address of the Last Line

The symbolic address for the last line of a file is the $ sign. To verify that the $ sign accesses the last line, access the try-me file with ed and specify this address on a line by itself. (Keep in mind that when you first access a file, your current line is always the last line of the file.)

```
$ ed try-me<CR>
110
.<CR>
This is the fourth line.
$<CR>
This is the fourth line.
```

Remember that the $ address within ed is not the same as the $ prompt from the shell.

Symbolic Address of the Set of All Lines

When used as an address, a comma (`,`) refers to all the lines of a file from the first through the last line. It is an abbreviated form of the string mentioned earlier that represents all lines in a file, `1,$`. Use this shortcut to print the contents of `try-me`:

```
,p<CR>
This is the first line of text.
This is the second line,
and this is the third line.
This is the fourth line.
```

Symbolic Address of the Current Line through the Last Line

The semi-colon (`;`) represents a set of lines beginning with the current line and ending with the last line of a file. It is equivalent to the symbolic address .,$. Use it with the file `try-me`:

```
2p<CR>
This is the second line,
;p<CR>
This is the second line,
and this is the third line.
This is the fourth line.
```

Address Relative to the Current Line

You may often want to address lines in relation to the current line. You can do this by adding or subtracting a number of lines from the current line with a plus (+) or a minus (–) sign. An address derived in this way is called a relative address. To experiment with relative line addresses, add several more lines to your file `try-me`, as shown in the following screen. Also, write the buffer contents to the file so your additions will be saved:

```
$ ed try-me<CR>
110
.<CR>
This is the fourth line.
a<CR>
five<CR>
six<CR>
seven<CR>
eight<CR>
nine<CR>
ten<CR>
.<CR>
w<CR>
140
```

Now try adding and subtracting line numbers from the current line.

```
4<CR>
This is the fourth line.
+3<CR>
seven
-5<CR>
This is a second line,
```

What happens if you ask for a line address that is greater than the last line, or if you try to subtract a number greater than the current line number?

```
5<CR>
five
-6<CR>
?
.=<CR>
5
+7<CR>
?
```

Notice that the current line remains at line 5 of the buffer. The current line changes only if you give ed a correct address. The ? response indicates an error. The section titled "Other Useful Commands and Information," at the end of this chapter, explains how to get a help message that describes the error.

Character String Address

You can search forward or backward in the file for a line containing a particular character string. To do so, specify a string, preceded by a delimiter.

Delimiters mark the boundaries of character strings; they tell ed where a string starts and ends. The most common delimiter is a / (slash), used in the following format:

/pattern

When you specify a pattern preceded by a / (slash), ed begins at the current line and searches forward (that is, through subsequent lines in the buffer) for the next line containing the pattern. When the search reaches the last line of the buffer, ed wraps around to the beginning of the file and continues its search from line 1.

The following rectangle represents the editing buffer. The path of the arrows shows the search initiated by a / :

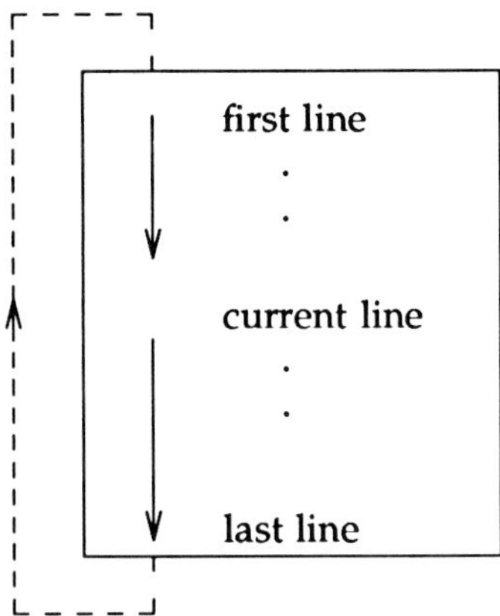

Another useful delimiter is ?. If you specify a pattern preceded by a ?, (?pattern), ed begins at the current line and searches backward (up through previous lines in the buffer) for the next line containing the pattern. If the search reaches the first line of the file, it wraps around and continues searching upward from the last line of the file.

The following rectangle represents the editing buffer. The path of the arrows shows the search initiated by a ? .

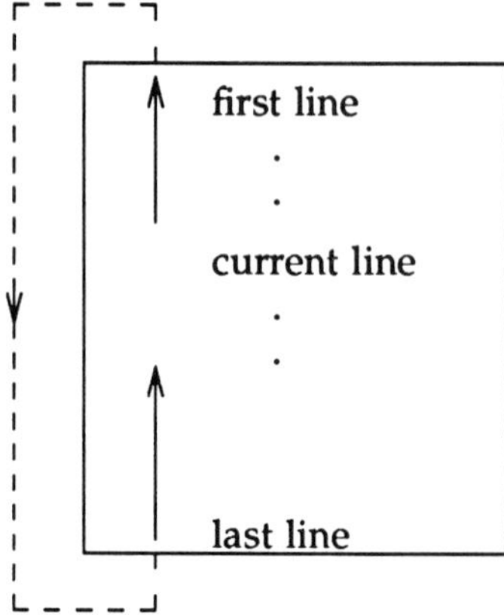

Experiment with these two methods of requesting address searches on the file try-me. What happens if ed does not find the specified character string?

```
$ ed try-me<CR>
140
.<CR>
ten
?first<CR>
This is the first line of text.
/fourth<CR>
This is the fourth line.
/junk<CR>
?
```

In this example, ed found the specified strings `first` and `fourth`. Then, because no command was given with the address, it executed the p command by default, displaying the lines it had found. When ed cannot find a specified string (such as `junk`), it responds with a ? .

You can also use the / (slash) to search for multiple occurrences of a pattern without typing it more than once. First, specify the pattern by typing */pattern*, as usual. After ed prints the first occurrence, it waits for another command. Type / and press the RETURN key; ed will continue to search forward through the file for the last pattern specified. Use this command by searching for the word `line` in the file `try-me`:

```
.<CR>
This is the first line of text.
/line<CR>
This is the second line,
/<CR>
and this is the third line.
/<CR>
This is the fourth line.
/<CR>
This is the first line of text.
```

Notice that after ed has found all occurrences of the pattern between the line where you requested a search and the end of the file, it wraps around to the beginning of the file and continues searching.

Specify a Range of Lines

You can request a group of lines in two ways. You can specify a range of lines, such as *address1* through *address2*, or you can specify a global search for all lines containing a specified pattern.

The simplest way to specify a range of lines is to use the line numbers of the first and last lines of the range, separated by a comma. Place this address before the command. For example, if you want to display lines 2 through 7 of the editing buffer, give *address1* as 2 and *address2* as 7 in the following format:

```
2,7p<CR>
```

Use this method on the file `try-me`:

```
2,7p<CR>
This is the second line,
and this is the third line.
This is the fourth line.
five
six
seven
```

Did you try typing 2,7 without the p? What happened? If you do not add the p command, ed prints only *address2,* the last line of the range of addresses.

You can also use relative line addresses to request a range of lines. Be sure that *address1* precedes *address2* in the buffer. Relative addresses are calculated from the current line, as the following example shows:

```
4<CR>
This is the fourth line
-2,+3p<CR>
This is the second line,
and this is the third line.
This is the fourth line.
five
six
seven
```

Specify a Global Search

Two commands do not follow the general format of ed commands: g and v. These are global search commands that specify addresses with a character string (pattern). The g command searches for all lines containing the string pattern and performs the command on those lines. The v command searches for all lines that do not contain the pattern and performs the command on those lines.

The general format for these commands is:

g/*pattern*/*command*<CR>
v/*pattern*/*command*<CR>

Try these commands by using them to search for the word `line` in `try-me`:

```
g/line/p<CR>
This is the first line of text.
This is the second line,
and this is the third line.
This is the fourth line
```

```
v/line/p<CR>
five
six
seven
eight
nine
ten
```

Notice the function of the `v` command: it finds all the lines that do not contain the word specified in the command line (`line`).

Once again, the default command for the lines addressed by `g` or `v` is `p`; you do not have to include a `p` as the last delimiter on your command line.

```
g/line<CR>
This is the first line of text.
This is the second line,
and this is the third line.
This is the fourth line
```

However, if you are giving line addresses to be used by other `ed` commands, you must include beginning and ending delimiters. You can use any of the methods discussed in this section to specify line addresses for `ed` commands. Table 6-2 summarizes the symbols and commands available for addressing lines.

Table 6-2: Summary of Line Addressing

Address	Description
n...	the number of a line in the buffer
.	the current line (the line most recently acted on by an ed command)
.=	the command used to request the line number of the current line
$	the last line of the file
43,	the set of lines from line 1 through the last line
;	the set of lines from the current line through the last line
+ *n*	the line that is located *n* lines after the current line
− *n*	the line that is located *n* lines before the current line
/*abc*	the command used to search forward in the buffer for the first line that contains the pattern *abc*
?*abc*	the command used to search backward in the buffer for the first line that contains the pattern *abc*
g/*abc*	the set of all lines that contain the pattern *abc*
v/*abc*	the set of all lines that do NOT contain the pattern *abc*

Exercise 2

2-1. Create a file called `towns` with the following lines:

My kind of town is
Chicago
Like being no where at all in
Toledo
I lost those little town blues in
New York
I lost my heart in
San Francisco
I lost $$ in
Las Vegas

2-2. Display line 3.

2-3. If you specify a range of lines with the relative address –2,+3p, what lines are displayed ?

2-4. What is the current line number? Display the current line.

2-5. What does the last line say?

2-6. What line is displayed by the following request for a search?

```
?town<CR>
```

After `ed` responds, type this command alone on a line:

```
?<CR>
```

What happened?

2-7. Search for all lines that contain the pattern `in`. Then search for all lines that do NOT contain the pattern `in`.

Displaying Text in a File

ed has three commands that display lines of text in the editing buffer: p, n, and l. (l is discussed in a later section of this chapter.)

Display Text Alone: the p Command

You have already used the p command in several examples. You are probably now familiar with its general format:

[*address1*,*address2*]p<CR>

p does not take arguments. However, it can be combined with a substitution command line. This will be discussed later in this chapter.

Experiment with the line addresses shown in Table 6-3 on a file in your home directory. Try the p command with each address and see if ed responds as described in the figure.

Table 6-3: Sample Addresses for Displaying Text

Specify this Address	Check for this Response
`1,$p<CR>`	ed should display the entire file on your terminal.
`-5p<CR>`	ed should move backward five lines from the current line and display the line found there.
`+2p<CR>`	ed should move forward two lines from the current line and display the line found there.
`1,/`*x*`/p<CR>`	ed displays the set of lines from line one through the first line after the current line that contains the character *x*. It is important to enclose the letter *x* between slashes so that ed can distinguish between the search pattern address (*x*) and the ed command (p).

Display Text with Line Addresses: the n Command

The n command displays text and precedes each line with its numerical line address. It is helpful when you are deleting, creating, or changing lines. The general command line format for n is the same as that for p.

[*address1,address2*]n<CR>

Like p, n does not take arguments, but it can be combined with the substitute command.

Use `n` on the `try-me` file:

```
$ ed try-me<CR>
140
1,$n<CR>
1       This is the first line of text.
2       This is the second line,
3       and this is the third line.
4       This is the fourth line.
5       five
6       six
7       seven
8       eight
9       nine
10      ten
```

Table 6-4 summarizes the `ed` commands for displaying text.

Table 6-4: Summary of Commands for Displaying Text

Command	Function
p	displays specified lines of text in the editing buffer on your terminal
n	displays specified lines of text in the editing buffer with their numerical line addresses on your terminal

Creating Text

ed has three basic commands for creating new lines of text:

a	append text
i	insert text
c	change text

Append Text: the a Command

The append command, a, allows you to add text AFTER the current line or a specified address in the file. You have already used this command in the "Getting Started" section of this chapter. The general format for the append command line is:

[*address1*]a<CR>

Specifying an address is optional. The default value of *address1* is the current line.

In previous exercises, you used this command with the default address. Now try using different line numbers for *address1*. In the following example, a new file called `new-file` is created. In the first append command line, the default address is the current line. In the second append command line, line 1 is specified as *address1*. The lines are displayed with n so that you can see their numerical line addresses. Remember, the append mode is ended by typing a period (.) on a line by itself.

```
$ ed new-file<CR>
?new-file
a<CR>
Create some lines<CR>
of text in<CR>
this file.<CR>
.<CR>
1,$n<CR>
1       Create some lines
2       of text in
3       this file.
1a<CR>
This will be line 2<CR>
This will be line 3<CR>
.<CR>
1,$n<CR>
1       Create some lines
2       This will be line 2
3       This will be line 3
4       of text in
5       this file.
```

Notice that after you append the two new lines, the line that was originally line 2 (`of text in`) becomes line 4.

You can take shortcuts to places in the file where you want to append text by combining the append command with symbolic addresses. The following three command lines allow you to move through and add to the text quickly in this way.

`.a<CR>`	appends text after the current line
`$a<CR>`	appends text after the last line of the file
`0a<CR>`	appends text before the first line of the file (at a symbolic address called line 0)

To use these addresses, create a one-line file called `lines` and type the examples shown in the following screens. (The examples appear in separate screens for easy reference only; it is not necessary to access the `lines` file three times to try each append symbol. You can access `lines` once and try all three consecutively.)

```
$ ed lines<CR>
?lines
a<CR>
This is the current line.<CR>
.<CR>
p<CR>
This is the current line.
.a<CR>
This line is after the current line.<CR>
.<CR>
-1,.p<CR>
This is the current line.
This line is after the current line.
```

```
$a<CR>
This is the last line now.<CR>
.<CR>
$<CR>
This is the last line now.
```

```
0a<CR>
This is the first line now.<CR>
This is the second line now.<CR>
The line numbers change<CR>
as lines are added.<CR>
.<CR>
1,4n<CR>
1       This is the first line now.
2       This is the second line now.
3       The line numbers change
4       as lines are added.
```

Because the append command creates text after a specified address, the last example refers to the line before line 1 as the line after line 0. To avoid such ambiguous references, use another command provided by the editor: the insert command, `i`.

Insert Text: the `i` Command

The insert command, `i`, allows you to add text BEFORE a specified line in the editing buffer. The general command line format for `i` is the same as that for `a`.

[*address1*]`i<CR>`

As with the append command, you can insert one or more lines of text. To quit input mode, you must type a period (.) alone on a line.

Create a file called `insert` in which you can try the insert command (`i`):

```
$ ed insert<CR>
?insert
a<CR>
Line 1<CR>
Line 2<CR>
Line 3<CR>
Line 4<CR>
.<CR>
w<CR>
28
```

Now insert one line of text above line 2 and another above line 1. Use the n command to display all the lines in the buffer:

```
2i<CR>
This is the new line 2.<CR>
.<CR>
1,$n<CR>
1       Line 1
2       This is the new line 2.
3       Line 2
4       Line 3
5       Line 4
1i<CR>
This is the beginning.<CR>
.<CR>
1,$n<CR>
1       This is the beginning.
2       Line 1
3       This is the new line 2.
4       Line 2
5       Line 3
6       Line 4
```

Experiment with the insert command by combining it with symbolic line addresses, as follows:

- .i<CR>
- $i<CR>

Change Text: the c Command

The change text command, c, erases all specified lines and allows you to create one or more lines of text in their place. Because c can erase a range of lines, the general format for the command line includes two addresses.

[*address1,address2*]c<CR>

The change command puts you in the text input mode. To leave the input mode, type a period alone on a line.

Address1 is the first line and *address2* is the last line of the range of lines to be replaced by new text. To erase one line of text, specify only *address1*. If you do not specify an address, `ed` assumes the current line is the line to be changed.

Now create a file called `change` in which you can try this command. After entering the text shown in the screen, change lines one through four by typing `1,4c`:

```
1,5n<CR>
1       line 1
2       line 2
3       line 3
4       line 4
5       line 5
1,4c<CR>
Change line 1<CR>
and lines 2 through 4<CR>
.<CR>
1,$n<CR>
1       change line 1
2       and lines 2 through 4
3       line 5
```

Now experiment with `c` and try to change the current line:

```
.<CR>
line 5
c<CR>
This is the new line 5.<CR>
.<CR>
.<CR>
This is the new line 5.
```

If you are not sure whether you have left the text input mode, it is a good idea to type another period. If the current line is displayed, you know you are in the command mode of `ed`.

Table 6-5 summarizes the ed commands for creating text.

Table 6-5: Summary of Commands for Creating Text

Command	Function
a	append text after the specified line in the buffer
i	insert text before the specified line in the buffer
c	change the text on the specified line(s) to new text
.	quit text input mode and return to ed command mode

Exercise 3

3-1. Create a new file called `ex3`. Instead of using the append command to create new text in the empty buffer, try the insert command. What happens?

3-2. Enter `ed` with the file `towns`. What is the current line?

Insert above the third line:

```
Illinois<CR>
```

Insert above the current line:

```
or<CR>
Naperville<CR>
```

Insert before the last line:

```
hotels in<CR>
```

Display the text in the buffer preceded by line numbers.

3-3. In the file `towns`, display lines 1 through 5 and replace lines 2 through 5 with:

```
London<CR>
```

Display lines 1 through 3.

3-4. After you have completed exercise 3-3, what is the current line?

Find the line of text containing:

```
Toledo
```

Replace

```
Toledo
```

with

```
Peoria
```

Display the current line.

3-5 With one command line search for and replace:

```
New York
```

with:

```
Iron City
```

Deleting Text and Undoing Changes

This section discusses commands for deleting text and undoing changes in `ed`. You may use them only when you are working in command mode. The command `d` deletes lines and `u` undoes the changes made by the last command.

Delete Lines in Command Mode: the `d` Command

You have already deleted lines of text with the delete command (`d`) in the "Getting Started" section of this chapter.

The general format for the `d` command line is:

[*address1*,*address2*]d<CR>

You can delete a range of lines (*address1* through *address2*) or you can delete one line only (*address1*). If no address is specified, `ed` deletes the current line.

The next example displays lines one through five and then deletes lines two through four:

```
1,5n<CR>
1         1 horse
2         2 chickens
3         3 ham tacos
4         4 cans of mustard
5         5 bails of hay
2,4d<CR>
1,$n<CR>
1         1 horse
2         5 bails of hay
```

How can you delete only the last line of a file? Using a symbolic line address makes this easy:

```
$d<CR>
```

How can you delete the current line? Because one of the most common errors in `ed` is forgetting to type a period to leave the text input mode, unwanted text may be added to the buffer. In the next example, a line containing a print command (`1,$p`) is accidentally added to the text before the user leaves input mode. Because this line was the last one added to the text, it becomes the current line. The symbolic address . is used to delete it.

```
a<CR>
Last line of text<CR>
1,$p<CR>
.<CR>
p<CR>
1,$p
.d<CR>
p<CR>
Last line of text.
```

Before experimenting with the delete command, you may first want to learn about the undo command, u.

Undo the Previous Command in Command Mode: the u Command

The command u (short for undo) nullifies the last command and restores any text changed or deleted by that command. It takes no addresses or arguments. The format is:

```
u<CR>
```

One purpose for which the u command is useful is to restore text you have mistakenly deleted. If you delete all the lines in a file and then type p, ed responds with a ? since no more lines are in the file. Use the u command to restore them.

```
1,$p<CR>
This is the first line.
This is the middle line.
This is the last line.
1,$d<CR>
p<CR>
?
u<CR>
p<CR>
This is the last line.
```

Now experiment with u; use it to undo the append command.

```
.<CR>
This is the only line of text
a<CR>
Add this line<CR>
.<CR>
1,$p<CR>
This is the only line of text
Add this line
u<CR>
1,$p<CR>
This is the only line of text
```

u cannot be used to undo the write command (w) or the quit command (q). However, u can undo an undo command (u).

Table 6-6 summarizes the ed commands and keys used to delete text in ed.

Table 6-6: Summary of Commands for Deleting Text

Command	Function
d	delete one or more lines of text
u	undo the previous command

Substituting Text

You can modify your text with the substitute command. This command replaces the first occurrence of a string of characters with new text. The general command line format is

[*address1,address2*]s/*old_text*/*new_text*/[*command*]<CR>

Each component of the command line is described below.

address1,address2 — The range of lines being addressed by s. The address can be one line, (*address1*), a range of lines (*address1* through *address2*), or a global search address. If no address is given, ed makes the substitution on the current line.

s — The substitute command

/old_text — The argument specifying the text to be replaced is usually delimited by slashes, but can be delimited by other characters such as a ? or a period. It consists of the words or characters to be replaced. By default, if an addressed line contains more than one occurrence of *old_text*, only the first occurrence on that line is replaced.

/new_text — The argument specifying the text to replace *old_text*. It is delimited by slashes or by the same delimiters used to specify the *old_text*. It consists of the words or characters that are to replace the *old_text*.

/command — Any one of the following four commands:

g	Change every occurrence of *old_text* on each specified line.
l	Display the last line of substituted text, including nonprinting characters. (See the last section of this chapter, "Other Useful Commands and Information.")
n	Display the last line of the substituted text preceded by its numerical line address.
p	Display the last line of substituted text.

Substitute on the Current Line

The simplest example of the substitute command is making a change to the current line. You do not have to give a line address for the current line.

s/*old_text*/*new_text*/<CR>

The next example contains a typing error. While the line that contains it is still the current line, you make a substitution to correct it. The old text is the `ai` of `airor` and the new text is `er`.

```
a<CR>
In the beginning, I made an airor.<CR>
.<CR>
.p<CR>
In the beginning, I made an airor.
s/ai/er/<CR>
```

Notice that `ed` gives no response to the substitute command. To verify that the command has succeeded in this case, you either have to display the line with `p` or `n`, or include `p` or `n` as part of the substitute command line. In the following example, `n` is used to verify that the word `file` has been substituted for the word `toad`.

```
.p<CR>
This is a test toad
s/toad/file/n<CR>
1       This is a test file
```

However, ed allows you a shortcut; it prints the results of the command automatically, if you omit the last delimiter after the *new_text* argument:

```
.p<CR>
This is a test file
s/file/frog<CR>
This is a test frog
```

Substitute on One Line

To substitute text on a line that is not the current line, include an address in the command line, as follows:

[*address1*]s/*old_text*/*new_text*/<CR>

For example, in the following screen the command line includes an address for the line to be changed (line 1) because the current line is line 3:

```
1,3p<CR>
This is a pest toad
testing testing
come in toad
.<CR>
come in toad
1s/pest/test<CR>
This is a test toad
```

As you can see, ed printed the new line automatically after the change was made, because the last delimiter was omitted.

Substitute on a Range of Lines

You can make a substitution on a range of lines by specifying the first address (*address1*) through the last address (*address2*).

[*address1*,*address2*]s/*old_text*/*new_text*/<CR>

If ed does not find the pattern to be replaced on a line, it makes no changes to that line.

In the following example, all the lines in the file are addressed for the substitute command. However, only the lines that contain the string es (the *old_text* argument) are changed.

```
1,$p<CR>
This is a test toad
testing testing
come in toad
testing 1, 2, 3
1,$s/es/ES/n<CR>
4       tESting 1, 2, 3
```

When you specify a range of lines and include p or n at the end of the substitute line, only the last line changed is printed.

To display all the lines in which text was changed, use the n or p command with the address 1,$.

```
1,$n<CR>
1       This is a tESt toad
2       tESting testing
3       come in toad
4       tESting 1, 2, 3
```

Notice that only the first occurrence of `es` (on line 2) has been changed. To change every occurrence of a pattern, use the `g` command, described in the next section.

Global Substitution

One of the most versatile tools in `ed` is global substitution. By placing the `g` command after the last delimiter on the substitute command line, you can change every occurrence of a pattern on each specified lines. Try changing every occurrence of the string `es` in the last example. If you are following along, doing the examples as you read this, remember that you can use `u` to undo the last substitute command.

```
u<CR>
1,$p<CR>
This is a test toad
testing, testing
come in toad
testing 1, 2, 3
1,$s/es/ES/g<CR>
1,$p<CR>
This is a tESt toad
tESting tESting
come in toad
tESting 1, 2, 3
```

Another method is to use a global search pattern as an address instead of the range of lines specified by `1,$`.

```
1,$p<CR>
This is a test toad
testing testing
come in toad
testing 1, 2, 3
g/test/s/es/ES/g<CR>
1,$p<CR>
This is a tESt toad
tESting tESting
come in toad
tESting 1, 2, 3
```

If the global search pattern is unique and matches the argument *old_text* (text to be replaced), you can use an ed shortcut: specify the pattern once as the global search address, and do not repeat it as an *old_text* argument. ed will remember the pattern from the search address and use it again as the pattern to be replaced.

g/*old_text*/s//*new_text*/g<CR>

Whenever you use this shortcut, be sure to include two slashes (//) after the s.

```
1,$p<CR>
This is a test toad
testing testing
come in toad
testing 1, 2, 3
g/es/s//ES/g<CR>
1,$p<CR>
This is a tESt toad
tESting tESting
come in toad
tESting 1, 2, 3
```

Experiment with other search pattern addresses:

/*pattern*<CR>
?*pattern*<CR>
v/*pattern*<CR>

See what they do when combined with the substitute command. In the following example, the `v/`*pattern* search format is used to locate lines that do not contain the pattern `testing`. Then the substitute command (`s`) is used to replace the existing pattern (`in`) with a new pattern (`out`) on those lines.

```
v/testing/s/in/out<CR>
This is a test toad
come out toad
```

Notice that the line `This is a test toad` was also printed, even though no substitution was made on it. When the last delimiter is omitted, all lines found with the search address are printed, regardless of whether or not substitutions have been made on them.

Now search for lines that do contain the pattern `testing` with the `g` command.

```
g/testing/s//jumping<CR>
jumping testing
jumping 1, 2, 3
```

Notice that this command makes substitutions only for the first occurrence of the pattern (`testing`) in each line. Once again, the lines are displayed on your terminal because the last delimiter has been omitted.

Exercise 4

4-1. In your file `towns` change `town` to `city` on all lines but the line with `little town` on it.

The file should read:

```
My kind of city is
London
Like being no where at all in
Peoria
I lost those little town blues in
Iron City
I lost my heart in
San Francisco
I lost $$ in
hotels in
Las Vegas
```

4-2. Try using ? as a delimiter. Change the current line

```
Las Vegas
```

to

```
Toledo
```

Because you are changing the whole line, you can also do this by using the change command, c.

4-3. Try searching backward in the file for the word

```
lost
```

and substitute

```
found
```

using the ? as the delimiter. Did it work?

4-4. Search forward in the file for

```
no
```

and substitute

```
NO
```

for it. What happens if you try to use `?` as a delimiter?

Experiment with the various command combinations available for addressing a range of lines and doing global searches.

What happens if you try to substitute something for the `$$`? Try to substitute `Big $` for `$` on line 9 of your file. Type:

```
9s/$/Big $<CR>
```

What happened?

Using Special Pattern-Matching Characters

If you try to substitute the $ sign in the line

```
I lost my $ in Las Vegas
```

you will find that instead of replacing the $, the new text is placed at the end of the line. The $ is a special character in ed that is symbolic for the end of the line.

ed has several special characters that give you a shorthand for search patterns and substitution patterns. If you tried to use these characters in a search or substitution pattern, the result was probably different from what you had expected.

Some of the special characters are:

.	Match any one character.
*	Match zero or more occurrences of the preceding character or expression in brackets.
.*	Match zero or more occurrences of any character.
^	Match the beginning of the line.
$	Match the end of the line.
\	Take away the meaning of the special character that follows.
%	Substitute the last replacement pattern.
&	Substitute the text matched by the substitution pattern in the replacement string.
[...]	Match the first occurrence of any character in the brackets.
[^...]	Match the first occurrence of any character that is NOT in the brackets.

In the following example, ed searches for any three-character sequence ending in the pattern at.

```
1,$p<CR>
rat
cat
turtle
cow
goat
g/.at<CR>
rat
cat
goat
```

Notice that the word goat is included because the string oat matches the pattern .at.

The * (asterisk) represents zero or more occurrences of a specified character in a search or substitute pattern. This can be useful in deleting repeated occurrences of a character that have been inserted by mistake. For example, suppose you hold down the R key too long while typing the word broke. You can use the * to delete every unnecessary r with one substitution command.

```
p<CR>
brrroke
s/br*/br<CR>
broke
```

Notice that the substitution pattern includes the b before the first r. If the b were not included in the search pattern, the * would interpret it, during the search, as a zero occurrence of r, make the substitution on it, and quit. (Remember, only the first occurrence of a pattern is changed in a substitution, unless you request a global search with g.) The following screen shows how the substitution would be made if you did not specify both the b and the r before the *.

```
p<CR>
brrroke
s/r*/r<CR>
rbrrroke
```

If you combine the period and the *, the combination will match all characters. With this combination you can replace all characters in the last part of a line:

```
p<CR>
Toads are slimy, cold creatures
s/are.*/are wonderful and warm<CR>
Toads are wonderful and warm
```

The .* can also replace all characters between two patterns.

```
p<CR>
Toads are slimy, cold creatures
s/are.*cre/are wonderful and warm cre<CR>
Toads are wonderful and warm creatures
```

If you want to insert a word at the beginning of a line, use the ^ (circumflex) for the old text to be substituted. This is particularly helpful when you want to insert the same pattern at the beginning of several lines. The next example places the word `all` at the beginning of each line:

```
1,$p<CR>
creatures great and small
things wise and wonderful
things bright and beautiful
1,$s/^/all /<CR>
1,$p<CR>
all creatures great and small
all things wise and wonderful
all things bright and beautiful
```

The $ sign is useful for adding characters at the end of a line or a range of lines:

```
1,$p<CR>
I love
I need
I use
The IRS wants my
1,$s/$/ money.<CR>
1,$p<CR>
I love money.
I need money.
I use money.
The IRS wants my money.
```

In these examples, you must remember to put a space after the word `all` or before the word `money` because `ed` adds the specified characters to the very beginning or the very end of the sentence. If you forget to leave a space before the word `money`, your file will look like this:

```
1,$s/$/money/<CR>
1,$p<CR>
I lovemoney
I needmoney
I usemoney
The IRS wants mymoney
```

The $ sign also provides a handy way to add punctuation to the end of a line:

```
1,$p<CR>
I love money
I need money
I use money
The IRS wants my money
1,$s/$/./<CR>
1,$p/<CR>
I love money.
I need money.
I use money.
The IRS wants my money.
```

Because . is not matching a character (old text), but replacing a character (new text), it does not have a special meaning. To change a period in the middle of a line, you must take away the special meaning of the period in the old text. To do this, simply precede the period with a backslash (\). This is how you take away the special meaning of some special characters that you want to treat as normal text characters in search or substitute arguments. For example, the following screen shows how to take away the special meaning of the period:

```
p<CR>
Way to go.  Wow!
s/\./!<CR>
Way to go!  Wow!
```

The same method can be used with the backslash character itself. If you want to treat a \ as a normal text character, be sure to precede it with a \. For example, if you want to replace the \ symbol with the word backslash, use the substitute command line shown in the following screen:

```
1,2p<CR>
This chapter explains
how to use the \.
s/\\/backslash<CR>
how to use the backslash.
```

If you want to change text without repeating the text in the replacement string, the & (ampersand) provides a useful shortcut. The & is replaced with the text matching the pattern, so you do not have to type the pattern twice. For example:

```
p<CR>fP
The neanderthal skeletal remains
s/thal/& man's/<CR>
p<CR>
The neanderthal man's skeletal remains
```

ed automatically remembers the last string of characters in a search pattern or the old text in a substitution. However, you must prompt ed to repeat the replacement characters in a substitution by using the % sign. The % sign allows you to make the same substitution on multiple lines without requesting a global substitution. For example, to change the word money to the word gold, repeat the last substitution from line 1 on line 3, but not on line 4.

```
1,$n<CR>
 1        I love money
 2        I need food
 3        I use money
 4        The IRS wants my money
1s/money/gold<CR>
I love gold
3s//%<CR>
I use gold
1,$n<CR>
 1        I love gold
 2        I need food
 3        I use gold
 4        The IRS wants my money
```

ed automatically remembers the word money (the old text to be replaced), so that string does not have to be repeated between the first two delimiters. The % sign tells ed to use the last replacement pattern, gold.

ed tries to match the first occurrence of one of the characters enclosed in brackets and substitute the specified old text with new text. The brackets can be at any position in the pattern to be replaced.

In the following example, ed changes the first occurrence of the numbers 6, 7, 8, or 9 to 4 on each line in which it finds one of those numbers:

```
1,$p<CR>
Monday        33,000
Tuesday       75,000
Wednesday     88,000
Thursday      62,000
1,$s/[6789]/4<CR>
Monday        33,000
Tuesday       45,000
Wednesday     48,000
Thursday      42,000
```

The next example deletes the Mr or Ms from a list of names:

```
1,$p<CR>
Mr Arthur Middleton
Mr Matt Lewis
Ms Anna Kelley
Ms M. L. Hodel
1,$s/M[rs] //<CR>
1,$p<CR>
Arthur Middleton
Matt Lewis
Anna Kelley
M. L. Hodel
```

If a ^ (circumflex) is the first character in brackets, ed interprets it as an instruction to match characters that are NOT within the brackets. However, if the circumflex is in any other position within the brackets, ed interprets it literally, as a circumflex.

```
1,$p<CR>
grade  A   Computer Science
grade  B   Robot Design
grade  A   Boolean Algebra
grade  D   Jogging
grade  C   Tennis
1,$s/grade [^AB]/grade A<CR>
1,$p<CR>
grade  A   Computer Science
grade  B   Robot Design
grade  A   Boolean Algebra
grade  A   Jogging
grade  A   Tennis
```

Whenever you use special characters in substitution patterns, use a distinctive pattern of characters. In the above example, if you had used only

```
1,$s/[^AB]/A<CR>
```

you would have changed the g in the word grade to A on every line. Try it.

Experiment with these special characters. Find out what happens when if you use them in different combinations.

Table 6-7 summarizes the special characters for search or substitute patterns.

Table 6-7: Summary of Special Characters

Character	Meaning
.	Match any character in a pattern.
*	Match zero or more occurrences of the preceding character or bracket expression.
.*	Match zero or more occurrences of any character.
^	Match the beginning of a line in the substitute pattern or in a search pattern.
$	Match the end of a line.
\	Remove the meaning of the special character that immediately follows in the pattern.
&	Substitute the text matched by the substitution pattern in the replacement string.
%	Substitute the last replacement pattern.
[...]	Match any character that is in the brackets.
[^...]	Match any character that is NOT in the brackets.

Exercise 5

5-1. Create a file containing the following lines of text.

```
A       Computer Science
D       Jogging
C       Tennis
```

What happens if you try this command line:

```
1,$s/[^AB]/A/<CR>
```

Undo the above command. How can you make the C and D unique? (Hint: they are at the beginning of the line, in the position shown by the ^.) Do not be afraid to experiment!

5-2. Insert the following line above line 2:

```
These are not really my grades.
```

Using brackets and the ^ character, create a search pattern that you can use to locate the line you inserted. There are several ways to address a line. When you edit text, use the way that is quickest and easiest for you.

5-3. Create a file containing the following lines:

```
I love money
I need money
The IRS wants my money
```

Now use one command to change them to:

```
It's my money
It's my money
The IRS wants my money
```

Using two command lines, do the following: change the word on the first line from `money` to `gold`, and change the last two lines from `money` to `gold` without using the words `money` or `gold` themselves.

5-4. How can you change the line

```
1020231020
```

to

```
10202031020
```

without repeating the old digits in the replacement pattern?

5-5. Create a line of text containing the following characters.

```
* . \ & % ^ *
```

Substitute a different letter for each character. Do you have to use a backslash for every substitution?

Moving Text

You have now learned to address lines, create and delete text, and make substitutions. **ed** has one more set of versatile and important commands. You can move, copy, or join lines of text in the editing buffer. You can also read in text from a file that is not in the editing buffer, or write lines of the file in the buffer to another file in the current directory. The commands that move text are:

`m`	move lines of text
`t`	copy lines of text
`j`	join contiguous lines of text
`w`	write lines of text to a file
`r`	read in the contents of a file

Move Lines of Text

The `m` command allows you to move blocks of text to another place in the file. The general format is:

[*address1*,*address2*]m[*address3*]<CR>

The components of this command line include:

address1,*address2*
: The range of lines to be moved. If only one line is moved, only *address1* is given. If no address is given, the current line is moved.

`m`
: The move command.

address3
: Place the text after this line.

Try the following example to see how the command works. Create a file that contains these three lines of text:

```
I want to move this line.
I want the first line
below this line.
```

Type:

```
1m3<CR>
```

ed will move line 1 below line 3.

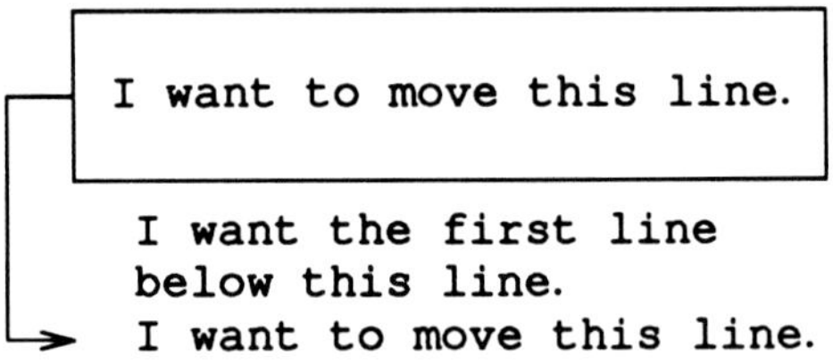

```
I want to move this line.

I want the first line
below this line.
I want to move this line.
```

The next screen shows how this will appear on your terminal:

```
1,$p<CR>
I want to move this line.
I want the first line
below this line.
1m3<CR>
1,$p<CR>
I want the first line
below this line.
I want to move this line.
```

If you want to move a paragraph of text, have *address1* and *address2* define the range of lines of the paragraph.

In the following example, a block of text (lines 8 through 12) is moved below line 65. Notice the n command that prints the line numbers of the file:

```
8,12n<CR>
8       This is line 8.
9       It is the beginning of a
10      very short paragraph.
11      This paragraph ends
12      on this line.
64,65n<CR>
64      Move the block of text
65      below this line.
8,12m65<CR>
59,65n<CR>
59      Move the block of text
60      below this line.
61      This is line 8.
62      It is the beginning of a
63      very short paragraph.
64      This paragraph ends
65      on this line.
```

How can you move lines above the first line of the file? Try the following command.

```
3,4m0<CR>
```

When *address3* is 0, the lines are placed at the beginning of the file.

Copy Lines of Text

The copy command `t` (transfer) acts like the `m` command except that the block of text is not deleted at the original address of the line. A copy of that block of text is placed after a specified line of text.

The general format of the `t` command looks like the `m` command.

[*address1,address2*]`t`[*address3*]`<CR>`

address1,address2 The range of lines to be copied. If only one line is copied, only *address1* is given. If no address is given, the current line is copied.

`t`	The copy command.
address3	Place the copy of the text after this line.

The next example shows how to copy three lines of text below the last line.

```
Safety procedures:

If there is a fire in the building:
Close the door of the room to seal off the fire
```

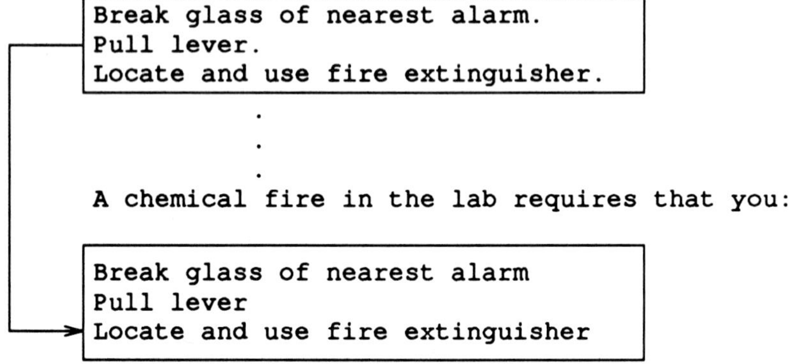
Break glass of nearest alarm.
Pull lever.
Locate and use fire extinguisher.
.
.
.
A chemical fire in the lab requires that you:
Break glass of nearest alarm
Pull lever
Locate and use fire extinguisher

The commands and ed's responses to them are displayed in the next screen. Again, the n command displays the line numbers:

```
5,8n<CR>
5          Close the door of the room, to seal off the fire.
6          Break glass of nearest alarm.
7          Pull lever.
8          Locate and use fire extinguisher.
30n<CR>
30         A chemical fire in the lab requires that you:
6,8t30<CR>
30,$n<CR>
30         A chemical fire in the lab requires that you:
31         Break glass of nearest alarm
32         Pull lever
33         Locate and use fire extinguisher
6,8n<CR>
6          Break glass of nearest alarm
7          Pull lever
8          Locate and use fire extinguisher
```

The text in lines 6 through 8 remains in place. A copy of those three lines is placed after line 50.

Experiment with `m` and `t` on one of your files.

Join Contiguous Lines

The `j` command joins contiguous lines. The general format is:

> [*address1*,*address2*]j<CR>

The components of this command line include:

address1,address2
: The range of lines to be joined. If no address is given, the current line is joined with the following line. If exactly one address is given, the command does nothing.

`j`
: The join command.

The next example shows how to join two lines.

```
1,2p<CR>
Now is the time to join
the team.
1,2j<CR>
1p<CR>
Now is the time to jointhe team.
```

Notice that there is no space between the last word (`join`) and the first word of the next line (`the`). You must place a space between them by using the `s` command.

Write Lines of Text to a File

The `w` command writes text from the buffer into a file. The general format is:

[*address1,address2*]`w` [*filename*]<CR>

address1,address2
: The range of lines to be placed in another file. If you do not use *address1* or *address2*, the entire file is written into a new file.

`w`
: The write command.

filename
: The name of the new file that contains a copy of the block of text.

In the following example, several lines of a letter are saved in a file called memo.

```
1,$n<CR>
1               March 20, 1990
2         Dear Kelly,
3         There will be a meeting in the
4         green room at 4:30 P.M. today.
5         Refreshments will be served.
6         Please plan to attend.
7         Other divisions and locations
8         will also be represented.
9         We will discuss plans
10        for marketing several
11        new products during the
12        coming fiscal year,
13        as well as long range
14        research activities that
15        should yield profitable products
16        during the next decade.
3,5w memo<CR>
91
```

The w command places a copy of lines three through five into a new file called memo. ed responds with the number of characters in the new file.

Potential Problems

The w command overwrites preexisting files; it erases the current file and puts the new text in the file without warning you. If, in our example, a file called memo had existed before we wrote our new file to that name, the original file would have been erased.

In "Special Commands," later in this chapter, you will learn how to execute shell commands from ed. Then you can list the file names in the directory to make sure that you are not overwriting a file.

Another potential problem is that you cannot write other lines to the file memo. If you try to add lines 13 through 16, the existing lines (3 through 5) will be erased and the file will contain only the new lines (13 through 16). However, you can use the W command to solve this problem. It will write the current ed buffer to the end of the file.

Read in the Contents of a File

The r command can be used to append text from a file to the buffer. The general format for the read command is:

[*address1*]r *filename*<CR>

address1	The text will be placed after the line *address1*. If *address1* is not given, the file is added to the end of the buffer.
r	The read command.
filename	The name of the file that will be copied into the editing buffer.

Using the example from the write command, the next screen shows a file being edited and new text being read into it.

```
1,$n<CR>
1               March 20, 1990
2       Dear Michael,
3       Are you free later today?
4       Hope to see you there.
3r memo<CR>
91
3,$n<CR>
3       Are you free later today?
4       There will be a meeting in the
5       green room at 4:30 P.M. today.
6       Refreshments will be served.
7       Hope to see you there.
```

ed responds to the read command with the number of characters in the file being added to the buffer (in the example, memo).

It is a good idea to display new or changed lines of text to be sure that they are correct.

Table 6-8 summarizes the ed commands for moving text.

Table 6-8: Summary of ed Commands for Moving Text

Command	Function
m	move lines of text
t	copy lines of text
j	join contiguous lines
w	write text into a new file
W	append text to an existing file
r	read in text from another file

Exercise 6

6-1. There are two ways to copy lines of text in the buffer: by issuing the copy command; or by using the write and read commands to write text to a file first and then read the file into the buffer.

Writing to a file and then reading the file into the buffer is a longer process. Can you think of an example where this method would be more practical?

What commands can you use to copy lines 10 through 17 of file `exer` into a file called `exer6` at line 7?

6-2. Lines 33 through 46 give an example that you want placed after line 3, and not after line 32. What command performs this task?

6-3. Say you are on line 10 of a file and you want to join lines 13 and 14. What commands can you issue to do this?

Other Useful Commands and Information

Four other commands and a special file will be useful to you during editing sessions.

`h,H`	access the help commands, which provide error messages
`l`	display characters that are not normally displayed
`f`	display the current filename
`!`	temporarily escape `ed` to execute a shell command
`ed.hup`	save the buffer in a special file called `ed.hup` if `ed` is interrupted.

Help Commands

You may have noticed when you were editing a file that `ed` responds to some of your commands with a ?. The ? is a diagnostic message issued by `ed` when it has found an error. The help commands give you a short message to explain the reason for the most recent diagnostic.

There are two help commands:

`h`	Display a short error message that explains the reason for the most recent ?.
`H`	Place `ed` into help mode so that a short error message is displayed every time the ? appears. (To cancel this request, type `H`.)

You know that if you try to quit `ed` without writing the changes in the buffer to a file, you will get a ?. Do this now. When the ? appears, type `h`:

```
q<CR>
?
h<CR>
warning: expecting 'w'
```

The ? is also displayed when you specify a new filename on the `ed` command line. Give `ed` a new filename. When the ? appears, type `h` to find out what the error message means.

```
ed newfile<CR>
?newfile
h<CR>
cannot open input file
```

This message means one of two things: either there is no file called `newfile` or there is such a file but `ed` is not allowed to read it.

As explained earlier, the `H` command responds to the ? and then turns on the help mode of `ed`, so that `ed` gives you a diagnostic explanation every time the ? is displayed subsequently. To turn off help mode, type `H` again. The next screen shows `H` used to turn on the help mode. Sample error messages are also displayed in response to some common mistakes:

```
$ ed newfile<CR>
H<CR>
cannot open input file
/hello<CR>
?
search string not found
1,22p<CR>
?
line out of range
a<CR>
I am appending this line to the buffer.<CR>
.<CR>
s/$ tea party<CR>
?
illegal or missing delimiter
,$s/$/ tea party<CR>
?
unknown command
H<CR>
q<CR>
?
h<CR>
warning: expecting 'w'
```

Some of the most common error messages that you may encounter during editing sessions are:

`search string not found`
: `ed` cannot find an occurrence of the search pattern `hello`.

`line out of range`
: `ed` cannot print any lines because the buffer is empty or the line specified is not in the buffer.

A line of text is appended to the buffer to show you some error messages associated with the `s` command.

`illegal or missing delimiter`
: The delimiter between the old text to be replaced and the new text is missing.

`unknown command`
: *address1* was not typed in before the comma; `ed` does not recognize `,$`.

Help mode is then turned off, and `h` is used to determine the meaning of the last `?`. While you are learning `ed`, you may want to leave the help mode turned on. If so, use the `H` command. However, once you become adept at using `ed`, you will only need to see error messages occasionally. Then you can use the `h` command.

Display Nonprinting Characters

Control characters usually do not appear on the terminal screen. For example, <^g> (control-g) rings the terminal bell but does not appear on the screen.

If you type a tab character, the terminal normally displays up to eight spaces covering the space up to the next tab setting. (Your tab setting may be more or fewer than eight spaces. See Chapter 9, "Shell Tutorial," on using `stty`).

If you want to see how many tabs or control characters you have inserted into your text, use the `l` (list) command. The general format for the `l` command is the same as for `n` and `p`.

[*address1*,*address2*]`l<CR>`

The components of this command line are:

address1,*address2*	The range of lines to be displayed. If no address is given, the current line is displayed. If only *address1* is given, only that line is displayed.
`l`	The command that displays the nonprinting characters along with the text.

The `l` command displays tabs with a > (greater than) character. To type control characters, hold down the CONTROL (CTRL) key and press the appropriate alphabetic key. The key that sounds the bell is ^g (control-g). It is displayed as \007 which is the octal representation (the computer code) for ^g.

Type in two lines of text that contain a <^g> (control-g) and a tab. Then use the `l` command to display the lines of text on your terminal.

```
a<CR>
Add a <^g> (control-g) to this line.<CR>
Add a <tab> (tab) to this line.<CR>
.<CR>
1,2l<CR>
Add a \007 (control-g) to this line.
Add a > (tab) to this line.
```

Did the bell sound when you typed <^g>?

The Current Filename

In a long editing session, you may forget the filename. The `f` command will remind you which file is currently in the buffer. Or, you may want to preserve the original file that you entered into the editing buffer and write the contents of the buffer to a new file. In a long editing session, you may forget and accidentally overwrite the original file with the customary `w` and `q` command sequence. You can prevent this by telling the editor to associate the contents of the buffer with a new filename while you are in the middle of the editing session. Do this with the `f` command and a new filename.

The format for displaying the current filename is `f` alone on a line:

```
f<CR>
```

To see how `f` works, enter `ed` with a file. For example, if your file is called `oldfile`, `ed` will respond as shown in the following screen:

```
ed oldfile<CR>
323
f<CR>
oldfile
```

To associate the contents of the editing buffer with a new filename use this general format:

```
f newfile<CR>
```

If you do not specify a filename with the write command, ed remembers the filename given at the beginning of the editing session and writes to that file. If you do not want to overwrite the original file, you must either use a new filename with the write command, or change the current filename using the `f` command followed by the new filename. Because you can use `f` at any point in an editing session, you can change the filename immediately. You can then continue with the editing session without worrying about overwriting the original file.

The next screen shows the commands for entering the editor with `oldfile` and then changing its name to `newfile`. A line of text is added to the buffer and then the write and quit commands are issued.

```
ed oldfile<CR>
323
f<CR>
oldfile
f newfile<CR>
newfile
a<CR>
Add a line of text.<CR>
.<CR>
w<CR>
343
q<CR>
```

Once you have returned to the shell, you can list your files and verify the existence of the new file, `newfile`. `newfile` should contain a copy of the contents of `oldfile` plus the new line of text.

Escape to the Shell

How can you make sure you are not overwriting an existing file when you write the contents of the editor to a new filename? You must return to the shell to list your files. The ! allows you to return temporarily to the shell, execute a shell command, and then return to the current line of the editor.

The general format for the escape sequence is:

```
!shell command line<CR>
shell response to the command line
!
```

When you type the ! as the first character on a line, the shell command must follow on that same line. The program response to your command will appear as the command is running. When the command has finished executing, the ! will appear alone on a line. This means that you are back in the editor at the current line.

For example, if you want to return to the shell to find out the correct date, type ! and the shell command `date`.

```
p<CR>
This is the current line
! date<CR>
Sun  Apr 1  14:24:22  EST  1990
!
p<CR>
This is the current line.
```

The screen first displays the current line. Then the command is given to temporarily leave the editor and display the date. After the date is displayed, you are returned to the current line of the editor.

If you want to execute more than one command on the shell command line, see the discussion on ; in the "Special Characters" section of Chapter 9, "The Shell Tutorial."

Recovering from Hangups

What happens if you are creating text in ed and the line connecting your terminal to the computer is disconnected, or your terminal is unplugged? When a hangup occurs, the UNIX system tries to save the contents of the editing buffer in a special file named ed.hup. Later you can retrieve your text from this file in one of two ways. First, you can use a shell command to move ed.hup to another filename, such as the name the file had while you were editing it (before the hangup). Second, you can enter ed and use the f command to rename the contents of the buffer. An example of the second method is shown in the following screen:

```
ed ed.hup<CR>
928
f myfile<CR>
myfile
```

If you use the second method to recover the contents of the buffer, be sure to remove the ed.hup file afterward.

Conclusion

You are now familiar with many useful commands in ed. The commands that were not discussed in this tutorial, such as G, P, and Q, and the use of the special pattern matching characters (,), {, and }, are discussed on the ed(1) page of the *User's Reference Manual*. You can experiment with these commands to see what tasks they perform.

Table 6-9 summarizes the functions of the commands introduced in this section.

Table 6-9: Summary of Other Useful Commands

Command	Function
`h`	Display a short error message for the preceding diagnostic ?.
`H`	Turn on help mode. An error message will be given with each diagnostic ?. The second `H` turns off help mode.
`l`	Display nonprinting characters in the text.
`f`	Display the current file name.
`f` *newfile*	Change the current file name associated with the editing buffer to *newfile.*
!cmd	Temporarily escape to the shell to execute a shell command *cmd.*
`ed.hup`	Save the buffer in a special file called `ed.hup` if ed is interrupted.

Exercise 7

7-1. Create a new file called `newfile1`. Access `ed` and change the name of the file to `current1`. Then create some text and write and quit `ed`. Run the `ls` command to verify that a file called `newfile1` does not exist in your directory.

7-2. Create a file called `file1`. Append some lines of text to the file. Leave append mode but do not write the file. Turn off your terminal. Then turn on your terminal and log in again. Issue the `ls` command in the shell. Is there a new file called `ed.hup`? Edit `ed.hup` using `ed`. How can you change the current file name to `file1`? Display the contents of the file. Are the lines the same lines you created before you turned off your terminal?

7-3. While you are in `ed`, temporarily escape to the shell and send a mail message to yourself.

Answers to Exercises

Exercise 1

1-1.

```
$ ed junk<CR>
?junk
a<CR>
Hello world.<CR>
.<CR>
w<CR>
13
q<CR>
$
```

```
$ ed stuff<CR>
?stuff
a<CR>
Goodby world.<CR>
.<CR>
w<CR>
15
q<CR>
$
```

1-2.

```
$ ed junk<CR>
13
1,$p<CR>
Hello world.
q<CR>
$
```

The system did not respond with the warning question mark because you did not make any changes to the buffer.

1-3.

```
$ ed junk<CR>
13
a<CR>
Wendy's horse came through the window.<CR>
.<CR>
1,$p<CR>
Hello world.
Wendy's horse came through the window.
q<CR>
?
w stuff<CR>
52
q<CR>
$
```

Exercise 2

2-1.

```
$ ed towns<CR>
?towns
a<CR>
My kind of town is<CR>
Chicago<CR>
Like being no where at all in<CR>
Toledo<CR>
I lost those little town blues in<CR>
New York<CR>
I lost my heart in<CR>
San Francisco<CR>
I lost $$ in<CR>
Las Vegas<CR>
.<CR>
w<CR>
163
```

2-2.

```
3<CR>
Like being no where at all in
```

2-3.

```
-2,+3p<CR>
My kind of town is
Chicago
Like being no where at all in
Toledo
I lost those little town blues in
New York
```

2-4.

```
.=<CR>
6
6<CR>
New York
```

2-5.

```
$<CR>
Las Vegas
```

2-6.

```
?town<CR>
I lost those little town blues in
?<CR>
My kind of town is
```

2-7.

```
g/in<CR>
My kind of town is
Like being no where at all in
I lost those little town blues in
I lost my heart in
I lost $$ in

v/in<CR>
Chicago
Toledo
New York
San Francisco
Las Vegas
```

Exercise 3

3-1.

```
$ ed ex3<CR>
?ex3
i<CR>
?
q<CR>
```

The ? after the i means there is an error in the command. There is no current line before which text can be inserted.

3-2.

```
$ ed towns<CR>
163
.n<CR>
10      Las Vegas
3i<CR>
Illinois<CR>
.<CR>
.i<CR>
or<CR>
Naperville<CR>
.<CR>
$i<CR>
hotels in<CR>
.<CR>
1,$n<CR>
1       my kind of town is
2       Chicago
3       or
4       Naperville
5       Illinois
6       Like being no where at all in
7       Toledo
8       I lost those little town blues in
9       New York
10      I lost my heart in
11      San Francisco
12      I lost $$ in
13      hotels in
14      Las Vegas
```

3-3.

```
1,5n<CR>
1       My kind of town is
2       Chicago
3       or
4       Naperville
5       Illinois
2,5c<CR>
London<CR>
.<CR>
1,3n<CR>
1       My kind of town is
2       London
3       Like being nowhere at all in
```

3-4.

```
.<CR>
Like being nowhere at all in
/Tol<CR>
Toledo
c<CR>
Peoria<CR>
.<CR>
.<CR>
Peoria
```

3-5.

```
.<CR>
/New Y/c<CR>
Iron City<CR>
.<CR>
.<CR>
Iron City
```

Your search string need not be the entire word or line. It only needs to be unique.

Exercise 4

4-1.

```
v/little town/s/town/city<CR>
My kind of city is
London
Like being no where at all in
Peoria
Iron City
I lost my heart in
San Francisco
I lost $$ in
hotels in
Las Vegas
```

The line

```
I lost those little town blues in
```

was not printed because it was NOT addressed by the `v` command.

4-2.

```
.<CR>
Las Vegas
s?Las Vegas?Toledo<CR>
Toledo
```

4-3.

```
?lost?s??found<CR>
I found $$ in
```

4-4.

```
/no?s??NO<CR>
?
/no/s//NO<CR>
Like being NO where at all in
```

You cannot mix delimiters such as / and ? in a command line.

The substitution command on line 9 produced this output:

```
I found $$ inBig $
```

It did not work correctly because the $ sign is a special character in ed.

Exercise 5

5-1.

```
$ ed file1<CR>
?file1
a<CR>
A  Computer Science<CR>
D  Jogging<CR>
C  Tennis<CR>
.<CR>
1,$s/[^AB]/A/<CR>
1,$p<CR>
AA  Computer Science
A  Jogging
A  Tennis
u<CR>
```

```
1,$s/^[^AB]/A/<CR>
1,$p<CR>
A  Computer Science
A  Jogging
A  Tennis
```

5-2.

```
2i<CR>
These are not really my grades.<CR>
.<CR>
1,$p<CR>
A  Computer Science
These are not really my grades.
A  Tennis
A  Jogging
/^[^A]<CR>
These are not really my grades
?^[T]<CR>
These are not really my grades
```

5-3.

```
1,$p<CR>
I love money
I need money
The IRS wants my money
g/^I/s/I.*m /It's my m<CR>
It's my money
It's my money
```

```
1s/money/gold<CR>
It's my gold
2,$s//%<CR>
The IRS wants my gold
```

5-4.

```
s/10202/&0<CR>
10202031020
```

5-5.

```
a<CR>
* . \ & % ^ *<CR>
.<CR>
s/*/a<CR>
a . \ & % ^ *
s/*/b<CR>
a . \ & % ^ b
```

Because there were no preceding characters, * substituted for itself.

```
s/ \./c<CR>
a c \ & % ^ b
s/ \\/d<CR>
a c d & % ^ b
s/&/e<CR>
a c d e % ^ b
s/%/f<CR>
a c d e f ^ b
```

The & and % are special characters only in the replacement text.

```
s/ \^/g<CR>
a c d e f g b
```

Exercise 6

6-1. Any time you have lines of text that you may want to have repeated several times, it may be easier to write those lines to a file and read in the file at those points in the text.

If you want to copy the lines into another file you must write them to a file and then read that file into the buffer containing the other file.

```
ed exer<CR>
725
10,17 w temp<CR>
210
q<CR>
ed exer6<CR>
305
7r temp<CR>
210
```

In this example, the temporary file happens to be called `temp`.

6-2.

```
33,46m3<CR>
```

6-3

```
13,14j<CR>
```

Exercise 7

7-1.

```
$ ed newfile1<CR>
?newfile1
f current1<CR>
current1
a<CR>
This is a line of text<CR>
Will it go into newfile1<CR>
or into current1<CR>
.<CR>
w<CR>
66
q<CR>
$ ls<CR>
bin
current1
```

7-2.

```
ed file1<CR>
?file1
a<CR>
I am adding text to this file.<CR>
Will it show up in ed.hup?<CR>
.<CR>
```

Turn off your terminal.

Log in again.

```
ed ed.hup<CR>
58
f file1<CR>
file1
1,$p<CR>
I am adding text to this file.
Will it show up in ed.hup?
```

7-3.

```
$ ed file1<CR>
58
! mail mylogin<CR>
You will get mail when<CR>
you are done editing!<CR>
.<CR>
!
```

7. SCREEN EDITOR (vi) TUTORIAL

7. SCREEN EDITOR (vi) TUTORIAL

7 Screen Editor (vi) Tutorial

Introduction

This chapter is a tutorial on the screen editor, `vi` (short for visual). The `vi` editor is a powerful and sophisticated tool for creating and editing files. It is designed for use with a video display terminal which is used as a window through which you can view the text of a file. A few simple commands allow you to make changes to the text that are quickly reflected on the screen.

The `vi` editor displays from one to many lines of text. It allows you to move the cursor to any point on the screen or in the file (by specifying places such as the beginning or end of a word, line, sentence, paragraph, or file) and create, change, or delete text from that point. You can also use some line editor commands, such as the powerful global commands that allow you to change multiple occurrences of the same character string by issuing one command. To move through the file, you can scroll the text forward or backward, revealing the lines below or above the current window, as shown in Figure 7-1.

Not all terminals have text scrolling capability; whether or not you can take advantage of the `vi` scrolling feature depends on the type of terminal you have.

Figure 7-1: Displaying a File with a `vi` Window

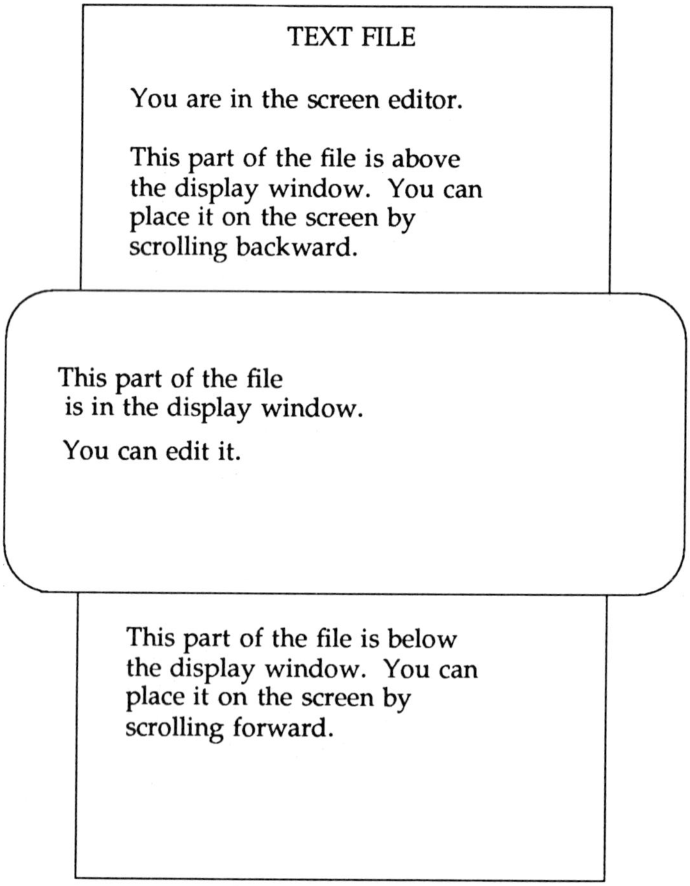

TEXT FILE

You are in the screen editor.

This part of the file is above the display window. You can place it on the screen by scrolling backward.

This part of the file is in the display window.

You can edit it.

This part of the file is below the display window. You can place it on the screen by scrolling forward.

There are more than 100 commands within `vi`. This chapter covers the basic commands that will enable you to use `vi` simply but effectively. Specifically, it explains how to do the following tasks:

- change your shell environment to set the configuration of your terminal
- enable automatic carriage return
- enter vi, create text, delete mistakes, write the text to a file, and quit
- move text within a file
- electronically cut and paste text
- use special commands and shortcuts
- use line editing commands available within vi
- temporarily escape to the shell to execute shell commands
- recover a file lost by an interruption to an editing session
- edit several files in the same session

Suggestions for Reading this Tutorial

As you read this tutorial, keep in mind the notation conventions described in the Preface. In the screens shown in this chapter, arrows are used to show the position of the cursor.

The commands discussed in each section are reviewed at the end of the section. A summary of vi commands is found in Appendix E, where they are listed by topic. At the end of some sections, exercises are given so you can experiment. The answers to all the exercises are at the end of this chapter. The best way to learn vi is by following the examples and doing the exercises as you read the tutorial. Log in on the UNIX system when you are ready to read this chapter.

Getting Started

This section describes how to set the terminal configuration, which is essential for using `vi` properly, and how to set the wrapmargin, or automatic carriage return, which is optional.

Setting the Terminal Configuration

Before you enter `vi`, you must set your terminal configuration. This simply means that you tell the UNIX system what type of terminal you are using, which is necessary because the software for the `vi` editor is executed differently on different terminals.

Each type of terminal has several code names that are recognized by the UNIX system. Appendix G, "Setting Up the Terminal," tells you how to find a recognized name for your terminal. Keep in mind that many computer installations add terminal types to the list of terminals supported on your UNIX system. It is a good idea to check with your local system administrator for the most up-to-date list of available terminal types.

To set your terminal configuration, type:

```
TERM=terminal_name<CR>
export TERM<CR>
tput init<CR>
```

The first line puts a value (a terminal type) in a variable called TERM. The second line exports this value; it conveys the value to all UNIX system programs whose execution depends on the type of terminal being used.

The `tput` command on the third line initializes (sets up) the software in your terminal so that it functions properly with the UNIX system. It is essential to run the `tput init` command when you are setting your terminal configuration because terminal functions such as tab settings may not work properly unless you do.

For example, if your terminal is a Teletype® 5425 this is how your commands will appear on the screen.

```
$ TERM=5425<CR>
$ export TERM<CR>
$ tput init<CR>
```

Do not experiment by entering names for terminal types other than your terminal. This may cause vi to display the screen incorrectly!

Changing Your Environment

If you are going to use vi regularly, you should change your login environment permanently so you do not have to configure your terminal each time you log in. Your login environment is controlled by a file in your home directory called .profile. For details, see Chapter 9, "Shell Tutorial."

If you specify the setting for your terminal configuration in your .profile, your terminal will be configured automatically every time you log in. You can do this by adding the three lines shown in the last screen (the TERM assignment, export command, and tput command) to your .profile. (For detailed instructions, see Chapter 9, "Shell Tutorial.")

Setting the Automatic Carriage Return

If you want the RETURN key to be entered automatically while you are using vi, create a file called .exrc in your home directory. You can use the .exrc file to contain options that control the vi editing environment.

To create a .exrc file, enter an editor with that filename. Then type in one line of text: a specification for the wrapmargin (automatic carriage return) option. The format for specifying this option is

```
:set wm=n<CR>
```

n represents the number of characters from the right-hand side of the screen where you want an automatic carriage return to occur. This can only occur between words, not between syllables of a word. For example, if you want a carriage return at twenty characters from the righthand side of the screen, type:

```
:set wm=20<C
```

Finally, write the contents of the buffer to the file and quit the editor (see "Text Editing Buffers" in Chapter 4, "Overview of the Tutorials"). The next time you use `vi`, this file will give you an automatic carriage return.

To check your settings for the terminal and wrapmargin when you are in `vi`, enter the command

```
:set<CR>
```

`vi` will report the terminal type and the wrapmargin, as well as any other options you have specified. You can also use the `:set` command to create or change the wrapmargin option. Try experimenting with it.

Creating a File

First, enter the editor; type `vi` and the name of the file you want to create or edit.

`vi` *filename*<CR>

For example, suppose you want to create a file called `stuff`. When you type the `vi` command with the filename `stuff`, `vi` clears the screen and displays a window in which you can enter and edit text.

```
_
~
~
~
~
~
~
~
~
~
"stuff" [New file]
```

The __ (underscore) on the top line shows the cursor. (On video display terminals, the cursor may be a blinking underscore or a reverse color block.) Every other line is marked with a ~ (tilde), the symbol for an empty line.

If you forgot to set your terminal configuration or you set it to the wrong type of terminal before entering `vi`, you will see an error message instead.

```
$ vi stuff<CR>
terminal_name: unknown terminal type
[Using open mode]
"stuff" [New file]
```

You cannot set the terminal configuration while you are in the editor; you must be in the shell. Leave the editor by typing

`:q<CR>`

Then set the correct terminal configuration.

Operating Modes

The `vi` editor operates in two modes: the input mode and the command mode. In the input mode you can add and modify text; in the command mode you can:

- edit and change existing text
- delete, move, and copy text
- move around in the file
- perform other tasks

How to Create Text in the Append Mode

If you have successfully entered `vi`, you are in the command mode and `vi` is waiting for your commands. How do you create text?

- Type a to enter the input mode of `vi`. (Do not press the `RETURN` key.) You can now add text to the file. (An a is not printed on the screen.)
- Type some text.
- To begin a new line, press the `RETURN` key.

  If you have specified the wrapmargin option in a `.exrc` file, you will start a new line whenever you reach the point for an automatic carriage return (see "Setting the Automatic Carriage Return").

How to Leave the Append Mode

When you finish creating text, press the `ESCAPE` key to leave the input mode and return to the command mode. Then you can edit any text you have created or write the text that is in the buffer to a file.

If you press the ESCAPE key and a bell sounds, you are already in the command mode. Pressing the ESCAPE key while you are in the command mode does not affect the text in the file, even if you do it several times.

On some types of terminals, vi flashes the screen instead of sounding the bell.

Editing Text in the Command Mode

To edit an existing file you must be able to add, change, and delete text. However, before you can perform those tasks you must be able to move to the part of the file you want to edit. `vi` offers an array of commands for moving from page to page, between lines, and between specified points inside a line. These commands, along with commands for deleting and adding text, are introduced in this section.

How to Move the Cursor

To edit your text, you need to move the cursor to the point on the screen where you will begin the correction. This is easily done with four keys that are grouped together on the keyboard: h, j, k, and l. (See Figure 7-2.)

`h`	moves the cursor one character to the left
`j`	moves the cursor down one line
`k`	moves the cursor up one line
`l`	moves the cursor one character to the right

The `j` and `k` commands maintain the column position of the cursor. For example, if the cursor is on the seventh character from the left, when you type `j` or `k` it goes to the seventh character on the new line. If there is no seventh character on the new line, the cursor moves to the last character.

Many people who use `vi` find it helpful to mark these four keys with arrows showing the direction in which each key moves the cursor.

Figure 7-2: Keyboard Showing Keys that Move the Cursor

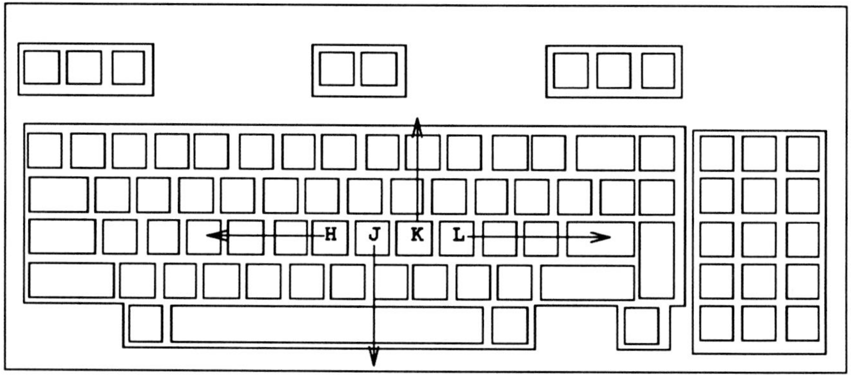

> **NOTE** Some terminals have special cursor control keys that are marked with arrows. Use them in the same way you use the `h`, `j`, `k`, and `l` commands.

Watch the cursor on the screen while you press the keys `h`, `j`, `k`, and `l`. Instead of pressing a motion command key a number of times to move the cursor a corresponding number of spaces or lines, you can precede the command with the desired number. For example, to move two spaces to the right, you can press `l` twice or enter `2l`. To move up four lines, press `k` four times or enter `4k`. If you cannot go any farther in the direction you have requested, `vi` sounds a bell.

Now experiment with the `j` and `k` motion commands. First, move the cursor up seven lines. Type:

```
7k
```

The cursor will move up seven lines above the current line. If there are fewer than seven lines above the current line, a bell will sound and the cursor will remain on the current line.

Now move the cursor down 35 lines. Type:

```
35j
```

`vi` will clear and redraw the screen. The cursor will be on the thirty-fifth line below the current line, appearing in the middle of the new window. If there are fewer than 35 lines below the current line, the bell will sound and the cursor will remain on the current line. Watch what happens when you type the next command.

```
35k
```

Like most `vi` commands, the `h`, `j`, `k`, and `l` motion commands are silent; they do not appear on the screen as you enter them. The only time you should see characters on the screen is when you are in input mode and are adding text to your file. If the motion command letters appear on the screen, you are still in the input mode. Press the `ESCAPE` key to return to the command mode and try the commands again.

Moving the Cursor to the Right or Left

In addition to the motion command keys `h` and `l`, the space bar and the `BACK-SPACE` key can be used to move the cursor right or left to a character on the current line.

<space bar>	move the cursor one character to the right
<*n*space bar>	move the cursor *n* characters to the right
<`BACKSPACE`>	move the cursor one character to the left
<*n*`BACKSPACE`>	move the cursor *n* characters to the left

Try typing a number before the command key. Notice that the cursor moves the specified number of characters to the left or right. In the example below, the cursor movement is shown by the arrows.

To move the cursor quickly to the right or left, type a number before the command. For example, suppose you want to create four columns on your screen and after you finish typing the headings for the first three columns, you notice a typing mistake, as shown in the screen below.

```
Column 1      Column 2      column
                                  ↑
~
~
~
```

<ESC>

You want to correct your mistake now, before you continue typing. Exit the insert/input mode and return to the command mode by pressing the ESCAPE key; the cursor will move to the n. Then use the h command to move back five spaces. This example, like many that follow, shows the original screen, your input, and the results in a second screen.

```
Column 1      Column 2      column
                                 ↑
~
~
~
```

5h

```
Column 1      Column 2      column
                            ↑
~
~
~
```

xiC<ESC>

Erase the c by typing x. Then change to input mode (i), enter a C, and press the ESCAPE key. Use the l motion command to return to your earlier position. A discussion of the x and i commands appears later in this chapter.

```
Column 1      Column 2      Column
                            ↑
~
~
~
```

5l

```
Column 1      Column 2      Column
                                 ↑
~
~
~
```

How to Delete Text

If you want to delete a character, move the cursor to that character and press the x. Watch the screen as you do so; the character will disappear and the line will readjust to the change. To erase three characters in a row, press x three times. In the following example, the arrows under the letters show the positions of the cursor.

x — delete one character

*n*x — delete *n* characters, where *n* is the number of characters you want to delete

```
Hello wurld!
       ↑
~
~
~
```

x

Now try preceding x with the number of characters you want to delete. For example, delete the second occurrence of the word deep from the text shown in the following screen. Put the cursor on the first letter of the string you want to delete, and delete five characters (for the four letters of deep plus an extra space).

```
Tomorrow the Loch Ness monster
shall slither forth from
the deep dark deep depths of the lake.
              ↑
~
~
~
```

5x

```
Tomorrow the Loch Ness monster
shall slither forth from
the deep dark depths of the lake.
              ↑
~
~
~
```

Notice that vi adjusts the text so that no gap appears in place of the deleted string. If, as in this case, the string you want to delete happens to be a word, you can also use the vi command for deleting a word. This command is described later in the section "Word Positioning."

How to Add Text

There are two basic commands for adding text: the insert (i) and append (a) commands. To add text with the insert command at a point in your file that is visible on the screen, move the cursor to that point by using h, j, k, and l. Then press i and start entering text. As you type, the new text will appear on the screen to the left of the character on which you put the cursor. That character and all characters to the right of the cursor will move right to make room for your new text. The vi editor will continue to accept the characters you type until you press the ESCAPE key. If necessary, the original characters will even wrap around onto the next line.

```
Hello Wrld!
      ↑
~
~
~
```

io

```
Hello World!
      ↑
~
~
~
```

<ESC>

You can use the append command in the same way. The only difference is that the new text will appear to the right of the character on which you put the cursor.

Later in this tutorial you will learn how to move around on the screen or scroll through a file to add or delete characters, words, or lines.

Quitting `vi`

When you have finished your text, you will want to write the buffer contents to a file and return to the shell. To do this, hold down the SHIFT key and press `Z` twice (`ZZ`). The editor remembers the file name you specified with the `vi` command at the beginning of the editing session, and moves the buffer text to the file of that name. A notice at the bottom of the screen gives the file name and the number of lines and characters in the file. Then the shell gives you a prompt.

```
<a>
This is a test file.<CR>
I am adding text to<CR>
a temporary buffer and<CR>
now it is perfect.<CR>
I want to write this file,<CR>
and return to the shell.<ESC><ZZ>
~
~
~
~
"stuff" [New file] 6 lines, 135 characters
$
```

You can also use the `:w` and `:q` commands of the line editor for writing and quitting a file. (Line editor commands begin with a colon and appear on the bottom line of the screen.) The `:w` command writes the buffer to a file. The `:q` command leaves the editor and returns you to the shell. You can type these commands separately or combine them into the single command `:wq`.

```
<a>This is a test file.<CR>
I am adding text to<CR>
a temporary buffer and<CR>
now it is perfect.<CR>
I want to write this file,<CR>
and return to the shell.<ESC>
~
~
~
~
:wq<CR>
```

Table 7-1 summarizes the basic commands you need to enter and use vi.

Table 7-1: Summary of Commands for the vi Editor

Command	Function
TERM=*terminal_name* export TERM	set the terminal configuration
tput init	initialize the terminal as defined by *terminal_name*
vi *filename*	enter vi editor to edit the file called *filename*
a	add text after the cursor
h	move one character to the left
j	move down one line
k	move up one line
l	move one character to the right
x	delete a character
<CR>	carriage return
<ESC>	leave input mode, and return to vi command mode
:w	write to a file
:q	quit vi
:wq	write to a file and quit vi
ZZ	write changes to a file and quit vi

Exercise 1

Answers to the exercises are given at the end of this chapter. However, keep in mind that there is often more than one way to perform a task in `vi`. If your method works, it is correct.

As you give commands in the following exercises, watch the screen to see how it changes or how the cursor moves.

1-1. If you have not logged in yet, do so now. Then set your terminal configuration.

1-2. Enter `vi` and append the following five lines of text to a new file called `exer1`.

```
This is an exercise!
Up, down,
left, right,
build your terminal's
muscles bit by bit
```

1-3. Move the cursor to the first line of the file and the seventh character from the right. Notice that as you move up the file, the cursor moves in to the last letter of the file, but it does not move out to the last letter of the next line.

1-4. Delete the seventh and eighth characters from the right.

1-5. Move the cursor to the last character on the last line of the text.

1-6. Append the following new line of text:

```
and byte by byte
```

1-7. Write the buffer to a file and quit `vi`.

1-8. Reenter `vi` and append two more lines of text to the file `exer1`. What does the notice at the bottom of the screen say once you have reentered `vi` to edit `exer1`?

Moving the Cursor Around the Screen

Until now you have been moving the cursor with the `h`, `j`, `k`, `l`, BACKSPACE key, and the space bar. There are several other commands that can help you move the cursor quickly around the screen. This section explains how to position the cursor in the following ways:

- by characters on a line
- by lines
- by text objects
  - words
  - sentences
  - paragraphs
- in the window

There are also commands that position the cursor within parts of the `vi` editing buffer that are not visible on the screen. These commands will be discussed in the next section, "Positioning the Cursor in Undisplayed Text."

To follow this section of the tutorial, you should enter `vi` with a file that contains at least forty lines. If you do not have a file of that length, create one now. Remember, to execute the commands described here, you must be in command mode of `vi`. Press the ESCAPE key to make sure that you are in command mode rather than input mode.

Positioning the Cursor on a Character

Three ways to position the cursor on a character in a line are:

- by moving the cursor right or left to a character
- by specifying the character at either end of the line
- by searching for a character on a line

The first method was discussed earlier in this chapter under "Moving the Cursor to the Right or Left." The following sections describe the other two methods.

Moving the Cursor to the Beginning or End of a Line

The second method of positioning the cursor on a line is by using one of three commands that put the cursor on the first or last character of a line.

$	puts the cursor on the last character of a line
0 (zero)	puts the cursor on the first character of a line
^ (circumflex)	puts the cursor on the first nonblank character of a line

The following examples show the movement of the cursor produced by each of these three commands.

```
Go to the end of the line!
            ↑
~
~
~
```

$

```
Go to the end of the line!
                         ↑
~
~
~
```

```
Go to the beginning of the line!
                               ↑
~
~
~
```

0

```
Go to the beginning of the line!
↑
~
~
~
```

```
Go to the first character
of the line
     that is not blank!
                    ↑
~
~
~
```

^

```
Go to the first character
of the line
     that is not blank!
     ↑
~
~
~
```

Searching for a Character on a Line

The third way to position the cursor on a line is to search for a specific character on the current line. If the character is not found on the current line, a bell sounds and the cursor does not move. (There is also a command that searches a file for patterns. This will be discussed in the next section.) You can use six commands to search within a line: `f`, `F`, `t`, `T`, `;`, and `,`. You must specify a character after all of them except the `;` and `,` commands.

`f`*x*	Move the cursor to the right to the specified character *x*.
`F`*x*	Move the cursor to the left to the specified character *x*.
`t`*x*	Move the cursor right to the character just before the specified character *x*.
`T`*x*	Move the cursor left to the character just after the specified character *x*.
`;`	Continue the search specified in the last command, in the same direction. The `;` remembers the character and seeks out the next occurrence of that character on the current line.
`,`	Continue the search specified in the last command, in the opposite direction. The `,` remembers the character and seeks out the previous occurrence of that character on the current line.

For example, in the following screen `vi` searches to the right for the first occurrence of the letter A on the current line.

```
Go forward to the letter A on this line.
             ↑
~
~
~
```

`fA`

```
Go forward to the letter A on this line.
                         ↑
~
~
~
```

Try the search commands on one of your files.

Line Positioning

Besides the `j` and `k` commands that you have already used, the `+`, `–`, and `<CR>` commands can be used to move the cursor to other lines.

The Minus Sign Motion Command

The – command moves the cursor up a line, positioning it at the first nonblank character, if there is one, on the line. To move more than one line at a time, specify the number of lines you want to move before the – command. For example, to move the cursor up 13 lines, type:

```
13-
```

The cursor will move up 13 lines. If some of those lines are above the current window, the window will scroll up to reveal them. This is a rapid way to move quickly up a file.

Now try to move up 100 lines. Type:

```
100-
```

What happened to the window? If there are fewer then 100 lines above the current line, a bell will sound telling you that you have made a mistake, and the cursor will remain on the current line.

The Plus Sign Motion Command

The plus sign command (+) or the `<CR>` command moves the cursor down a line to the first non-blank character. Specify the number of lines you want to move before the + command. For example, to move the cursor down nine lines, type:

```
9+
```

The cursor will move down nine lines. If some of those lines are below the current screen, the window will scroll down to reveal them.

Now try to do the same thing by pressing the RETURN key. Are the results the same as they were when you pressed the + key?

Word Positioning

The vi editor considers a word to be a string of characters that may include letters, numbers, or underscores. There are six word positioning commands: w, b, e, W, B, and E. The lower case commands (w, b, and e) treat any character other than a letter, digit, or underscore as a delimiter, signifying the beginning or end of a word. Punctuation before or after a white space is considered a word. The beginning or end of a line is also a delimiter.

The upper case commands (W, B, and E) treat punctuation as part of the word; words are delimited by white space, which consists of white space, tabs, and newlines.

The following is a summary of the word positioning commands.

w Move the cursor forward to the first character in the next word. You may press w as many times as you want to reach the word you want, or you can prefix the necessary number to the w command.

*n*w Move the cursor forward *n* number of words to the first character of that word. The end of the line does not stop the movement of the cursor; instead, the cursor wraps around and continues counting words from the beginning of the next line.

```
The <w> command
leaps word by word through the
file.  Move from THIS word forward

six words to THIS word.
~
~
```

6w

```
The w command
leaps word by word through the
file.  Move from THIS word forward
six words to THIS word.
                ↑
~
~
```

W Ignore all punctuation and move the cursor forward to the word after the next blank.

e Moves the cursor forward in the line to the last character in the next word.

```
Go forward one word to the end of
the next word in this line
   ↑
~
~
```

e

```
Go forward one word to the end of
the next word in this line
         ↑
~
~
```

```
Go to the end of the third word after the current word.
           ↑
~
~
```

3e

```
Go to the end of the third word after the current word.
                          ↑
~
~
```

E Ignore all punctuation except white space, delimiting words only by white space.

b Move the cursor backward in the line to the first character of the previous word.

*n*b Move the cursor backward *n* number of words to the first character of the *n*th word. The b command does not stop at the beginning of a line, but moves to the end of the line above and continues moving backward.

B Can be used just like the b command, except that it delimits the word only by blank spaces and newlines. It treats all other punctuation as letters of a word.

```
Leap backward word by word through
the file. Go back four words from here.
                             ↑
~
~
```

4b

```
Leap backward word by word through
the file. Go back four words from here.
         ↑
~
~
~
```

Positioning the Cursor by Sentences

The `vi` editor also recognizes sentences. In `vi` a sentence ends in `!` or `.` or `?`. If these delimiters appear in the middle of a line, they must be followed by two spaces for `vi` to recognize them. You should get used to the convention of typing two spaces after a period as the end of a sentence, because it is often useful to be able to operate on a sentence as a unit.

You can move the cursor from sentence to sentence in the file with the `(` (open parenthesis) and `)` (close parenthesis) commands.

`(`	Move the cursor to the beginning of the current sentence.
n`(`	Move the cursor to the beginning of the *n*th sentence above the current sentence.
`)`	Move the cursor to the beginning of the next sentence.
n`)`	Move the cursor to the beginning of the *n*th sentence following the current sentence.

The example in the following screens shows how the open parenthesis moves the cursor around the screen.

```
Suddenly we spotted whales in the
distance.  Daniel was the first to see them.
                     ↑
~
~
```

(

```
Suddenly we spotted whales in the
distance.  Daniel was the first to see them.
           ↑
~
~
~
```

Now repeat the command, preceding it with a number. For example, type:

`3(` (or)
`5)`

Did the cursor move the correct number of sentences?

Positioning the Cursor by Paragraphs

Paragraphs are recognized by `vi` if they begin after a blank line. If you want to be able to move the cursor to the beginning of a paragraph (or later in this tutorial, to delete or change a whole paragraph), then make sure each paragraph ends in a blank line.

{	Move the cursor to the beginning of the current paragraph, which is delimited by a blank line above it.

n{	Move the cursor to the beginning of the *n*th paragraph above the current paragraph.
}	Move the cursor to the beginning of the next paragraph.
n}	Move the cursor to the *n*th paragraph below the current line.

The following two screens show how the cursor can be moved to the beginning of another paragraph.

```
Suddenly, we spotted whales in the
distance.  Daniel was the first to see them.
           ↑



"Hey look!  Here come the whales!" he cried excitedly.
~
~
```

}

```
Suddenly, we spotted whales in the
distance.  Daniel was the first to see them.

<————————
"Hey look!  Here come the whales!" he cried excitedly.
~
~
```

Positioning in the Window

The `vi` editor also provides three commands that help you position yourself in the window. Try out each command. Be sure to type them in upper case.

`H`	Move the cursor to the first line on the screen.
`M`	Move the cursor to the middle line on the screen.
`L`	Move the cursor to the last line on the screen.

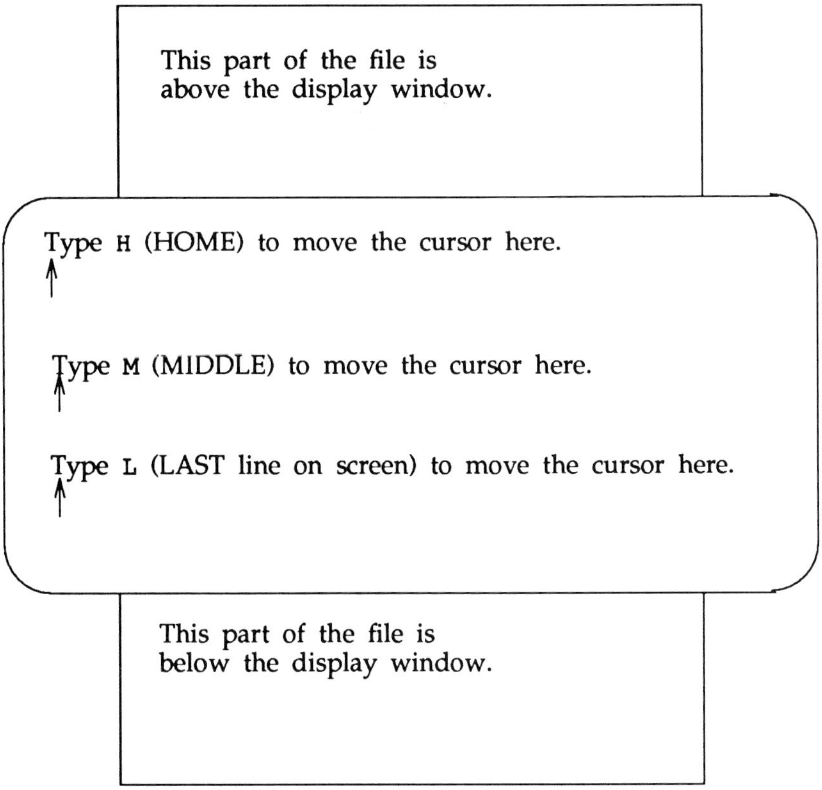

This part of the file is above the display window.

Type `H` (HOME) to move the cursor here.

Type `M` (MIDDLE) to move the cursor here.

Type `L` (LAST line on screen) to move the cursor here.

This part of the file is below the display window.

Table 7-2 (sheets 1 through 4) summarizes the `vi` commands for moving the cursor by positioning it on a character, line, word, sentence, paragraph, or position on the screen. (Additional `vi` commands for moving the cursor are summarized in Table 7-3, which appears later in the chapter.)

Table 7-2: Summary of `vi` Motion Commands

Positioning on a Character	
`h`	Move the cursor one character to the left.
`l`	Move the cursor one character to the right.
`<BACKSPACE>`	Move the cursor one character to the left.
`<space bar>`	Move the cursor one character to the right.
`f`*x*	Move the cursor to the right to the specified character *x*.
`F`*x*	Move the cursor to the left to the specified character *x*.
`t`*x*	Move the cursor to the right, to the character just before the specified character *x*.
`T`*x*	Move the cursor to the left, to the character just after the specified character *x*.
`;`	Continue searching in same direction on the line for the last character requested with `f`, `F`, `t`, or `T`. The `;` remembers the character and finds the next occurrence of it on the current line.
`,`	Continue searching in opposite direction on the line for the last character requested with `f`, `F`, `t`, or `T`. The `,` remembers the character and finds the next occurrence of it on the current line.

Table 7-2: Summary of `vi` Motion Commands (continued)

	Positioning on a Character
`k`	Move the cursor up to the same column in the previous line (if a character exists in that column).
`j`	Move the cursor down to the same column in the next line (if a character exists in that column).
`-`	Move the cursor up to the beginning of the previous line.
`+`	Move the cursor down to the beginning of the next line.
`<CR>`	Move the cursor down to the beginning of the next line.
	Positioning on a Line
`$`	Move the cursor to the last character on the line.
`0 (zero)`	Move the cursor to the first character on the line.
`^ (circumflex)`	Move the cursor to the first nonblank character on the line.

Table 7-2: Summary of `vi` Motion Commands (continued)

Positioning on a Word	
`w`	Move the cursor forward to the first character in the next word.
`W`	Ignore all punctuation and move the cursor forward to the next word delimited only by white space.
`b`	Move the cursor backward one word to the first character of that word.
`B`	Move the cursor to the left one word, which is delimited only by white space.
`e`	Move the cursor to the end of the current word.
`E`	Delimit the words by white space only. The cursor is placed on the last character before the next white space, or end of the line.

Table 7-2: Summary of vi Motion Commands (continued)

	Positioning on a Sentence
(	Move the cursor to the beginning of the current sentence.
)	Move the cursor to the beginning of the next sentence.
	Positioning on a Paragraph
{	Move the cursor to the beginning of the current paragraph.
}	Move the cursor to the beginning of the next paragraph.
	Positioning in the Window
H	Move the cursor to the first line on the screen (the home position).
M	Move the cursor to the middle line on the screen.
L	Move the cursor to the last line on the screen.

Positioning the Cursor in Undisplayed Text

How do you move the cursor to text that is not shown in the current editing window? One option is to use the `20j` or `20k` command. However, if you are editing a large file, you need to move quickly and accurately to another place in the file. This section covers those commands that can help you move around within the file by:

- scrolling forward or backward in the file
- going to a specified line in the file
- searching for a pattern in the file

Scrolling the Text

Four commands allow you to scroll the text of a file. The `^f` (control-f) and `^d` (control-d) commands scroll the screen forward. The `^b` (control-b) and `^u` (control-u) commands scroll the screen backward.

The Control-f Command

The `^f` (control-f) command scrolls the text forward one full window of text below the current window. To do this, `vi` clears the screen and redraws the window. The two lines that were at the bottom of the current window are placed at the top of the new window. If too few lines are left in the file to fill the window, the screen displays a ~ (tilde) to show that there are empty lines.

`vi` clears and redraws the screen as follows:

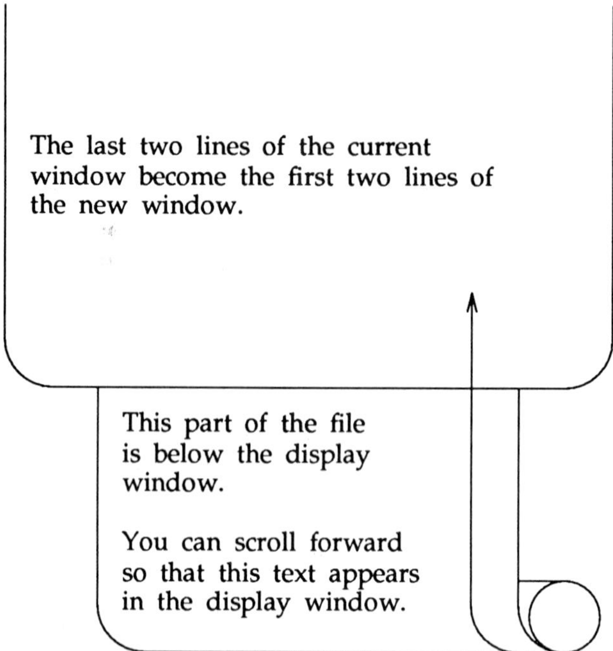
The last two lines of the current window become the first two lines of the new window.
This part of the file is below the display window.
You can scroll forward so that this text appears in the display window.

The Control-d Command

The ^d (control-d) command scrolls down a half screen to reveal text below the window. When you type ^d, the text appears to be rolled up at the top and unrolled at the bottom. This allows the lines below the screen to appear on the screen, while the lines at the top of the screen disappear. If the cursor is on the last line of the file and you type ^d, a bell will sound.

The Control-b Command

The ^b (control-b) command scrolls the screen back a full window to reveal the text above the current window. To do this, vi clears the screen and redraws the window with the text that is above the current screen. Unlike the ^f command, ^b does not leave any reference lines from the previous window. If not enough lines are above the current window to fill a full new window, a bell will sound and the current window will remain on the screen.

This part of the file is above the display window.

You can scroll backward so that this text appears in the display window.

Any text that currently appears in the display window is placed below the current window. The current window is cleared and redrawn so that the text above the window appears within the window.

Now try scrolling backward. Type:

```
<^b>
```

`vi` clears the screen and draws a new screen. Any text that was in the display window is placed below the current window.

The Control-u Command

The `^u` (control-u) command scrolls up a half screen of text to reveal the lines just above the window. The lines at the bottom of the window are erased. Now scroll up in the text, moving the portion above the screen into the window. Type:

```
<^u>
```

When the cursor reaches the top of the file, a bell will sound to notify you that the file cannot scroll further.

Go to a Specified Line

The G command positions the cursor on a specified line in the window; if that line is not currently on the screen, G clears the screen and redraws the window around it. If you do not specify a line, the G command sends the cursor to the last line of the file.

G	go to the last line of the file
*n*G	go to the *n*th line of the file

Line Numbers

Each line of the file has a line number corresponding to its position in the buffer. To get the number of a particular line, position the cursor on the line and type ^g. The ^g command gives you a status notice at the bottom of the screen which tells you:

- the name of the file
- whether the buffer has been modified since it was last written to a file
- the line number on which the cursor rests
- the total number of lines in the buffer
- the percentage of the total lines in the buffer represented by the current line

```
This line is the 35th line of the buffer.
The cursor is on this line.
                   ↑



There are several more lines in the
buffer.
The last line of the buffer is line 116.
~
```

(continued on next page)

```
~
```

<^g>

```
This line is the 35th line of the buffer.
The cursor is on this line.
                    ↑


There are several more lines in the
buffer.
The last line of the buffer is line 116.
~
~
"file.name" [modified] line 36 of 116 --34%--
```

Searching for a Pattern of Characters: the / and ? Commands

The fastest way to reach a specific place in your text is to use one of the search commands: /, ?, n, or N. These commands allow you to search forward or backward in the buffer for the next occurrence of a specified character pattern. The / and ? commands are not silent; they appear as you type them, along with the search pattern, on the bottom of the screen. The n and N commands allow you to repeat the previous search.

The /, followed by a pattern (*/pattern*), searches forward in the buffer for the next occurrence of the characters in the pattern, and puts the cursor on the first of those characters. For example, the command line

```
/Hello world<CR>
```

finds the next occurrence in the buffer of the words `Hello world` and puts the cursor under the `H`.

The `?`, followed by a pattern (?*pattern*), searches backward in the buffer for the first occurrence of the characters in the pattern, and puts the cursor on the first of those characters. For example, the command line

```
?data set design<CR>
```

finds the previous occurrence in the buffer of the words `data set design` and puts the cursor under the `d` in `data`.

These search commands do not wrap around the end of a line while searching for two words. For example, you are searching for the words `Hello world`. If `Hello` is at the end of one line and `world` is at the beginning of the next, the search command will not find that occurrence of `Hello world`.

However, the search commands do wrap around the end or the beginning of the buffer to continue a search. For example, if you are near the end of the buffer and the pattern for which you are searching (with the /*pattern* command) is at the top of the buffer, the command will find the pattern.

The `n` and `N` commands allow you to continue searches you have requested with /*pattern* or ?*pattern* without retyping them.

`n`	Repeat the last search command.
`N`	Repeat the last search command in the opposite direction.

For example, you want to search backward in the file for the three-letter pattern `the`. Initiate the search with `?the` and continue it with `n`. The following screens offer a step-by-step illustration of how the `n` command searches backward through the file and finds four occurrences of the character string `the`.

```
↓
Suddenly, we spotted whales in the
distance.  Daniel was the first to see them.

"Hey look!  Here come the whales!" he cried excitedly.
~
~
~
?the
```

```
Suddenly, we spotted whales in the
distance.  Daniel was the first to see them.

"Hey look!  Here come the whales!" he cried excitedly.
                     ↑
~
~
~
```

n

```
Suddenly, we spotted whales in the
distance.  Daniel was the first to see them.
                                        ↑

"Hey look!  Here come the whales!" he cried excitedly.
~
~
~
```

n

```
Suddenly, we spotted whales in the
distance.  Daniel was the first to see them.
                      ↑

"Hey look!  Here come the whales!" he cried excitedly.
~
~
```

n

```
                                          ↓
Suddenly, we spotted whales in the
distance.  Daniel was the first to see them.

"Hey look!  Here come the whales!" he cried excitedly.
~
~
```

The / and ? search commands do not allow you to specify particular occurrences of a pattern with numbers. You cannot, for example, request the third occurrence (after your current position) of a pattern.

Table 7-3 summarizes the `vi` commands for moving the cursor by scrolling the text, specifying a line number, and searching for a pattern.

Table 7-3: Summary of Additional `vi` Motion Commands

Scrolling	
`^f`	Scroll the screen forward a full window, revealing the window of text below the current window.
`^d`	Scroll the screen down a half window, revealing lines below the current window.
`^b`	Scroll the screen back a full window, revealing the window of text above the current window.
`^u`	Scroll the screen up a half window, revealing the lines of text above the current window.
Positioning on a Numbered Line	
`1G`	Go to the first line of the file.
`G`	Go to the last line of the file.
`^g`	Give the line number and file status.
Searching for a Pattern	
/*pattern*	Search forward in the buffer for the next occurrence of the pattern. Position the cursor on the first character of the pattern.
?*pattern*	Search backward in the buffer for the first occurrence of the pattern. Position the cursor under the first character of the pattern.
`n`	Repeat the last search command.
`N`	Repeat the search command in the opposite direction.

Exercise 2

2-1. Create a file called `exer2`. Type a number on each line, numbering the lines sequentially from 1 to 50. Your file should look similar to the following:

2-2. Try using each of the scroll commands, noticing how many lines scroll through the window. Try the following:

```
^f
^b
^u
^d
```

2-3. Go to the end of the file. Append the following line of text.

```
123456789 123456789
```

What number does the command `7h` place the cursor on? What number does the command `3l` place the cursor on?

2-4. Try the command `$` and the command `0` (number zero).

2-5. Go to the first character on the line that is not a blank. Move to the first character in the next word. Move back to the first character of the word to the left. Move to the end of the word.

2-6. Go to the first line of the file. Try the commands that place the cursor in the middle of the window, on the last line of the window, and on the first line of the window.

2-7. Search for the number 8. Find the next occurrence of the number 8. Find 48.

Creating Text

Three basic commands enable you to create text:

`a`	append text
`i`	insert text
`o`	open a new line on which text can be entered

After you finish creating text with any one of these commands, you can return to the command mode of `vi` by pressing the `ESCAPE` key.

Appending Text

`a`	append text after the cursor
`A`	append text at the end of the current line

You have already experimented with the a command in the "Creating a File" section. Make a new file named `junk2`. Append some text using the a command. To return to the command mode of `vi`, press the `ESCAPE` key. Then compare the `a` command to the `A` command.

Inserting Text

`i`	insert text before the cursor
`I`	insert text at the beginning of the current line before the first character that is not a blank

To return to the command mode of `vi`, press the `ESCAPE` key.

In the following examples you can compare the append and insert commands. The arrows show the position of the cursor, where new text will be added.

```
Append three spaces AFTER the H of Here.
                                   ↑
~
~
~
```

a <ESC>

```
Append three spaces AFTER the H of H   ere.
                                      ↑
~
~
~
```

```
Insert three spaces BEFORE the H of Here.
                                    ↑
```

i <ESC>

```
Insert three spaces BEFORE the H of    Here.
                                    ↑
~
~
~
```

Notice that, in both cases, the user has left text input mode by pressing the ESCAPE key.

Opening a Line for Text

o Create text from the beginning of a new line below the current line. You can issue this command from any point in the current line.

O Create text from the beginning of a new line above the current line. This command can also be issued from any position in the current line.

The open command creates a line directly above or below the current line, and puts you into the text input mode. For example, in the following screens the O command opens a line above the current line, and the o command opens a line below the current line. In both cases, the cursor waits for you to enter text from the beginning of the new line.

```
Create text ABOVE the current line.
               ↑
~
~
```

O

```
↓
 Create text ABOVE the current line.
~
~
```

```
Now create text BELOW the current line.
               ↑
~
~
```

o

```
Now create text BELOW the current line.

↑
~
~
```

Table 7-4 summarizes the commands for creating and adding text with the `vi` editor.

Table 7-4: Summary of `vi` Commands for Creating Text

Command	Function
`a`	Create text after the cursor.
`A`	Create text at the end of the current line.
`i`	Create text in front of the cursor.
`I`	Create text before the first character that is not a blank on the current line.
`o`	Create text at the beginning of a new line below the current line.
`O`	Create text at the beginning of a new line above the current line.
`<ESC>`	Return `vi` to command mode from any of the above text input modes.

Exercise 3

3-1. Create a text file called `exer3`.

3-2. Insert the following four lines of text.

```
Append text
Insert text
a computer's
job is boring.
```

3-3. Add the following line of text above the last line:

```
financial statement and
```

3-4. Using a text insert command, add the following line of text above the third line:

```
Delete text
```

3-5. Add the following line of text below the current line:

```
byte of the budget
```

3-6. Using an append command, add the following line of text below the last line:

```
But, it is an exciting machine.
```

3-7. Move to the first line and add the word `some` before the word text.

Now practice using each of the six commands for creating text.

3-8. Leave `vi` and go on to the next section to find out how to delete any mistakes you made in creating text.

Deleting Text

You can delete text with various commands in the command mode, and undo the entry of small amounts of text in the text input mode. In addition, you can entirely undo the effects of your most recent command.

Deleting Entered Text in the Text Input Mode

To delete a character at a time when you are in the text input mode, use the BACKSPACE key.

<BACKSPACE> Delete the current character (the character to the left of the cursor).

The BACKSPACE key moves the cursor backward in the text input mode and deletes each character that the cursor backs across. However, the deleted characters are not erased from the screen until you type over them or press the ESCAPE key to return to the command mode.

In the following example, the arrows represent the cursor.

```
Mary had a litttl
                 ↑
~
~
```

<BACKSPACE> <BACKSPACE>

```
Mary had a litttl
               ↑
~
~
```

<ESC>

```
Mary had a litt
             ↑
~
~
~
```

Notice that the characters are not erased from the screen until you press the ESCAPE key.

Two other keys can also delete text in the text input mode. Although you may not use them often, you should be aware that they are available. To remove the special meanings of these keys so that they can be typed as text, precede the key with ^v.

^w	undo the entry of the current word
@	delete all text entered on current line since text input mode was entered
^v	remove the special meaning, if any, of the following input character

When you type ^w, the cursor backs up over the word last typed and waits on the first character of that word. It does not erase the word from the screen until you press the ESCAPE key or enter new characters over the old ones. The @ sign behaves in a similar manner, except that it removes all text you have typed on the current line since you last entered the input mode.

Undo the Last Command

Before you experiment with the delete commands, you should try the u command. This command undoes the last command you issued.

u	undo the last command
U	restore the current line to its state before you changed it

If you delete lines by mistake, type u; your lines will reappear on the screen. If you type the wrong command, type u and it will be nullified. The U command will nullify all changes made to the current line as long as the cursor has not been moved from it.

If you type u twice in a row, the second command will undo the first; your undo will be undone! For example, if you delete a line by mistake and restore it by typing u, typing u a second time will delete the line again. Knowing this command can save you a lot of trouble.

Delete Commands in the Command Mode

You know that you can precede a command by a number. Many of the commands in `vi`, such as the delete and change commands, also allow you to enter a cursor movement command after another command. The cursor movement command can specify a text object such as a word, line, sentence, or paragraph. The general format of a `vi` command is:

[*number*][*command*]*text_object*

The brackets around some components of the command format show that those components are optional.

All delete commands issued in the command mode immediately remove unwanted text from the screen and, on most terminals, redraw the affected part of the screen.

The delete command follows the general format of a `vi` command.

[*number*]d*text_object*

Deleting Words

You can delete a word or part of a word with the `d` command. Move the cursor to the first character to be deleted and type `dw`. The character under the cursor and all subsequent characters in that word are erased.

```
the deep dark depths of the lake.
    ↑
~
~
```

2dw

```
the depths of the lake.
    ↑
~
~
```

The dw command deletes one word or punctuation mark and the space(s) that follow it. You can delete several words or marks at once by specifying a number before the command. For example, to delete three words and two commas, type 5dw.

```
the deep, deep, dark depths of the lake
    ↑
~
~
```

5dw

```
the depths of the lake
    ↑
~
~
~
```

Deleting Paragraphs

To delete paragraphs, use the following commands:

`d{` or `d}`

Observe what happens to your file. Remember, you can restore the deleted text with `u`.

Deleting Lines

To delete a line, type `dd`. To delete multiple lines, specify a number before the command. For example, typing

```
10dd
```

erases ten lines. If you delete more than a few lines, `vi` displays the following notice on the bottom of the screen:

```
10 lines deleted
```

If fewer than ten lines are below the current line in the file, a bell sounds and no lines are deleted.

Deleting Text After the Cursor

To delete all text on a line after the cursor, put the cursor on the first character to be deleted and type:

`D` or `d$`.

Neither of these commands allows you to specify a number of lines; they can be used only on the current line.

Table 7-5 summarizes the `vi` commands for deleting text.

Table 7-5: Summary of Delete Commands

Command	Function
For Insert/Input Mode:	
`<BACKSPACE>`	Delete the current character.
`<^w>`	Delete the current word.
`@`	Delete the current line of new text or delete all new text on the current line.
For COMMAND Mode:	
`u`	Undo the last command.
`U`	Restore current line to its previous state.
`x`	Delete the current character.
*n*d*x*	Delete *n* number of text objects of type *x*.
`dw`	Delete the word at the cursor through the next space or to the next punctuation mark.
`dW`	Delete the word and punctuation at the cursor through the next space.
`dd`	Delete the current line.
`D`	Delete the portion of the line to the right of the cursor.
`d)`	Delete from the current position to the end of the current sentence.
`d}`	Delete from the current position to the end of the current paragraph.

Exercise 4

4-1. Create a file called `exer4` and put the following four lines of text in it:

```
When in the course of human events
there are many repetitive, boring
chores, then one ought to get a
robot to perform those chores.
```

4-2. Move the cursor to line two and append to the end of that line:

```
, tedious, and unsavory
```

Delete the word unsavory while you are in append mode.

Delete the word boring while you are in command mode.

What is another way you could have deleted the word boring?

4-3. Insert at the beginning of line four:

```
congenial and computerized
```

Delete the line.

How can you delete the contents of the line without removing the line itself?

Delete all the lines with one command.

4-4. Leave the screen editor and remove the empty file from your directory.

Modifying Text

The delete commands and text input commands provide one way for you to modify text. Another way you can change text is by using a command that lets you delete and create text simultaneously. There are three basic change commands: `r`, `s`, and `c`.

Replacing Text

`r`*x* — Replace the current character (the character shown by the cursor) with *x*. This command does not initiate text input mode, and so does not have to be followed by pressing the `ESCAPE` key.

n`r`*x* — Replace *n* characters with *x*. This command automatically terminates after the *nth* character is replaced. It does not have to be followed by pressing the `ESCAPE` key.

`R` — Replace only those characters typed over until the `ESCAPE` command is given. If the end of the line is reached, this command appends the input as new text.

The `r` command replaces the current character with the next character that is typed in. For example, suppose you want to change the word acts to ants in the following sentence:

```
The circus has many acts.
```

Place the cursor under the `c` of `acts` and type:

```
rn
```

The sentence becomes

```
The circus has many ants.
```

To change many to `7777`, place the cursor under the `m` of many and type:

```
4r7
```

The `r` command changes the four letters of many to four occurrences of the number seven.

```
The circus has 7777 ants.
```

Substituting Text

The substitute command replaces characters, but then allows you to continue to insert text from that point until you press the ESCAPE key.

s	Delete the character shown by the cursor and append text. End the text input mode by pressing the ESCAPE key.
*n*s	Delete *n* characters and append text. End the text input mode by pressing the ESCAPE key.
S	Replace all the characters in the line.

When you enter the s command, the last character in the string of characters to be replaced is overwritten by a $ sign. The characters are not erased from the screen until you type over them, or leave the text input mode by pressing the ESCAPE key.

Notice that you cannot use a text-object argument with either r or s. Did you try?

Suppose you want to substitute the word million for the word hundred in the sentence `My salary is one hundred dollars.` Put the cursor under the h of hundred and type 7s. Notice where the $ sign appears.

```
My salary is one hundred dollars.
                 ↑
~
~
~
```

```
7s million<ESC>
```

```
My salary is one million dollars.
                         ↑
~
~
~
```

Changing Text

The substitute command replaces characters. The change command replaces text- objects, and then continues to append text from that point until you press the ESCAPE key. To end the change command, press the ESCAPE key.

The change command can take a text-object argument. You can replace a character, word, an entire line, and so on, with new text.

*n*c*x*	Replace *n* text-objects of type *x*, such as sentences (shown by `)`) and paragraphs (shown by `}`).
cw	Replace a word or the remaining characters in a word with new text. The `vi` editor prints a `$` sign to show the last character to be changed.
*n*cw	Replace *n* words.
cc	Replace all the characters in the line.
*n*cc	Replace all characters in the current line and up to *n* lines of text.
C	Replace the remaining characters in the line, from the cursor to the end of the line.
*n*C	Replace the remaining characters from the cursor in the current line and replace all the lines following the current line up to *n* lines.

The change command, c, uses a $ sign to mark the last letter to be replaced. Notice how this works in the following example:

```
They are now due to arrive on Tuesday.
                              ↑
~
~
```

cw

```
They are now due to arrive on Tuesda$.
                              ↑
~
~
```

Wednesday<ESC>

```
They are now due to arrive on Wednesday.
                                      ↑
~
~
~
```

Notice that the new word (Wednesday) has more letters than the word it replaced (Tuesday). Once you have executed the change command, you are in the text input mode and can enter as much text as you want. The buffer will accept text until you press the ESCAPE key.

The C command, when used to change the remaining text on a line, works in the same way. When you enter the command it uses a $ sign to mark the end of the text that will be deleted, puts you in text input mode, and waits for you to type new text over the old. The following screens show the use of the C command.

```
This is line 1.
Oh, I must have the wrong number.
↑
This is line 3.
This is line 4.
~
~
```

C

```
This is line 1.
Oh, I must have the wrong number$
↑
This is line 3.
This is line 4.
~
~
```

This is line 2.<ESC>

```
This is line 1.
This is line 2.
              ↑
This is line 3.
This is line 4.
~
~
```

Now try combining arguments. For example, type:

c{

Because you know the undo command, do not hesitate to experiment with different arguments or to precede the command with a number. You must press the `ESCAPE` key before using the `u` command, since the `c` command places you in the text input mode.

Compare the `S` and `cc` commands. Both produce the same results.

Table 7-6 summarizes the `vi` commands for changing text.

Table 7-6: Summary of `vi` Commands for Changing Text

Command	Function
`r`	Replace the current character.
`R`	Replace only those characters typed over with new characters until the `ESCAPE` key is pressed.
`s`	Delete the character the cursor is on and append text. End the input mode by pressing the `ESCAPE` key.
`S`	Replace all the characters in the line.
`cc`	Replace all the characters in the line.
ncx	Replace *n* number of text objects of type *x*, such as sentences (shown by `)`) and paragraphs (shown by `}`).
`cw`	Replace a word or the remaining characters in a word with new text.
`C`	Replace the remaining characters in the line, from the cursor to the end of the line.

Cutting And Pasting Text Electronically

`vi` provides a set of commands that cut and paste text in a file. Another set of commands copies a portion of text and places it in another section of a file.

Moving Text

You can move text from one place to another in the `vi` buffer by deleting the lines and then placing them at the required point. The last text that was deleted is stored in a temporary buffer. If you move the cursor to that part of the file where you want the deleted lines to be placed and press the `p` key, the deleted lines will be added below the current line.

`p`	Place the contents of the temporary buffer after the cursor or below the current line.

A partial line that was deleted by the `D` command can be placed in the middle of another line. Position the cursor in the space between two words, then press the `p` key. The partial line is placed after the cursor.

Characters deleted by *n*`x` also go into a temporary buffer. Any text object that was just deleted can be placed somewhere else in the text with the `p` command.

The `p` command should be used right after a delete command since the temporary buffer only stores the results of one command at a time. The `p` command is also used to copy text placed in the temporary buffer by the yank command. The yank command (`y`) is discussed in the section titled "Copying Text."

Fixing Transposed Letters

A quick way to fix transposed letters is to combine the `x` and the `p` commands as `xp`. The `x` deletes the letter, and `p` places it after the next character.

Notice the error in the following line:

```
A line of tetx
```

This error can be changed quickly by placing the cursor under the `t` in `tx` and then pressing the `x` and `p` keys, in that order. The result is:

```
A line of text
```

Try this. Make a typing error in your file and use the `xp` command to correct it. Why does this command work?

Copying Text

You can yank (copy) one or more lines of text into a temporary buffer, and then put a copy of that text anywhere in the file. To put the text in a new position, type `p`; the text will appear on the next line.

The yank command follows the general format of a `vi` command.

[*number*]`y`[*text_object*]

Yanking lines of text does not delete them from their original position in the file. If you want the same text to appear in more than one place, this provides a convenient way to avoid typing the same text several times. However, if you do not want the same text in multiple places, be sure to delete the original text after you have put the text into its new position.

Table 7-7 summarizes the ways you can use the yank command.

Table 7-7: Summary of the Yank Command

Command	Function
*n*y*x*	Yank *n* number of text-objects of type *x*, (such as sentences) and paragraphs }).
yw	Yank a copy of a word.
yy	Yank a copy of the current line.
*n*yy	Yank *n* lines.
y)	Yank all text up to the end of the sentence.
y}	Yank all text up to the end of the paragraph.

Notice that this command allows you to specify the number of text objects to be yanked.

Try the following command lines and see what happens on your screen. Remember, you can always undo your last command. Type:

```
5yw
```

Move the cursor to another spot. Type:

```
p
```

Now try yanking a paragraph (y}) and placing it after the current paragraph. Then move to the end of the file (G) and place that same paragraph at the end of the file.

Copying or Moving Text Using Registers

Moving or copying several sections of text to a different part of the file is tedious work. `vi` provides a shortcut for this: named registers in which you can store text until you want to move it. To store text you can either yank or delete the text you wish to store.

Using registers is useful if a piece of text must appear in many places in the file. The extracted text stays in the specified register until you either end the editing session, or yank or delete another section of text to that register.

The general format of the command is:

[*number*]["*x*]*command*[*text_object*]

The *x* is the name of the register and can be any single, lower-case letter. It must be preceded by a double quotation mark. For example, place the cursor at the beginning of a line. Type:

```
3"ayy
```

Type in more text and then go to the end of the file. Type:

```
"ap
```

Did the lines you saved in register `a` appear at the end of the file?

Table 7-8 summarizes the cut and paste commands.

Table 7-8: Summary of `vi` Commands for Cutting and Pasting Text

Command	Function
`p`	Place the contents of the temporary buffer containing the text obtained from the most recent delete or yank command into the text after the cursor.
`yy`	Yank a line of text and place it into a temporary buffer.
nyx	Yank a copy of *n* number of text objects of type *x* and place them in a temporary buffer.
"xy*n*	Place a copy of a text object of type *n* in the register named by the letter x.
`"xp`	Place the contents of the register x after the cursor.

Exercise 5

5-1. Enter `vi` with the file called `exer2` that you created in Exercise 2.

Go to line eight and change its contents to `END OF FILE`.

5-2. Yank the first eight lines of the file and place them in register `z`. Put the contents of register `z` after the last line of the file.

5-3. Go to line eight and change its contents to `eight is great`.

5-4. Go to the last line of the file. Substitute `EXERCISE` for `FILE`. Replace `OF` with `TO`.

Special Commands

Here are some special commands that you will find useful:

`.`	repeat the last command
`J`	join two lines together
`^l`	clear the screen and redraw it
`~`	change lower case to upper case and vice versa

Repeating the Last Command

The `.` (period) repeats the last command to create, delete, or change text in the file. It is often used with the search command.

For example, suppose you forget to capitalize the S in United States. However, you do not want to capitalize the s in chemical states. One way to correct this problem is by searching for the word states. The first time you find it in the expression United States, you can change the s to S. Then continue your search. When you find another occurrence, you can simply type a period; `vi` will remember your last command and repeat the substitution of S for s.

Experiment with this command. For example, if you try to add a period at the end of a sentence while in command mode, the last text change will suddenly appear on the screen. Watch the screen to see how the text is affected.

Joining Two Lines

The `J` command joins lines. To enter this command, place the cursor on the current line, and press the SHIFT and `j` keys simultaneously. The current line is joined with the line that follows it.

For example, suppose you have the following two lines of text:

```
Dear Mr.
Smith:
```

To join these two lines into one, place the cursor under any character in the first line and type:

```
J
```

You will immediately see the following on your screen:

```
Dear Mr. Smith:
```

Notice that `vi` automatically places a space between the last word on the first line and the first word on the second line.

Clearing and Redrawing the Window

If another UNIX system user sends you a message using the write command while you are editing with `vi`, the message will appear in your current window, over part of the text you are editing. To restore your text after you have read the message, you must be in the command mode. (If you are in the text input mode, press the `ESCAPE` key to return to the command mode.) Then type `^l` (control-l). `vi` erases the message and redraws the window exactly as it appeared before the message arrived.

Changing Lower Case to Upper Case and Vice Versa

A quick way to change any lower case letter to upper case, or vice versa, is to put the cursor on the letter to be changed and type a ~ (tilde). For example, to change the letter a to A, press ~. You can change several letters by typing ~ several times, or you can precede the command with a number to change several letters with that one command.

Table 7-9 summarizes the special commands.

Table 7-9: Summary of Special Commands

Command	Function
.	Repeat the last command.
J	Join the line below the current line with the current line.
^l	Clear and redraw the current window.
~	Change lower case to upper case, or vice versa.

Using Line Editing Commands in vi

The vi editor has access to many of the commands provided by a line editor called ex. (For a complete list of ex commands see the ex(1) page in the *User's Reference Manual.*) This section discusses some of those most commonly used.

The ex commands are very similar to the ed commands discussed in Chapter 6. If you are familiar with ed, you may want to experiment on a test file to see how many ed commands also work in vi.

Line editor commands begin with a : (colon). After you type the colon, the cursor drops to the bottom of the screen and displays the colon. The remainder of the command also appears at the bottom of the screen as you type it.

Temporarily Returning to the Shell: the :sh and :! Commands

When you enter vi, the contents of the buffer fills your screen, making it impossible to issue any shell commands. However, you may want to do so. For example, you may want to get information from another file to incorporate into your current text. You could get that information by running one of the shell commands that displays the text of a file on your screen, such as the cat or pg command. However, quitting and reentering the editor is time consuming and tedious. vi offers two methods of escaping the editor temporarily so that you can issue shell commands (and even edit other files) without having to write your buffer and quit. These temporary escape commands are the :! command and the :sh command.

The :! command allows you to escape the editor and run a shell command on a single command line. From the command mode of vi, type :!. These characters are printed at the bottom of your screen. Type a shell command immediately after the !. The shell will run your command, give you output, and print the message [Hit return to continue]. When you press the RETURN key vi refreshes the screen and the cursor reappears exactly where you left it.

The ex command :sh allows you to do the same thing, but behaves differently on the screen. From the command mode of vi type :sh and press the RETURN key. A shell command prompt appears on the next line. Type your command(s) after the prompt, as you would normally do while working in the shell. When you are ready to return to vi, type ^d or exit; your screen is refreshed with contents of your buffer and the cursor appears where you left it.

Even changing directories while you are temporarily in the shell will not prevent you from returning to the `vi` buffer where you were editing your file when you type `exit` or `^d`.

Writing Text to a New File: the :w Command

The `:w` (for write) command allows you to create a file by copying lines of text from the file you are currently editing into a file that you specify. To create your new file, you must specify a line or range of lines (with their line numbers), along with the name of the new file, on the command line. You can write as many lines as you like. The general format is:

:*line_number[,line_number]*w *filename*

For example, to write the third line of the buffer to a line named `three`, type:

```
:3w three<CR>
```

`vi` reports the successful creation of your new file with the following information:

```
"three" [New file] 1 line, 20 characters
```

To write your current line to a file, you can use a . (period) as the line address:

```
:.w junk<CR>
```

A new file called `junk` is created. It will contain only the current line in the `vi` buffer.

You can also write a whole section of the buffer to a new file by specifying a range of lines. For example, to write lines 23 through 37 to a file, type the following:

:23,37w *newfile*<CR>

Going to a Specified Line

You can move the cursor to any line in the buffer by typing : and the line number. The command line

`:`*n*`<CR>`

means to go to the *n*th line of the buffer.

Deleting the Rest of the Buffer

One of the easiest ways to delete all the lines between the current line and the end of the buffer is by using the line editor command `d` with the special symbols for the current and last lines.

```
:.,$d<CR>
```

The . represents the current line; the `$` sign represents the last line.

Adding a File to the Buffer

To add text from a file below a specific line in the editing buffer, use the `:r` (read) command. For example, to put the contents of a file called `data` into your current file, place the cursor on the line above the place where you want it to appear. Type:

```
:r data<CR>
```

You may also specify the line number instead of moving the cursor. For example, to insert the file `data` below line 56 of the buffer, type:

```
:56r data<CR>
```

Do not be afraid to experiment; you can use the u command to undo `ex` commands, too.

Making Global Changes

One of the most powerful commands in ex is the global command. The global command is given here to help those users who are familiar with the line editor. Even if you are not familiar with a line editor, you may want to try the command on a test file.

For example, say you have several pages of text about the DNA molecule in which you refer to its structure as a helix. Now you want to change every occurrence of the word helix to the words double helix. The ex editor's global command allows you to do this with one command line. First, you have to understand a series of commands.

:g/*pattern*/*command*<CR>

For each line containing *pattern*, execute the ex command named *command*. For example, type: :g/helix/p<CR>. The line editor prints all lines that contain the pattern helix.

:s/*pattern*/*new_words*/<CR>

This is the substitute command. The line editor searches for the first instance of the characters *pattern* on the current line and changes them to *new_words*.

:s/*pattern*/*new_words*/g<CR>

If you add the letter g after the last delimiter of this command line, ex changes every occurrence of *pattern* on the current line. If you do not add the letter g, ex changes only the first occurrence.

:g/helix/s//double helix/g<CR>

This command line searches for the word helix. Each time the word helix is found, the substitute command substitutes two words, double helix, for every instance of helix on that line. The delimiters after the s command do not require that the word helix be typed in again. The command remembers the word from the delimiters after the global command g. This is a powerful command. For a more detailed explanation of global and substitution commands, see Chapter 6, "Line Editor (ed) Tutorial."

Table 7-10 summarizes the line editor commands available in vi.

Table 7-10: Summary of Line Editor Commands

Command	Function
:	Indicate that the commands following are line editor commands.
:sh<CR>	Temporarily return to the shell to perform shell commands.
^d	Escape the temporary shell and return to the current window of vi to continue editing.
:*n*<CR>	Go to the *n*th line of the buffer.
:*x,y*w *data*<CR>	Write lines from the number *x* through the number *y* into a new file (*data*).
:$<CR>	Go to the last line of the buffer.
:.,$d<CR>	Delete all the lines in the buffer from the current line to the last line.
:r *shell.file*<CR>	Insert the contents of *shell.file* after the current line of the buffer.
:s/*text*/*new_words*/<CR>	Replace the first instance of the characters *text* on the current line with *new_words*.
:s/*text*/*new_words*/g<CR>	Replace every occurrence of *text* on the current line with *new_words*.
:g/*text*/s//*new_words*/g<CR>	Replace every occurrence of *text* in the file with *new_words*.

Quitting `vi`

Five basic command sequences can be used to quit the `vi` editor. Commands that are preceded by a colon (`:`) are line editor commands.

`:wq`<CR>	Write the contents of the `vi` buffer to the UNIX file currently being edited and quit `vi`.
`ZZ`	Write the buffer only if the contents of the buffer changed since the last write command and quit `vi`.
`:w` *filename*<CR> `:q`<CR>	Write the temporary buffer to a new file named *filename*, and quit `vi`.
`:w!` *filename*<CR> `:q`<CR>	Overwrite an existing file called *filename* with the contents of the buffer and quit `vi`.
`:q!`<CR>	Quit `vi` without writing the buffer to a file, and discard all changes made to the buffer.
`:q`<CR>	Quit `vi` without writing the buffer to a UNIX file. This works only if you have made no changes to the buffer; otherwise `vi` warns you that you must either save the buffer or use the `:q!`<CR> command to terminate.

The `:wq` command and the `ZZ` command, under the circumstances explained above, write the contents of the buffer to a file, quit `vi`, and return you to the shell. You have tried the `ZZ` command. Now try to exit `vi` with `:wq`. `vi` remembers the name of the file currently being edited, so you do not have to specify it when you want to write the contents of the buffer back into the file. Type:

```
:wq<CR>
```

The `vi` editor tells you the name of the file and reports the number of lines and characters in the file.

What must you do to give the file a different name? For example, suppose you want to write to a new file called `junk`. Type:

```
:w junk<CR>
```

After you write to the new file, leave `vi`. Type:

```
:q<CR>
```

If you try to write to an existing file, you will receive a warning. For example, if you try to write to a file called `johnson`, the system responds with:

```
"johnson" File exists - use "w! johnson" to overwrite
```

If you want to replace the contents of the existing file with the contents of the buffer, use the `:w!` command to overwrite `johnson`.

```
:w! johnson<CR>
```

Your new file will overwrite the existing one.

If you edit a file called `memo`, make some changes to it, and then decide you don't want to keep the changes, leave `vi` without writing to the file. Type:

```
:q!<CR>
```

Table 7-11 summarizes the quit commands.

Table 7-11: Summary of the Quit Commands

Command	Function
`ZZ`	Write the file if it has changed since the last write command and quit `vi`.
`:wq<CR>`	Write the file and quit `vi`.
`:w` *filename*<CR> `:q<CR>`	Write the editing buffer to a new file (*filename*) and quit `vi`.
`:w!` *filename*<CR> `:q<CR>`	Overwrite an existing file (*filename*) with the contents of the editing buffer and quit `vi`.
`:q!<CR>`	Quit `vi` without writing the buffer to a file even if the buffer changed.
`:q<CR>`	Quit `vi` without writing the buffer to a file only if the buffer has not changed.

Special Options for `vi`

The `vi` command has some special options. It allows you to:

- recover a file lost if `vi` is interrupted
- place several files in the editing buffer and edit each in sequence
- view the file without risk of accidentally changing the file

Recovering a File Lost by an Interrupt

If an interrupt or disconnect occurs, `vi` exits without writing the text in the buffer back to its file. However, `vi` stores a copy of the buffer for you. When you log back in to the UNIX system, you are able to recover the file with the `-r` option of the `vi` command. Type:

`vi -r` *filename*<CR>

All or most of the changes you made to *filename* before the interrupt occurred are now in the `vi` buffer. You can continue editing the file, or you can write the file and quit `vi`. The `vi` editor will remember the filename and write to that file.

Editing Multiple Files

If you want to edit more than one file in the same editing session, issue the `vi` command, specifying each filename. Type:

`vi` *file1 file2*<CR>

`vi` responds by telling you how many files you are going to edit. For example:

```
2 files to edit
```

After you have edited the first file, write your changes (in the buffer) to the file (*file1*). Type

`:w`<CR>

The system response to the `:w<CR>` command is a message at the bottom of the screen giving the name of the file and the number of lines and characters in that file. Then you can edit the next file by using the `:n` command. Type:

```
:n<CR>
```

The system responds by printing a notice at the bottom of the screen, telling you the name of the next file to be edited and the number of characters and lines in that file.

Select two of the files in your current directory; then enter `vi` and place the two files in the editing buffer at the same time. Notice the system responses to your commands at the bottom of the screen.

Viewing a File

It is often convenient to be able to inspect a file by using the powerful search and scroll capabilities of `vi`. However, you might want to protect yourself against accidentally changing a file during an editing session. The read-only option prevents you from writing in a file. To avoid accidental changes, you can set this option by invoking the editor as `view` rather than `vi`.

Table 7-12 summarizes the special options for `vi`.

Table 7-12: Summary of Special Options for vi

Option	Function
vi *file1 file2 file3*<CR>	Enter three files (*file1*, *file2*, and *file3*) into the vi buffer to be edited.
:w<CR> :n<CR>	Write the current file and start editing the next file.
vi -r *file1*<CR>	Recover the changes made to *file1*.
view *file*<CR>	Inspect file with the read-only option set, preventing accidental changes to *file*.

Exercise 6

6-1. Try to restore a file lost by an interrupt.

Enter `vi`, create some text in a file called `exer6`. Turn off your terminal without writing to a file or leaving `vi`. Turn your terminal back on, and log in again. Then try to get back into `vi` and edit `exer6`.

6-2. Place `exer1` and `exer2` in the `vi` buffer to be edited. Write `exer1` and call in the next file in the buffer, `exer2`.

Write `exer2` to a file called `junk`.

Quit `vi`.

6-3. Try out the command:

```
vi exer*<CR>
```

What happens? Try to quit all the files as quickly as possible.

6-4. Look at `exer4` in read-only mode.

Scroll forward.

Scroll down.

Scroll backward.

Scroll up.

Quit and return to the shell.

Answers To Exercises

There is often more than one way to perform a task in vi. Any method that works is correct. The following are suggested ways of doing the exercises.

Exercise 1

1-1. Ask your system administrator for your terminal's system name. Type:

```
TERM=terminal_name<CR>
export TERM<CR>
tput init<CR>
```

1-2. Enter the vi command for a file called exer1:

```
vi exer1<CR>
```

Then use the append command (a) to enter the following text in your file:

```
This is an exercise!<CR>
Up, down,<CR>
left, right,<CR>
build your terminal's<CR>
muscles bit by bit<ESC>
~
~
```

1-3. Use the k and h commands.

1-4. Use the x command.

1-5. Use the j and l commands.

1-6. Use the append command (a) to enter the following text:

```
<CR>
and byte by byte<ESC>
```

1-7. Type:

```
ZZ
```

1-8. Type:

```
vi exer1<CR>
```

Notice the system response:

```
"exer1" 6 lines, 100 characters
```

Exercise 2

2-1. Type:

```
vi exer2<CR>
a
1<CR>
2<CR>
3<CR>
   .
   .
   .
48<CR>
49<CR>
50<ESC>
```

2-2. Type:

```
<^f>
<^b>
<^u>
<^d>
```

Notice the line numbers as the screen changes.

2-3. Type:

```
G
$
a
```

```
<CR>
123456789 123456789<ESC>
7h
3l
```

Typing 7h puts the cursor on the 2 in the second set of numbers. Typing 3l puts the cursor on the 5 in the second set of numbers.

2-4. $ = end of line
0 = first character in the line

2-5. Type:

```
^
w
b
e
```

2-6. Type:

```
1G
M
L
H
```

2-7. Type:

```
/8<CR>
n
/48<CR>
```

Exercise 3

3-1. Type:

```
vi exer3<CR>
```

3-2. Type:

```
a
Append text<CR>
Insert text<CR>
a computer's<CR>
job is boring.<ESC>
```

3-3. Type:

```
o
financial statement and<ESC>
```

3-4. Type:

```
3G
iDelete text<CR><ESC>
```

The text in your file now reads:

```
Append text
Insert text
Delete text
a computer's
financial statement and
job is boring.
```

3-5. The current line is a `computer's`. To create a line of text below that line, use the o command.

3-6. The current line is `byte of the budget`.
`G` puts you on the bottom line.
`A` lets you begin appending at the end of the line.
<CR> creates the new line.
Add the sentence: `But, it is an exciting machine.`
<ESC> leaves input mode.

3-7. Type:

```
1G
/text
i
some<space bar><ESC>
```

3-8. `ZZ` writes the buffer to `exer3` and returns you to the shell.

Exercise 4

4-1. Type:

```
vi exer4<CR>
a
When in the course of human events<CR>
there are many repetitive, boring<CR>
chores, then one ought to get a<CR>
robot to perform those chores.<ESC>
```

4-2. Type:

```
2G
A
, tedious, and unsavory<^w><ESC>
```

Press `Fb` to get to the `b` of `boring`. Then type: `dw`. (You can also use `6x`.)

4-3. You are at the second line. Type:

```
2j
I congenial and computerized <ESC>
dd
```

To delete the line and leave it blank, type in:

u (to undo the dd)
0 (zero moves the cursor to the beginning of the line)
D

```
d1G
```

4-4. Write and quit `vi`.

```
ZZ
```

Remove the file.

```
rm exer4<CR>
```

Exercise 5

5-1. Type:

```
vi exer2<CR>
8G
cc
END OF FILE<ESC>
```

5-2. Type:

```
1G
8"zyy
G
"zp
```

5-3. Type:

```
8G
cc
8 is great<ESC>
```

5-4. Type:

```
G
2w
cw
EXERCISE<ESC>
2b
cw
TO<ESC>
```

Exercise 6

6-1. Type:

```
vi exer6<CR>
```

a (append several lines of text)

```
<ESC>
```

Turn off the terminal.

Turn on the terminal.
Log in on your UNIX system. Type:

```
vi -r exer6<CR>
:wq<CR>
```

6-2. Type:

```
vi exer1 exer2<CR>
:w<CR>
:n<CR>

:w junk<CR>
ZZ
```

6-3. Type:

```
vi exer*<CR>
```

(Response:)

`8 files to edit` (`vi` calls all files with names that begin with `exer`.)

```
:q!
```

6-4. Type:

```
view exer4<CR>
<^f>
<^d>
<^b>
<^u>
:q<CR>
```

8 LP Print Service Tutorial

Introduction

The LP print service is a set of UNIX system programs that help you print files on paper. The name "LP" stands for "line printer," the type of printing device for which the print service was designed originally. Now, however, because the print service can accommodate many types of printing devices, the name "LP" is more historical than descriptive.

The simplest way to use this print service is by running the `lp` command and specifying the name of the file you want to print. The `lp` command routes a job request to a destination (such as a line printer or a laser printer) where it is placed in a queue to await printing. The destination may be a printer or a class of printers. If you don't specify a destination, the request is routed to the default destination.

When you enter such a command line, the system responds with a message that (a) confirms the name of the printer doing the job, (b) assigns an ID number to your print request, and (c) acknowledges the number of files you've asked to have printed.

```
$ lp filename
request id is laser-9885 (1 file)
```

The system response shows that your job will be printed on a printer named "laser" (the default printer for your system) and consists of one file. The string (set of characters) `laser-9885` is called a "request-ID"; use it to refer to a job when you are checking its status.

If you print a file with this simple command, you don't need to make decisions about issues such as the size of the paper; you can assume that when your system administrator set up the print service he or she chose default values for specifications such as paper size. (If you are the administrator of the print service for your computer, see the "LP Print Service Administration" chapter in the *System Administrator's Guide.*) You are not limited to the use of these default values, however. The following section explains how you can customize your print job.

Providing Your Own Print Specifications

The LP print service allows you to provide your own specifications for many aspects of a print job.

- Do you want your file to be printed by a particular printer or a particular type of printer?
  (Default: assigned by the print service administrator)
- Do you want to print your file on plain paper (the stock selected by the administrator)? Or do you want to use pre-printed forms, such as invoices or invitations?
  (Default: plain paper)
- Do you want a particular font?
  (Default: assigned by the print service administrator)
- Do you want pages of a particular size?
  (Default: assigned by the print service administrator)
- Do you want to increase or decrease the number of lines of text that appear in each inch on the page?
  (Default: assigned by the print service administrator)
- Do you want a "banner page" to be printed along with your file?
  (Default: a banner page is printed)
- If you're printing more than one file, do you want them to be printed as one job (so that there are no page breaks to mark separate files) or do you want them to be printed in discrete segments, so that each file begins on a new page?
  (Default: files are printed separately)
- Do you want more than one copy?
  (Default: one copy is printed)

If you specify only a file name when you run the `lp` command (as discussed above), you do not need to answer any of these questions; your administrator will have answered them when setting up your print service. If you want "non-default" specifications for your job, however, you will have to provide them on the command line.

There are several options you can include on your command line that will let you provide your own job specifications. To understand these options, a brief look at the main components of a print job will help you.

Components of the LP Printing Process

Printing a document with the `lp` command requires the interaction of five key components: (1) your electronic file, (2) the `lp` program, (3) any filters your administrator has installed (and you have requested), (4) any character sets (CS) or print wheels your administrator has installed (and you have requested), and (5) the paper on which your file is printed. The role of each component in the printing process is summarized in Figure 8-1.

Figure 8-1: Main Components of a Print Job

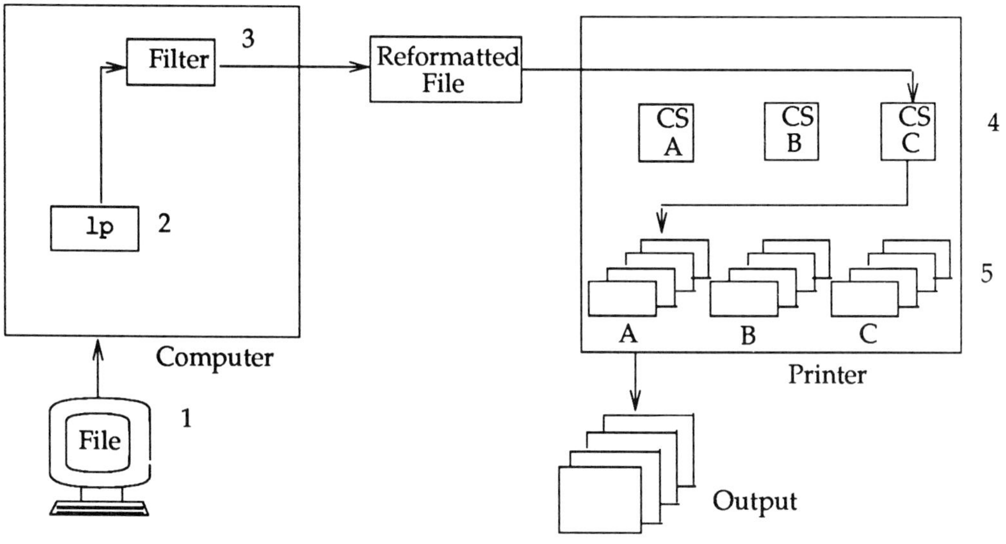

In the example shown in Figure 8-1, the person printing the file has selected type C character set and type A forms. Both of these selections are made when you request a print job.

About This Chapter

This chapter describes three functions you may do while printing files:

- enabling and disabling a printer
- controlling the appearance of the finished document by providing print specifications such as fonts and the page size
- controlling the process of printing by selecting a printer, monitoring the printing process through messages and status reports, and, when necessary, changing and canceling requests.

Controlling the Printing Process

The LP print service makes it possible for you to monitor and control the printing process by allowing you to do the following:

- Specify a printer for your job
- Identify high priority jobs that need to be "pushed to the front" of the job queue
- Request status reports about printers, print service resources (such as forms and character sets), and jobs in progress
- Change the specifications of a job request already submitted
- Cancel a job in progress

This section explains how to do these tasks.

Selecting a Print Destination

The term "print destination" refers to any device that your system administrator has defined to be a printer or a class of printers. A class is a set of printers grouped together by an administrator for reasons of convenience. For example, one administrator might group all printers of a similar type (such as laser printers or line printers) together into a class. Another administrator might assign all the printers on the second floor of a building to the same class. A class can be defined in any way that is convenient for the administrator and/or the users of a print service; the LP print service does not require a printer to meet any prerequisites before it is assigned to a class. In this sense, a class is an arbitrary grouping.

The `-d` *dest* (short for destination) option on the command line causes your file to be printed at the destination specified in the *dest* argument, as long as a printer is available and capable of meeting your specifications for the job. In the following example, a request is made to have a file called `memo` printed on printer3.

```
$ lp -d printer3 memo RETURN
```

Using a Remote Printer

The LP print service allows computers connected through a network to share printing tasks. If the printer you choose is connected to a remote computer, there may be some delays in having files printed, and in receiving responses to queries about job and printer status from a remote machine. Otherwise, however, the location of a printer to which you are sending print requests and related commands should not be obvious to you: follow the same procedures every time you use the print service, regardless of whether the printer being used is local or remote.

Controlling Priorities in the Job Queue

As you and other users send requests for print jobs to the printers on your system, your requests are arranged in a queue that determines the order of printing. Highest priority is given to requests that have been assigned level 0 priority; lowest priority to requests with a level of 39. Whether your job is assigned high or low priority depends on several factors.

First, the default value for job priority on your system is 20, unless your system administrator has defined it otherwise. Every job you submit to a printer will be given this medium-level priority. If your administrator has redefined the default priority level so that it is now, for example, 10, all jobs that you send to the printer will be given this higher priority.

You can change this priority level, however, by requesting a level other than the default; to do so, use the `-q` option to the `lp` command. For example, if you need a memo printed immediately, you can send it to the front of the queue by assigning it the highest priority: 0.

```
$ lp -d printer3 -q 0 urgent.memo RETURN
```

Note that the system administrator can limit the priority level that you can use. If your administrator has limited the priority level available to you and you request a priority higher than that, the priority level will remain, by default, at the level set by the administrator. Check with your system administrator to find out what the default priority level is and whether there is a limit on the priority level you can request.

Requesting Messages from the Print Service

The LP print service does not automatically notify you when your job has been printed. To make sure you will be notified, list the `-w` option on the `lp` command line, as follows:

`$ lp -d printer3 -w` *filename* **RETURN**

The print service will display a message on your terminal screen to let you know when your files have been printed. If you are not logged in when the message is ready to be sent, the message will be sent to you via electronic mail, instead.

If you want to be notified through electronic mail that your files have been printed, include the `-m` option after the `lp` command, as follows:

`$ lp -d printer3 -m` *filename* **RETURN**

Requesting Status Reports on Printers

At some time after issuing a request for a print job, you may want to find out whether it is proceeding properly or if problems have arisen. You can check the status of all print requests by executing the `lpstat` command. When issued alone (without any options), this command will tell you the status of all requests you have made to the LP print service, as shown in the following example:

```
$ lpstat
dqp10_1-25        pr2cms   1942    July 19 13:09
dqp10_1-26        pr2cms   3893    July 19 13:15
dqp10_1-27        pr2cms    942    July 19 14:09
```

If you do not want to know about all print requests, you can specify a subset of requests by listing the request ID numbers for those jobs on the command line. (Whenever a print request is issued, a request ID number for it is displayed on the screen.)

`$ lpstat laser-6885 printer-227` **RETURN**

In this example, you are asking for the status of two print requests with the ID numbers `laser-6885` and `printer-227`.

In addition, by using various options, you can request the following types of information from `lpstat`:

- the status of local printers
- a list of available pre-printed forms
- a list of available character sets and print wheels
- a list of available printers

The rest of this section contains instructions for getting these types of information by issuing the options to `lpstat`.

What is the Status of the Printers?

First, if you do not already know them, you may want to find out the names of the printers in your system. Which printers are available to you depends on your UNIX system facility. Ask your system administrator for the names of available printers, or type the following command line:

```
$ lpstat -p all RETURN
```

A list of printers will be displayed, showing which printers are enabled and which are disabled, as follows:

```
printer printer1 enabled since Aug 22 16:00. available.
printer printer1 disabled since Aug 26 22:00. available.
```

If you already have the names of the printers on your system, you can get a status report on one or more of them by listing the appropriate names in place of the argument `all` in the preceding example.

```
$ lpstat -p printer1,printer3 RETURN
```

More detailed status reports can be obtained by adding the `-l` option to the `lpstat` command line, as follows:

```
$ lpstat -p printer1,printer3 -l RETURN
```

For each printer you have specified, a status report will be displayed. Each report will include the following: the printer type, the types of forms allowed and mounted on it, acceptable content types, the names of users allowed to use the printer, the default dimensions for page size and character pitch, and so on.

The system administrator may restrict access to certain printers. If you are not allowed access to a printer for this reason, the phrase `not available` will appear.

Which Forms are Available?

To find out which pre-printed forms are available on your system, issue the `lpstat` command with the `-f` option and the argument `all`, as follows:

```
$ lpstat -f all [RETURN]
```

The command prints a list of all the forms that your system recognizes and can handle. Forms that are mounted on printers in your system are identified as follows:

```
form payroll_check is available to you, mounted on printer4
```

Forms that are recognized and can be handled by your system but that are not mounted on printers are listed as follows:

```
form payroll_check is available to you
```

The system administrator may restrict access to certain forms. If you are not allowed access to a form for this reason, the phrase `is not available to you` will appear.

If you want to know whether specific forms are available on your system, list them after the `-f` option in place of the argument `all`, as in this example:

```
$ lpstat -f laser2,laser2 [RETURN]
```

If you want detailed information about any or all of the available forms, use the `-l` option with `lpstat -f`, as follows:

```
$ lpstat -f all -l [RETURN]
```

A description of each form, including page length, page width, number of pages, ribbon color, and so on, will be displayed.

Which Character Sets or Print Wheels are Available?

First, you may want to find out which character sets and/or print wheels are available on your LP print service. Issue the `lpstat` command with the `-S` option and the argument `all`, as follows:

```
$ lpstat -S all [RETURN]
```

A list of all character sets and print wheels that can be used on printers in your system will be displayed. If you want to know whether one or more specific character sets or print wheels are available, list them on the command line in place of the argument `all`.

```
$ lpstat -S "charset_1 wheel_3" RETURN
```

The double quotes that appear around the two arguments (`charset_1` and `wheel_3`) to the `-S` option are necessary because these arguments are separated by a space. (If the arguments are separated by commas, double quotes are not required.)

To obtain detailed output from the `lpstat` command, add the `-l` option to the command line. The output will include the following information about each item specified: a list of the printers on which each character set or print-wheel is available, whether the character set or print-wheel is mounted, and what built-in character set it maps.

Changing a Print Request

Suppose you have just noticed that when submitting a request to the print service a little while ago, you forgot to request a longer than usual page length for the job, as you had originally planned to do. Don't worry; it may not be too late to change your request! As long as the job has not actually been printed, you may submit changes to your original request. Simply execute the `lp` command again, this time including the `-i` option, followed by the request-ID assigned to your request. The `-i` option signals your intent to change the previous request to the printer.

For example, suppose your original request was for a page length of 50, a width of 70, no banner, and 3 copies:

```
$ lp -d printer2-23 -o "length=50,width=70,nobanner"\
-n 3 july.report
 request id is printer2-23
```

(The third line in the above example is the response from the system to your command line.) When you later remembered to request a longer page, you reissued the command as follows:

```
$ lp -i printer2-23 -o "length=60,width=70,\
nobanner" RETURN
```

Notice that although there were two options in the original command line (-o and -n), only one of them (-o) is included in the change request. A change request should specify only those options from the original command line that you want to change.

However, as this example also shows, when changing the values in a -o option, you must not only request additional arguments or request different arguments in place of existing ones, you must also repeat those arguments that you want to preserve. (This requirement also applies to the -y option.) Look again at the command lines in the preceding example. Notice that three arguments are given for the -o option: `length`, `width`, and `nobanner`. Although only one argument to -o is being changed (from `"length=50"` to `"length=60"`), all three arguments are listed in the change request. Repeating the `width` and `nobanner` arguments is necessary; they are not otherwise preserved from the original command line.

Canceling a Request: the `cancel` Command

You can cancel a print request that has already been submitted to the print service as long as you are the person who submitted the print request, and you request the cancellation on the same system on which you submitted the print request. To stop a request, run the `cancel` command.

You can execute the `cancel` command with either of two types of arguments: request IDs or printer names. To cancel one print request, run `cancel` *request_ID*. To cancel only the job that is currently printing, run `cancel` *printer_name*; no other requests in the queue for the named printer will be canceled. Arguments of both types may be intermixed.

To cancel a request to a printer, type the command `cancel` and specify a request ID. For example, to cancel the printing of the file `letters` (request ID `laser-6885`), type:

```
$ cancel laser-6885 (RETURN)
```

If you want to cancel more than one print request include the -u option after the `cancel` command. To cancel all requests that you submitted to a particular printer, type the following:

`cancel -u` *login_ID printer*

To cancel all requests that you submitted to all printers, type the following:

```
cancel -u login_ID all
```

Once the `cancel` command has been run, the specified job is removed from the queue.

You can invoke this command anytime before a print job has been completed.

Enabling and Disabling a Printer

The `enable` and `disable` commands are not always available to users. Because enabling and disabling printers is an administrative function, it is left to the discretion of the system administrator to decide who should have access to these commands.

Before a printer is able to start printing files requested through the `lp` command, it must be activated. You can activate a printer by issuing the `enable` command with one argument: one printer or a list of printers.

```
$ enable printer1 printer2 printer3 RETURN
```

You can verify that you have enabled a printer by requesting a status report for it (see "Requesting Status Reports on Printers" later in this chapter).

There may be times when you want a printer to stop printing jobs. For example, hardware malfunctions, paper jams, running out of paper, and shutdowns at the end of the day are all situations that may require stopping the printer. To stop printing, deactivate the printer by issuing the `disable` command.

```
$ disable printer1 RETURN
```

The printer will stop printing the current job and save it to complete later (when the printer has been enabled again).

There are other ways to have the current job handled, however. You may have the current job completed immediately, before the printer is disabled, by using the `-W` option.

On the other hand, you may not care whether or not it is completed at all. For example, if the output being produced is full of printing errors (such as parts of the text being illegible because of a lack of toner in the printer), you'll have to start the job over from the beginning anyway, once you have resolved the problem. In cases such as this, you'll want to disable the printer and cancel the job at the same time. To do so, specify the -c option; the job currently being printed will be thrown out as the printer is disabled. The -W and -c options are mutually exclusive.

The -c and -W options will not work for jobs being sent to a printer on a remote system. This is because the `enable` and `disable` commands do not actually activate or deactivate printers on remote systems; instead, they activate or deactivate the transfer of files to a remote system. As a result, the -c and -W options are ignored when requested with the `disable` command for a remote printer.

Finally, when you disable a printer, it is a good idea to record the reason for your action so that other users may understand why a particular printer is unavailable. To record your reason, add the -r option, followed by a reason, to the command line. Be sure to enclose the words that make up your reason in double quotes, so that they will be treated as a single argument.

```
$ disable -r "disabling for reconfiguration"\
printer4 RETURN
```

The reason you provide will be displayed by the `lpstat` command when a user requests a status report on that printer. For example, if you specify `paper jam` as the reason when you disable printer pdq10, a user who later runs `lpstat` to determine the status of pdq10 will receive the response shown below:

```
$ lpstat -p pdq10
printer pdq10 disabled since July 18 10:15-
     paper jam
$
```

If you disable a printer without supplying a reason, subsequent output from the `disable` command will include the message `unknown reason`.

Customizing Printed Output With the lp Command

The LP print service allows you to determine the appearance of your printed output by using any of numerous options to the `lp` command. This section describes those parameters for which you can specify values:

- content type
- page size and pitch settings
- whether to have breaks between multiple files
- whether to have a "banner" page printed with your output
- whether to have your text printed on plain paper or on pre-printed forms (such as invoices or invitations)
- a non-standard character set or print wheel
- miscellaneous job specifications (such as one-sided or two-sided printing) known as "special modes"
- number of copies

Selecting the Content Type

To print a file, a printer must be capable of correctly interpreting the file's contents. Different printers have different capabilities in this sense; not every printer is able to print every type of content. You can make sure that the LP print service assigns your request to a printer capable of printing it by using the `-T` option to the `lp` command.

The `-T` option allows you to specify the format of the content of the file to be printed. For example, suppose you want to print a file containing your monthly report for July (`july.report`). The contents of this file are arranged in a 455 type format, which means that they can be interpreted by an AT&T Model 455 printer. You know that your system has several 455 printers but you don't know the names of any of them. The `-T` option lets you request a Model 455 printer without specifying one by name, as follows:

```
$ lp -T 455 -d any july.report RETURN
```

The -T option instructs the printer service to select any printer that can print a file with contents of type 455. If you want a particular printer to be used—even if it is the default printer—use the -d option to identify the printer.

What happens if there are no Model 455 printers? The answer depends on whether any filters have been defined for your system. (Your system administrator can tell you whether any filters are available.) A filter is a program that converts data from one format to another; in this case, from the format in which it was typed in the file to a format that can be "read" by a printer. If there are no printers that can handle the content type of your file, and some filters have been defined for your system, your print request will be sent to a filter. (If necessary, your file will be sent to multiple filters. For example, your file could be sent through a `troff` filter, a `postscript` filter, a `page`selection filter, and a filter for downloading fonts, all of which perform different operations on your file.) The contents of the file will be converted, by the filter, to a content type that the printer can handle. If, however, there is no printer that can handle the content type of your file, and there is no filter that will convert the file, your print request will be rejected.

Filters make it possible to have files printed by a variety of printers. There may be situations, however, in which the content type is a critical factor of the job. In such a case you do not want to have a file printed unless it can be printed with the original content type. If your system supports filters and you do not want your print request to be sent to one, specify the -r option after the -T option to the lp command, as follows:

```
$ lp -T 455 -r july.report (RETURN)
```

Note that with the -r option, if your print request cannot be handled by any printer on your system (because of content type), your print request will be rejected.

Filters are installed and maintained on your LP print service by your system administrator. Ask your administrator for a list of content types available to your system.

Defining the Page Size and Pitch Settings

Page size consists of two measurements: length and width. Pitch settings are specifications for the number of lines per inch (vertical measurement) and the number of characters per inch (horizontal measurement). When a file is printed, these dimensions may be determined in one of the following four ways:

- by the printer's default dimensions
- by the default dimensions established by your system administrator
- by the dimensions provided with a particular form that you have selected
- by your specification for that particular job

To request your own specification for a print job, use the `-o` option to `lp`, and specify the desired sizes in "scaled decimal numbers."

The term "scaled-decimal-number" refers to a non-negative number used to show a unit of size. (The type of unit is shown by a "trailing" letter attached to the number.) Three types of scaled decimal numbers are discussed for the LP print service: numbers that show sizes in centimeters (marked with a trailing "c"), numbers that show sizes in inches (marked with a trailing "i"), and numbers that show sizes in units appropriate to use (without a trailing letter), such as lines, columns, lines per inch, or characters per inch.

The following command line shows how to request a print job with your own specifications for page size and pitch settings. (Specifications are shown in *sdn* or scaled decimal numbers.)

```
$ lp -d any -o "length=sdn width=sdn lpi=sdn\
cpi=sdn" filename (RETURN)
```

Your job will be printed according to the default dimensions for the type of printer you are using under either of two circumstances: (1) if you do not specify page dimensions for your print request; or (2) if you do not use a printer for which specific dimensions have been defined by an administrator. These default dimensions are listed in a database called Terminfo; your system administrator is responsible for maintaining this database and can give you details about it.

For example, if you are using an AT&T Model 455 printer, the default dimensions for your printer will be as follows:

Page length: 66 lines
Page width: 132 columns
Line pitch: 6 lines per inch
Character pitch: 12 characters per inch

If, however, you are using an AT&T Model 470 printer, the default dimensions will be slightly different:

Page length: 66 lines
Page width: 80 columns
Line pitch: 6 lines per inch
Character pitch: 10 characters per inch

Canceling Breaks Between Files

Your print request may consist of more than one file. By default, the LP print service will assume that you want each file to be printed separately. If you want the set of files to be printed continuously, without having each file begin on a new page, specify the -o option, as follows:

`$ lp -d any -o nofilebreak` *filenames* [RETURN]

Canceling the Banner Page

The LP print service automatically prints a title page (known here as a "banner page") with every job printed. If you do not want a banner page printed with your job, include the -o option, as follows:

`$ lp -d any -o nobanner` *filename* [RETURN]

Your system administrator may disallow this option for particular printers. If your administrator has done so, any request you make for such a printer will be printed with a banner page.

Using Pre-Printed Forms

Many companies frequently need to issue specialized documents, such as payroll checks and invoices. The LP print service allows you to print your files on pre-printed forms that your administrator loads on your printer. To find out which, if any, special forms are available on your printer, ask your system administrator. If you want to use a particular form, and you know it's available, include the `-f` option on the `lp` command line, followed by the name of the form. For example, say you want to have a file called `april.payroll` printed on a type of form called `paycheck` by a printer called "printer4." Enter the following:

`$ lp -d printer4 -f paycheck april.payroll` (RETURN)

If the printer you have requested is not capable of handling this form, your request will be rejected. To make sure your request is accepted by any printer on which the desired form can be mounted, include the `-d` option, followed by the argument `any`, as shown in the following command line:

`$ lp -d any -f` *form_name filename* (RETURN)

The LP print service will then send your request to any printer that is capable of handling the type of form required for your job. If your LP print service contains both local and remote printers, the command will try to send your job to a local printer before sending it to a remote printer.

Using a Character Set or Print Wheel

The `lp` command allows you to select a character set or print wheel with which your job will be printed. To find out which character sets and print wheels are available on your system, run the command `lpstat -S`.

To request a character set or print wheel for your print job, include the `-S` option on the `lp` command line, as follows:

`$ lp -d any -S` *character_set filename* (RETURN)

If you have no preference, and if you haven't chosen a form that requires a particular character set or print wheel, you can skip this option.

Special Printing Modes

The final appearance of the document you are printing depends not only on its content, but also on certain other features that affect the composition of the page. For example, you might want to have an unusual font used in your document. The number of special printing modes available to you depends on the available printer(s).

To request special printing modes for your print job, include the -y option on the command line, as follows:

`$ lp -d any -y` *list_of_modes filename* (RETURN)

Each item in the list of modes must be a one-word name consisting of any combination of letters and numbers.

The printer will accept your request if all the modes you requested in the list are known by the "filter" being used as an interface between your print request and the printer. To find out which filters are available on your system, and which -y options are allowed, check with your system administrator.

Requesting Multiple Copies

If you want to have more than one copy made, you can request a multiple printing by issuing the -n ("number") option. For example, to have four copies made, enter a command line such as the following:

`$ lp -d any -n 4` *filename* (RETURN)

When you do not use this option, only one copy is made by default.

Using PostScript Printers

PostScript is a general purpose programming language, like C or Pascal. In addition to providing the usual features of a language, however, PostScript allows you to specify the appearance of both text and graphics on a page in ways that are more sophisticated than those allowed by other printers. For example, you can create geometric figures and place them anywhere on a page in any size, arranged at any angle. For your text, you can use a variety of fonts in any position, size, or orientation on a page. Graphics and text can be combined easily. In addition, PostScript files can be printed on either low-resolution or high-resolution printers. In short, PostScript printers allow you to produce more varied and sophisticated looking documents than other printers.

PostScript files can be printed only on PostScript printers. These printers are actually special purpose computers capable of interpreting PostScript language files. Unless special provisions have been made by a printer manufacturer, files submitted to a PostScript printer must be written in the PostScript language. It is not necessary for you to write files in PostScript, however.

Many popular software packages, including word-processing, spreadsheet, desktop publishing, and computer-aided design packages, support PostScript. If your computer runs one of these packages, you need only create a file in the usual way; the software will translate it into PostScript. To find out whether your software supports PostScript, ask your system administrator.

Once the PostScript printers and filters have been installed, LP manages PostScript files like any others. To request that a PostScript file be printed on a PostScript printer, simply specify the appropriate printer on the command line, and identify the file content type, as follows:

`lp -d`*psprinter* `-Tpostscript` *psfile*

As long as the printer (*psprinter*) has been defined with the LP print service as a PostScript printer, the print service will schedule your request and transmit it to the printer.

Support of Non-PostScript Print Requests

The LP print service offers a "translation service": you can create a file in the format you usually use, and the print service will translate it into PostScript language before sending it to a PostScript printer. The print service does this by passing your file through a filter that translates from the "content type" (the formatting language) used in your file to PostScript. Having these filters available means you can use PostScript printers while continuing to write files with your usual formats.

Because each content type requires a separate filter, and UNIX system users create files with many different content types, the print service has many filters for translating files to PostScript. Therefore, if you want to have a file translated, you must request a translation and specify the content type of your file when you submit your print request (that is, when you issue the `lp` command). The following is a list of content types that require translation before they can be handled by a PostScript printer.

`troff`	Print the output from `troff`.
`simple`	Print an ASCII ("simple") text file.
`dmd`	Print the contents of a bit-mapped display from a terminal such as an AT&T 630.
`tek4014`	Print files formatted for a Tektronix 4014 device.
`daisy`	Print files intended for a Diablo 630 ("daisy-wheel") printer.
`plot`	Print plot-formatted files

For example, to convert a file containing ASCII to PostScript code, the filter takes that text and writes a program around it, specifying printing parameters such as fonts and the layout of the text on a page.

The filters that do these translations are invoked automatically by LP when a user specifies one of the content-types listed above for a print request with the `-T` option. For example,

```
lp -dpsprinter -Tsimple report2
```

automatically converts the ASCII file `report2` (a file with an ASCII or "simple" format) to PostScript (as long as the destination printer `psprinter` has been defined to the system as a PostScript printer). The default content-type is `simple`.

Additional PostScript Capabilities Provided by Filters

The filters previously described also take advantage of PostScript capabilities to provide additional printing flexibility. Most of these features may be accessed through the "mode option" (invoked by the `-y` option) to the `lp` command. These filters allow you to use several unusual options for your print jobs. The following list describes these options and shows the option you should include on the `lp` command line for each one.

Content Type	Type of Print Request
`-yreverse`	Reverse the order in which pages are printed.
`-ylandscape`	Change the orientation of a logical page from portrait to landscape.
`-yx=x`*number*`,y=y`*number*	Change the default position of a logical page on a physical page by moving the origin.
`-ygroup=`*number*	Group multiple logical pages on a single physical page.
`-ymagnify=`*number*	Increase or decrease the size of the logical page.
`-P`*number*	Select, by page numbers, a subset of a document to be printed.
`-n`*number*	Print multiple copies of a document.

NOTE

If these filters are to be used with an application that creates PostScript output, make sure that the application conforms to the PostScript file structuring comments. In particular, the beginning of each PostScript page must be marked by the comment

`%%Page:label` *ordinal*

where *ordinal* is a positive integer that specifies the position of the page in the sequence of pages in the document.

For example, say you have a file called `report2` that has a content type `simple` (meaning that the content of this file is in ASCII format). You want to print six pages of this file (pages 4-9) with two logical pages on each physical page. Because one of the printers on your system (psprinter) is a PostScript printer, you can do this, by entering the following command:

```
lp -dpsprinter -Tsimple -P4-9 -ygroup=2 myfile
```

The filter that groups these logical pages tries to position the pages on the physical page to maximize space utilization. Thus, the pages are printed side by side, so that the physical page appears in landscape mode. Landscape mode, which controls the orientation of the logical page rather than the physical page, causes the logical pages to be positioned one on top of the other.

In addition, the LP print service offers a special filter that can print a gray-scale representation of a matrix. (A gray-scale representation of matrix is a picture in which each cell is colored one of seven shades of gray to show the value of the cell. Darker shades correspond to larger values.) To print a gray-scale representation, specify `matrix` as the content type of your source file by giving the `-T` option (`-Tmatrix`).

The dimension of the matrix is assumed to be the square root of the number of elements in the matrix unless you specify the number of rows and columns in it by using the *-ydimen=nrowsxncols* option. The cell values represented by each level of gray may be specified by *-yinterval=slash-separated list.* The default list is -1/0/1. This separates the elements of the matrix into seven regions: $x<-1$, $x=-1$, $-1<x<0$, $x=0$, $0<x<1$, $x=1$, $1<x$. The list may contain a maximum of three numbers.

How to Use PostScript Fonts

One of the advantages of PostScript is that it allows you to manage fonts. Fonts are stored in outline form, either on a printer or on a computer that communicates with a printer. When a document is printed, the PostScript interpreter generates each character as needed (in the appropriate size) from the outline description of it. If a font required for a document is not stored on the printer being used, it must be transmitted to that printer before the document can be printed. This transmission process is called "downloading fonts."

Fonts are stored and accessed in several ways.

- Fonts may be stored on a printer. The fonts may reside permanently on the printer's disk, or they may be loaded by the administrator into the printer's memory each time the printer is turned on. Ask your printer service administrator for a list of fonts available on your printers.
- Fonts may be stored in your own directory, so they're available for your print requests. When you issue a print request that requires a font from your own directory, the font will be transmitted to the printer, along with the source file, as part of your request. This arrangement is preferable for fonts that are not used frequently. Generally, the application program that creates the PostScript file will prepend the font to your PostScript file before delivering it to the print service.

- Fonts may be stored in a public directory on a system shared by many users. These fonts are described as "host-resident." To access these fonts, a user requests fonts to be printed through an application program that creates a PostScript document. When the application program creates a PostScript document file, it must include requests for any desired fonts. This method is useful when the number of fonts is too large to store on the printer.

The LP print service allows you to manage fonts with any of these methods.

The LP print service provides a special download filter to manage fonts using the last method described above. The print service manages this process for you automatically.

Downloading Host-Resident Fonts

The filter that downloads host-resident fonts performs the following tasks:

- It searches the PostScript document to determine which fonts have been requested. Font requests appear in the header comments in the format of PostScript structuring comments:

  `%%DocumentFonts:` *font1 font2* . . .

- It searches the list of fonts resident on the destination printer to see if the requested font must be downloaded. If the font is not resident on that printer, the filter searches the directory containing host-resident fonts to see if the requested font is available. If it is, the filter takes the file for that font and prepends it to the file to be printed.

The download filter relies on the PostScript structuring comments to determine which fonts must be downloaded. If you plan to use this downloading option, make sure the font requests in your application program conform to the PostScript structuring conventions.

Summary of the LP Print Service Commands

Figure 8-2: Print Commands and their Functions

Command	Function
`lp`	Requests a paper copy of a file from a printer
`cancel`	Cancels a request for a paper copy of a file
`lpstat`	Displays information on the screen about the current status of the LP print service
`enable`	Activates the printer(s) specified so jobs that are requested through the `lp` command can be printed
`disable`	Deactivates the printer(s) specified so jobs that are requested through the `lp` command can no longer be printed

Figures 8-3 through 8-7 summarize the syntax and capabilities of each of these commands.

Figure 8-3: Summary of the `lp` Command

	Command Recap `lp` – request paper copy of a file from a printer	
command	*options*	*arguments*
`lp`	*(as listed)*	*file(s)*

Description: The `lp` command requests that specified files be printed by a printer, thus providing paper copies of the contents.

Options:

`-d` *dest*	Allows you to choose *dest* as the printer or class of printers to produce the paper copy. You do not have to use this option if the administrator has set a default destination or if you have set the LPDEST environment variable.
`-y` *mode*	Requests special printing modes, such as portrait or landscape. (This option requires a special filter; check with your system administrator to find out whether your system has one.)
`-o` *option*	Defines page dimensions: length and width, number of lines per inch, and number of characters per inch. (`-o` performs other tasks, too; see `lp`(1) in the *User's Reference Manual.*)
`-P` *pages*	Specifies subset of pages to be printed. (This option requires a special filter; check with your system administrator to find out whether your system has an appropriate filter.)
`-n` *copies*	Specifies number of copies to be made.
`-f` *form*	Specifies pre-printed form on which files are to be printed.
`-S` *char_set*	Specifies character set or print wheel to be used.
`-T` *type*	Specifies content type of print request.

Figure 8-3: Summary of the `lp` Command (continued)

Command Recap		
	`lp` – request paper copy of a file from a printer	
command	*options*	*arguments*
`lp`	*(as listed)*	*file(s)*
	`-w`	Notifies you by screen message when print job is complete.
	`-m`	Notifies you by mail when print job is complete.
	`-i` *req_ID*	Allows you to change a print request already issued (but not yet printed).
	`-q` *level*	Allows you to specify a priority level for your job request.
Remarks:	You can cancel a request to the printer by typing `cancel` and the request ID given to you by the system when the request was acknowledged. Check with your system administrator for information on additional and/or different commands for printers that may be available at your location.	

Figure 8-4: Summary of the `lpstat` Command

Command Recap		
`lpstat` – display information about status of LP print service		
command	*options*	*arguments*
`lpstat`	(*as listed*)	*file(s)*

Description: The `lpstat` command reports the status of print requests, printers, and the LP request scheduler, and provides other information related to the status of the print service.

Options:

`-a` *list*	Reports whether print requests are being accepted by specified printers or classes of printers.
`-c` *list*	Displays, for each class in the list, members (printers) of the class.
`-d`	Shows the default destination for your LP print service.
`-f` *list* [`-l`]	Verifies that the forms named in *form-list* are recognized by the LP print service. The `-l` option lists the form descriptions.
`-o` *list* [`-l`]	Reports the status of print requests. *List* may include names of printers or printer classes, or request IDs.
`-p` *list* [`-D`] [`-l`]	Reports the status of printers named in *list*. The `-D` option adds a description of each printer, and `-l` requests a full description of each printer's configuration.
`-R`	Shows the rank of all print requests in the queue.
`-r`	Reports the status of the LP request scheduler.
`-s`	Prints a status summary of the whole LP print

Figure 8-4: Summary of the `lpstat` Command (continued)

Command Recap		
`lpstat` – display information about status of LP print service		
command	*options*	*arguments*
`lpstat`	(*as listed*)	*file(s)*
		service.
	`-S` *list* [`-l`]	Verifies that the character sets or print wheels specified in *list* are recognized by the LP print service. The `-l` option requests a list of printers that can handle each character set and print wheel.
	`-t`	Prints all status information.
	`-u` *list*	Reports status of users' print requests. *List* is a list of login names.
	`-v` *list*	Lists printers and the pathnames of the devices associated with them. *List* is a list of printer names.
Remarks:	In each case where *list* is specified, you have the choice of providing a list or specifying `all`. If you do not specify any options, the `-o` option is assumed.	

Figure 8-5: Summary of the `cancel` Command

Command Recap		
`cancel` – cancels printer requests made by `lp`		
command	*options*	*arguments*
`lp`	*(as listed)*	*file(s)*

Description: The `cancel` command cancels printer requests made by the `lp` command.

Options:

[*request-ID* ...] Allows you to cancel print requests you have issued, as specified by the ID numbers of those requests.

[*printers*] Allows you to cancel whatever print request you have submitted that is currently being printed on the printer specified.

Figure 8-6: Summary of the `enable` Command

Command Recap		
`enable` – activates any printers in an LP print service		
command	*options*	*arguments*
`enable`	*(as listed)*	*file(s)*
Description:	The `enable` command activates a printer that is part of an LP print service. Your system administrator may or may not authorize users on your system to execute this command.	
Options:	none	
Remarks:	Run `lpstat` to determine the status of printers.	

Figure 8-7: Summary of the `disable` Command

Command Recap

`disable` – deactivates any printers in an LP print service

command	*options*	*arguments*
`disable`	*(as listed)*	*file(s)*

Description: The `disable` command deactivates a printer that is part of an LP print service. Your system administrator may or may not authorize users on your system to execute this command.

Options:

`-c`	Cancels any requests that are currently printing on any of the designated printers. (This option cannot be used with the `-W` option.)
`-r` *reason*	Assigns a *reason* for the disabling of the printers. This *reason* applies to all printers mentioned up to the next `-r` option. This *reason* is reported by `lpstat`. If the `-r` option is not present, then a default reason will be used.
`-W`	Waits until the request currently being printed is finished before disabling the specified printer. (This option cannot be used with the `-c` option.)

9. SHELL TUTORIAL

9. SHELL TUTORIAL

9 Shell Tutorial

Introduction

This chapter shows you how the UNIX system shell can help you do routine tasks. For example, it tells you how to use the shell to manage your files, to manipulate file contents, and to group commands together in programs the shell can execute for you.

The chapter has two major sections. The first section, "Shell Command Language," covers in detail the use of the shell as a command interpreter. It tells you how to use shell commands and characters with special meanings to manage files, redirect standard input and output, and execute and terminate processes. The second section, "Shell Programming," details the use of the shell as a programming language. It tells you how to create, execute, and debug programs made up of commands, variables, and programming constructs like loops and case statements. Finally, it tells you how to modify your login environment.

The chapter offers many examples. To get the most benefit from this tutorial you should log into your UNIX system and recreate the examples as you read the text. As in the other examples in this guide, different typefaces (*italic* and `constant width`) are used to distinguish substitutable from literal input and output. For details see "Notation Conventions" in the "Preface" to this book.

In addition to the examples, exercises appear at the ends of both the "Shell Command Language" and "Shell Programming" sections. These exercises can help you better understand the topics discussed. The answers to the exercises are at the end of the chapter.

Your UNIX system might not have all commands referenced in this chapter. If you cannot access a command, check with your system administrator.

If you want an overview of how the shell functions as both command interpreter and programming language, see Chapters 1 and 4 before reading this chapter. Also, refer to Appendix F, "Summary of Shell Command Language".

Shell Command Language

This section introduces commands and, more importantly, some characters with special meanings that let you

- find and manipulate a group of files by using pattern matching
- run a command in the background or at a specified time
- run a group of commands sequentially
- redirect standard input and output from and to files and other commands
- terminate running programs

First the section covers the characters having special meanings to the shell, and then it discusses the commands and notations for carrying out the tasks listed above. For your convenience, Table 9-1 summarizes the characters that have special meanings discussed in this chapter.

Table 9-1: Characters with Special Meanings in the Shell Language

Character	Function
* ? [ ]	metacharacters (asterisk, question mark, and brackets) that provide a shortcut for specifying filenames by pattern matching
&	ampersand places commands in background mode, leaving your terminal free for other tasks
;	semicolon separates multiple commands on one command line
\	turns off the meaning of special characters such as *, ?, [ ], &, ;, >, <, and |.
'...'	single quotes turn off the delimiting meaning of a space and the special meaning of all special characters
"..."	double quotes turn off the delimiting meaning of a space and the special meaning of all special characters *except* $ and `
>	redirects output of a command into a file (replaces existing contents)
<	redirects input for a command to come from a file
>>	redirects output of a command to be added to the end of an existing file
|	creates a pipe of the output of one command to the input of another command
`...`	used in pairs, allows the grave accents allow the output of a command to be used directly as arguments on a command line
$	used with positional parameters and user-defined variables; also used as the default shell prompt symbol

Metacharacters

Metacharacters, a subset of the special characters, represent other characters. They are sometimes called wild cards, because they are like the joker that can be used for any card in card games. The metacharacters * (asterisk), ? (question mark), and [ ] (brackets) are discussed here.

These characters are used to match filenames or parts of filenames, thereby simplifying the task of specifying files or groups of files as command arguments. (The files whose names match the patterns formed from these metacharacters must already exist.) This is known as filename expansion. For example, you may want to refer to all filenames containing the letter "a", all filenames consisting of five letters, and so on.

The Metacharacter That Matches All Characters: the Asterisk (*)

The asterisk (*) matches any string of characters, including a null (empty) string. You can use the * to specify a full or partial filename. The * alone matches all the file and directory names in the current directory, except those starting with a .(dot). To see the effect of the *, try it as an argument to the echo(1) command. Type:

```
echo *<CR>
```

The echo command displays its arguments on your screen. Notice that the system response to echo * is a listing of all the filenames in your current directory.

Table 9-2 summarizes the syntax and capabilities of the echo command.

Table 9-2: Summary of the echo Command

Command echo write any arguments to the output		
command	*options*	*arguments*
echo	none	any character(s)
Description:	echo writes arguments, which are separated by blanks and ended with <CR>, to the output.	
Remarks:	In shell programming, echo is used to issue instructions, to redirect words or data into a file, and to pipe data into a command. All these uses are discussed later in this chapter.	

The * is a character that matches everything. For example, if you type `rm *` you will erase all the files in your current directory. Be very careful how you use the asterisk!

For another example, say you have written several reports and have named them `report`, `report1`, `report1a`, `report1b.01`, `report25`, and `report316`. By typing `report1*` you can refer to all files that are part of report1, collectively. To find out how many reports you have written, you can use the `ls` command to list all files that begin with the string "`report`", as shown in the following example.

```
$ ls report*<CR>
report
report1
report1a
report1b.01
report25
report316
$
```

The * matches any characters after the string "report", including no letters at all. Notice that * matches the files in numerical and alphabetical order. A quick and easy way to print the contents of your report files in order on your screen is by typing the following command:

```
pr report*<CR>
```

Now try another exercise. Suppose you have a current directory called appraisals that contains files called Andrew_Adams, Paul_Lang, Jane_Peters, and Fran_Smith, choose a character that all the filenames in your directory have in common, such as a lower case "a". Then request a listing of those files by referring to that character. For example, if you choose a lower case "a", type the following command line:

```
ls *a*<CR>
```

The system responds by printing the names of all the files in your current directory that contain a lower case "a".

The * can represent characters in any part of the filename. For example, if you know that several files have their first and last letters in common, you can request a list of them on that basis. If, for example, you had a directory containing files named FATE, FE, FADED_LINE, F123E, Fig3.4E, FIRE_LANE, FINE_LINE, FREE_ENTRY, and FAST_LANE, you could use this command to obtain a list of files starting with F and ending with E. For such a request, your command line might look like this:

```
ls F*E<CR>
```

The system response will be a list of filenames that begin with F, end with E, and are in the following order:

```
F123E
FADED_LINE
FAST_LANE
FATE
FE
FINE_LINE
FIRE_LANE
Fig3.4E
```

The order is determined by the collating sequences of the language being used, in this case, English: (1) numbers, (2) upper case letters, (3) lower case letters.

The * is even more powerful; it can help you find all files named memo in system directory when you use:

```
ls */memo
```

The Metacharacter That Matches One Character: the Question Mark (?)

The question mark (?) matches any single character of a filename except a leading dot or period. Let's suppose you have written several chapters in a book that has 12 chapters, and you want a list of those you have finished through Chapter 9. If your directory contains the following files:

Chapter 1,
Chapter 2,
Chapter 5,
Chapter 9, and
Chapter 11,

use the `ls` command with the ? to list all chapters that begin with the string "`chapter`" and end with any single character, as shown below:

```
$ ls chapter?<CR>
chapter1
chapter2
chapter5
chapter9
$
```

The system responds by printing a list of all filenames that match.

Although ? matches any one character, you can use it more than once in a filename. To list the rest of the chapters in your book, type:

```
ls chapter??<CR>
```

Of course, if you want to list all the chapters in the current directory, use the * (asterisk):

```
ls chapter*
```

The Metacharacters That Match One of a Set: Brackets ([ ])

Use brackets ([ ]) when you want the shell to match any one of several possible characters that may appear in one position in the filename. Suppose your directory contains the following files: cat, fat, mat, rat. If you include [crf] as part of a filename pattern, the shell will look for filenames that have the letter "c", the letter "r", or the letter "f" in the specified position, as the following example shows.

```
$ ls [crf]at<CR>
cat
fat
rat
$
```

This command displays all filenames that begin with the letter "c", "r", or "f" and end with the letters "at". Characters that can be grouped within brackets in this way are collectively called a "character class."

Brackets can also be used to specify a range of characters, whether numbers or letters. Suppose you have a directory containing the following files: `chapter 1`, `chapter 2`, `chapter 3`, `chapter4`, `chapter 5` and `chapter 6`. If you specify

```
chapter[1-5]
```

the shell will match the files named `chapter1` through `chapter5`. This is an easy way to handle only a few chapters at a time.

Try the `pr` command with an argument in brackets:

```
$ pr chapter[2-4]<CR>
```

This command prints the contents of `chapter2`, `chapter3`, and `chapter4`, in that order, on your terminal.

A character class may also specify a range of letters. If you specify `[A-Z]`, the shell will look only for upper case letters; if `[a-z]`, only lower case letters.

The uses of the metacharacters are summarized in Table 9-3. Try to use the metacharacters on the files in your current directory.

Table 9-3: Summary of Metacharacters

Character	Function
*	matches any string of characters, including an empty (null) string, except a leading dot or period
?	matches any single character, except a leading dot or period
[ ]	matches one of the sequence of characters specified within the brackets
[-]	matches one of the range of characters specified

Special Characters

The shell language has other special characters that perform a variety of useful functions. Some of these additional special characters are discussed in this section; others are described in the next section, "Input and Output Redirection."

Running a Command in Background: the Ampersand (&)

Some shell commands take a long time to execute. The ampersand (&) is used to execute commands in background mode, thus freeing your terminal for other tasks. The general format for running a command in background mode is

command &<CR>

You should not run interactive shell commands, for example `read` (see "Using the `read` Command" in this chapter), in the background.

In the example below, the shell is performing a long search in background mode. Specifically, the `grep(1)` command is searching for the string "`delinquent`" in the file `accounts`. Notice the & is the last character of the command line:

```
$ grep delinquent accounts &<CR>
21940
$
```

When you run a command in the background, the UNIX system outputs a process number; `21940` is the process number in the example. You can use this number to terminate the execution of a background command. (Stopping the execution of processes is discussed in the "Executing and Terminating Processes" section.) The prompt on the last line means that the terminal is free and waiting for your commands; `grep` has started running in background mode.

Running a command in background mode affects only the availability of your terminal; it does not affect the output of the command. Whether or not a command is run in background, it prints its output on your terminal screen, unless you redirect it to a file. (See the section titled "Redirecting Output" later in this chapter, for details.)

If you want a command to continue running in background after you log out, you can execute it with the nohup(1) command. (This is discussed in the section titled "Using the nohup Command," later in this chapter.)

Executing Commands Sequentially: the Semicolon (;)

You can type two or more commands on one line as long as each is separated by a semicolon (;) or an ampersand (&), as follows:

command1; *command2*; *command3*<CR>

The UNIX system executes the commands in the order that they appear in the line and prints all output on the screen. This process is called sequential execution.

Try this exercise to see how the ; works. First, type:

```
cd; pwd; ls<CR>
```

The shell executes these commands sequentially:

1. cd changes your location to your login directory
2. pwd prints the full pathname of your current directory
3. ls lists the files in your current directory

If you do not want the system responses to these commands to appear on your screen, refer to the section titled "Redirecting Output" for instructions.

Turning Off Special Meanings: the Backslash (\)

The shell interprets the backslash (\) as an escape character that allows you to turn off any special meaning of the character immediately after it. To see how this works, try the following exercise. Create a two-line file called trial that contains the following text:

```
The all * game
was held in Summit.
```

Use the grep command to search for the asterisk in the file, as shown in the following example:

```
$ grep \* trial<CR>
The all * game
$
```

The grep command finds the * in the text and displays the line in which it appears. Without the \ (backslash), the * would be a metacharacter to the shell and would match all filenames in the current directory.

Turning Off Special Meanings: Quotation Marks

Another way to escape the meaning of a special character is to use quotation marks. Single quotes ('...') turn off the special meaning of any character except single quotes. Double quotes ("...") turn off the special meaning of all characters except double quotes, the $ and the ` (grave accent), which retain their special meanings within double quotes. An advantage of using quotes is that numerous special characters can be enclosed in the quotes; this can be more concise than using the backslash.

For example, if your file named trial also contained the line:

```
He really wondered why? Why???
```

you could use the grep command to match the line with the three question marks as follows:

```
$ grep '???' trial<CR>
He really wondered why? Why???
$
```

If you had instead entered the command

```
grep ??? trial<CR>
```

the three question marks would have been used as shell metacharacters and matched all filenames, if any, of length three.

Using Quotes to Turn Off the Meaning of a Space

Quotes, like backslashes, are commonly used as escape characters for turning off the special meaning of the blank space. The shell interprets a space on a command line as a delimiter between the arguments of a command. Both single and double quotes allow you to escape that meaning.

For example, to locate two or more words that appear together in text, make the words a single argument (to the `grep` command) by enclosing them in quotes. To find the two words "The all" in your file `trial`, enter the following command line:

```
$ grep ′The all′ trial<CR>
The all * game
$
```

`grep` finds the string "`The all`" and prints the line that contains it. What would happen if you did not put quotes around that string?

The ability to escape the special meaning of a space is especially helpful when you are using the `banner`(1) command. This command prints a message across a terminal screen in large, poster-size letters.

To execute `banner`, specify a message consisting of one or more arguments (in this case, usually words), separated on the command line by spaces. The `banner` will use these spaces to delimit the arguments and print each argument on a separate line.

To print more than one argument on the same line, enclose the words, together, in double quotes. For example, to print a birthday greeting, type:

```
banner happy birthday to you<CR>
```

The command prints your message as a four-line banner. Now print the same message as a three-line banner. Type:

```
banner happy birthday "to you"<CR>
```

Notice that the words "`to`" and "`you`" now appear on the same line. The space between them has lost its meaning as a delimiter.

Table 9-4 summarizes the syntax and capabilities of the `banner` command.

Table 9-4: Summary of the `banner` Command

Command `banner` make posters		
command	*options*	*arguments*
`banner`	none	characters
Description:	`banner` displays up to ten characters in large letters	
Remarks:	Later in this chapter you will learn how to redirect the `banner` command into a file to be used as a poster.	

Input and Output Redirection

In the UNIX system, some commands expect to receive their input only from the keyboard (standard input) and most commands display their output at the terminal (standard output). However, the UNIX system lets you redirect both input and output to other files and programs. With such redirection, you can tell the shell to

- take its input from a file rather than from the keyboard
- send its output to a file rather than to the terminal
- use a program as the source of data for another program

The operators, the less than sign (<), the greater than sign (>), two greater than signs (>>) to redirect input and output are the pipe symbol (|), and two less than signs (described in the section titled "Shell Programming").

Redirecting Input: the < Sign

To redirect input, specify a filename after a less than sign (<) on a command line:

command < *file*<CR>

For example, assume that you want to use the `mail(1)` command (described in Chapter 11, "Electronic Mail Tutorial") to send a message to another user with the login `colleague` and that you already have the message in a file named `report`. You can avoid retyping the message by specifying the filename as the source of input:

```
mail colleague < report<CR>
```

Redirecting Output to a File: the > Sign

To redirect output, specify a filename after the greater than sign (>) on a command line:

command > *file*<CR>

If you redirect output to a file that already exists, the output of your command will overwrite the contents of the existing file.

Before redirecting the output of a command to a particular file, make sure that a file by that name does not already exist, unless you do not mind overwriting it. Because the shell does not allow you to have two files of the same name in a directory, it will overwrite the contents of the existing file with the output of your command if you redirect the output to a file with the same name as an existing file. The shell does not warn you about overwriting the original file.

To make sure that no file exists with the name you plan to use, run the `ls` command, specifying your proposed filename as an argument. If a file with that name exists, `ls` will list it; if not, you will receive a message that the file was not found in the current directory. For example, checking for the existence of the files `temp` and `junk` would give you the following output:

```
$ ls temp<CR>
temp
$ ls junk<CR>
junk:  no such file or directory
$
```

This means you can name your new output file `junk`, but you cannot name it `temp` unless you no longer want the contents of the existing `temp` file.

Appending Output to an Existing File: the >> Symbol

To keep from destroying an existing file, you can also use the double greater than symbol (>>), as follows:

command >> *file*<CR>

This appends the output of a command to the end of the file *file*. If *file* does not exist, it is created when you use the >> symbol this way.

The following example shows how to append the output of the `cat` command, described in the section titled "Shell Programming," to an existing file. The `cat` command prints its argument filenames to the standard output. If it has no arguments, it prints its standard input to the standard output. First, the `cat` command is executed on both files without output redirection to show their respective contents. Then the contents of `trial2` are added after the last line of `trial1` by executing the `cat` command on `trial2` and redirecting the output to `trial1`.

```
$ cat trial1<CR>
This is the first line of trial1.
Hello.
This is the last line of trial1.
$
$ cat trial2<CR>
This is the beginning of trial2.
Hello.
This is the end of trial2.
$
$ cat trial2 >> trial1<CR>
$ cat trial1<CR>
This is the first line of trial1.
Hello.
This is the last line of trial1.
This is the beginning of trial2.
Hello.
This is the end of trial2.
$
```

Useful Applications of Output Redirection

Redirecting output is useful when you do not want it to appear on your screen immediately or when you want to save it. Output redirection is also especially useful when you run commands that perform clerical chores on text files. Two such commands are `spell` and `sort`.

The `spell` Command

The `spell` program compares every word in a file against its internal vocabulary list and prints a list of all potential misspellings on the screen. If `spell` does not have a listing for a word (such as a person's name), it will report that as a misspelling, too.

Running `spell` on a lengthy text file can take a long time and may produce a list of misspellings that is too long to fit on your screen. `spell` prints all its output at once; if it does not fit on the screen, the command scrolls it continuously off the top until it has all been displayed. A long list of misspellings will roll off your screen quickly and may be difficult to read.

You can avoid this problem by redirecting the output of `spell` to a file. In the following example, `spell` searches a file named memo and places a list of misspelled words in a file named `misspell`:

```
$ spell memo > misspell<CR>
```

Table 9-5 summarizes the syntax and capabilities of the `spell` command.

Table 9-5: Summary of the `spell` Command

Command `spell` find spelling errors		
command	*options*	*arguments*
`spell`	available*	*file*
Description:	`spell` collects words from a specified file or files and looks them up in a spelling list. Words that are not on the spelling list are displayed on your terminal.	
Options:	`spell` has several options, including one for checking British spellings.	
Remarks:	The list of misspelled words can be redirected into a file.	

* See the **spell**(1) manual page in the *User's Reference Manual* for all available options and an explanation of the capabilities of each.

The `sort` Command

The `sort` command arranges the lines of a specified file in alphabetical or numerical order (see Chapter 3, "Using the File System," for details). Because users generally want to keep a file that has been alphabetized, output redirection greatly enhances the value of the `sort` command.

Be careful to choose a new name for the file that will receive the output of the `sort` command (the alphabetized list). When `sort` is executed, the shell first empties the file that will accept the redirected output. Then it performs the sort and places the output in the blank file. If you type

```
sort list > list<CR>
```

the shell will empty `list` and then sort nothing into `list`.

Combining Background Mode and Output Redirection

Running a command in background does not affect the output of the command; unless it is redirected, output is always printed on the terminal screen. If you are using your terminal to perform other tasks while a command runs in background, you will be interrupted when the command displays its output on your screen. However, if you redirect that output to a file, you can work undisturbed, except when an error occurs.

For example, in the section titled "Special Characters," you learned how to execute the `grep` command in background with `&`. Now suppose you want to find occurrences of the word "`test`" in a file named `schedule`. Run the `grep` command in background and redirect its output to a file called `testfile`:

```
$ grep test schedule > testfile &<CR>
```

You can then use your terminal for other work and examine `testfile` when you have finished it.

Redirecting Output to a Command: the Pipe (|)

The | character is called a pipe. Pipes are powerful tools that allow you to take the output of one command and use it as input for another command without creating temporary files. A multiple command line created in this way is called a pipeline.

The general format for a pipeline is:

command1 | *command2* | *command3*...<CR>

The output of *command1* is used as the input of *command2*. The output of *command2* is then used as the input for *command3*.

To understand the efficiency and power of a pipeline, consider the contrast between two methods that achieve the same results.

- To use the input/output redirection method, run one command and redirect its output to a temporary file. Then run a second command that takes the contents of the temporary file as its input. Finally, remove the temporary file after the second command has finished running.
- To use the pipeline method, run one command and pipe its output directly into a second command.

For example, suppose you want to mail a happy birthday message in a banner to the owner of the login `david`. Doing this without a pipeline is a three-step procedure. You must:

1. Enter the `banner` command and redirect its output to a temporary file:

   ```
   banner happy birthday > message.tmp
   ```

2. Enter the `mail` command using `message.tmp` as its input:

   ```
   mail david < message.tmp
   ```

3. Remove the temporary file:

   ```
   rm message.tmp
   ```

However, by using a pipeline you can do this in one step:

```
banner happy birthday | mail david<CR>
```

A Pipeline Using the `cut` and `date` Commands

The `cut` and `date` commands provide a good example of how pipelines can increase the versatility of individual commands. The `cut` command allows you to extract part of each line in a file. It looks for characters in a specified part of the line and prints them. To specify a position in a line, use the `-c` option and identify the part of the file you want by the numbers of the spaces it occupies on the line, counting from the left-hand margin.

For example, suppose you want to display only the dates from a file called `birthdays`. The file contains the following list:

```
Anne     12/26
Klaus    7/4
Mary     10/18
Peter    11/9
Nandy    4/23
Sam      8/12
```

The birthdays appear between the ninth and thirteenth spaces on each line. To display them, type:

```
cut -c9-13 birthdays<CR>
```

The output is shown below:

```
12/26
7/4
10/18
11/9
4/23
8/12
```

Table 9-6 summarizes the syntax and capabilities of the `cut` command.

Table 9-6: Summary of the `cut` Command

Command		
`cut` cut out selected fields from each line of a file		
command	options	arguments
`cut`	−clist −`f`list [−`d`]	*file*
Description:	`cut` extracts columns from a table or fields from each line of a file	
Options:	−`c` lists the number of character positions from the left. A range of numbers such as characters 1−9 can be specified by `−c1−9` −`f` lists the field number from the left separated by a delimiter described by −`d`. −`d` gives the field delimiter for −`f`. The default is a space. If the delimiter is a colon, this would be specified by `−d :` .	
Remarks:	If you find the `cut` command useful, you may also want to use the `paste` command and the `split` command.	

The `cut` command is usually executed on a file; however, piping makes it possible to run this command on the output of other commands, too. This is useful if you want only part of the information generated by another command. For example, you may want to have the time printed. The `date` command prints the day of the week, date, and time, as follows:

```
$ date<CR>
Sat Dec 24 13:12:32 EST 1988
$
```

Notice that the time is given between spaces 12 and 19 of the line. You can display the time (without the date) by piping the output of `date` into `cut`, specifying spaces `12-19` with the `-c` option. Your command line and its output will look like this:

```
$ date | cut -c12-19<CR>
13:14:56
$
```

Table 9-7 summarizes the syntax and capabilities of the `date` command.

Table 9-7: Summary of the `date` Command

Command `date` display the date and time		
command	options	arguments
`date`	`+%m%d%y*` `+%H%%M%S`	available*
Description:	`date` displays the current date and time on your terminal	
Options:	`+%` followed by `m` (for month), `d` (for day), `y` (for year), `H` (for hour), `M` (for month), and `S` (for second) will echo these back to your terminal. You can add explanations such as: `date ´+%H:%M is the time´`	
Remarks:	If you are working on a small computer system, of which you are both a user and the system administrator, you may be allowed to set the date and time using optional arguments to the `date` command. Check your reference manual for details. When working in a multiuser environment, the arguments are available only to the system administrator.	

* See the **`date`**(1) manual page in the *User's Reference Manual* for all available options and an explanation of the capabilities of each.

Substituting Output for an Argument

The output of most commands may be captured and used as arguments on a command line. This is done by enclosing the command in grave accents (`...`) and placing it on the command line in the position where the output should be treated as arguments. This is known as command substitution.

For example, you can substitute the output of the `date` and `cut` pipeline command used previously for the argument in a `banner` printout by typing the following command line:

```
$ banner `date | cut -c12-19`<CR>
```

Notice the results: the system prints a banner with the current time.

The section titled "Shell Programming" in this chapter shows you how you can also use the output of a command line as the value of a variable.

Executing, Stopping, and Restarting Processes

This section discusses the following topics:

- how to run commands to run at a later time with the `batch` and `at` commands
- how to obtain the status of running processes
- how to terminate active processes
- how to restart a stopped processes
- how to keep background processes running after you have logged out
- how to move processes in foreground to background, and processes in background to foreground.

Running Commands at a Later Time With the `batch` and `at` Commands

The `batch` and `at` commands allow you to specify a command or sequence of commands to be run at a later time. With the `batch` command, the system determines when the commands run; with the `at` command, you determine when the commands run. Both commands expect input from standard input (the terminal); the list of commands entered as input from the terminal must be ended by pressing <^d> (control-d).

The `batch` command is useful if you are running a process or shell program that uses a large amount of system time. The `batch` command submits a batch job (containing the commands to be executed) to the system. The job is put in a queue, and runs when the system load falls to an acceptable level. This frees the system to respond rapidly to other input and is a courtesy to other users.

The general format for `batch` is:

```
batch<CR>
first command<CR>
      .
      .
      .
last command<CR>
<^d>
```

If there is only one command to be run with `batch`, you can enter it as follows:

```
batch command_line<CR>
<^d>
```

The next example uses `batch` to execute the `grep` command at a convenient time. Here `grep` searches all files in the current directory and redirects the output to the file `dol.file`.

```
$ batch<CR>
grep dollar * > dol-file<CR>
<^d>
job 155223141.b at Sun Dec 3 11:14:54 1989
$
```

After you submit a job with `batch`, the system responds with a job number, date, and time. This job number is not the same as the process number that the system generates when you run a command in the background.

Table 9-8 summarizes the syntax and capabilities of the batch Command.

Table 9-8: Summary of the batch Command

Command batch execute commands at a later time		
command	*options*	*input*
batch	none	*command_lines*
Description:	batch submits a batch job, which is placed in a queue and executed when the load on the system falls to an acceptable level.	
Remarks:	The list of commands must end with a <^d> (control-d).	

The at command allows you to specify an exact time to execute the commands. The general format for the at command is

at *time*<CR>
first command<CR>
.
.
.
last command<CR>
<^d>

The *time* argument consists of the time of day and, if the date is not today, the date.

The following example shows how to use the at command to mail a happy birthday banner to the person having login emily on her birthday:

```
$ at 8:15am Feb 27<CR>
banner happy birthday | mail emily<CR>
<^d>
job 453400603.a at Thurs Feb 23 08:15:00 1989
$
```

Notice that the at command, like the batch command, responds with the job number, date, and time.

If you decide you do not want to execute the commands currently waiting in a batch or at job queue, you can erase those jobs by using the -r option of the at command with the job number or you can save the job number by redirecting it. The general format is

at -r *jobnumber*<CR>

Try erasing the previous at job for the happy birthday banner. Type:

at -r 453400603.a<CR>

If you have forgotten the job number, the at -l command will give you a list of the current jobs in the batch or at queue, as the following screen shows:

```
$ at -l<CR>CW
user = mylogin 168302040.a at Sat Nov 25 13:00:00 1989
user = mylogin 453400603.a at Fri Feb 24 08:15:00 1989
$
```

Notice that the system displays the job number and the time the job will run.

Using the at command, mail yourself the file memo at noon, to tell you it is lunch time. (You must redirect the file into mail unless you use the "here document," described in the section titled "Shell Programming.") Then try the at command with the -l option.

```
$ at 12:00pm<CR>
mail mylogin < memo<CR>
<^d>
job 263131754.a at Jun 25 12:00:00 1989
$
$ at -l<CR>
user = mylogin 263131754.a at Jun 25 12:00:00 1989
$
```

Table 9-9 summarizes the syntax and capabilities of the at command.

Table 9-9: Summary of the `at` Command

Command `at` execute commands at a specified time		
command	*options*	*arguments*
`at`	`-r` `-l`	*time (date)* *jobnumber*
Description:	Executes commands at the time specified. You can use between one and four digits, and "am" or "pm" to show the time. To specify the date, give a month name followed by the number for the day. You do not need to enter a date if you want your job to run the same day. See the `at`(1) entry in the *User's Reference Manual* for other default times.	
Options:	The `-r` option with the job number removes previously scheduled jobs. The `-l` option (no arguments) reports the job number and status of all scheduled `at` and `batch` jobs.	

Remarks:	Examples of how to specify times and dates with the `at` command are shown below. For other ways, see the *Programmer's Reference Manual*.
	
	`at 08:15am Feb 27`
	`at 5:14pm Sept 24`	

Obtaining the Status of Running Processes

The ps command gives you the status of all the processes currently being run. For example, you can use the ps command to show the status of all processes that you run in the background mode using & (described earlier in the section titled "Special Characters").

The next section, "Terminating Active Processes," discusses how you can use the PID (process identification) number to stop a command from executing. A PID is a unique number that the UNIX system assigns to each active process.

In the following example, grep is run in the background, and then the ps command is issued. The system responds with the process identification (PID) and the terminal identification (TTY) number. It also gives the cumulative execution time for each process (TIME), and the name of the command that is being executed (COMMAND).

```
$ grep word * > temp &<CR>
28223
$
$ ps<CR>
PID            TTY   TIME   COMD
28124          tty10 0:00   sh
28223          tty10 0:04   grep
28224          tty10 0:04   ps
$
```

Notice that the system reports a PID number for the grep command, as well as for the other processes that are running: the ps command itself, and the sh (shell) command that runs while you are logged in. The shell program sh interprets the shell commands and is discussed in Chapters 1 and 4.

Table 9-10 summarizes the syntax and capabilities of the ps command.

Table 9-10: Summary of the ps Command

Command ps report process status		
command	*options*	*arguments*
ps	available*	none
Description:	ps displays information about active processes.	
Options:	Several. If none is specified, ps displays the status of all active processes you are running.	
Remarks:	Gives you the PID (process ID) which is needed to kill a process (stop the process from executing).	

* See the **ps**(1) manual page in the *User's Reference Manual* for all available options and an explanation of the capabilities of each.

You can suspend and restart programs if your login has been configured for job control. See your system administrator to have your login set up to include job control. The jobs command also gives you a listing of current background processes, running or stopped. However, in addition to the PID, the jobs command gives you a number called the "job identifier" (JID) and the original command typed to initiate the job (*job name*). You will need to know the JID of a process to restart a stopped "job", or to resume a background process in foreground. The JID is printed on the screen whenever you enter a command to start or stop a process. To obtain information about your stopped or background jobs, type:

```
jobs <CR>
```

and information resembling the following will appear:

[*JID*] - `Stopped` (signal)   *<job name>*
or
[*JID*] + `Running`   *<job name>*

Terminating Active Processes

The `kill` command terminates active shell processes in background mode and the `stop` command temporarily suspends the process if job control is active. The general format for these commands is:

`kill` *PID*<CR>
or
`stop` *JID*<CR>

Note that you cannot terminate background processes by pressing the `BREAK` or `DELETE` key. The following example shows how you can terminate the `grep` command that you started executing in background mode in the previous example.

```
$ kill 28223<CR>
28223 Terminated
$
```

Notice that the system responds with a message and a `$` prompt, showing that the process has been killed. If the system cannot find the PID number you specify, it responds with an error message:

```
kill:28223:No such process
```

To suspend a foreground process in the job shell (only when job control is active), type:

```
ctrl Z
```

A message appears on the screen resembling the following:

<JID>   Stopped (user)   *<job name>*

Table 9-11 summarizes the syntax and capabilities of the `kill` command.

Table 9-11: Summary of the `kill` Command

Command `kill` terminate a process		
command	*options*	*arguments*
`kill`	available*	*PID*
Description:	`kill` terminates the process specified by the PID number.	

* See the `kill`(1) manual page in the *User's Reference Manual* for all available options and an explanation of the capabilities of each.

Restarting a Stopped Process

When job control is active you can restart a suspended process. To restart a process with the `stop` command, you must first determine the JID by using the `jobs` command. You can then use the JID with the following commands:

fg `<JID>` `resumes a stopped or background job in foreground`
bg `<JID>` `restarts a stopped job in background`

Using the `nohup` Command

All processes, except the `at` and batch requests, are killed when you log out. If you want a background process to continue running after you log out, you must use the nohup command to submit that background command.

To execute the nohup command, use the following format:

```
nohup command &<CR>
```

Notice that you place the nohup command before the command you intend to run as a background process.

For example, suppose you want the `grep` command to search all the files in your current directory for the string "`word`" and redirect the output to a file called `word.list`, and you wish to log out immediately afterward. Type the command line as follows:

```
nohup grep word * > word.list & <CR>
```

You can terminate the nohup command by using the `kill` command. Table 9-12 summarizes the syntax and capabilities of the nohup command.

Table 9-12: Summary of the nohup Command

Command nohup prevents interruption of command execution by hang ups		
command	*options*	*arguments*
nohup	*none*	*command line*
Description:	Executes a command line, even if you hang up or quit the system.	

Now that you have mastered these basic shell commands and notations, use them in your shell programs! The exercises that follow will help you practice using the shell command language. Answers to the exercises appear at the end of the chapter.

Command Language Exercises

1-1. What happens if you use an * (asterisk) at the beginning of a filename? Try to list some of the files in a directory using the * with the last letter of one of your filenames. What happens?

1-2. Try to enter the following two commands:

```
cat[0-9]*<CR>
echo *<CR>
```

1-3. Is it acceptable to use a `?` at the beginning or in the middle of a pattern? Try it.

1-4. Do you have any files that begin with a number? Can you list them without listing the other files in your directory? Can you list only those files that begin with a lower case letter between a and m? (Hint: use a range of numbers or letters in `[ ]`).

1-5. Is it acceptable to place a command in background mode on a line that is executing several other commands sequentially? Try it. What happens? (Hint: use `;` and `&`.) Can the command in background mode be placed in any position on the command line? Try placing it in various positions. Experiment with each new character that you learn to see the full power of the character.

1-6. Redirect the output of `pwd` and `ls` into a file by using the following command line:

```
cd; pwd; trial; ls >> trial <CR>
```

Remember, if you want to redirect both commands to the same file, you have to use the >> (append) sign for the second redirection. If you do not, you will wipe out the information from the `pwd` command.

1-7. Instead of cutting the time out of the `date` response, try redirecting only the date, without the time, into `banner`. What is the only part you need to change in the following command line?

```
banner `date | cut -c12-19`<CR>
```

Shell Programming

You can use the shell to create programs—new commands. Such programs are also called "shell procedures." This section tells you how to create and execute shell programs using commands, variables, positional parameters, return codes, and basic programming control structures.

The examples of shell programs in this section are shown two ways. First, the `cat` command is used in a screen to display the contents of a file containing a shell program:

```
$ cat testfile<CR>
first command
    .
    .
    .
last command
$
```

Second, the results of executing the shell program appear after a command line:

```
$ testfile<CR>
program_output
$
```

You should be familiar with an editor before you try to create shell programs. Refer to the tutorials in Chapter 6 (for the `ed` editor) and Chapter 7 (for the `vi` editor).

Shell Programs

Creating a Simple Shell Program

We'll begin by creating a simple shell program that will do the following tasks, in order:

- print the current directory
- list the contents of that directory

- display this message on your terminal:

  "This is the end of the shell program."

Create a file called dl (short for directory list) using your editor of choice, and enter the following:

```
pwd<CR>
ls<CR>
echo This is the end of the shell program.<CR>
```

Now write and quit the file. You have just created a shell program! You can cat the file to display its contents, as the following screen shows:

```
$ cat dl<CR>
pwd
ls
echo This is the end of the shell program.
$
```

Executing a Shell Program

One way to execute a shell program is to use the sh command. Type:

```
sh dl<CR>
```

The dl command is executed by sh, and the pathname of the current directory is printed first, then the list of files in the current directory, and finally, the comment This is the end of the shell program. The sh command provides a good way to test your shell program to make sure it works.

If dl is a useful command, you can use the chmod command (see the *Programmer's Reference Manual* for a description of chmod) to make it an executable file; then you can type dl by itself to execute the command it contains. The following example shows how to use the chmod command to make a file executable and then run the ls -l command (see the *Programmer's Reference Manual* for a description of the ls -l command) to verify the changes you have made in the permissions.

```
$ chmod u+x dl<CR>
$  ls -l<CR>
total 2
-rw-------         1  login  login    3661  Nov  2     10:28 mbox
-rwx------         1  login  login      48  Nov 15     10:50 dl
$
```

Notice that chmod turns on permission to execute (+x) for the user (u). Now dl is an executable program. Try to execute it. Type:

```
dl<CR>
```

You get the same results as before, when you entered sh dl to execute it. For further details about the chmod command, see Chapter 3.

Creating a bin Directory for Executable Files

To make your shell programs accessible from all your directories, you can make a bin directory from your login directory and move the shell files to your bin.

You must also set your shell variable PATH to include your bin directory:

```
PATH=$PATH:$HOME/bin
```

See "Variables" and "Using Shell Variables" in this chapter for more information about PATH.

The following example reminds you which commands are necessary. In this example, dl is in the login directory. Type these command lines:

```
cd<CR>
mkdir bin<CR>
mv dl bin/dl<CR>
```

Move to the bin directory and type the ls -l command. Does dl still have execute permission?

Now move to a directory other than the login directory, and type the following command:

```
dl<CR>
```

What happened?

Table 9-13 summarizes your new shell program, `dl`.

Table 9-13: Summary of the `dl` Shell Program

Shell Program `dl` display the directory path and directory contents (user defined)	
command	*arguments*
`dl`	none
Description:	`dl` displays the name and contents of the current directory.

It is possible to give the `bin` directory another name; if you do so, you must change your shell variable `PATH` again.

Warnings about Naming Shell Programs

You can give your shell program any appropriate filename; however, you should not give your program the same name as a system command. If you do, the system will execute your command instead of the system command. For example, if you had named your `dl` program `mv`, each time you tried to move a file, the system would have executed your directory list program instead of `mv`.

Another problem can occur if you name the `dl` file `ls`, and then try to execute the file. You would create an infinite loop, since your program executes the `ls` command. After some time, the system would give you the following error message:

```
Too many processes, cannot fork
```

What happened? You typed in your new command, `ls`. The shell read and executed the `pwd` command. Then it read the `ls` command in your program and tried to execute your `ls` command. This formed an infinite loop. For this reason, the UNIX system limits the number of times an infinite loop can execute. One way to prevent such looping is to give the pathname for the system `ls` command, `/usr/bin/ls`, when you write your own shell program.

The following `ls` shell program would work:

```
$ cat ls<CR>
pwd
/bin/ls
echo This is the end of the shell program
```

If you name your command `ls`, then you can only execute the system `ls` command by using its full pathname, `/usr/bin/ls`.

Variables

Variables are the basic data objects that, in addition to files, shell programs manipulate. Here we discuss three types of variables and how to use them:

- positional parameters
- special parameters
- named variables

Positional Parameters

A positional parameter is a variable within a shell program; its value is set from an argument specified on the command line that invokes the program. Positional parameters are numbered and are referred to with a preceding `$`: `$1`, `$2`, `$3`, and so on.

A shell program may reference up to nine positional parameters. If a shell program is invoked with a command line that appears like this:

```
shell.prog pp1 pp2 pp3 pp4 pp5 pp6 pp7 pp8 pp9<CR>
```

then positional parameter `$1` within the program is assigned the value `pp1`, positional parameter `$2` within the program is assigned the value `pp2`, and so on, at the time the shell program is invoked.

To practice positional parameter substitution, create a file called pp (short for positional parameters). Then enter the echo commands shown in the following screen. Enter the command lines so that running the cat command on your completed file will produce the following output:

```
$ cat pp<CR>
echo  The first positional parameter is: $1<CR>
echo  The second positional parameter is: $2<CR>
echo  The third positional parameter is: $3<CR>
echo  The fourth positional parameter is: $4<CR>
$
```

If you execute this shell program with the arguments one, two, three, and four, you will obtain the following results (but first you must make the shell program pp executable using the chmod command):

```
$ chmod u+x pp<CR>
$
$ pp one two three four<CR>
The first positional parameter is: one
The second positional parameter is: two
The third positional parameter is: three
The fourth positional parameter is: four
$
```

The following screen shows the shell program bbday, which mails a greeting to the login entered in the command line:

```
$ cat bbday<CR>
banner happy birthday | mail $1
```

Try sending yourself a birthday greeting. If your login name is sue, your command line will be:

```
bbday sue<CR>
```

Table 9-14 summarizes the syntax and capabilities of the bbday shell program.

Table 9-14: Summary of the bbday Command

Shell Program bbday mail a banner birthday greeting	
command	*arguments*
bbday	*login*
Description:	bbday mails the message happy birthday, in poster-size letters, to the specified login.

The who command lists all users currently logged in on the system. How can you make a simple shell program called whoson, that will tell you if the owner of a particular login is currently working on the system?

Type the following command line into a file called whoson:

```
who | grep $1<CR>
```

The who command lists all current system users, and grep searches that output for a line with the string contained as a value in the positional parameter $1.

Now try using your login as the argument for the new program whoson. For example, suppose your login is sue. When you issue the whoson command, the shell program substitutes sue for the parameter $1 in your program and executes as if it were:

```
who | grep sue <CR>
```

The output is shown on the following screen:

```
$ whoson sue<CR>
sue    tty26      Jan 24 13:35
$
```

If the owner of the specified login is not currently working on the system, `grep` fails and the `whoson` prints no output.

Table 9-15 summarizes the syntax and capabilities of the `whoson` command.

Table 9-15: Summary of the `whoson` Command

Shell Program `whoson` display login information if user is logged in (user defined)	
command	*arguments*
`whoson`	*login*
Description:	If a user is on the system, `whoson` displays the user's login, the TTY number, and the time and date the user logged in.

The shell allows a command line to contain at least 128 arguments; however, a shell program is restricted to referencing only nine positional parameters, `$1` through `$9`, at a given time. You can work around this restriction by using the `shift` command, described in the manual *Shell Commands and Programming*. The special parameter `$*`, described in the next section, can also be used to access the values of all command line arguments.

Special Parameters

`$#` This parameter, when referenced in a shell program, contains the number of arguments with which the shell program was invoked. Its value can be used anywhere in the shell program.

Enter the command line, shown in the following screen, in the executable shell program called `get.num`. Then run the `cat` command on the file:

```
$ cat get.num<CR>
echo The number of arguments is: $#
$
```

The program simply displays the number of arguments with which it is invoked. For example:

```
$ get.num test out this program<CR>
The number of arguments is: 4
$
```

Table 9-16 summarizes the `get.num` shell program.

Table 9-16: Summary of the `get.num` Shell Program

Shell Program `get.num` count and display the number of arguments (user defined)	
command	*arguments*
`get.num`	*(character_string)*
Description:	`get.num` counts the number of arguments given to the command and then displays the total.
Remarks:	This command demonstrates the special parameter `$#`.

`$*` This special parameter, when referenced in a shell program, contains a string with all the arguments with which the shell program was invoked, starting with the first. You are not restricted to nine parameters as you are with the positional parameters `$1` through `$9`..

You can write a simple shell program to demonstrate `$*`. Create a shell program called `show.param` that will `echo` all the parameters. Use the command line shown in the following completed file:

```
$ cat show.param<CR>
echo The parameters for this command are: $*
$
```

The program `show.param` will echo all the arguments you give to the command. Make `show.param` executable and try it using these parameters:

```
Hello. How are you?
```

```
$ show.param Hello. How are you?<CR>
The parameters for this command are: Hello.  How are you?
$
```

Notice that show.param echoes `Hello.  How are you?` Now try show.param using more than nine arguments:

```
$ show.param one two 3 4 5 six 7 8 9 10 11<CR>
The parameters for this command are: one two 3 4 5 six 7 8 9 10 11
$
```

Once again, show.param echoes all the arguments you give. The $* parameter can be useful if you use filename expansion to specify arguments to the shell command.

Use the filename expansion feature with your show.param command. For example, suppose you have several files in your directory named for chapters of a book: chap1, chap2, and so on, through chapF. The show.param command prints a list of all those files.

```
$ show.param chap?<CR>
The parameters for this command are: chap1 chap2 chap3
chap4 chap5 chapB chapF
$
```

Table 9-17 summarizes the show.param shell program.

Table 9-17: Summary of the `show.param` Shell Program

Shell Program `show.param` display all positional parameters (user defined)	
command	*arguments*
`show.param`	(any positional parameters)
Description:	`show.param` displays all the parameters.
Remarks:	If the parameters are filename generations, the command displays each of those filenames.

Named Variables

Another form of variable that you can use in a shell program is a named variable. You assign values to named variables yourself. The format for assigning a value to a named variable is:

named_variable=*value*<CR>

Notice that there are no spaces on either side of the equals (=) sign.

In the following example, `var1` is a named variable, and `myname` is the value or character string assigned to that variable:

```
var1=myname<CR>
```

A `$` is used in front of a variable name in a shell program to reference the value of that variable. Using the example above, the reference `$var1` tells the shell to substitute the value `myname` (assigned to `var1`), for any occurrence of the character string `$var1`.

The first character of a variable name must be a letter or an underscore. The rest of the name can consist of letters, underscores, and digits. Like shell program filenames, variable names should not be shell command names. Also, the shell reserves some variable names that you should not use for your variables. A brief explanation of these reserved shell variable names follows:

- `CDPATH` defines the search path for the `cd` command.
- `HOME` is the default variable for the `cd` command (home directory).
- `IFS` defines the internal field separators (normally the space, the tab, and the carriage return).
- `LOGNAME` is your login name.
- `MAIL` names the file that contains your electronic mail.
- `PATH` determines the search path used by the shell to find commands.
- `PS1` defines the primary prompt (default is `$`).
- `PS2` defines the secondary prompt (default is >).
- `TERM` identifies your terminal type. It is important to set this variable if you are editing with `vi`.
- `TERMINFO` identifies the directory to be searched for information about your terminal, for example, its screen size.
- `TZ` defines the time zone (default is `EST5EDT`).

Many of these variables are explained in "Modifying Your Login Environment" later in this chapter. You can also read more about them on the `sh`(1) manual page in the *User's Reference Manual*.

You can see the value of these variables in your shell in two ways. First, you can type

```
echo $variable_name
```

The system outputs the value of *variable_name*. Second, you can use the `env`(1) command to print out the value of all defined variables in the shell. To do this, type `env` on a line by itself; the system outputs a list of the variable names and values.

Assigning a Value to a Variable

If you edit with `vi`, you know you can set the `TERM` variable by entering the following command line:

```
TERM=terminal_name<CR>
EXPORT TERM
```

This is the simplest way to assign a value to a variable. However, there are several other ways to do this:

- Use the `read` command to assign input to the variable.
- Redirect the output of a command into a variable by using command substitution with grave accents (\` ... \`).
- Assign a positional parameter to the variable.

The following sections discuss each of these methods in detail.

Using the `read` Command

The `read` command used within a shell program allows you to prompt the user of the program for the values of variables. The general format for the `read` command is:

```
read variable<CR>
```

The values assigned by `read` to *variable* will be substituted for `$`*variable* wherever it is used in the program. If a program executes the `echo` command just before the `read` command, the program can display directions such as `Type in ....` The `read` command will wait until you type a character string, followed by a `RETURN` key, and then make that string the value of the variable.

The following example shows how to write a simple shell program called `num.please` to keep track of your telephone numbers. This program uses the following commands for the purposes specified:

`echo`	to prompt you for a person's last name
`read`	to assign the input value to the variable name
`grep`	to search the file `list` for this variable

Your finished program should look like the one displayed here:

```
$ cat num.please<CR>
echo Type in the last name:
read name
grep $name home/list
$
```

Create a file called `list` that contains several last names and telephone numbers. Then try running `num.please`.

The next example is a program called `mknum`, which creates a list. `mknum` includes the following commands for the purposes shown.

- `echo` prompts for a person's name
- `read` assigns the person's name to the variable *name*
- `echo` asks for the person's number
- `read` assigns the telephone number to the variable *num*
- `echo` adds the values of the variables *name* and *num* to the file `list`

If you want the output of the `echo` command to be added to the end of `list`, you must use >> to redirect it. If you use >, `list` will contain only the last telephone number you added.

Running the `cat` command on `mknum` displays the contents of the program. When your program looks like this, you will be ready to make it executable (with the `chmod` command):

```
$ cat mknum<CR>
echo Type in name
read name
echo Type in number
read num
echo $name $num >> list
$ chmod u+x mknum<CR>
$
```

Try out the new programs for your telephone list. In the next example, mknum creates a new listing for Mr. Niceguy. Then num.please gives you Mr. Niceguy's telephone number:

```
$ mknum<CR>
Type in name
Mr. Niceguy<CR>
Type in number
668-0007<CR>
$ num.please<CR>
Type in last name
Niceguy<CR>
Mr. Niceguy 668-0007
$
```

Notice that the variable name accepts both Mr. and Niceguy as the value.

Tables 9-18 and 9-19 summarize the mknum and num.please shell programs, respectively.

Table 9-18: Summary of the `mknum` Shell Program

Shell Program `mknum` place name and number on a telephone list	
command	*arguments*
`mknum`	(interactive)
Description:	Asks you for the name and number of a person and adds that name and number to your telephone list.
Remarks:	This is an interactive command.

Table 9-19: Summary of the `num.please` Shell Program

Shell Program `num.please` display a person's name and number	
command	*arguments*
`num.please`	(interactive)
Description:	Asks you for a person's last name, and then displays the person's full name and telephone number.
Remarks:	This is an interactive command.

Substituting Command Output for the Value of a Variable

You can substitute a command's output for the value of a variable by using *command substitution.* This has the following format:

variable=`*command*`<CR>

The output from *command* becomes the value of *variable.*

In one of the previous examples on piping, the `date` command was piped into the `cut` command to get the correct time. That command line was the following:

```
date | cut -c12-19<CR>
```

You can put this in a simple shell program called `t` that gives you the time.

```
$ cat t<CR>
time=`date | cut -c12-19`
echo The time is: $time
$
```

Remember, there are no spaces on either side of the equal sign. Make the file executable, and you will have a program that gives you the time:

```
$ chmod u+x t<CR>
$ t<CR>
The time is: 10:36
$
```

Figure 9-20 summarizes your `t` program.

Table 9-20: Summary of the t Shell Program

Shell Program t display the correct time	
command	*arguments*
t	none
Description:	t gives you the correct time in hours and minutes.

Assigning Values with Positional Parameters

You can assign a positional parameter to a named parameter by using the following format:

var1=$1<CR>

The next example is a simple program called `simp.p` that assigns a positional parameter to a variable. The following screen shows the commands in `simp.p`:

```
$ cat simp.p<CR>
var1=$1
echo $var1
$
```

Of course, you can also assign to a variable the output of a command that uses positional parameters, as follows:

```
person=`who | grep $1`<CR>
```

In the next example, the program `log.time` keeps track of your `whoson` program results. The output of `whoson` is assigned to the variable `person`, and added to the file `login.file` with the `echo` command. The last `echo` displays the value of `$person`, which is the same as the output from the `whoson` command:

```
$ cat log.time<CR>
person=`who | grep $1`
echo $person >> $home/login.file
echo $person
$
```

The system response to `log.time` is shown in the following screen:

```
$ log.time maryann<CR>
maryann     tty61          Apr 11 10:26
$
```

Figure 9-21 summarizes the `log.time` shell program.

Table 9-21: Summary of the `log.time` Shell Program

Shell Program `log.time` log and display a specified login (user defined)	
command	*arguments*
`log.time`	*login*
Description:	If the specified login is currently on the system, `log.time` places the line of information from the `who` command into the file `login.file` and then displays that line of information on your terminal.

Shell Programming Constructs

The shell programming language has several constructs that give added flexibility to your programs:

- Comments let you document the function of a a program.
- The "here document" allows you to include within the shell program itself lines to be redirected as input to some command in the shell program.
- The `exit` command lets you terminate a program at a point other than the end of the program and use return codes.
- The looping constructs, `for` and `while`, allow a program to iterate through groups of commands in a loop.
- The conditional control commands, `if` and `case`, execute a group of commands only if a particular set of conditions is met.

- The break command allows a program to exit unconditionally from a loop.

Comments

You can place comments in a shell program in either of two ways. The shell ignores all text on a line following a word that begins with a # (pound) sign. If the # sign appears at the beginning of a line, the comment uses the entire line; if it appears after a command, the command is executed but the remainder of the line is ignored. The end of a line always ends a comment. The general format for a comment line is

#*comment*<CR>

For example, a program that contains the following lines will ignore them when it is executed:

```
# This program sends a generic birthday greeting.<CR>
# This program needs a login as<CR>
# the positional parameter.<CR>
```

Comments are useful for documenting the function of a program and should be included in any program you write.

The Here Document

A "here document" allows you to place into a shell program lines that are redirected to be the input of a command in that program. It is a way to provide input to a command in a shell program without using a separate file. The notation consists of the redirection symbol ≪ and a delimiter that specifies the beginning and end of the lines of input. The delimiter can be one character or a string of characters; the ! is often used.

Figure 9-1 shows the general format for a here document.

Figure 9-1: Format of a Here Document

```
command <<delimiter<CR>
...input lines . . . <CR>
delimiter<CR>
```

In the next example, the program `gbday` uses a here document to send a generic birthday greeting by redirecting lines of input into the `mail` command:

```
$ cat gbday<CR>
mail $1 <<!
Best wishes to you on your birthday.
!
$
```

When you use this command, you must specify the recipient's login as the argument to the command. The input included with the use of the here document is:

```
Best wishes to you on your birthday
```

For example, to send this greeting to the owner of login `mary`, type:

```
$ gbday mary<CR>
```

User `mary` will receive your greeting the next time she reads her mail messages:

```
$ mail<CR>
From mylogin Wed May 14 14:31 CDT 1986
Best wishes to you on your birthday
$
```

Table 9-22 summarizes the format and capabilities of the gbday command.

Table 9-22: Summary of the gbday Command

Shell Program gbday send a generic birthday greeting (user defined)	
command	*arguments*
gbday	*login*
Description:	gbday sends a generic birthday greeting to the owner of the login specified in the argument.

Using ed in a Shell Program

The here document offers a convenient and useful way to use ed in a shell script. For example, suppose you want to make a shell program that will enter the ed editor, make a global substitution to a file, write the file, and then quit ed. The following screen shows the contents of a program called ch.text which does these tasks.

```
$ cat ch.text<CR>
echo Type in the filename.
read file1
echo Type in the exact text to be changed.
read old_text
echo Type in the exact new text to replace the above.
read new_text
ed - $file1 <<!
g/$old_text/s//$new_text/g
w
q
!
$
```

Notice the – (minus) option to the ed command. This option prevents the character count from being displayed on the screen. Notice, also, the format of the ed command for global substitution:

g/*old_text*/s//*new_text*/g<CR>

The program uses three variables: *file1*, *old_text*, and *new_text*. When the program is run, it uses the read command to obtain the values of these variables. The variables provide the following information:

file	the name of the file to be edited
old_text	the exact text to be changed
new_text	the new text

Once the variables are entered in the program, the here document redirects the global substitution, the write command, and the quit command into the ed command. Try the new ch.text command. The following screen shows sample responses to the program prompts:

```
$ ch.text<CR>
Type in the filename.
memo<CR>
Type in the exact text to be changed.
Dear John:<CR>
Type in the exact new text to replace the above.
To whom it may concern:<CR>
$ cat memo<CR>
To whom it may concern:
$
```

Notice that by running the cat command on the changed file, you could examine the results of the global substitution.

Table 9-23 summarizes the format and capabilities of the ch.text command.

Table 9-23: Summary of the ch.text Command

Shell Program ch.text change text in a file	
command	*arguments*
ch.text	(interactive)
Description:	Replaces text in a file with new text.
Remarks:	This shell program is interactive. It prompts you to type in the arguments.

If you want to become more familiar with ed, see Chapter 6, "Line Editor (ed) Tutorial." The stream editor sed can also be used in shell programming.

Return Codes

Most shell commands issue return codes that indicate whether the command executed properly. By convention, if the value returned is 0 (zero), then the command executed properly; any other value indicates that it did not. The return code is not printed automatically, but is available as the value of the shell special parameter `$?`.

Checking Return Codes

After executing a command interactively, you can see its return code by typing

```
echo $?
```

Consider the following example:

```
$ cat hi
This is file hi.
$ echo $?
0
$ cat hello
cat: cannot open hello
$ echo $?
2
$
```

In the first case, the file `hi` exists in your directory and has read permission for you. The `cat` command behaves as expected and outputs the contents of the file. It exits with a return code of 0, which you can see using the parameter `$?`. In the second case, the file either does not exist or does not have read permission for you. The `cat` command prints a diagnostic message and exits with a return code of 2.

Using Return Codes With the `exit` Command

A shell program normally terminates when the last command in the file is executed. However, you can use the `exit` command to terminate a program at some other point. Perhaps more importantly, you can also use the `exit` command to issue return codes for a shell program. For more information about `exit`, see the `exit` command on the `sh` manual page in the *Programmer's Reference Manual*.

Looping

In the previous examples in this chapter, the commands in shell programs have been executed in sequence. The `for` and `while` looping constructs allow a program to execute a command or sequence of commands several times.

The `for` Loop

The `for` loop executes a sequence of commands once for each member of a list. It has the format shown in Figure 9-2

Figure 9-2: Format of the `for` Loop Construct

```
for variable<CR>
        in a_list_of_values<CR>
do<CR>
      command 1<CR>
      command 2<CR>
             .
             .
             .
      last command<CR>
done<CR>
```

For each iteration of the loop, the next member of the list is assigned to the variable given in the `for` clause. References to that variable may be made anywhere in the commands within the `do` clause.

It is easier to read a shell program if the looping constructs are visually clear. Since the shell ignores spaces at the beginning of lines, each section of commands can be indented as it was in the above format. Also, if you indent each command section, you can easily check to make sure each `do` has a corresponding `done` at the end of the loop.

The variable can be any name you choose. For example, if you call it `var`, then the values given in the list after the keyword `in` will be assigned in turn to `var`; references within the command list to `$var` will make the value available. If the `in` clause is omitted, the values for `var` will be the complete set of arguments given to the command and available in the special parameter `$*`. The command list between the keywords do and done will be executed once for each value.

When the commands have been executed for the last value in the list, the program will execute the next line below done. If there is no line, the program will end.

The easiest way to understand a shell programming construct is to try an example. Create a program that will move files to another directory. Include the following commands for the purposes shown:

`echo`	to prompt the user for a pathname to the new directory.
`read`	to assign the pathname to the variable `path`
`for` *variable*	to call the variable `file`; it can be referenced as `$file` in the command sequence.
`in` *list_of_values*	to supply a list of values. If the `in` clause is omitted, the list of values is assumed to be `$*` (all the arguments entered on the command line).
`do` *command_sequence*	to provide a command sequence. The construct for this program will be:

```
do
    mv $file $path/$file<CR>
done
```

The following screen shows the text for the shell program `mv.file`:

```
$ cat mv.file<CR>
echo Please type in the directory path
read path
for file
   in memo1 memo2 memo3
do
   mv $file $path/$file
done
$
```

In this program the values for the variable `file` are already in the program. To change the files each time the program is invoked, assign the values using positional parameters or the `read` command. When positional parameters are used, the `in` keyword is not needed, as the next screen shows:

```
$ cat mv.file<CR>
echo type in the directory path
read path
for file
do
   mv $file $path/$file
done
$
```

You can move several files at once with this command by specifying a list of file names as arguments to the command. (This can be done most easily using the filename expansion mechanism described earlier).

Table 9-24 summarizes the `mv.file` shell program.

Table 9-24: Summary of `mv.file` Shell Program

Shell Program `mv.file` move files to another directory (user defined)	
command	*arguments*
`mv.file`	*filenames* (interactive)
Description:	Moves files to a new directory.
Remarks:	This program requires filenames to be given as arguments. The program prompts for the path to the new directory.

The `while` Loop

Another loop construct, the `while` loop, uses two groups of commands. It will continue executing the sequence of commands in the second group, the `do...done` list, as long as the final command in the first group, the `while` list, returns a status of (true), meaning the statements after the `do` can be executed.

The general format of the `while` loop is shown in Figure 9-3.

Figure 9-3: Format of the `while` Loop Construct

```
while<CR>
      command 1<CR>
          .
          .
          .
     last command<CR>
do<CR>
     command 1<CR>
          .
          .
          .
     last command<CR>
done<CR>
```

For example, a program called `enter.name` uses a `while` loop to enter a list of names into a file. The program consists of the following command lines:

```
$ cat enter.name<CR>
while
   read x
do
   echo $x>>xfile
done
$
```

With some added refinements, the program becomes:

```
$ cat enter.name<CR>
echo Please type in each person's name and then a <CR>
echo Please end the list of names with a <^d>
while read x
do
   echo $x>>xfile
done
echo xfile contains the following names:
cat xfile
$
```

Notice that, after the loop is completed, the program executes the commands below the `done`.

You used special characters in the first two `echo` command lines, so you must use quotes to turn off the special meaning. The next screen shows the results of `enter.name`:

```
$  enter.name<CR>
Please type in each person's name and then a <CR>
Please end the list of names with a <^d>
Mary Lou<CR>
Janice<CR>
<^d>
xfile contains the following names:
Mary Lou
Janice
$
```

Notice that after the loop completes, the program prints all the names contained in `xfile`.

The Shell's Garbage Can: `/dev/null`

The file system has a file called `/dev/null` where you can have the shell deposit any unwanted output.

Try `/dev/null` by ignoring the results of the `who` command. First, type in the `who` command. The response tells you who is on the system. Now, try the `who` command, but redirect the output into `/dev/null`:

```
who > /dev/null<CR>
```

Notice that the system responded with a prompt. The output from the `who` command was placed in `/dev/null` and was effectively discarded.

Conditional Constructs

`if...then`

The `if` command tells the shell program to execute the `then` sequence of commands only if the final command in the `if` command list is successful. The `if` construct ends with the keyword `fi`.

The general format for the `if` construct is shown in Figure 9-4.

Figure 9-4: Format of the `if...then` Conditional Construct

```
if<CR>
     command1<CR>
        .
        .
        .
     last command<CR>
   then<CR>
        command1<CR>
           .
           .
           .
        last command<CR>
fi<CR>
```

For example, a shell program called `search` demonstrates the use of the `if...then` construct. The `search` program uses the `grep` command to search for a word in a file. If `grep` is successful, the program `echos` that the word is found in the file. Copy the `search` program (shown on the following screen) and try it yourself:

```
$ cat search<CR>
echo Type in the word and the file name.
read word file
if grep $word $file
   then echo $word is in $file
fi
$
```

Notice that the `read` command assigns values to two variables. The first characters you type, up until a space, are assigned to `word`. The rest of the characters, including embedded spaces, are assigned to `file`.

A problem with this program is the unwanted display of output from the `grep` command. If you want to dispose of the system response to the `grep` command in your program, use the file `/dev/null`, changing the `if` command line to the following:

```
if grep $word $file > /dev/null<CR>
```

Now execute your `search` program. It should respond only with the message specified after the `echo` command.

if...then...else

The `if...then` construction can also issue an alternate set of commands with `else`, when the `if` command sequence is false. when the `if` command sequence is false. It has the general format shown in Figure 9-5.

Figure 9-5: Format of the `if...then...else` Conditional Construct

```
if<CR>
    command1<CR>
        .
        .
        .
    last command<CR>
  then<CR>
      command1<CR>
          .
          .
          .
      last command<CR>
  else<CR>
      command1<CR>
          .
          .
          .
      last command<CR>
fi<CR>
```

You can now improve your `search` command so it will tell you when it cannot find a word, as well as when it can. The following screen shows how your improved program will look:

```
$ cat search<CR>
echo Type in the word and the file name.
read word file
if
   grep $word $file >/dev/null
then
   echo $word is in $file
else
   echo $word is NOT in $file
fi
$
```

Table 9-25 summarizes your enhanced `search` program.

Table 9-25: Summary of the `search` Shell Program

Shell Program `search` tells you if a word is in a file (user defined)	
command	*arguments*
`search`	interactive
Description:	Reports whether a word is in a file.
Remarks:	The command prompts you for the arguments (the word and the file)

The `test` Command for Loops

The `test` command, which checks to see if certain conditions are true, is a useful command for conditional constructs. If the condition is true, the loop will continue. If the condition is false, the loop will end and the next command will be executed. Some of the useful options for the `test` command are:

`test -r` *file*<CR>	true if the file exists and is readable
`test -w` *file*<CR>	true if the file exists and has write permission
`test -x` *file*<CR>	true if the file exists and is executable
`test -s` *file*<CR>	true if the file exists and has at least one character
`test` *var1* `-eq` *var2*<CR>	true if *var1* equals *var2*
`test` *var1* `-ne` *var2*<CR>	true if *var1* does not equal *var2*

You may want to create a shell program to move all the executable files in the current directory to your `bin` directory. You can use the `test -x` command to select the executable files. Review the example of the `for` construct that occurs in the `mv.file` program, shown in the following screen:

```
$ cat mv.file<CR>
echo type in the directory path
read path
for file
do
  mv $file $path/$file
done
$
```

Create a program called mv.ex that includes an if test -x statement in the do...done loop to move executable files only. Your program will be as follows:

```
$ cat mv.ex<CR>
echo type in the directory path
read path
for file
  do
    if test -x $file
       then
          mv $file $path/$file
    fi
  done
$
```

The directory path is the path from the current directory to the bin directory. However, if you use the value for the shell variable HOME, you will not need to type in the path each time. $HOME gives the path to the login directory. $HOME/bin gives the path to your bin.

In the following example, mv.ex does not prompt you to type in the directory name, and therefore, does not read the path variable:

```
$ cat mv.ex<CR>
for file
  do
    if test -x $file
       then
         mv $file $HOME/bin/$file
    fi
  done
$
```

Test the command, using all the files in the current directory, specified with the `*` metacharacter as the command argument. The command lines shown in the following example execute the command from the current directory and then changes to `bin` and lists the files in that directory. All executable files should be there.

```
$ mv.ex *<CR>
$ cd; cd bin; ls<CR>
list_of_executable_files
$
```

Figure 9-26 summarizes the format and capabilities of the `mv.ex` shell program.

Table 9-26: Summary of the `mv.ex` Shell Program

Shell Program `mv.ex` move all executable files in the current directory to the `bin` directory	
command	*arguments*
`mv.ex`	a list of files in the current directory
Description:	Moves all files in the current directory with execute permission to the `bin` directory.
Remarks:	All executable files in the `bin` directory (or any directory shown by the `PATH` variable) can be executed from any directory.

`case..esac`

The `case...esac` construction has a multiple choice format that allows you to choose one of several patterns and then execute a list of commands for that pattern. The pattern statements must begin with the keyword `in`, and a `)` must be placed after the last character of each pattern. The command sequence for each pattern is ended with `;;`. The `case` construction must be ended with `esac` (the letters of the word case reversed).

The general format for the `case` construction is shown in Figure 9-6:

Figure 9-6: The `case...esac` Conditional Construct

```
case word<CR>
in<CR>
    pattern1)<CR>
        command line 1<CR>
            .
            .
            .
        last command line<CR>
    ;;<CR>
    pattern2)<CR>
        command line 1<CR>
            .
            .
            .
        last command line<CR>
    ;;<CR>
    pattern3)<CR>
        command line 1<CR>
            .
            .
            .
        last command line<CR>
    ;;<CR>
    *)<CR>
        command 1<CR>
            .
            .
            .
        last command<CR>
    ;;<CR>
esac<CR>
```

The `case` construction tries to match the *word* following the word `case` with the *pattern* in the first pattern section. If a match exists, the program executes the command lines after the first pattern and up to the corresponding *;;*.

If the first pattern is not matched, the program proceeds to the second pattern. Once a pattern is matched, the program does not try to match any more of the patterns, but goes to the command following `esac`.

The `*` used as a pattern matches any *word*, and so allows you to give a set of commands to be executed if no other pattern matches. To do this, it must be placed as the last possible pattern in the `case` construct, so that the other patterns are checked first. This helps you detect incorrect or unexpected input.

The patterns that can be specified in the *pattern* part of each section may use the metacharacters `*`, `?`, and `[]` as described earlier in this chapter for the filename expansion capability of the shell. This provides useful flexibility.

The `set.term` program contains a good example of the `case...esac` construction. This program sets the shell variable `TERM` according to the type of terminal you are using. It uses the following command line:

`TERM=`*terminal_name*`<CR>`

For an explanation of the commands used, see Chapter 7, "Screen Editor Tutorial (`vi`)." In the following example, the terminal is a Teletype 4420, Teletype 5410, or Teletype 5420.

The `set.term` program first checks to see whether the value of `term` is 4420. If it is, the program makes T4 the value of `TERM`, and terminates. If it the value of `term` is not 4420, the program checks for other values: 5410 and 5420. It executes the commands under the first pattern that it finds, and then goes to the first command after the `esac` command.

The pattern `*` , meaning everything else, is included at the end of the terminal patterns. It warns that you do not have a pattern for the terminal specified and it allows you to exit the `case` construct:

```
$ cat set.term<CR>
echo If you have a TTY 4420 type in 4420
echo If you have a TTY 5410 type in 5410
echo If you have a TTY 5420 type in 5420
read term
case $term
        in
            4420)
                TERM=T4
            ;;
            5410)
                TERM=T5
            ;;
            5420)
                TERM=T7
            ;;
            *)
            echo not a correct terminal type
            ;;
esac
export TERM
echo end of program
$
```

Notice the use of the `export` command in the preceding screen. You use `export` to make a variable available within your environment and to other shell procedures. What would happen if you placed the * pattern first? The `set.term` program would never assign a value to `TERM`, since it would always match the first pattern *, which means everything.

Table 9-27 summarizes the format and capabilities of the `set.term` shell program.

Table 9-27: Summary of the `set.term` Shell Program

Shell Program `set.term` assign a value to TERM (user defined)	
command	*arguments*
`set.term`	interactive
Description:	Assigns a value to the shell variable TERM and then exports that value to other shell procedures.
Remarks:	This command asks for a specific terminal code to be used as a pattern for the `case` construction.

Unconditional Control Statements: the `break` and `continue` Commands

The `break` command unconditionally stops the execution of any loop in which it is encountered, and goes to the next command after the `done`, `fi`, or `esac` statement. If no commands follow that statement, the program ends.

In the example for `set.term`, you could have used the `break` command instead of `echo` to leave the program, as the next example shows:

```
$ cat set.term<CR>
echo If you have a TTY 4420 type in 4420
echo If you have a TTY 5410 type in 5410
echo If you have a TTY 5420 type in 5420
read term
case $term
        in
            4420)
            TERM=T4
        ;;
        5410)
            TERM=T5
        ;;
        5420)
            TERM=T7
        ;;
        *)
            break
        ;;
esac
export TERM
echo end of program
$
```

The `continue` command causes the program to go immediately to the next iteration of a `while` or `for` loop without executing the remaining commands in the loop.

Debugging Programs

At times you may need to debug a program to find and correct errors. Two options to the `sh` command (listed below) can help you debug a program:

`sh –v` *shellprogramname*	prints the shell input lines as they are read by the system
`sh –x` *shellprogramname*	prints commands and their arguments as they are executed

To try these two options, create a shell program that has an error in it. For example, create a file called bug that contains the following list of commands:

```
$ cat bug<CR>
today=`date`
echo enter person
read person
mail $1
$person
When you log off come into my office please.
$today.
MLH
$
```

Notice that today equals the output of the date command, which must be enclosed in grave accents for command substitution to occur.

The mail message sent to Tom ($1) at login tommy ($1) should look like the following screen:

```
$ mail<CR>
From mlh  Mon  Apr 10  11:36  CST  1989
Tom
When you log off come into my office please.
Mon  Apr 10  11:36:32  CST  1989
MLH
?
.
```

To execute bug, you have to press the BREAK or DELETE key to end the program.

To debug this program, try executing bug using sh -v. This will print the lines of the file as they are read by the system, as shown below:

```
$ sh -v bug tommy<CR>
today=`date`
echo enter person
enter person
read person
tom
mail $1
```

Notice that the output stops on the `mail` command, since there is a problem with `mail`. You must use the here document to redirect input into `mail`.

Before you fix the `bug` program, try executing it with `sh -x`, which prints the commands and their arguments as they are read by the system.

```
$ sh -x bug tommy<CR>
+date
today=Mon  Apr 10  11:07:23  CST  1989
+ echo enter person
enter person
+ read person
tom
+ mail tom
$
```

Once again, the program stops at the `mail` command. Notice that the substitutions for the variables have been made and are displayed.

The corrected `bug` program is as follows:

```
$ cat bug<CR>
today=`date`
echo enter person
read person
mail $1 <<!
$person
When you log off come into my office please.
$today
MLH
!
$
```

The `tee` command is a helpful command for debugging pipelines. While simply passing its standard input to its standard output, it also saves a copy of its input into the file whose name is given as an argument.

The general format of the `tee` command is:

> *command1* | `tee` *saverfile* | *command2*<CR

`saverfile` is the file that saves the output of *command1* for you to study.

For example, suppose you want to check on the output of the `grep` command in the following command line:

```
who | grep $1 | cut -c1-9<CR>
```

You can use `tee` to copy the output of `grep` into a file called `check`, without disturbing the rest of the pipeline.

```
who | grep $1 | tee check | cut -c1-9<CR>
```

The file `check` contains a copy of the `grep` output, as shown in the following screen:

```
$ who | grep mlhmo | tee check | cut -c1-9<CR>
mlhmo
$ cat check<CR>
mlhmo   tty61   Apr 10   11:30
$
```

Modifying Your Login Environment

The UNIX system lets you modify your login environment in several ways. For example, users frequently want to change the default values of the erase (`^H`) and line kill (`@`) characters.

When you log in, the shell first examines a file in your login directory named `.profile` (pronounced "dot profile"). This file contains commands that control your shell environment.

Because the `.profile` is a shell script, it can be edited and changed to suit your needs. On some systems you can edit this file yourself, whereas on others, the system administrator must do this for you. To see whether you have a `.profile` in your home directory, type:

```
ls -al $HOME
```

If you can edit the file yourself, you may want to be cautious the first few times. Before making any changes to your `.profile`, make a copy of it in another file called `safe.profile`. Type:

```
cp .profile safe.profile<CR>
```

You can add commands to your `.profile` just as you add commands to any other shell program. You can also set some terminal options with the `stty` command, and set some shell variables.

Adding Commands to Your `.profile`

Practice adding commands to your `.profile`. Edit the file and add the following `echo` command to the last line of the file:

```
echo Good Morning! I am ready to work for you.
```

Write and quit the editor.

Whenever you make changes to your `.profile` and you want to initiate them in the current work session, you may cause the commands in `.profile` to be executed directly using the `.` (dot) shell command. The shell reinitializes your environment by reading executing the commands in your `.profile`. Try this now. Type:

```
. .profile<CR>
```

The system should respond with the following:

```
Good Morning! I am ready to work for you.
$
```

Setting Terminal Options

The `stty` command can make your shell environment more convenient. You can use these options with `stty`: `-tabs` and `echoe`.

`stty -tabs` This option preserves tabs when you are printing. It expands the tab setting to eight spaces, which is the default. The number of spaces for each tab can be changed. (See `stty`(1) in the *User's Reference Manual* for details.)

`stty echoe` If you have a terminal with a screen, this option erases characters from the screen as you erase them with the BACKSPACE key.

If you want to use these options for the `stty` command, you can create those command lines in your `.profile` just as you would create them in a shell program. If you use the `tail` command, which displays the last few lines of a file, you can see the results of adding those three command lines to your `.profile`:

```
$ tail -3 .profile<CR>
echo Good Morning! I am ready to work for you
stty -tabs
stty echoe
$
```

Table 9-28 summarizes the format and capabilities of the `tail` command.

Table 9-28: Summary of the `tail` Command

Command `tail` display the last portion of a file		
command	*options*	*arguments*
`tail`	*−n*	*filename*
Description:	Displays the last lines of a file.	
Options:	Use *−n* to specify the number of lines *n* (default is ten lines). You can specify a number of blocks (−*n*b) or characters (−*n*c) instead of lines.	

Using Shell Variables

Several of the variables reserved by the shell are used in your `.profile`. You can display the current value for any shell variable by entering the following command:

echo *$variable_name*

Four of the most basic of these variables are discussed next.

`HOME` This variable gives the pathname of your login directory. Use the `cd` command to go to your login directory and type:

```
pwd<CR>
```

What was the system response? Now type:

```
echo $HOME<CR>
```

Was the system response the same as the response to `pwd`?

`$HOME` is the default argument for the `cd` command. If you do not specify a directory, `cd` will move you to `$HOME`.

`PATH` This variable gives the search path for finding and executing commands. To see the current values for your `PATH` variable type:

```
echo $PATH<CR>
```

The system will respond with your current PATH value.

```
$ echo $PATH<CR>
:/mylogin/bin:/bin:/usr/bin
$
```

The colon (:) is a delimiter between pathnames in the string assigned to the $PATH variable. When nothing is specified before a : , then the current directory is understood. Notice how, in the last example, the system looks for commands in the current directory first, then in `/mylogin/bin`, then in `/usr/bin`, then in `/usr/bin`, and finally in `/usr/lib`.

If you are working on a project with several other people, you may want to set up a group `bin`, a directory of special shell programs used only by your project members. The path might be named `/project1/bin`. Edit your `.profile`, and add `:/project1/bin` to the end of your `PATH`, as in the next example.

```
PATH="$PATH:/project1/bin"<CR>
```

`TERM` This variable tells the shell what kind of terminal you are using. To assign a value to it, you must execute the following three commands in this order:

```
TERM=terminal_name<CR>
export TERM<CR>
tput init
```

The first two lines, together, are necessary to tell the computer what type of terminal you are using. The last line, containing the `tput` command, tells the terminal that the computer is expecting to communicate with the type of terminal specified in the `TERM` variable. Therefore, this command must always be entered after the variable has been exported.

If you do not want to specify the `TERM` variable each time you log in, add these three command lines to your `.profile`; they will be executed automatically whenever you log in. To determine what terminal name to assign to the `TERM` variable, see the instructions in Appendix G, "Setting Up the Terminal." This appendix also contains details about the `tput` command.

If you log in on more than one type of terminal, it would also be useful to have your `set.term` command in your `.profile`.

`PS1` This variable sets the primary shell prompt string (the default is the `$` sign). You can change your prompt by changing the `PS1` variable in your `.profile`.

Try the following example. Note that to use a multi-word prompt, you must enclose the phrase in quotes. Type the following variable assignment in your `.profile`.

```
PS1="Your command is my wish<CR>"
```

Now execute your `.profile` (with the `.` command) and watch for your new prompt sign.

```
$ . .profile<CR>
Your command is my wish
```

The `$` sign is gone forever, or at least until you delete the `PS1` variable from your `.profile`.

Shell Programming Exercises

2-1. Create a shell program called `time` from the following command line:

```
banner `date | cut -c12-19`<CR>
```

2-2. Write a shell program that will give only the date in a banner display. Be careful not to give your program the same name as a UNIX system command.

2-3. Write a shell program that will send a note to several people on your system.

2-4. Redirect the `date` command without the time into a file.

2-5. Echo the phrase Dear colleague in the same file as the previous exercise, without erasing the date.

2-6. Using the above exercises, write a shell program that will send a memo to the same people on your system mentioned in Exercise 2-3. Include in your memo:

   The current date and the two words Dear colleague at the top of the memo

   The body of the memo (stored in an existing file)

   The closing statement

2-7. How can you `read` variables into the `mv.file` program?

2-8. Use a `for` loop to move a list of files in the current directory to another directory. How can you move all your files to another directory?

2-9. How can you change the program `search`, so that it searches through several files?

   Hint:

```
for file
 in $*
```

2-10. Set the `stty` options for your environment.

2-11. Change your prompt to the word Hello.

2-12. Check the settings of the variables `$HOME`, `$TERM`, and `$PATH` in your environment.

Answers To Exercises

Command Language Exercises

1-1. The * at the beginning of a filename refers to all files that end in that filename, including that file name.

```
$ ls *t<CR>
cat
123t
new.t
t
$
```

1-2. The command `cat [0-9]*` produces the following output:

```
1memo
100data
9
05name
```

The command `echo *` produces a list of all the files in the current directory.

1-3. You can place `?` in any position in a filename.

1-4. The command `ls [0-9]*` lists only those files that start with a number.

The command `ls [a-m]*` lists only those files that start with the letters "a" through "m".

1-5. If you placed the sequential command line in the background mode, the immediate system response was the PID number for the job.

No, the `&` (ampersand) must be placed at the end of the command line.

1-6. The command line would be:

```
cd; pwd > junk; ls >> junk <CR>
```

1-7. Change the –c option of the command line to read:

```
banner `date | cut -c1-10`<CR>
```

Shell Programming Exercises

2-1.

```
$ cat time<CR>
banner `date | cut -c12-19`
$
$ chmod u+x time<CR>
$ time<CR>
(banner display of the time 10:26)
$
```

2-2.

```
$ cat mydate<CR>
banner `date | cut -c1-10`
$
```

2-3.

```
$ cat tofriends<CR>
echo Type in the name of the file containing the note.
read note
mail janice marylou bryan < $note
$
```

Or, if you used parameters for the logins, instead of the logins themselves, your program may have looked like this:

```
$ cat tofriends<CR>
echo Type in the name of the file containing the note.
read note
mail $* < $note
$
```

2-4. `date | cut -c1-10 > file1<CR>`

2-5. `echo Dear colleague >> file1<CR>`

2-6.

```
$ cat send.memo<CR>
date | cut -c1-10 > memo1
echo Dear colleague >> memo1
cat memo >> memo1
echo A memo from M. L. Kelly >> memo1
mail janice marylou bryan < memo1
$
```

2-7.

```
$ cat mv.file<CR>
echo type in the directory path
read path
echo type in file names, end with <^d>
  while
  read file
    do
      mv $file $path/$file
    done
echo all done
$
```

2-8.

```
$ cat mv.file<CR>
echo Please type in directory path
read path
for file in $*
  do
    mv $file $path/$file
  done
$
```

The command line for moving all files in the current directory is:

```
$ mv.file *<CR>
```

2-9. See hint given with exercise 2-9.

```
$ cat search<CR>
for file
  in $*
  do
    if grep $word $file >/dev/null
    then echo $word is in $file
    else echo $word is NOT in $file
    fi
  done
$
```

2-10. Add the following lines to your `.profile`.

```
stty -tabs<CR>
stty erase <^h><CR>
stty echoe<CR>
```

2-11. Add the following command lines to your `.profile`

```
PS1=Hello<CR>
export PS1
```

2-12. To check the values of these variables in your home environment:

- $ echo $HOME<CR>
- $ echo $TERM<CR>
- $ echo $PATH<CR>

10. awk TUTORIAL

10. awk TUTORIAL

10 awk Tutorial

Introduction

This chapter describes a programming language that enables you to handle easily the tasks associated with data processing and information retrieval. With awk, you can tabulate survey results stored in a file, print various reports summarizing these results, generate form letters, count the occurrences of a string in a file, or reformat a data file used for one application package so it can be used for another application package.

The name awk is an acronym formed from the initials of its developers. The name awk denotes both the language and the UNIX system command you use to run an awk program.

This chapter explains the new version of the awk language as described in the *Programmer's Reference Manual* under nawk(1). The earlier version is described in that book under awk(1) and will be replaced in a later release of the UNIX system.

awk is an easy language to learn. It automatically does many things that in other languages you have to program yourself. As a result, many useful awk programs are only one or two lines long. Because awk programs are usually smaller than equivalent programs in other languages, and because they are interpreted, not compiled, awk is also a good language for prototyping.

The first part of this chapter introduces you to the basics of awk and is intended to make it easy for you to start writing and running your own awk programs. The rest of the chapter describes the complete language and is somewhat less tutorial. If you are an experienced awk user, you will find the skeletal summary of the language at the end of the chapter particularly useful.

You should be familiar with the UNIX system and shell programming to use this chapter. Although you don't need other programming experience, some knowledge of the C programming language is beneficial because many constructs found in awk are also found in C.

Basic awk

This section provides enough information for you to write and run some of your own programs. Each topic presented in this section is discussed in more detail in later sections.

Program Structure

The basic operation of awk is to scan a set of input lines one after another, searching for lines that match any of a set of patterns or conditions you specify. For each pattern, you can specify an action; this action is performed on each line that matches the pattern. Accordingly, an awk program is a sequence of pattern-action statements, as Figure 10-1 shows.

Figure 10-1: awk Program Structure and Example

Structure:

```
pattern    { action }
pattern    { action }
...
```

Example:

```
$1 == "address"  { print $2, $3 }
```

The example in the figure is a typical awk program, consisting of one pattern-action statement. The program prints the second and third fields of each input line whose first field is `address`. In general, awk programs work by matching each line of input against each of the patterns in turn. For each pattern that matches, the associated action (which may involve multiple steps) is executed. Then the next line is read and the matching starts again. This process typically continues until all the input has been read.

Either the pattern or the action in a pattern-action statement may be omitted. If there is no action with a pattern, as in

```
$1 == "name"
```

the matching line is printed. If there is no pattern with an action, as in

```
{ print $1, $2 }
```

the action is performed for every input line. Since patterns and actions are both optional, actions are enclosed in braces to distinguish them from patterns.

Usage

You can run an awk program two ways. First, you can type the command line

awk '*pattern-action statements*'   *optional list of input files*

to execute the pattern-action statements on the set of named input files. For example, you could say

```
awk '{ print $1, $2 }' file1 file2
```

Notice that the pattern-action statements are enclosed in single quotes. This protects characters like $ from being interpreted by the shell and also allows the program to be longer than one line.

If no files are mentioned on the command line, awk reads from the standard input. You can also specify that input comes from the standard input by using the hyphen (–) as one of the input files. For example,

```
awk '{ print $3, $4 }' file1 -
```

says to read input first from file1 and then from the standard input.

The arrangement above is convenient when the awk program is short (a few lines). If the program is long, it is often more convenient to put it into a separate file and use the -f option to fetch it:

awk -f *program_file* *optional list of input files*

For example, the following command line says to fetch and execute myprogram on input from the file file1:

```
awk  -f myprogram file1
```

Fields

Normally, awk reads its input one line, or record, at a time; a record is, by default, a sequence of characters ending with a newline. Then awk splits each record into fields, where, by default, a field is a string of non-blank, non-tab characters.

As input for many of the awk programs in this chapter, we use the file - countries, which contains information about the ten largest countries in the world. (See Figure 10-2.) Each record contains the name of a country, its area in thousands of square miles, its population in millions, and the continent on which it is located. (Data are from 1978; the U.S.S.R. has been arbitrarily placed in Asia.) The white space between fields is a tab in the original input; a single blank separates North and South from America .

Figure 10-2: The Sample Input File countries

```
USSR        8650    262     Asia
Canada      3852    24      North America
China       3692    866     Asia
USA         3615    219     North America
Brazil      3286    116     South America
Australia   2968    14      Australia
India       1269    637     Asia
Argentina   1072    26      South America
Sudan       968     19      Africa
Algeria     920     18      Africa
```

This file is typical of the kind of data awk is good at processing—a mixture of words and numbers separated into fields by blanks and tabs.

The number of fields in a record is determined by the field separator. Fields are normally separated by sequences of blanks and/or tabs, so that the first record of countries would have four fields, the second five, and so on. It's possible to set the field separator to just tab, so each line would have four fields, matching the meaning of the data; we'll show how to do this shortly. For the time being, we'll use the default: fields separated by blanks and/or tabs. The first field within a line is called $1, the second $2, and so forth. The entire record is called $0.

Printing

If the pattern in a pattern-action statement is omitted, the action is executed for all input lines. The simplest action is to print each line; you can accomplish this with an awk program consisting of a single print statement

```
{ print }
```

so the command line

```
awk '{ print }' countries
```

prints each line of countries, copying the file to the standard output. The print statement can also be used to print parts of a record; for instance, the program

```
{ print $1, $3 }
```

prints the first and third fields of each record. Thus

```
awk '{ print $1, $3 }' countries
```

produces as output the following sequence of lines:

```
USSR 262
Canada 24
China 866
USA 219
Brazil 116
Australia 14
India 637
Argentina 26
Sudan 19
Algeria 18
```

When printed, items separated by a comma in the print statement are separated by the output field separator which, by default, is a single blank. Each line printed is terminated by the output record separator which, by default, is a newline.

In the remainder of this chapter, we only show **awk** programs, without the command line that invokes them. Each complete program can be run either by enclosing it in quotes as the first argument of the **awk** command, or by putting it in a file and invoking **awk** with the **-f** flag, as discussed earlier in the section titled "Usage." For example, if no input is mentioned, the input is assumed to be the file `countries`.

Formatted Printing

For more carefully formatted output, `awk` provides a C-like `printf` statement

`printf` *format*, $expr_1$, $expr_2$, . . ., $expr_n$

which prints the $expr_i$'s according to the specification in the string *format*. For example, the `awk` program

```
{ printf "%10s %6d\n", $1, $3 }
```

prints the first field (`$1`) as a string of 10 characters (right justified), then a space, then the third field (`$3`) as a decimal number in a six-character field, then a newline (`\n`). With input from the file `countries`, this program prints an aligned table:

```
      USSR    262
    Canada     24
     China    866
       USA    219
    Brazil    116
 Australia     14
     India    637
 Argentina     26
     Sudan     19
   Algeria     18
```

With `printf`, no output separators or newlines are produced automatically; you must create them yourself by using `\n` in the format specification. The section "The `printf` Statement" in this chapter contains a full description of `printf`.

Simple Patterns

You can select specific records for printing or other processing by using simple patterns. awk has three kinds of patterns. First, you can use patterns called relational expressions that make comparisons. For example, the operator == tests for equality. To print the lines for which the fourth field equals the string Asia, we can use the program consisting of the single pattern

```
$4 == "Asia"
```

With the file countries as input, this program yields

```
USSR  8650  262   Asia
China 3692  866   Asia
India 1269  637   Asia
```

The complete set of comparisons is >, >=, <, <=, == (equal to) and != (not equal to). These comparisons can be used to test both numbers and strings. For example, suppose we want to print only countries with a population greater than 100 million. The program

```
$3 > 100
```

is all that is needed. It prints all lines in which the third field exceeds 100. (Remember that the third field in the file countries is the population in millions.)

Second, you can use patterns called regular expressions that search for specified characters to select records. The simplest form of a regular expression is a string of characters enclosed in slashes:

```
/US/
```

This program prints each line that contains the (adjacent) letters US anywhere; with the file countries as input, it prints

```
USSR  8650  262   Asia
USA   3615  219   North America
```

We will have a lot more to say about regular expressions later in this chapter.

Third, you can use two special patterns, BEGIN and END, that match before the first record has been read and after the last record has been processed. This program uses BEGIN to print a title:

```
BEGIN    { print "Countries of Asia:" }
/Asia/   { print "      ", $1 }
```

The output is

```
Countries of Asia:
      USSR
      China
      India
```

Simple Actions

We have already seen the simplest action of an awk program: printing each input line. Now let's consider how you can use built-in and user-defined variables and functions for other simple actions in a program.

Built-in Variables

Besides reading the input and splitting it into fields, awk counts the number of records read and the number of fields within the current record; you can use these counts in your awk programs. The variable NR is the number of the current record, and NF is the number of fields in the record. So the program

```
{ print NR, NF }
```

prints the number of each line and how many fields it has, while

```
{ print NR, $0 }
```

prints each record preceded by its record number.

User-defined Variables

Besides providing built-in variables like NF and NR, awk lets you define your own variables, which you can use for storing data, doing arithmetic, and the like. To illustrate, consider computing the total population and the average population represented by the data in the file countries:

```
  { sum = sum + $3 }
END { print "Total population is", sum, "million"
      print "Average population of", NR, "countries is",
        sum/NR }
```

awk initializes sum to zero before using it.

The first action accumulates the population from the third field; the second action, which is executed after the last input, prints the sum and average:

```
Total population is 2201 million
Average population of 10 countries is 220.1
```

Functions

Built-in functions of awk handle common arithmetic and string operations for you. For example, one of the arithmetic functions computes square roots; a string function substitutes one string for another. awk also lets you define your own functions. Functions are described in detail in the section titled "Actions" in this chapter.

A Handful of Useful One-liners

Although awk can be used to write large programs of some complexity, many programs are not much more complicated than what we've seen so far. Here is a collection of other short programs that you may find useful and instructive. Although these programs are not explained here, new constructs they may contain are discussed later in this chapter.

Print last field of each input line:

```
{ print $NF }
```

Print 10th input line:

```
NR == 10
```

Print last input line:

```
        { line = $0}
END     { print line }
```

Print input lines that don't have four fields:

```
NF != 4     { print $0, "does not have 4 fields" }
```

Print input lines with more than four fields:

```
NF > 4
```

Print input lines with last field more than 4:

```
$NF > 4
```

Print total number of input lines:

```
END     { print NR }
```

Print total number of fields:

```
        { nf = nf + NF }
END     { print nf }
```

Print total number of input characters:

```
        { nc = nc + length($0) }
END     { print nc + NR }
```

(Adding NR includes in the total the number of newlines.)

Print the total number of lines that contain the string Asia:

```
/Asia/        { nlines++ }
END     { print nlines }
```

(nlines++ has the same effect as nlines = nlines + 1.)

Error Messages

If you make an error in your awk program, you generally get an error message. For example, trying to run the program

```
$3 < 200 { print ( $1 }
```

generates the error messages

```
awk: syntax error at source line 1
 context is
        $3 < 200 { print ( >>> $1 } <<<
awk: illegal statement at source line 1
         1 extra (
```

Some errors may be detected while your program is running. For example, if you try to divide a number by zero, awk stops processing and reports the input record number (NR) and the line number in the program.

Patterns

In a pattern-action statement, the pattern is an expression that selects the records for which the associated action is executed. This section describes the kinds of expressions that may be used as patterns.

`BEGIN` and `END`

`BEGIN` and `END` are two special patterns that give you a way to control initialization and wrap-up in an `awk` program. `BEGIN` matches before the first input record is read, so any statements in the action part of a `BEGIN` are done once, before the `awk` command starts to read its first input record. The pattern `END` matches the end of the input, after the last record has been processed.

The following `awk` program uses `BEGIN` to set the field separator to tab (`\t`) and to put column headings on the output. The field separator is stored in a built-in variable called `FS`. Although `FS` can be reset at any time, usually the only sensible place is in a `BEGIN` section, before any input has been read. The second `printf` statement of the program which is executed for each input line, formats the output into a table, neatly aligned under the column headings. The `END` action prints the totals. (Notice that a long line can be continued after a comma.)

```
BEGIN { FS = "\t"
        printf "%10s %6s %5s   %s\n",
               "COUNTRY", "AREA", "POP", "CONTINENT" }
      { printf "%10s %6d %5d   %s\n", $1, $2, $3, $4
        area = area + $2; pop = pop + $3 }
END   { printf "\n%10s %6d %5d\n", "TOTAL", area, pop }
```

With the file `countries` as input, this program produces

```
  COUNTRY   AREA   POP  CONTINENT
     USSR   8650   262  Asia
   Canada   3852    24  North America
    China   3692   866  Asia
      USA   3615   219  North America
   Brazil   3286   116  South America
Australia   2968    14  Australia
    India   1269   637  Asia
Argentina   1072    26  South America
    Sudan    968    19  Africa
  Algeria    920    18  Africa

    TOTAL  30292  2201
```

Relational Expressions

An awk pattern can be any expression involving comparisons between strings of characters or numbers. awk has six relational operators, and two regular expression matching operators, ~ (tilde) and !~, which are discussed in the next section, for making comparisons. Table 10-1 lists these operators and their meanings.

Table 10-1: awk Comparison Operators

Operator	Meaning
<	less than
<=	less than or equal to
==	equal to
!=	not equal to
>=	greater than or equal to
>	greater than
~	matches
!~	does not match

In a comparison, if both operands are numeric, a numeric comparison is made; otherwise, the operands are compared as strings. (Every value might be either a number or a string; usually `awk` can tell what is intended. The section "Number or String?" contains more information about this.) Thus, the pattern `$3>100` selects lines where the third field exceeds 100, and the program

```
$1 >= "S"
```

selects lines that begin with the letters S through Z, namely,

```
USSR      8650  262   Asia
USA       3615  219   North America
Sudan     968   19    Africa
```

In the absence of any other information, `awk` treats fields as strings, so the program

```
$1 == $4
```

compares the first and fourth fields as strings of characters, and with the file `countries` as input, prints the single line for which this test succeeds:

```
Australia   2968   14   Australia
```

If both fields appear to be numbers, the comparisons are done numerically.

Regular Expressions

`awk` provides more powerful patterns for searching for strings of characters than the comparisons illustrated in the previous section. These patterns are called regular expressions, and are like those in `egrep`(1) and `lex`(1). The simplest regular expression is a string of characters enclosed in slashes, like

```
/Asia/
```

This program prints all input records that contain the substring `Asia`. (If a record contains `Asia` as part of a larger string like `Asian` or `Pan-Asiatic`, it is also printed.) In general, if *re* is a regular expression, then the pattern

/*re*/

matches any line that contains a substring specified by the regular expression *re*.

To restrict a match to a specific field, you use the matching operators ~ (matches) and !~ (does not match). The program

```
$4 ~ /Asia/ { print $1 }
```

prints the first field of all lines in which the fourth field matches `Asia`, while the program

```
$4 !~ /Asia/ { print $1 }
```

prints the first field of all lines in which the fourth field does not match `Asia`.

In regular expressions, the symbols

```
\ ^ $ . [] * + ? () |
```

are metacharacters with special meanings like the metacharacters in the UNIX shell. For example, the metacharacters ^ and $ match the beginning and end, respectively, of a string, and the metacharacter . ("dot") matches any single character. Thus,

```
/^.$/
```

matches all records that contain exactly one character.

A group of characters enclosed in brackets matches any one of the enclosed characters; for example, `/[ABC]/` matches records containing any one of `A`, `B`, or `C` anywhere. Ranges of letters or digits can be abbreviated within brackets: `/[a-zA-Z]/` matches any single letter.

If the first character after the `[` is a `^`, this complements the class so it matches any character not in the set: `/[^a-zA-Z]/` matches any non-letter. The character + means "one or more." Thus, the program

```
$2 !~ /^[0-9]+$/
```

prints all records in which the second field is not a string of one or more digits (^ for beginning of string, `[0-9]+` for one or more digits, and `$` for end of string). Programs of this type are often used for data validation.

Parentheses `()` are used for grouping and the character `|` is used for alternatives. The program

```
/(apple|cherry) (pie|tart)/
```

matches lines containing any one of the four substrings `apple pie`, `apple tart`, `cherry pie`, or `cherry tart`.

To turn off the special meaning of a metacharacter, precede it by a \ (backslash). Thus, the program

```
/b\$/
```

prints all lines containing b followed by a dollar sign.

In addition to recognizing metacharacters, awk recognizes the following C programming language escape sequences within regular expressions and strings:

\b	backspace
\f	formfeed
\n	newline
\r	carriage return
\t	tab
ddd	octal value *ddd*
\"	quotation mark
c	any other character *c* literally

For example, to print all lines containing a tab, use the program

```
/\t/
```

awk interprets any string or variable on the right side of a ~ or !~ as a regular expression. For example, we could have written the program

```
$2 !~ /^[0-9]+$/
```

as

```
BEGIN      { digits = "^[0-9]+$" }
$2 !~ digits
```

Suppose you want to search for a string of characters like ^[0-9]+$ When a literal quoted string like "^[0-9]+$" is used as a regular expression, one extra level of backslashes is needed to protect regular expression metacharacters. This is because one level of backslashes is removed when a string is originally parsed. If a backslash is needed in front of a character to turn off its special meaning in a regular expression, then that backslash needs a preceding backslash to protect it in a string.

For example, suppose you want to match strings containing b followed by a dollar sign. The regular expression for this pattern is b\$. If you want to create a string to represent this regular expression, you must add one more backslash: `"b\\$"`. The two regular expressions on each of the following lines are equivalent:

```
x ~ "b\\$"          x ~ /b\$/
x ~ "b\$"           x ~ /b$/
x ~ "b$"            x ~ /b$/
x ~ "\\t"           x ~ /\t/
```

The precise form of regular expressions and the substrings they match is in Table 10-2. The unary operators `*`, `+`, and `?` have the highest precedence, then concatenation, and then alternation `|`. All operators are left associative. *r* stands for any regular expression.

Table 10-2: awk Regular Expressions

Expression	Matches
c	any non-metacharacter *c*
c	character *c* literally
^	beginning of string
$	end of string
.	any character but newline
[*s*]	any character in set *s*
[^*s*]	any character not in set *s*
*r**	zero or more *r*'s
r+	one or more *r*'s
r?	zero or one *r*
(*r*)	*r*
r_1r_2	r_1 then r_2 (concatenation)
$r_1 \mid r_2$	r_1 or r_2 (alternation)

Combinations of Patterns

A compound pattern combines simpler patterns with parentheses and the logical operators `||` (or), `&&` (and), and `!` (not). For example, suppose you want to print all countries in Asia with a population of more than 500 million. The following program does this by selecting all lines in which the fourth field is `Asia` and the third field exceeds 500:

```
$4 == "Asia" && $3 > 500
```

The program

```
$4 == "Asia" || $4 == "Africa"
```

selects lines with `Asia` or `Africa` as the fourth field. Another way to write the latter query is to use a regular expression with the alternation operator `|` :

```
$4 ~ /^(Asia|Africa)$/
```

The negation operator `!` has the highest precedence, then `&&`, and finally `||`. The operators `&&` and `||` evaluate their operands from left to right; evaluation stops as soon as truth or falsehood is determined.

Pattern Ranges

A pattern range consists of two patterns separated by a comma, as in

pat_1, pat_2 `{ . . . }`

In this case, the action is performed for each line between an occurrence of pat_1 and the next occurrence of pat_2 (inclusive). For example, the pattern

```
/Canada/, /Brazil/
```

matches lines starting with the first line that contains the string Canada up through the next occurrence of the string Brazil:

```
Canada      3852     24      North America
China       3692     866     Asia
USA         3615     219     North America
Brazil      3286     116     South America
```

Similarly, since `FNR` is the number of the current record in the current input file (and `FILENAME` is the name of the current input file), the program

```
FNR == 1, FNR == 5 { print FILENAME, $0 }
```

prints the first five records of each input file with the name of the current input file prepended.

Actions

In a pattern-action statement, the action determines what is to be done with the input records that the pattern selects. Actions frequently are simple printing or assignment statements, but they may also be a combination of one or more statements. This section describes the statements that can make up actions.

Built-in Variables

Table 10-3 lists the built-in variables that awk maintains. You have already learned some of these; others appear in this and later sections.

Table 10-3: awk Built-in Variables

Variable	Meaning	Default
ARGC	number of command-line arguments	-
ARGV	array of command-line arguments	-
FILENAME	name of current input file	-
FNR	record number in current file	-
FS	input field separator	blank&tab
NF	number of fields in current record	-
NR	number of records read so far	-
OFMT	output format for numbers	%.6g
OFS	output field separator	blank
ORS	output record separator	newline
RS	input record separator	newline
RSTART	index of first character matched by match()	-
RLENGTH	length of string matched by match()	-
SUBSEP	subscript separator	"\034"

Arithmetic

Actions can use conventional arithmetic expressions to compute numeric values. As a simple example, suppose you want to print the population density for each country in the file `countries`. Since the second field is the area in thousands of square miles and the third field is the population in millions, the expression `1000 * $3 / $2` gives the population density in people per square mile. The program

```
{ printf "%10s %6.1f\n", $1, 1000 * $3 / $2 }
```

when applied to the file `countries`, prints the name of each country and its population density:

```
      USSR   30.3
    Canada    6.2
     China  234.6
       USA   60.6
    Brazil   35.3
 Australia    4.7
     India  502.0
 Argentina   24.3
     Sudan   19.6
   Algeria   19.6
```

Arithmetic is done internally in floating point. The arithmetic operators are `+`, `-`, `*`, `/`, `%` (remainder) and `^` (exponentiation; `**` is a synonym). Arithmetic expressions can be created by applying these operators to constants, variables, field names, array elements, functions, and other expressions, all of which are discussed later. Note that `awk` recognizes and produces scientific (exponential) notation: `1e6`, `1E6`, `10e5`, and `1000000` are numerically equal.

`awk` has assignment statements like those found in the C programming language. The simplest form is the assignment statement

v = *e*

where *v* is a variable or field name, and *e* is an expression. For example, to compute the number of Asian countries and their total population, you could write

```
$4 == "Asia"    { pop = pop + $3; n = n + 1 }
END             { print "population of", n,
                    "Asian countries in millions is", pop }
```

Applied to `countries`, this program produces

```
population of 3 Asian countries in millions is 1765
```

The action associated with the pattern `$4 == "Asia"` contains two assignment statements, one to accumulate population and the other to count countries. The variables are not explicitly initialized, yet everything works properly because `awk` initializes each variable with the string value `""` and the numeric value `0`.

The assignments in the previous program can be written more concisely using the operators += and ++:

```
$4 == "Asia"    { pop += $3; ++n }
```

The operator += is borrowed from the C programming language; therefore,

```
pop += $3
```

has the same effect as

```
pop = pop + $3
```

but the += operator is shorter and runs faster. The same is true of the ++ operator, which adds one to a variable.

The abbreviated assignment operators are `+=`, `-=`, `*=`, `/=`, `%=`, and `^=`. Their meanings are similar:

v op= e

has the same effect as

v = v op e.

The increment operators are ++ and --. As in C, they may be used as prefix (++x) or postfix (x++) operators. If `x` is 1, then `i=++x` increments `x`, then sets `i` to 2, while `i=x++` sets `i` to 1, then increments `x`. An analogous interpretation applies to prefix and postfix --.

Assignment and increment and decrement operators may all be used in arithmetic expressions.

We use default initialization to advantage in the following program, which finds the country with the largest population:

```
maxpop < $3   { maxpop = $3; country = $1 }
END           { print country, maxpop }
```

Note, however, that this program would not be correct if all values of `$3` were negative.

`awk` provides the built-in arithmetic functions listed in Table 10-4.

Table 10-4: `awk` Built-in Arithmetic Functions

Function	Value Returned
`atan2`(*y*,*x*)	arctangent of y/x in the range $-\pi$ to π
`cos`(*x*)	cosine of *x*, with *x* in radians
`exp`(*x*)	exponential function of *x*
`int`(*x*)	integer part of *x* truncated towards 0
`log`(*x*)	natural logarithm of *x*
`rand()`	random number between 0 and 1
`sin`(*x*)	sine of *x*, with *x* in radians
`sqrt`(*x*)	square root of *x*
`srand`(*x*)	*x* is new seed for rand()

x and *y* are arbitrary expressions. The function `rand()` returns a pseudo-random floating point number in the range (0,1), and `srand`(*x*) can be used to set the seed of the generator. If `srand()` has no argument, the seed is derived from the time of day.

Strings and String Functions

A string constant is created by enclosing a sequence of characters inside quotation marks, as in `"abc"` or `"hello, everyone"`. String constants may contain the C programming language escape sequences for special characters listed in the "Regular Expressions" section in this chapter.

String expressions are created by concatenating constants, variables, field names, array elements, functions, and other expressions. The program

```
{ print NR ":" $0 }
```

prints each record preceded by its record number and a colon, with no blanks. The three strings representing the record number, the colon, and the record are concatenated and the resulting string is printed. The concatenation operator has no explicit representation other than juxtaposition.

`awk` provides the built-in string functions shown in Table 10-5. In this table, *r* represents a regular expression (either as a string or as /*r*/), *s* and *t* string expressions, and *n* and *p* integers.

Table 10-5: awk Built-In String Functions

Function	Description
`gsub`(*r*,*s*)	substitute *s* for *r* globally in current record, return number of substitutions
`gsub`(*r*,*s*,*t*)	substitute *s* for *r* globally in string *t*, return number of substitutions
`index`(*s*,*t*)	return position of string *t* in *s*, 0 if not present
`length`(*s*)	return length of *s*
`match`(*s*,*r*)	return the position in *s* where *r* occurs, 0 if not present
`split`(*s*,*a*)	split *s* into array *a* on FS, return number of fields
`split`(*s*,*a*,*r*)	split *s* into array *a* on *r*, return number of fields
`sprintf`(*fmt*,*expr-list*)	return *expr-list* formatted according to format string *fmt*
`sub`(*r*,*s*)	substitute *s* for first *r* in current record, return number of substitutions
`sub`(*r*,*s*,*t*)	substitute *s* for first *r* in *t*, return number of substitutions
`substr`(*s*,*p*)	return suffix of *s* starting at position *p*
`substr`(*s*,*p*,*n*)	return substring of *s* of length *n* starting at position *p*

The functions `sub` and `gsub` are patterned after the substitute command in the text editor `ed`(1). The function `gsub`(*r*,*s*,*t*) replaces successive occurrences of substrings matched by the regular expression *r* with the replacement string *s* in the target string *t*. (As in `ed`, the leftmost match is used, and is made as long as possible.) It returns the number of substitutions made. The function `gsub`(*r*,*s*) is a synonym for `gsub`(*r*,*s*,`$0`). For example, the program

```
{ gsub(/USA/, "United States"); print }
```

transcribes its input, replacing occurrences of `USA` by `United States`. The `sub` functions are similar, except that they only replace the first matching substring in the target string.

The function `index`(*s*,*t*) returns the leftmost position where the string *t* begins in *s*, or zero if *t* does not occur in *s*. The first character in a string is at position 1. For example,

```
index("banana", "an")
```

returns 2.

The `length` function returns the number of characters in its argument string; thus,

```
{ print length($0), $0 }
```

prints each record, preceded by its length. (`$0` does not include the input record separator.) The program

```
length($1) > max   { max = length($1); name = $1 }
END                { print name }
```

when applied to the file `countries`, prints the longest country name: `Australia`.

The `match`(*s*, *r*) function returns the position in string *s* where regular expression *r* occurs, or 0 if it does not occur. This function also sets two built-in variables `RSTART` and `RLENGTH`. `RSTART` is set to the starting position of the match in the string; this is the same value as the returned value. `RLENGTH` is set to the length of the matched string. (If a match does not occur, `RSTART` is 0, and `RLENGTH` is −1.) For example, the following program finds the first occurrence of the letter `i` followed by at most one character followed by the letter `a` in a record:

```
{ if (match($0, /i.?a/))
      print RSTART, RLENGTH, $0 }
```

It produces the following output on the file `countries`:

```
17 2 USSR 8650    262     Asia
26 3 Canada        3852    24      North America
3 3 China 3692    866     Asia
24 3 USA  3615    219     North America
27 3 Brazil        3286    116     South America
8 2 Australia      2968    14      Australia
4 2 India 1269    637     Asia
7 3 Argentina      1072    26      South America
17 3 Sudan         968     19      Africa
6 2 Algeria        920     18      Africa
```

match() matches the leftmost longest matching string. For example, with the record

```
AsiaaaAsiaaaaan
```

as input, the program

```
{ if (match($0, /a+/))  print RSTART, RLENGTH, $0 }
```

matches the first string of a's and sets RSTART to 4 and RLENGTH to 3.

The function sprintf(*format*, $expr_1$, $expr_2$, . . ., $expr_n$) returns (without printing) a string containing $expr_1$, $expr_2$, . . ., $expr_n$ formatted according to the printf specifications in the string *format*. The section titled "The printf Statement" in this chapter contains a complete specification of the format conventions. The statement

```
x = sprintf("%10s %6d", $1, $2)
```

assigns to x the string produced by formatting the values of $1 and $2 as a ten-character string and a decimal number in a field of width at least six; x may be used in any subsequent computation.

The function substr(*s*,*p*,*n*) returns the substring of *s* that begins at position *p* and is at most *n* characters long. If substr(*s*,*p*) is used, the substring goes to the end of *s*; that is, it consists of the suffix of *s* beginning at position *p*. For example, we could abbreviate the country names in countries to their first three characters by invoking the program

```
{ $1 = substr($1, 1, 3); print }
```

on this file to produce

```
USS 8650 262 Asia
Can 3852 24 North America
Chi 3692 866 Asia
USA 3615 219 North America
Bra 3286 116 South America
Aus 2968 14 Australia
Ind 1269 637 Asia
Arg 1072 26 South America
Sud 968 19 Africa
Alg 920 18 Africa
```

Note that setting `$1` in the program forces `awk` to recompute `$0` and, therefore, the fields are separated by blanks (the default value of `OFS`), not by tabs.

Strings are stuck together (concatenated) merely by writing them one after another in an expression. For example, when invoked on the file `countries`,

```
    { s = s substr($1, 1, 3) " " }
END { print s }
```

prints

```
USS Can Chi USA Bra Aus Ind Arg Sud Alg
```

by building `s` up a piece at a time from an initially empty string.

Field Variables

The fields of the current record can be referred to by the field variables `$1`, `$2`, . . ., `$NF`. Field variables share all of the properties of other variables—they may be used in arithmetic or string operations, and they may have values assigned to them. So, for example, you can divide the second field of the file `countries` by 1000 to convert the area from thousands to millions of square miles:

```
{ $2 /= 1000; print }
```

or assign a new string to a field:

```
BEGIN                       { FS = OFS = "\t" }
$4 == "North America"       { $4 = "NA" }
$4 == "South America"       { $4 = "SA" }
                            { print }
```

The `BEGIN` action in this program resets the input field separator `FS` and the output field separator `OFS` to a tab. Notice that the `print` in the fourth line of the program prints the value of `$0` after it has been modified by previous assignments.

Fields can be accessed by expressions. For example, `$(NF-1)` is the second to last field of the current record. The parentheses are needed: the value of `$NF-1` is 1 less than the value in the last field.

A field variable referring to a nonexistent field, for example, `$(NF+1)`, has as its initial value the empty string. A new field can be created, however, by assigning a value to it. For example, the following program invoked on the file `countries` creates a fifth field giving the population density:

```
BEGIN  { FS = OFS = "\t" }
       { $5 = 1000 * $3 / $2; print }
```

The number of fields can vary from record to record, but usually the implementation limit is 100 fields per record.

Number or String?

Variables, fields and expressions can have both a numeric value and a string value. They take on numeric or string values according to context. For example, in the context of an arithmetic expression like

```
pop += $3
```

pop and `$3` must be treated numerically, so their values will be coerced to numeric type if necessary.

In a string context like

```
print $1 ":" $2
```

`$1` and `$2` must be strings to be concatenated, so they will be coerced if necessary.

In an assignment $v = e$ or v *op*= e, the type of v becomes the type of e. In an ambiguous context like

```
$1 == $2
```

the type of the comparison depends on whether the fields are numeric or string, and this can only be determined when the program runs; it may well differ from record to record.

In comparisons, if both operands are numeric, the comparison is numeric; otherwise, operands are coerced to strings, and the comparison is made on the string values. All field variables are of type string; in addition, each field that contains only a number is also considered numeric. This determination is done at run time. For example, the comparison `"$1 == $2"` will succeed on any pair of the inputs

```
1     1.0     +1     0.1e+1     10E-1    001
```

but will fail on the inputs

```
(null)  0
(null)  0.0
0a      0
1e50    1.0e50
```

There are two idioms for coercing an expression of one type to the other:

number ""	concatenate a null string to a *number* to coerce it to type string
string + 0	add zero to a *string* to coerce it to type numeric

Thus, to force a string comparison between two fields, use

```
$1 "" == $2 ""
```

The numeric value of a string is the value of any prefix of the string that looks numeric; thus the value of `12.34x` is 12.34, while the value of `x12.34` is zero. The string value of an arithmetic expression is computed by formatting the string with the output format conversion `OFMT`.

Uninitialized variables have numeric value 0 and string value `""`. Nonexistent fields and fields that are explicitly null have only the string value `""`; they are not numeric.

Control Flow Statements

`awk` provides `if-else`, `while`, `do-while`, and `for` statements, and statement grouping with braces, as in the C programming language.

The `if` statement syntax is

`if` (*expression*) $statement_1$ `else` $statement_2$

The *expression* acting as the conditional has no restrictions; it can include the relational operators <, <=, >, >=, ==, and `!=`; the regular expression matching operators ~ and `!~`; the logical operators `||`, `&&`, and `!`; juxtaposition for concatenation; and parentheses for grouping.

In the `if` statement, `awk` first evaluates the *expression*. If it is non-zero and non-null, $statement_1$ is executed; otherwise $statement_2$ is executed. The `else` part is optional.

A single statement can always be replaced by a statement list enclosed in braces. The statements in the statement list are terminated by newlines or semicolons.

Rewriting the maximum population program from the "Arithmetic Functions" section with an `if` statement results in

```
{    if (maxpop < $3) {
          maxpop = $3
          country = $1
     }
}
END  { print country, maxpop }
```

The `while` statement is exactly that of the C programming language:

`while` (*expression*) *statement*

The *expression* is evaluated; if it is non-zero and non-null the *statement* is executed and the *expression* is tested again. The cycle repeats as long as the *expression* is non-zero. For example, to print all input fields one per line,

```
{   i = 1
    while (i <= NF) {
        print $i
        i++
    }
}
```

The `for` statement is like that of the C programming language:

`for` (*expression*$_1$; *expression*; *expression*$_2$) *statement*

It has the same effect as

```
expression1
while (expression) {
            statement
            expression2
}
```

so

```
{ for (i = 1; i <= NF; i++)   print $i }
```

does the same job as the `while` example shown above. An alternate version of the `for` statement is described in the next section.

The do statement has the form

do *statement* `while` (*expression*)

The *statement* is executed repeatedly until the value of the *expression* becomes zero. Because the test takes place after the execution of the *statement* (at the bottom of the loop), it is always executed at least once. As a result, the do statement is used much less often than `while` or `for`, which test for completion at the top of the loop.

The following example of a do statement prints all lines except those between `start` and `stop`.

```
/start/ {
        do {
            getline x
        } while (x !~ /stop/)
        }
        { print }
```

The `break` statement causes an immediate exit from an enclosing `while` or `for`; the `continue` statement causes the next iteration to begin. The `next` statement causes `awk` to skip immediately to the next record and begin matching patterns starting from the first pattern-action statement.

The `exit` statement causes the program to behave as if the end of the input had occurred; no more input is read, and the `END` action, if any, is executed. Within the `END` action,

`exit` *expr*

causes the program to return the value of *expr* as its exit status. If there is no *expr*, the exit status is zero.

Arrays

`awk` provides one-dimensional arrays. Arrays and array elements need not be declared; like variables, they spring into existence by being mentioned. An array subscript may be a number or a string.

As an example of a conventional numeric subscript, the statement

```
x[NR] = $0
```

assigns the current input line to the `NR`th element of the array `x`. In fact, it is possible in principle (though perhaps slow) to read the entire input into an array with the awk program

```
        { x[NR] = $0 }
END     { ... processing ... }
```

The first action merely records each input line in the array x, indexed by line number; processing is done in the END statement.

Array elements may also be named by nonnumeric values. For example, the following program accumulates the total population of Asia and Africa into the associative array pop. The END action prints the total population of these two continents.

```
/Asia/      { pop["Asia"] += $3 }
/Africa/    { pop["Africa"] += $3 }
END         { print "Asian population in millions is", pop["Asia"]
              print "African population in millions is", pop["Africa"]
            }
```

On the file countries, this program generates

```
Asian population in millions is 1765
African population in millions is 37
```

In this program if you had used pop[Asia] instead of pop["Asia"] the expression would have used the value of the variable Asia as the subscript, and since the variable is uninitialized, the values would have been accumulated in pop[""] .

Suppose your task is to determine the total area in each continent of the file countries. Any expression can be used as a subscript in an array reference. Thus

```
area[$4] += $2
```

uses the string in the fourth field of the current input record to index the array area and, in that entry, accumulates the value of the second field:

```
BEGIN { FS = "\t" }
      { area[$4] += $2 }
END   { for (name in area)
                  print name, area[name] }
```

Invoked on the file `countries`, this program produces

```
Africa 1888
North America 7467
South America 4358
Asia 13611
Australia 2968
```

This program uses a form of the `for` statement that iterates over all defined subscripts of an array:

`for (`*i* `in` *array*`)` *statement*

executes *statement* with the variable *i* set in turn to each value of *i* for which *array[i]* has been defined. The loop is executed once for each defined subscript, which is chosen in a random order. Results are unpredictable when *i* or *array* is altered during the loop.

`awk` does not provide multi-dimensional arrays, but it does permit a list of subscripts. They are combined into a single subscript with the values separated by an unlikely string (stored in the variable `SUBSEP`). For example,

```
for (i = 1; i <= 10; i++)
        for (j = 1; j <= 10; j++)
                arr[i,j] = ...
```

creates an array which behaves like a two-dimensional array; the subscript is the concatenation of *i*, `SUBSEP`, and *j*.

You can determine whether a particular subscript *i* occurs in an array *arr* by testing the condition *i* in *arr*, as in

```
if ("Africa" in area) ...
```

This condition performs the test without the side effect of creating `area["Africa"]`, which would happen if you used

```
if (area["Africa"] != "") ...
```

Note that neither is a test of whether the array `area` contains an element with the value `"Africa"` .

It is also possible to split any string into fields in the elements of an array using the built-in function `split`. The function

```
split("s1:s2:s3", a, ":")
```

splits the string `s1:s2:s3` into three fields, using the separator `:` , and stores `s1` in `a[1]`, `s2` in `a[2]`, and `s3` in `a[3]` . The number of fields found, here three, is returned as the value of `split`. The third argument of `split` is a regular expression to be used as the field separator. If the third argument is missing, `FS` is used as the field separator.

An array element may be deleted with the `delete` statement:

`delete` *arrayname* [*subscript*]

User-Defined Functions

`awk` provides user-defined functions. A function is defined as

`function` *name* (*argument-list*) {
    statements
}

The definition can occur anywhere a pattern-action statement can. The argument list is a list of variable names separated by commas; within the body of the function these variables refer to the actual parameters when the function is called. No space must be left between the function name and the left parenthesis of the argument list when the function is called; otherwise it looks like a concatenation. For example, the following program defines and tests the usual recursive factorial function (of course, using some input other than the file `countries`):

```
function fact(n) {
     if (n <= 1)
          return 1
     else
          return n * fact(n-1)
}
{ print $1 "! is " fact($1) }
```

Array arguments are passed by reference, as in C, so it is possible for the function to alter array elements or create new ones. Scalar arguments are passed by value, however, so the function cannot affect their values outside. Within a function, formal parameters are local variables, but all other variables are global. (You can have any number of extra formal parameters that are used only as local variables.) The `return` statement is optional, but the returned value is undefined if it is not included.

Some Lexical Conventions

Comments may be placed in `awk` programs; they begin with the character `#` and end at the end of the line, as in

```
print x, y     # this is a comment
```

Statements in an `awk` program normally occupy a single line. Several statements may occur on a single line if they are separated by semicolons. A long statement may be continued over several lines by terminating each continued line by a backslash. (It is not possible to continue a "..." string.) This explicit continuation is rarely necessary, however, since statements continue automatically if the line ends with a comma. (For example, this might occur in a `print` or `printf` statement) or after the operators `&&` and `||`.

Several pattern-action statements may appear on a single line if separated by semicolons.

Output

The `print` and `printf` statements are the two primary constructs that generate output. The `print` statement is used to generate simple output; `printf` is used for more carefully formatted output. Like the shell, `awk` lets you redirect output, so that output from `print` and `printf` can be directed to files and pipes. This section describes the use of these two statements.

The `print` Statement

The statement

```
print expr1, expr2, . . ., exprn
```

prints the string value of each expression separated by the output field separator followed by the output record separator. The statement

```
print
```

is an abbreviation for

```
print $0
```

To print an empty line, use

```
print ""
```

Output Separators

The output field separator and record separator are held in the built-in variables `OFS` and `ORS`. Initially, `OFS` is set to a single blank and `ORS` to a single newline, but these values can be changed at any time. For example, the following program prints the first and second fields of each record with a colon between the fields and two newlines after the second field:

```
BEGIN  { OFS = ":"; ORS = "\n\n" }
       { print $1, $2 }
```

Notice that

```
{ print $1 $2 }
```

prints the first and second fields with no intervening output field separator because `$1 $2` is a string consisting of the concatenation of the first two fields.

The `printf` Statement

awk's `printf` statement is the same as that in C except that the * format specifier is not supported. The `printf` statement has the general form

`printf` *format*, $expr_1$, $expr_2$, . . ., $expr_n$

where *format* is a string that contains both information to be printed and specifications on what conversions are to be performed on the expressions in the argument list, as in Figure 10-8. Each specification begins with a `%`, ends with a letter that determines the conversion, and may include:

–	Left-justify expression in its field.
width	Pad field to this width as needed; fields that begin with a leading 0 are padded with zeros.
.*prec*	Specify maximum string width or digits to right of decimal point.

Table 10-6 lists the `printf` conversion characters.

Table 10-6: `awk printf` Conversion Characters

Character	Prints Expression as
c	single character
d	decimal number
e	[–]*d.dddddd*E[+–]*dd*
f	[–]*ddd.dddddd*
g	e or f conversion, whichever is shorter, with nonsignificant zeros suppressed
o	unsigned octal number
s	string
x	unsigned hexadecimal number
%	print a %; no argument is converted

Below are some examples of `printf` statements along with the corresponding output:

```
printf "%d", 99/2                      49
printf "%e", 99/2                      4.950000e+01
printf "%f", 99/2                      49.500000
printf "%6.2f", 99/2                   49.50
printf "%g", 99/2                      49.5
printf "%o", 99                        143
printf "%06o", 99                      000143
printf "%x", 99                        63
printf "|%s|", "January"               |January|
printf "|%10s|", "January"             |   January|
printf "|%-10s|", "January"            |January   |
printf "|%.3s|", "January"             |Jan|
printf "|%10.3s|", "January"           |       Jan|
printf "|%-10.3s|", "January"          |Jan       |
printf "%%"                            %
```

The default output format of numbers is `%.6g`; this can be changed by assigning a new value to `OFMT`. `OFMT` also controls the conversion of numeric values to strings for concatenation and creation of array subscripts.

Output to Files

You can print output to files instead of to the standard output by using the > and >> redirection operators. For example, the following program invoked on the file `countries` prints all lines where the population (third field) is bigger than 100 into a file called `bigpop`, and all other lines into a file called `smallpop`:

```
$3 > 100    { print $1, $3 >"bigpop" }
$3 <= 100   { print $1, $3 >"smallpop" }
```

Notice that the filenames have to be quoted; without quotes, `bigpop` and `smallpop` are merely uninitialized variables. If the output filenames were created by an expression, they would also have to be enclosed in parentheses:

```
$4 ~ /North America/ { print $1 > ("tmp" FILENAME) }
```

because the > operator has higher precedence than concatenation; without parentheses, the concatenation of `tmp` and `FILENAME` would not work.

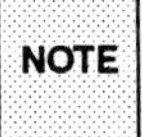

Files are opened once in an awk program. If > is used to open a file, its original contents are overwritten. But if >> is used to open a file, its contents are preserved and the output is appended to the file. Once the file has been opened, the two operators have the same effect.

Output to Pipes

You can also direct printing to a pipe with a command on the other end, instead of to a file. The statement

```
print | "command-line"
```

causes the output of `print` to be piped into the *command-line*.

Although they are shown here as literal strings enclosed in quotes, the *command-line* and filenames can come from variables and the return values from functions.

Suppose you want to create a list of continent-population pairs, sorted alphabetically by continent. The `awk` program below accumulates the population values in the third field for each of the distinct continent names in the fourth field in an array called pop. Then it prints each continent and its population, and pipes this output into the `sort` command.

```
BEGIN   { FS = "\t" }
        { pop[$4] += $3 }
END     { for (c in pop)
              print c ":" pop[c] | "sort" }
```

Invoked on the file `countries`, this program yields

```
Africa:37
Asia:1765
Australia:14
North America:243
South America:142
```

In all these `print` statements involving redirection of output, the files or pipes are identified by their names (that is, the pipe above is literally named `sort`), but they are created and opened only once in the entire run. So, in the last example, for all `c` in pop, only one sort pipe is open.

There is a limit to the number of files that can be open simultaneously. The statement `close` (*file*) closes a file or pipe; *file* is the string used to create it in the first place, as in

```
close("sort")
```

When opening or closing a file, different strings are different commands.

Input

The most common way to give input to an awk program is to name on the command line the file(s) that contains the input. This is the method used in this chapter; however, several other methods can be used. Each of these is described in this section.

Files and Pipes

You can provide input to an awk program by putting the input data into a file, say awkdata, and then executing

```
awk 'program' awkdata
```

If no filenames are given, awk reads its standard input (see the section titled "Usage" in this chapter); thus, a second common arrangement is to have another program pipe its output into awk. For example, egrep(1) selects input lines containing a specified regular expression, but it can do so faster than awk, since this is the only thing it does. We could, therefore, invoke the pipe

```
egrep 'Asia' countries | awk '...'
```

egrep quickly finds the lines containing Asia and passes them on to the awk program for subsequent processing.

Input Separators

With the default setting of the field separator FS, input fields are separated by blanks or tabs, and leading blanks are discarded, so each of these lines has the same first field:

```
    field1   field2
  field1
field1
```

When the field separator is a tab, however, leading blanks are not discarded.

The field separator can be set to any regular expression by assigning a value to the built-in variable FS. For example,

```
BEGIN { FS = ",[ \t]*|([ \t]+" }
```

makes into field separators every string consisting of a comma followed by blanks or tabs and every string of blanks or tabs with no comma. `FS` can also be set on the command line with the `-F` argument:

```
awk -F'(,[ \t]*)|([ \t]+)' '. . .'
```

behaves the same as the previous example. Regular expressions used as field separators match the leftmost longest occurrences (as in `sub()`), but do not match null strings.

Multi-line Records

Records are normally separated by newlines, so that each line is a record; but this too can be changed, though only in a limited way. If the built-in record separator variable `RS` is set to the empty string, as in

```
BEGIN   { RS = "" }
```

then input records can be several lines long; a sequence of empty lines separates records. A common way to process multiple-line records is to use

```
BEGIN   { RS = ""; FS = "\n" }
```

to set the record separator to an empty line and the field separator to a newline. Each line is then one field. However, the length of a record is limited; it is usually about 2500 characters. "The `getline` Function" and "Cooperation with the Shell" sections in this chapter show other examples of processing multi-line records.

The `getline` Function

`awk`'s facility for automatically breaking its input into records that are more than one line long is not adequate for some tasks. For example, if records are not separated by blank lines, but by something more complicated, merely setting `RS` to null doesn't work. In such cases, the program must manage the splitting of each record into fields. Here are some suggestions.

The function `getline` can be used to read input either from the current input or from a file or pipe, by redirection analogous to `printf`. By itself, `getline` fetches the next input record and performs the normal field-splitting operations on it. It sets `NF`, `NR`, and `FNR`. `getline` returns 1 if there was a record present, 0 if the end-of-file was encountered, and −1 if some error occurred (such as failure to open a file).

To illustrate, suppose you have input data consisting of multi-line records, each of which begins with a line beginning with `START` and ends with a line beginning with `STOP`. The following `awk` program processes these multi-line records, a line at a time, putting the lines of the record into consecutive entries of an array

```
f[1] f[2] ... f[nf]
```

Once the line containing `STOP` is encountered, the record can be processed from the data in the `f array`:

```
/^START/ {
        f[nf=1] = $0
        while (getline && $0 !~ /^STOP/)
            f[++nf] = $0
        # now process the data in f[1]...f[nf]
        ...
}
```

Notice that this code uses the fact that `&&` evaluates its operands left to right and stops as soon as one is true.

The same job can also be done by the following program:

```
/^START/ && nf==0          { f[nf=1] = $0 }
nf > 1                     { f[++nf] = $0 }
/^STOP/                    { # now process the data in f[1]...f[nf]
                             ...
                             nf = 0
}
```

The statement

```
getline x
```

reads the next record into the variable x. No splitting is done; NF is not set. The statement

```
getline <"file"
```

reads from file instead of the current input. It has no effect on NR or FNR, but field splitting is performed and NF is set. The statement

```
getline x <"file"
```

gets the next record from file into x; no splitting is done, and NF, NR and FNR are untouched.

If a filename is an expression, it should be in parentheses for evaluation:

```
while ( getline x < (ARGV[1] ARGV[2]) ) {  ... }
```

because the < has precedence over concatenation. Without parentheses, a statement such as

```
getline x < "tmp" FILENAME
```

sets x to read the file tmp and not tmp *<value of FILENAME>*. Also, if you use this getline statement form, a statement like

```
while ( getline x < file ) { ... }
```

loops forever if the file cannot be read because getline returns −1, not zero if an error occurs. A better way to write this test is

```
while ( getline x < file > 0) { ... }
```

You can also pipe the output of another command directly into getline. For example, the statement

```
while ("who" | getline)
      n++
```

executes who and pipes its output into getline. Each iteration of the while loop reads one more line and increments the variable n, so after the while loop terminates, n contains a count of the number of users. Similarly, the statement

```
"date" | getline d
```

pipes the output of date into the variable d, thus setting d to the current date.

Table 10-7 summarizes the `getline` function.

Table 10-7: `getline` Function

Form	Sets
`getline`	`$0, NF, NR, FNR`
`getline` *var*	*var*, `NR, FNR`
`getline <`*file*	`$0, NF`
`getline` *var* `<`*file*	*var*
cmd `| getline`	`$0, NF`
cmd `| getline` *var*	*var*

Command-line Arguments

The command-line arguments are available to an `awk` program: the array `ARGV` contains the elements `ARGV[0], ..., ARGV[ARGC-1]`; as in C, `ARGC` is the count. `ARGV[0]` is the name of the program (generally `awk`); the remaining arguments are whatever was provided (excluding the program and any optional arguments) when `awk` is invoked. The following command line contains an `awk` program that echoes the arguments that appear after the program name:

```
awk '
BEGIN {
   for (i = 1; i < ARGC; i++)
         printf "%s ", ARGV[i]
   printf "\n"
}' $*
```

The arguments may be modified or added to; `ARGC` may be altered. As each input file ends, `awk` treats the next non-null element of `ARGV` (up to the current value of `ARGC-1`) as the name of the next input file.

One exception to the rule that an argument is a filename is when it is in the form

var=value

Then the variable *var* is set to the value *value*, as if by assignment. Such an argument is not treated like a filename. If *value* is a string, no quotes are needed.

Using awk with Other Commands and the Shell

awk is most powerful when it is used in conjunction with other programs. This section discusses some of the ways in which awk programs cooperate with other commands.

The system Function

The built-in function system(*command-line*) executes the command *command-line*, which may be a string computed by, for example, the built-in function sprintf. The value returned by system is the return status of the command executed.

For example, the program

```
$1 == "#include"  { gsub(/[<>"]/, "", $2);
  system("cat " $2) }
```

calls the command cat to print the file named in the second field of every input record whose first field is #include, after stripping any <, >, or " that might be present.

Cooperation with the Shell

In all the examples thus far, the awk program was in a file and was fetched from there using the -f flag, or it appeared on the command line enclosed in single quotes, as in

```
awk '{ print $1 }' . . .
```

Since awk uses many of the same characters as the shell does, such as $ and ", surrounding the awk program with single quotes ensures that the shell will pass the entire program unchanged to the awk interpreter.

Now, consider writing a command addr that will search a file addresslist for name, address and telephone information. Suppose that addresslist contains names and addresses in which a typical entry is a multi-line record such as

```
G. R. Emlin
600 Mountain Avenue
Murray Hill, NJ 07974
201-555-1234
```

Records are separated by a single blank line.

You want to search the address list by issuing commands like

```
addr Emlin
```

That is easily done by a program of the form

```
awk '
BEGIN { RS = "" }
/Emlin/
' addresslist
```

The problem is how to get a different search pattern into the program each time it is run.

There are several ways to do this. One way is to create a file called `addr` that contains

```
awk '
BEGIN { RS = "" }
/'$1'/
' addresslist
```

The quotes are critical here. The `awk` program is only one argument, even though there are two sets of quotes because quotes do not nest. The `$1` is outside the quotes, visible to the shell, which therefore replaces it by the pattern `Emlin` when the command `addr Emlin` is invoked. On a UNIX system, `addr` can be made executable by changing its mode with the following command:

```
chmod +x addr
```

A second way to implement `addr` relies on the fact that the shell substitutes for `$` parameters within double quotes:

```
awk "
BEGIN { RS = \"\" }
/$1/
" addresslist
```

Therefore, you must protect the quotes defining `RS` with backslashes, so that the shell passes them on to `awk` without interpretation. `$1` is recognized as a parameter, however, so the shell replaces it by the pattern when the command `addr` *pattern* is invoked.

A third way to implement `addr` is to use `ARGV` to pass the regular expression to an `awk` program that explicitly reads through the address list with `getline`:

```
awk '
BEGIN   { RS = ""
          while (getline < "addresslist")
             if ($0 ~ ARGV[1])
                print $0
} ' $*
```

All processing is done in the `BEGIN` action.

Notice that any regular expression can be passed to `addr`; in particular, it is possible to retrieve by parts of an address or telephone number as well as by name.

Example Applications

awk has been used in surprising ways: to implement database systems and a variety of compilers and assemblers, in addition to the more traditional tasks of information retrieval, data manipulation, and report generation. Invariably, the awk programs are significantly shorter than equivalent programs written in more conventional programming languages such as Pascal or C. This section presents a few more examples to illustrate some additional awk programs.

Generating Reports

awk is especially useful for producing reports that summarize and format information. Suppose you want to produce a report from the file countries in which the continents are listed alphabetically, and the countries on each continent are listed after in decreasing order of population:

```
Africa:
            Sudan          19
            Algeria        18

Asia:
            China         866
            India         637
            USSR          262

Australia:
            Australia      14

North America:
            USA           219
            Canada         24

South America:
            Brazil        116
            Argentina      26
```

As with many data processing tasks, it is much easier to produce this report in several stages. First, create a list of continent-country-population triples, in which each field is separated by a colon. This can be done with the following program triples, which uses an array pop indexed by subscripts of the form *continent*:*country* to store the population of a given country. The print statement in the END section of the program creates the list of continent-country-population triples that are piped to the sort routine.

```
BEGIN { FS = "\t" }
      { pop[$4 ":" $1] += $3 }
 END  { for (cc in pop)
            print cc ":" pop[cc] | "sort -t: +0 -1 +2nr" }
```

The arguments for sort deserve special mention. The -t: argument tells sort to use : as its field separator. The +0 -1 arguments make the first field the primary sort key. In general, *+i −j* makes fields *i+1*, *i+2*, . . ., *j* the sort key. If *−j* is omitted, the fields from *i+1* to the end of the record are used. The +2nr argument makes the third field, numerically decreasing, the secondary sort key (n is for numeric, r for reverse order). Invoked on the file countries, this program produces as output

```
Africa:Sudan:19
Africa:Algeria:18
Asia:China:866
Asia:India:637
Asia:USSR:262
Australia:Australia:14
North America:USA:219
North America:Canada:24
South America:Brazil:116
South America:Argentina:26
```

This output is in the right order but the wrong format. To transform the output into the desired form, run it through a second awk program format:

```
BEGIN  { FS = ":" }
{       if ($1 != prev) {
             print "\n" $1 ":"
             prev = $1
        }
        printf "\t%-10s %6d\n", $2, $3
}
```

This is a control-break program that prints only the first occurrence of a continent name and formats the country-population lines associated with that continent in the desired manner. The command line

```
awk -f triples countries | awk -f format
```

gives the desired report. As this example suggests, complex data transformation and formatting tasks can often be reduced to a few simple awks commands and sorts.

Additional Examples

Word Frequencies

Our first example illustrates associative arrays for counting. Suppose you want to count the number of times each word appears in the input, where a word is any contiguous sequence of non-blank, non-tab characters. The following program prints the word frequencies, sorted in decreasing order.

```
      { for (w = 1; w <= NF; w++) count[$w]++ }
END   { for (w in count) print count[w], w | "sort -nr" }
```

The first statement uses the array count to accumulate the number of times each word is used. Once the input has been read, the second for loop pipes the final count along with each word into the sort command.

Accumulation

Suppose we have two files, deposits and withdrawals, of records containing a name field and an amount field. For each name we want to print the net balance determined by subtracting the total withdrawals from the total deposits for each name. The net balance can be computed by the following program:

```
awk '
FILENAME == "deposits"      { balance[$1] += $2 }
FILENAME == "withdrawals"   { balance[$1] -= $2 }
END                         { for (name in balance)
                                   print name, balance[name]
} ' deposits withdrawals
```

The first statement uses the array `balance` to accumulate the total amount for each name in the file `deposits`. The second statement subtracts associated withdrawals from each total. If only withdrawals are associated with a name, an entry for that name is created by the second statement. The `END` action prints each name with its net balance.

Random Choice

The following function prints (in order) `k` random elements from the first `n` elements of the array `A`. In the program, `k` is the number of entries that still need to be printed, and `n` is the number of elements yet to be examined. The decision of whether to print the *i*th element is determined by the test `rand() < k/n`.

```
function choose(A, k, n, i) {
        for (i = 1; n > 0; i++)
                if (rand() < k/n--) {
                        print A[i]
                        k--
                }
        }
}
```

Shell Facility

The following awk program roughly simulates the history facility of the UNIX system shell. A line containing only = re-executes the last command executed. A line beginning with = *cmd* re-executes the last command whose invocation included the string *cmd*. Otherwise, the current line is executed.

```
$1 == "=" { if (NF == 1)
                system(x[NR] = x[NR-1])
            else
                for (i = NR-1; i > 0; i--)
                        if (x[i] ~ $2) {
                                system(x[NR] = x[i])
                                break
                        }
            next }

/./         { system(x[NR] = $0) }
```

Form-Letter Generation

The following program generates form letters, using a template stored in a file called `form.letter`:

```
This is a form letter.
The first field is $1, the second $2, the third $3.
The third is $3, second is $2, and first is $1.
```

and replacement text of this form:

```
field 1|field 2|field 3
one|two|three
a|b|c
```

The `BEGIN` action stores the template in the array `template;` the remaining action cycles through the input data, using `gsub` to replace template fields of the form $\$n$ with the corresponding data fields.

```
BEGIN {   FS = "|"
                    while (getline <"form.letter")
                line[++n] = $0
}
{         for (i = 1; i <= n; i++) {
                s = line[i]
                for (j = 1; j <= NF; j++)
                        gsub("\\$"j, $j, s)
                print s
          }
}
```

In all such examples, a prudent strategy is to start with a small version and expand it, trying out each aspect before moving on to the next.

awk Summary

Command Line

awk *program filenames*
awk -f *program-file filenames*
awk -F*s* sets field separator to string *s*; -Ft sets separator to tab

Patterns

BEGIN
END
/regular expression/
relational expression
pattern && *pattern*
pattern || *pattern*
(*pattern*)
!*pattern*
pattern, *pattern*

Control Flow Statements

if (*expr*) *statement* [else *statement*]
if (*subscript* in *array*) *statement* [else *statement*]
while (*expr*) *statement*
for (*expr*; *expr*; *expr*) *statement*
for (*var* in *array*) *statement*
do *statement* while (*expr*)
break
continue
next
exit [*expr*]
return [*expr*]

Input–Output

`close` (*filename*)	close file
`getline`	set `$0` from next input record; set `NF`, `NR`, `FNR`
`getline` <*file*	set `$0` from next record of *file*; set `NF`
`getline` *var*	set *var* from next input record; set `NR`, `FNR`
`getline` *var* <*file*	set *var* from next record of *file*
`print`	print current record
`print` *expr-list*	print expressions
`print` *expr-list* >*file*	print expressions on *file*
`printf` *fmt*, *expr-list*	format and print
`printf` *fmt*, *expr-list* >*file*	format and print on *file*
`system` (*cmd-line*)	execute command *cmd-line*, return status

In `print` and `printf` above, >>*file* appends to the *file*, and | *command* writes on a pipe. Similarly, *command* | `getline` pipes into `getline`. `getline` returns 0 on end of file, and −1 on error.

Functions

`func` *name* (*parameter list*) { *statement* }
`function` *name* (*parameter list*) { *statement* }
function-name (*expr*, *expr*, . . .)

String Functions

`gsub`(*r*,*s*,*t*)	substitute string *s* for each substring matching regular expression *r* in string *t*, return number of substitutions; if *t* omitted, use `$0`
`index`(*s*,*t*)	return index of string *t* in string *s*, or 0 if not present
`length`(*s*)	return length of string *s*
`match`(*s*,*r*)	return position in *s* where regular expression *r* occurs, or 0 if *r* is not present

`split(`*s,a,r*`)`	split string *s* into array *a* on regular expression *r*, return number of fields; if *r* omitted, `FS` is used in its place
`sprintf(`*fmt, expr-list*`)`	print *expr-list* according to *fmt*, return resulting string
`sub(`*r,s,t*`)`	like `gsub` except only the first matching substring is replaced
`substr(`*s,i,n*`)`	return *n*-char substring of *s* starting at *i*; if *n* omitted, use rest of *s*

Arithmetic Functions

`atan2(`*y,x*`)`	arctangent of *y*/*x* in radians
`cos(`*expr*`)`	cosine (angle in radians)
`exp(`*expr*`)`	exponential
`int(`*expr*`)`	truncate to integer
`log(`*expr*`)`	natural logarithm
`rand()`	random number between 0 and 1
`sin(`*expr*`)`	sine (angle in radians)
`sqrt(`*expr*`)`	square root
`srand(`*expr*`)`	new seed for random number generator; use time of day if no *expr*

Operators (Increasing Precedence)

`= += -= *= /= %= ^=`	assignment
`?:`	conditional expression
`||`	logical OR
`&&`	logical AND
`~ !~`	regular expression match, negated match
`< <= > >= != ==`	relationals
`blank`	string concatenation
`+ -`	add, subtract
`* / %`	multiply, divide, mod

+ - !	unary plus, unary minus, logical negation
^	exponentiation (** is a synonym)
++ --	increment, decrement (prefix and postfix)
$	field

Regular Expressions (Increasing Precedence)

c	matches non-metacharacter *c*
c	matches literal character *c*
.	matches any character but newline
^	matches beginning of line or string
$	matches end of line or string
[*abc...*]	character class matches any of *abc...*
[^*abc...*]	negated class matches any but *abc...* and newline
r1 | *r2*	matches either *r1* or *r2*
r1r2	concatenation: matches *r1*, then *r2*
r+	matches one or more *r*'s
*r**	matches zero or more *r*'s
r?	matches zero or one *r*'s
(*r*)	grouping: matches *r*

Built-in Variables

ARGC	number of command-line arguments
ARGV	array of command-line arguments (0..ARGC-1)
FILENAME	name of current input file
FNR	input record number in current file
FS	input field separator (default blank)
NF	number of fields in current input record
NR	input record number since beginning
OFMT	output format for numbers (default %.6g)
OFS	output field separator (default blank)
ORS	output record separator (default newline)
RS	input record separator (default newline)

`RSTART`	index of first character matched by `match()`; 0 if no match
`RLENGTH`	length of string matched by `match()`; −1 if no match
`SUBSEP`	separates multiple subscripts in array elements; default `\034`

Limits

Any particular implementation of awk enforces some limits. Here are typical values:

100 fields
2500 characters per input record
2500 characters per output record
1024 characters per individual field
1024 characters per printf string
400 characters maximum quoted string
400 characters in character class
15 open files
1 pipe
numbers are limited to what can be represented on the local machine, e.g., 1e−38..1e+38

Initialization, Comparison, and Type Coercion

Each variable and field can potentially be a string or a number or both at any time. When a variable is set by the assignment

var = *expr*

its type is set to that of the expression. (Assignment includes +=, −=, etc.) An arithmetic expression is of type number, a concatenation is of type string, and so on. If the assignment is a simple copy, as in

```
v1 = v2
```

then the type of `v1` becomes that of `v2`.

In comparisons, if both operands are numeric, the comparison is made numerically. Otherwise, operands are coerced to string if necessary, and the comparison is made on strings. The type of any expression can be coerced to numeric by subterfuges such as

```
expr + 0
```

and to string by

```
expr ""
```

(that is, concatenation with a null string).

Uninitialized variables have the numeric value `0` and the string value `""`. Accordingly, if `x` is uninitialized,

```
if (x) ...
```

is false, and

```
if (!x) ...
if (x == 0) ...
if (x == "") ...
```

are all true. But the following is false:

```
if (x == "0") ...
```

The type of a field is determined by context when possible; for example,

```
$1++
```

clearly implies that `$1` is to be numeric, and

```
$1 = $1 "," $2
```

implies that `$1` and `$2` are both to be strings. Coercion is done as needed.

In contexts where types cannot be reliably determined, for example,

```
if ($1 == $2) ...
```

the type of each field is determined on input. All fields are strings; in addition, each field that contains only a number is also considered numeric.

Fields that are explicitly null have the string value `""` ; they are not numeric. Non-existent fields (i.e., fields past `NF`) are treated this way, too.

As it is for fields, so it is for array elements created by `split()`.

Mentioning a variable in an expression causes it to exist, with the value `""` as described above. Thus, if `arr[i]` does not currently exist,

```
if (arr[i] == "") ...
```

causes it to exist with the value `""` so the `if` is satisfied. The special construction

```
if (i in arr) ...
```

determines if `arr[i]` exists without the side effect of creating it if it does not.

11. ELECTRONIC MAIL TUTORIAL

11 Electronic Mail Tutorial

Introduction

The UNIX system offers a choice of commands that enable you to communicate with other UNIX system users. Specifically, they allow you to: send and receive messages from other users (on either your system or another UNIX system); exchange files; and form networks with other UNIX systems. Through networking, a user on one system can exchange messages and files between computers, and execute commands on remote computers.

To help you take advantage of these capabilities, this chapter will teach you how to use the following commands.

For exchanging messages: `mail`, `mailx`, `uname`, and `uuname`

To help you exchange files, and for information on networking, see Chapter 12.

Exchanging Messages

To send messages you can use either the `mail` or `mailx` command. These commands deliver your message to a file belonging to the recipient. When the recipient logs in (or while already logged in), he or she receives a message that says `you have mail`. The recipient can use either the `mail` or `mailx` command to read your message and reply at his or her leisure.

The main difference between `mail` and `mailx` is that only `mailx` offers the following features:

- a choice of text editors (`ed` or `vi`) for handling incoming and outgoing messages
- several options for saving files
- commands for replying to messages and sending copies (of both incoming and outgoing messages) to other users

You can also use `mail` or `mailx` to send short files containing memos, reports, and so on. However, if you want to send someone a file that is over a page long, use one of the commands designed for transferring files: `uuto` or `uucp`. (See "Sending Files" in chapter 12 for descriptions of these commands.)

mail

This section presents the mail command. It discusses the basics of sending mail to one or more people simultaneously, whether they are working on the local system (the same system as you) or on a remote system. It also covers receiving and handling incoming mail.

Sending Messages

The basic command line format for sending mail is

mail *login*<CR>

where *login* is the recipient's login name on a UNIX system. This login name can be either of the following:

- a login name if the recipient is on your system (for example, bob)
- a system name and login name if the recipient is on another UNIX system that can communicate with yours (for example, sys2!bob)

For the moment, assume that the recipient is on the local system. (We will deal with sending mail to users on remote systems later.) Type the mail command at the system prompt, type the recipient's login id, press the RETURN key, and start typing the text of your message on the next line. When you have finished typing it, send the message by typing a period (.) or a <cntrl-d> at the beginning of a new line.

The following example shows how this procedure will appear on your screen.

```
$ mail phyllis<CR>
My meeting with Smith's<CR>
group tomorrow has been moved<CR>
up to 3:00 so I won't be able to<CR>
see you then.  Could we meet<CR>
in the morning instead?<CR>
.<CR>
$
```

The prompt on the last line means that your message has been queued (placed in a waiting line of messages) and will be sent.

Undeliverable Mail

If you make an error when typing the recipient's login, the mail command will not be able to deliver your mail. Instead, it will print two messages telling you that it has failed and that it is returning your mail. Then it will return your mail in a message that includes the system name and login name of both the sender and intended recipient, and an error message stating the reason for the failure.

For example, say you (owner of the login kol) want to send a message to a user with the login chris. Your message says The meeting has been changed to 2:00. Failing to notice that you have incorrectly typed the login as cris, you try to send your message.

```
$ mail cris<CR>
The meeting has been changed to 2:00.
.<CR>
mail: Can't send to cris
mail: Return to kol
you have mail
$
```

The message you have mail is presented by the shell; different shells may use slightly different wording for this message.

The mail that is waiting for you in /var/mail will be useful if you do not know why the mail command has failed, or if you want to retrieve your mail so that you can resend it without typing it in again. It contains the following:

```
$ mail<CR>
From kol Mon Jan 23 16:00 EST 1989
Date: Mon Jan 23 11:00:01 GMT 1989
Original-Date:  Mon Jan 23 15:59 EST 1989
Not-Delivered-To: marmaduk!cris  due to 02  Ambiguous Originator/Recipient Name
     ORIGINAL MESSAGE ATTACHED
     (mail: Error # 8 'Invalid recipient')
Content-Length: 77

Content-Type: text
Content-Length: 38

The meeting has been changed to 2:00.

?
```

To learn how to display and handle this message see "Managing Incoming Mail" later in this chapter.

Sending Mail to One Person

The following screen shows a typical message.

```
$ mail tommy<CR>
Tom,<CR>
There's a meeting of the review committee<CR>
at 3:00 this afternoon.  D.F. wants your<CR>
comments and an idea of how long you think<CR>
the project will take to complete.<CR>
B.K.<CR>
.<CR>
$
```

When Tom logs in at his terminal (or while he is already logged in), he receives a message that tells him he has mail waiting:

```
you have mail
```

To find out how he can read his mail, see the section "Managing Incoming Mail" in this chapter.

You can practice using the mail command by sending mail to yourself. Type in the mail command and your login ID, and then write a short message to yourself. When you type the final period or <cntrl-d>, the mail will be sent to a file named after your login ID in the /var/mail directory, and you will receive a notice that you have mail.

Sending mail to yourself can also serve as a handy reminder system. For example, suppose you (login ID bob) want to call someone the next morning. Send yourself a reminder in a mail message.

```
$ mail bob<CR>
Call Accounting and find out<CR>
why they haven't returned my 1988 figures!<CR>
.<CR>
$
```

When you log in the next day, a notice will appear on your screen informing you that you have mail waiting to be read.

Sending Mail to Several People Simultaneously

You can send a message to several people by including their login names on the mail command line. For example:

```
$ mail tommy jane wombat dave<CR>
Diamond cutters,<CR>
The game is on for tonight at diamond three.<CR>
Don't forget your gloves!<CR>
Your Manager<CR>
.<CR>
$
```

Sending Mail to Remote Systems: the uname and uuname Commands

Until now we have assumed that you are sending messages to users on the local UNIX system. However, your company may have three separate computer systems, each in a different part of a building, or you may have offices in several locations, each with its own system.

If your system has the Basic Networking Utilities package installed, you can send mail to users on other systems simply by adding the name of the recipient's system before the login ID on the command line.

```
mail sys2!bob<CR>
```

Notice that the system name and the recipient's login ID are separated by an exclamation mark.

Before you can run this command, however, you need three pieces of information:

- the name of the remote system
- whether or not your system and the remote system communicate
- the recipient's login name

The uname and uuname commands allow you to find this information.

If you can, get the name of the remote system and the recipient's login name from the recipient. If the recipient does not know the system name, have him or her issue the following command on the remote system:

```
uname -n<CR>
```

The command will respond with the name of the system. For example:

```
$ uname -n<CR>
dumbo
$
```

Once you know the remote system name, the uuname command can help you verify that your system can communicate with the remote system. At the prompt, type:

```
uuname<CR>
```

This generates a list of remote systems with which your system can communicate. If the recipient's system is on that list, you can send messages to it by mail.

You can simplify this step by using the grep command to search through the uuname output. At the prompt, type:

```
uuname | grep system<CR>
```

(Here *system* is the recipient's system name.) If grep finds the specified system name, it prints it on the screen. For example:

```
$ uuname | grep dumbo<CR>
dumbo
$
```

This means that dumbo can communicate with your system. If dumbo does not communicate with your system, a prompt is returned.

```
$ uuname | grep dumbo<CR>
$
```

To summarize our discussion of uname and uuname, consider an example. Suppose you want to send a message to login sarah on the remote system dumbo. Verify that dumbo can communicate with your system and send your message. The following screen shows both steps.

```
$ uuname | grep dumbo<CR>
dumbo
$ mail dumbo!sarah<CR>
Sarah,<CR>
The final counts for the writing seminar<CR>
are as follows:<CR>
<CR>
Our department - 18<CR>
Your department - 20<CR>
<CR>
Tom<CR>
.<CR>
$
```

Figures 11-1 and 11-2 summarize the syntax and capabilities of the uname and uuname commands, respectively.

Figure 11-1: Summary of the uname Command

Command Recap uname – displays the system name		
command	*options*	*arguments*
uname	–n and others*	none
Description:	uname –n displays the name of the system on which your login resides.	

* See **uname**(1) in the *User's Reference Manual* for all available options and an explanation of their capabilities.

Figure 11-2: Summary of the uuname Command

Command Recap uuname – displays a list of networked systems		
command	*options*	*arguments*
uuname	none	none
Description:	uuname displays a list of remote systems that can communicate with your system.	

In addition to the addressing style described above, another addressing syntax known as Domain-style addressing is supported. Here the address would be in the form

recipient@remote_system

or

recipient@remote_system.domain_info

The above two addresses are equivalent to the addresses

remote_system!*recipient*

or

remote_system.domain_info!*recipient*

Other addressing syntaxes may be set up by your local System Administrator. Your local System Administrator may also have set it up (check with your local System Administrator to be sure), such that it may not be necessary to verify that your local system can directly communicate with the remote system. If the remote system cannot be contacted directly the message may be automatically forwarded to another system that can service the indicated remote system.

Figure 11-3 summarizes the syntax and capabilities of the `mail` command.

Figure 11-3: Summary of Sending Messages with the `mail` Command

Command Recap `mail` – sends a message to another user's login		
command	*options**	*arguments*
`mail`	none required	[*system_name!*]*login*
Description:	Typing `mail` followed by one or more login names (which may include a system name), sends the message typed on the lines following the command line to the specified login(s).	
Remarks:	Typing a period (`.`) (followed by the `RETURN` key) or a <cntrl-d> at the beginning of a new line sends the message.	

* See the **mail**(1) manual page in the *User's Reference Manual* for all available options and an explanation of their capabilities.

Managing Incoming Mail

As stated earlier, the `mail` command also allows you to display messages sent to you by other users on your screen so you can read them. If you are logged in when someone sends you mail, the following message is printed on your screen:

```
you have mail
```

This means that one or more messages are being held for you in a file called `/var/mail/`*your_login*, usually referred to as your mailbox. To display these messages on your screen, type the `mail` command without any arguments:

```
mail<CR>
```

The messages will be displayed one at a time, beginning with the one most recently received. A typical `mail` message display looks like this:

```
$ mail
>From tommy Wed May 21 15:33 CST 1989
Content-Length: 104

Bob,
Looks like the meeting has been canceled.
Do you still want the material for the technical review?
Tom

?
```

The first set of lines, called the message header, provides information about the message: the login name of the sender, the date and time the message was sent, and how many characters long the contents of the message is. The lines after the first blank line (up to the line containing the ?) comprise the contents of the message.

If a long message is being displayed on your terminal screen, you may not be able to read it all at once. You can interrupt the printing by typing <cntrl-s>. This will freeze the screen, giving you a chance to read. When you are ready to continue, type <cntrl-q> and the printing will resume.

After displaying each message, the `mail` command prints a `?` prompt and waits for a response. You have many options, for example, you can leave the current message in your mailbox while you read the next message; you can delete the current message; or you can save the current message for future reference. For a list of `mail`'s available options, type a `?` in response to `mail`'s ? prompt.

To display the next message without deleting the current message, press the `RETURN` key after the question mark.

?<CR>

The current message remains in your mailbox and the next message is displayed. If you have read all the messages in your mailbox, the shell prompt appears.

To delete a message, type a d after the question mark:

```
? d<CR>
```

The message is deleted from your mailbox. If there is another message waiting, it is then displayed.

To save a message for later reference, type an s after the question mark:

```
? s<CR>
```

This saves the message, by default, in a file called mbox in your home directory. To save the message in another file, type the name of that file after the s command.

For example, to save a message in a file called mailsave (in your current directory), enter the response shown after the question mark:

```
? s mailsave<CR>
```

If mailsave is an existing file, the mail command appends the message to it. If there is no file by that name, the mail command creates one and stores your message in it. You can later verify the existence of the new file by using the ls command. (ls lists the contents of your current directory.)

You can also save the message in a file in a different directory by specifying a path name. For example:

```
? s project1/memo<CR>
```

This is a relative path name that identifies a file called memo (where your message will be saved) in a subdirectory (project1) of your current directory. You can use either relative or full path names when saving mail messages. (For instructions on using path names, see Chapter 3, "Using the File System.")

To quit reading messages, enter the response shown after the question mark:

```
? q<CR>
```

Any messages that you have not read are kept in your mailbox until the next time you use the mail command.

To stop the printing of a message entirely, press the BREAK key. The mail command will stop the display, print a ? prompt, and wait for a response from you.

Figure 11-4 summarizes the syntax and capabilities of the `mail` command for reading messages.

Figure 11-4: Summary of Reading Messages with the `mail` Command

Command Recap		
`mail` – reads messages sent to your login		
command	*options*	*arguments*
`mail`	available*	none
Description:	When issued without options, the `mail` command displays any messages waiting in your mailbox (the system file `/var/mail/`*your_login*).	
Remarks:	A question mark (`?`) at the end of a message means that a response is expected. A full list of possible responses is given in the *User's Reference Manual.*	

* See the **mail**(1) manual page in the *User's Reference Manual* for all available options and an explanation of their capabilities.

The `vacation` and `notify` commands

Two other programs related to managing incoming messages are *notify*(1) and *vacation*(1). The *notify* command provides a mechanism for notifying the recipient (if they are currently logged on) of newly arrived messages. The *vacation* command provides a way to automatically answer incoming messages with a canned response while also saving the incoming messages for later perusal. See the *User's Reference Manual* for additional details.

mailx

This section introduces the mailx facility. It explains how to set up your mailx environment, send messages with the mailx command, and handle messages that have been sent to you. The material is presented in four parts:

- mailx Overview
- Sending Messages
- Managing Incoming Mail
- The .mailrc File

mailx Overview

The mailx(1) command is an enhanced version of the mail(1) command. There are many options to mailx that are not available in mail for sending and reading mail. For example, you can define an alias for a single login or for a group. This allows you to send mail to an individual using a name or word other than their login ID, and to send mail to a whole group of people using a single name or word. When you use mailx to read incoming mail you can save it in various files, edit it, forward it to someone else, respond to the person who originated the message, and so forth. By using mailx environment variables you can develop an environment to suit your individual tastes.

If you type the mailx command with one or more logins as arguments, mailx decides you are sending mail to the named users, prompts you for a summary of the subject, and then waits for you to type in your message or issue a command. The section "How to Send Messages" describes features that are available to you for editing, incorporating other files, adding names to copy lists, and more.

If you enter the mailx command with no arguments, mailx checks incoming mail for you in a file named /var/mail/*your_login*. If there is mail for you in that file, you are shown a list of the items and given the opportunity to read, store, remove or transfer each one to another file. The section entitled "How to Manage Incoming Mail" provides some examples and describes the options available.

If you choose to customize mailx, you should create a start-up file in your home directory called .mailrc. The section on "The .mailrc File" describes variables you can include in your start-up file.

mailx has two modes of functioning: input mode and command mode. You must be in input mode to create and send messages. Command mode is used to read incoming mail. You can use any of the following methods to control the way mailx works for you:

- by entering options on the command line. (See the mailx(1) manual page in the *User's Reference Manual.*)
- by issuing commands when you are in input mode, for example, creating a message to send. These commands are always preceded by a ~(tilde) and are referred to as tilde escapes. (See the mailx(1) manual page in the *User's Reference Manual.*)

- by issuing commands when you are in command mode, for example, reading incoming mail.
- by storing commands and environment variables in a start-up file in your home directory called `$HOME/.mailrc`.

Tilde escapes are discussed in "Sending Messages," command mode commands in "Managing Incoming Mail," and the `.mailrc` file in "The `.mailrc` File."

Command Line Options

In this section, we will look at command line options.

The syntax for the `mailx` command is:

`mailx [`*options*`] [`*name...*`]`

The *options* are flags that control the action of the command, and *name...* represents the intended recipients.

Anything on the command line other than an option preceded by a hyphen is read by `mailx` as a *name;* that is, the login or alias of a person to whom you are sending a message.

One valuable command line option that is also available in `mail`, is

`-f` [*filename*]: Allows you to read messages from *filename* instead of your mailbox.

Because `mailx` lets you store messages in any file you name, you need the `-f` option to review these stored options. The default storage file is `$HOME/mbox`, so the command `mailx -f` is used to review messages stored there.

How to Send Messages: the Tilde Escapes

To send a message to another UNIX system user, enter the following command:

```
$ mailx login<CR>
Subject:
```

The login name specified belongs to the person who is to receive the message. The system puts you into input mode and prompts you for the subject of the message. (You may have to wait a few seconds for the `Subject:` prompt if the system is very busy.) This is the simplest way to run the `mailx` command; it differs little from the way you run the `mail` command.

The following examples show how you can edit messages you are sending, incorporate existing text into your messages, change the header information, and do other tasks that take advantage of the `mailx` command's capabilities. Each example is followed by an explanation of the key points illustrated in the example.

```
$ mailx sms<CR>
Subject:
```

Whether to include a subject or not is optional. If you elect not to, press the `RETURN` key. The cursor moves to the next line and the program waits for you to enter the text of the message.

```
$ mailx sms<CR>
Subject: meeting notice<CR>
We're having a meeting for novice mailx users in<CR>
the auditorium at 9:00 tomorrow.<CR>
Would you be willing to give a demonstration?<CR>
Bob<CR>
~. <CR>
EOT
$
```

There are two important things to notice about the above example:

- You break up the lines of your message by pressing the `RETURN` key at the end of each line. This makes it easier for the recipient to read the message, and prevents you from overflowing the line buffer.
- You end the text and send the message by entering a tilde and a period together (`~.`), or a `cntrl-d`, at the beginning of a line. The system responds with an end-of-text notice (`EOT`) and a prompt.

There are several commands available to you when you are in input mode (as we were in the example). Each of them consists of a tilde (~), followed by an alphabetic character, entered at the beginning of a line. Together they are known as tilde escapes. (See the `mailx`(1) manual page in the *User's Reference Manual*.) Most of them are used in the examples in this section.

You can include the subject of your message on the command line by using the `-s` option. For example, the command line:

```
$ mailx -s "meeting notice" sms<CR>
```

is equivalent to:

```
$ mailx sms<CR>
Subject: meeting notice<CR>
```

The subject line will look the same to the recipient of the message. Notice that when putting the subject on the command line, you must enclose a subject that has more than one word in quotation marks.

Editing the Message

When you are in the input mode of `mailx`, you can invoke an editor by entering the <tilde e> escape at the beginning of a line. The following example shows how to use tilde:

```
$ mailx sms<CR>
Subject: Testing my tilde<CR>
When entering the text of a message<CR>
that has somehow gotten grabled<CR>
you may invoke your favorite editor<CR>
by means of a <tilde e> (~e).
                    .
                    .
                    .
```

Notice that you have misspelled a word in your message. To correct the error, use ~e to invoke the editor, in this case the default editor, ed.

```
                    .
                    .
                    .
~e<CR>
12
/grabled/p
that has somehow gotten grabled
s/gra/gar/p
that has somehow gotten garbled
w
132
q
(continue)
What more can I tell you?
                    .
                    .
                    .
```

In this example the ed editor was used. Your .profile or a .mailrc file controls which editor will be invoked when you issue a ~e escape command. The ~v (tilde v) escape invokes an alternate editor (most commonly, vi).

When you exited from ed (by typing q), the mailx command returned you to input mode and prompted you to continue your message. At this point you may want to preview your corrected message by entering a ~p (tilde p) escape. The ~p escape prints out the entire message up to the point where the ~p was entered. Thus, at any time during text entry, you can review the current contents of your message.

```
                    .
                    .
                    .
~p
Message contains:
To: sms
Subject: Testing my tilde

When entering the text of a message
that has somehow gotten garbled
you may invoke your favorite editor
by means of a <tilde e> (~e).
What more can I tell you?
(continue)
~.
EOT
$
```

Incorporating Existing Text into Your Message

`mailx` provides four ways to incorporate material from another source into the message you are creating. You can:

- read a file into your message
- read a message you have received into a reply
- incorporate the value of a named environment variable into a message
- execute a shell command and incorporate the output of the command into a message

The following examples show the first two of these functions. These are the most commonly used of these four functions. For information about the other two, see the `mailx`(1) manual page of the *User's Reference Manual.*

Reading a File into a Message

```
$ mailx sms<CR>
Subject: Work Schedule<CR>
As you can see from the following<CR>
~r letters/file1
"letters/file1"   10/725
we have our work cut out for us.
Please give me your thoughts on this.
- Bob
~.
EOT
$
```

As the example shows, the ~r (tilde r) escape is followed by the name of the file you want to include. The system displays the file name and the number of lines and characters it contains. You are still in input mode and can continue with the rest of the message. When the recipient gets the message, the text of letters/file1 is included. (You can, of course, use the ~p (tilde p) escape to preview the contents before sending your message.)

Incorporating a Message from Your Mailbox into a Reply

```
$ mailx<CR>
mailx version 4.0  Type ? for help.
"/var/mail/roberts": 2 messages 1 new
>N   1 abc        Tue May 1  08:09  8/155  Meeting Notice
     2 hqtrs      Mon Apr 30 16:57  4/127  Schedule
? m jones<CR>
Subject: Hq Schedule<CR>
Here is a copy of the schedule from headquarters...<CR>
~f 2<CR>
Interpolating: 2
(continue)
As you can see, the boss will be visiting our district on<CR>
the 14th and 15th.<CR>
- Robert
~.
EOT
?
```

There are several important points illustrated in this example:

- The sequence begins in command mode, where you read and respond to your incoming mail. Then you switch into input mode by issuing the command `m jones` (meaning send a message to `jones`).
- The `~f` escape is used in input mode to forward a message in your mailbox and make it part of the outgoing message. The number 2 after the `~f` means message 2 is to be interpolated (read in).
- `mailx` tells you that message 2 is being interpolated and then tells you to continue.
- When you finish creating and sending the message, you are back in command mode, shown by the ? prompt. You may now do something else in command mode, or exit `mailx` by typing q.

An alternate command, the `~m` (tilde m) escape, works the way that `~f` does except the read-in message is indented one tab stop. Both the `~m` and `~f` commands work only if you start out in command mode and then enter a command that puts you into input mode. Other commands that work this way will be covered in the section "How to Manage Incoming Mail."

Changing Parts of the Message Header

The header of a `mailx` message has four components:

- subject
- recipient(s)
- copy-to list
- blind-copy list (a list of intended recipients that is not shown on the copies sent to other recipients)

When you enter the `mailx` command followed by a login or an alias you are put into input mode and prompted for the subject of your message. Once you end the subject line by pressing the RETURN key, `mailx` expects you to type the text of the message. If, at any point in input mode, you want to change or supplement some of the header information, there are four tilde escapes that you can use: `~h`, `~t`, `~c`, and `~b`.

`~h` displays all the header fields: subject, recipient, copy-to list, and blind copy list, with their current values. You can change a current value, add to it, or, by pressing the RETURN key, accept it.

`~t` lets you add names to the list of recipients. Names can be either login names or aliases.

`~c` lets you create or add to a copy-to list for the message. Enter either login names or aliases of those to whom a copy of the message should be sent.

`~b` lets you create or add to a blind-copy list for the message.

All tilde escapes must be in the first position on a line. For the `~t`, `~c` or `~b`, any additional material on the line is taken to be input for the list in question. Entering a tilde escape with no additional material will display the header line in question, allowing you to backspace and make changes. Any additional material on a line that begins with a `~h` is ignored.

Adding Your Signature

If you want, you can establish two different signatures with the `sign` and `Sign` environment variables. These can be invoked with the `~a` (tilde a) or `~A` (tilde A) escape, respectively. Assume you have set the value Supreme Commander to be called by the `~A` escape. Here's how it would work:

```
$ mailx -s orders bll<CR>
Be ready to move out at 0400 hours.<CR>
~A<CR>
Supreme Commander
~.<CR>
EOT
$
```

Having both escapes (`~a` and `~A`) allows you to set up two forms for your signature. However, because the sender's login automatically appears in the message header when the message is read, no signature is required to identify you.

Keeping a Record of Messages You Send

The `mailx` command offers several ways to keep copies of outgoing messages. Two that you can use without setting any special environment variables are the `~w` (tilde w) escape and the `-F` option on the command line.

The `~w` followed by a file name causes the text of the message to be written to the named file if the file does not already exist. For example:

```
$ mailx bdr<CR>
Subject: Saving Copies<CR>
When you want to save a copy of<CR>
the text of a message, use the tilde w.<CR>
~w savemail
"savemail" 2/71
~.
EOT
$
```

If you now display the contents of `savemail`, you will see this:

```
$ cat savemail<CR>
When you want to save a copy of
the text of a message, use the tilde w.
$
```

The drawback to this method, as you can see, is that none of the header information is saved.

The `-F` option appends the text of the message to a file named after the first recipient. If you have used an alias for the recipient(s) the alias is first converted into the appropriate login(s) and the first login is used as the file name. As noted above, if you have a file by that name in your current directory, the text of the message is appended to it.

Using the `-F` option on the command line does preserve the header information. It works as follows:

```
$ mailx -F bdr<CR>
Subject:  Savings
This method appends this message to a
file in my current directory named bdr.
~.
EOT
$
```

We can check the results by looking at the file `bdr`.

```
$ cat bdr<CR>
From: kol  Fri May 2  11:14:45  1989
To: bdr
Subject: Savings

This method appends this message to a
file in my current directory named bdr.
$
```

Exiting from `mailx`

When you have finished composing your message, you can leave `mailx` by typing any of the following three commands:

~. tilde period (`~.`), or `cntrl-d`, is the standard way of leaving input mode. It also sends the message. If you entered input mode from the command mode of `mailx`, you now return to the command mode (shown by the ? prompt you receive after typing this command). If you started out in input mode, you now return to the shell (shown by the shell prompt).

~q tilde q (~q) simulates an interrupt. It lets you exit the input mode of `mailx`. If you have entered text for a message, it will be appended to the file called `dead.letter` in your home directory.

`~x` tilde x (`~x`) simulates an interrupt. It lets you exit the input mode of `mailx` without saving anything.

Summary

In the preceding paragraphs we have described and shown examples of some of the tilde escape commands available when sending messages via the `mailx` command. (See the `mailx`(1) manual page in the *User's Reference Manual.*)

How to Manage Incoming Mail

mailx has over fifty commands that help you manage your incoming mail. See the mailx(1) manual page in the *User's Reference Manual* for a list of all of them (and their synonyms) in alphabetic order. The most commonly used commands (and arguments) are described in the following subsections:

- the *msglist* argument
- commands for reading and deleting mail
- commands for saving mail
- commands for replying to mail
- commands for getting out of mailx

The msglist Argument

Many commands in mailx take a form of the *msglist* argument. This argument provides the command with a list of messages on which to operate. If a command expects a *msglist* argument and you do not provide one, the command is performed on the current message. Any of the following formats can be used for a *msglist*:

n	use message number *n* as the current message
^	the first undeleted message
$	the last message
*	all messages
n-m	an inclusive range of message numbers
user	all messages from *user*
/*string*	All messages with *string* in the subject line (case is ignored)
:*c*	all messages of type *c* where *c* is: d - deleted messages n - new messages o - old messages r - read messages u - unread messages

The context of the command determines whether this type of specification makes sense.

Here are two examples (the ? is the command mode prompt):

```
? d 1-3          [ Delete messages 1, 2 and 3 ]
? s bdr bdrmail  [ Save all messages from user bdr in a file named bdrmail. ]
?
```

Additional examples may be found throughout the next three subsections.

Commands for Reading and Deleting Mail

When a message arrives in your mailbox the following notice appears on your screen:

```
you have mail
```

The notice appears when you log in or when you return to the shell from another procedure.

Reading Mail

To read your mail, enter the `mailx` command with or without arguments. Execution of the command places you in the command mode of `mailx`. The next thing that appears on your screen is a display that looks something like this:

```
mailx version 4.0  Type ? for help.
"/var/mail/bdr":   3 messages  3 new
> N 1 rbt         Thur Apr 30 14:20   8/190  Review Session
  N 2 admin       Thur Apr 30 15:56   5/84   New printer
  N 3 sms         Fri  May  1 08:39  64/1574 Reorganization
?
```

The first line identifies the version of `mailx` used on your system, and reminds you that help is available by typing a question mark (?). The second line shows the path name of the file used as input to the display (the file name is normally the same as your login name) together with a count of the total number of messages and their status. The rest of the display is header information from the incoming messages. The messages are numbered in sequence with the last one received at the bottom of the list. To the left of the numbers there may be a status indicator; N for new, U for unread. A greater than sign (>) points to the current message. Other fields in the header line show the login of the originator of the message, the day, date and time it was delivered, the number of lines and characters in the message, and the message subject. The last field may be blank.

When the header information is displayed on your screen, you can print messages either by pressing the RETURN key or entering a command followed by a *msglist* argument. If you enter a command with no *msglist* argument, the command acts on the message pointed at by the > sign. Pressing the RETURN key is equivalent to typing the `p` (for print) command without a *msglist* argument; the message displayed is the one pointed at by the > sign. To read some other message (or several others in succession), enter a `p` (for print) or `t` (for type) followed by the message number(s). Here are some examples:

```
? <CR>              [ Print the current message. ]
? p 2<CR>         [ Print message number 2.       ]
? p sms<CR>     [ Print all messages from user sms. ]
```

The command `t` (for type) is a synonym of `p` (for print).

Scanning Your Mailbox

The `mailx` command lets you look through the messages in your mailbox while you decide which ones need your immediate attention.

When you first enter the `mailx` command mode, the banner tells you how many messages you have and displays the header line for twenty messages. (If you are connected to the computer over a slow communication line, only the header lines for ten messages are displayed.) If the total number of messages exceeds one screenful, you can display the next screen by entering the `z` command. Typing `z-` causes a previous screen (if there is one) to be displayed. If you want to see the header information for a specific group of messages, enter the `f` (for from) command followed by the *msglist* argument.

Here are examples of those commands:

```
? z        [ Scroll forward one screenful of header lines. ]
? z-       [ Scroll backward one screenful. ]
? f sms    [ Display headers of all messages from user sms. ]
```

Switching to Other Mail Files

When you enter `mailx` by issuing the command:

```
$ mailx<CR>
```

you are looking at the file `/var/mail/`*your_login*.

`mailx` lets you switch to other mail files and use any of the `mailx` commands on their contents. (You can even switch to a non-mail file, but if you try to use `mailx` commands you are told `No applicable messages.`) The switch to another file is done with the `fi` or `fold` command (they are synonyms) followed by the *filename*. The following special characters work in place of the *filename* argument:

%	the user's default mailbox (`/var/mail/`*your_login*)
%*login*	the mailbox of the owner of *login* (if you have the required permissions)
#	the previous file
&	the current mbox

Here is an example of how this might look on your screen:

```
$ mailx<CR>
mailx version 4.0  Type ? for help.
"/var/mail/sms":  3 messages 2 new 3 unread
  U 1 jaf          Sat May 9 07:55   7/137    test25
> N 2 todd         Sat May 9 08:59   9/377    UNITS requirements
  N 3 has          Sat May 9 11:08  29/1214   access to bailey

? fi &              [ Enter this command to transfer to your mbox. ]

Held 3 messages in /var/mail/sms
"+mbox":  74 messages 10 unread
   .                [ Enter any commands for your mbox. ]
   .
   .
? q<CR>
$
```

Deleting Mail

To delete a message, enter a d followed by a *msglist* argument. If the *msglist* argument is omitted, the current message is deleted. The messages are not deleted until you leave the mailbox file you are processing. Until you do, the u (for undelete) gives you the opportunity to change your mind. Once you have issued the quit command (q) or switched to another file, however, the deleted messages are gone.

`mailx` permits you to combine the delete and print command and enter a dp. This is like saying, "Delete the message I just read and show me the next one." Here are some examples of the delete command:

```
? d *      [ Delete all my messages. ]
? d :r     [ Delete all messages that have been read. ]
? dp       [ Delete the current message and print the next one. ]
? d 2-5    [ Delete messages 2 through 5. ]
```

Commands for Saving Mail

All messages not specifically deleted are saved when you quit `mailx`. Messages that have been read are saved in a file in your home directory called `mbox`. Messages that have not been read are held in your mailbox (`/var/mail/`*your_login*).

The command to save messages comes in two forms: with an upper case or a lower case `s`. The syntax for the upper case version is:

`S` [*msglist*]

Messages specified by the *msglist* argument are saved in a file in the current directory named for the login of the first message in the list.

The syntax for the lower case version is:

`s` [*msglist*] *filename*
or
`s`

Messages specified by the *msglist* argument are saved in the file named in the *filename* argument. If you omit the *msglist* argument, the current message is saved. If you are using logins for file names, this can lead to some ambiguity. If `mailx` is puzzled, you will get an error message. Finally, if both the *msglist* and the *filename* are omitted, the mail is saved in a file called `mbox` in your home directory.

Commands for Replying to Mail

The command for replying to mail comes in two forms: with an upper case or a lower case `r`. The difference between the two forms is that the upper case form (`R`) causes your response to be sent only to the originator of the message, while the lower case form (`r`) causes your response to be sent not only to the originator but also to all other recipients.

When you reply to a message, the original subject line is picked up and used as the subject of your reply. Here's an example of the way it looks:

```
$ mailx<CR>

mailx version 4.0  Type ? for help.
"/var/mail/sms":  3 messages 2 new 3 unread
  U 1 jaf        Wed May 9 07:55   7/137   test25
> N 2 todd       Wed May 9 08:59   9/377   UNITS requirements
  N 3 has        Wed May 9 11:08  29/1214  access to bailey

? R 2
To: todd
Subject: Re: UNITS requirements
```

Assuming the message about "UNITS requirements" had been sent to some additional people, and the lower case `r` had been used, the header might have appeared like this:

```
? r 2
To: todd eg has jcb bdr
Subject: Re:  UNITS requirements
```

Commands for Getting Out of `mailx`

There are two standard ways of leaving `mailx`: with a `q` or with an `x`. If you leave `mailx` with a `q`, you see messages that summarize what you did with your mail. They look like this:

```
? q<CR>
Saved 1 message in /fs1/bdr/mbox
Held 1 message in /var/mail/bdr
$
```

From the example we can surmise that user bdr had at least two messages, read one and either left the other unread or issued a command asking that it be held in /var/mail/bdr. If there were more than two messages, the others were deleted or saved in other files. mailx does not issue a message about those.

If you leave mailx with an x, it is almost as if you had never entered. Mail read and messages deleted are retained in your mailbox. However, if you have saved messages in other files, that action has already taken place and is not undone by the x.

mailx Command Summary

In the preceding subsections we have described some of the most frequently used mailx commands. (See the mailx(1) manual page in the *User's Reference Manual* for a complete list.) If you need help while you are in the command mode of mailx, type either a ? or help at the ? prompt. A list of mailx commands and what they do will be displayed on your terminal screen.

The `.mailrc` File

The `.mailrc` file contains commands to be executed when you invoke `mailx`.

There may be a system-wide start-up file (`/etc/mail/mailx.rc`) on your system. If it exists it is used by the system administrator to set common variables. Variables set in your `.mailrc` file take precedence over those in `mailx.rc`.

Most `mailx` commands are legal in the `.mailrc` file. However, the following commands are NOT legal entries:

`!` (or) `shell`	escape to the shell
`Copy`	save messages in *msglist* in a file whose name is derived from the author
`edit`	invoke the editor
`visual`	invoke vi
`followup`	respond to a message
`Followup`	respond to a message, sending a copy to *msglist*
`mail`	switch into input mode
`reply`	respond to a message
`Reply`	respond to the author of each message in *msglist*

You can create your own `.mailrc` with any editor, or copy a friend's. Figure 11-5 shows a sample `.mailrc` file.

Figure 11-5: Sample `.mailrc` File

```
if r
  cd $HOME/mail
endif
set allnet append asksub askcc autoprint dot
set metoo quiet save showto header hold keep keepsave
set outfolder
set folder='mail'
set record='outbox'
set crt=24
set EDITOR='/bin/ed'
set sign='Roberts'
set Sign='Jackson Roberts, Supervisor'
set toplines=10
alias fred  fjs
alias bob  rcm
alias alice  ap
alias donna  dr
alias pat  pat
group robertsgrp  fred bob alice mark pat
group accounts  robertsgrp donna
```

The example in Figure 11-5 includes the commands you are most likely to find useful: the `set` command and the `alias` or `group` commands.

The `set` command is used to establish values for environment variables. The command syntax is:

> `set`
> `set` *name*
> `set` *name=string*
> `set` *name=number*

When you issue the `set` command without any arguments, `set` produces a list of all defined variables and their values. The argument *name* refers to an environmental variable. More than one *name* can be entered after the `set` command. Some variables take a string or numeric value. String values are enclosed in single quotes.

When you put a value in an environment variable by making an assignment such as `HOME=`*my_login*, you are telling the shell how to interpret that variable. However, this type of assignment in the shell does not make the value of the variable accessible to other UNIX system programs that need to reference environment variables. To make it accessible, you must export the variable. If you set the `TERM` variable in your environment in Chapter 7 or Chapter 9), you will remember using the `export` command shown in the following example:

```
$ TERM=5425
$ export TERM
```

When you export variables from the shell in this way, programs that reference environment variables are said to import them. Some of these variables (such as `EDITOR` and `VISUAL`) are not peculiar to `mailx`, but may be specified as general environment variables and imported from your execution environment. If a value is set in `.mailrc` for an imported variable it overrides the imported value. There is an `unset` command, but it works only against variables set in `.mailrc`; it has no effect on imported variables.

There are too many environment variables that can be defined in your `.mailrc` to be fully described in this document. For complete information, consult the `mailx`(1) manual page in the *User's Reference Manual*.

Three variables used in the example in Figure 11-5 deserve special attention because they show how to organize the filing of messages. These variables are: `folder`, `record`, and `outfolder`. All three are interrelated and control the directories and files in which copies of messages are kept.

To put a value into the `folder` variable, use the following format:

`set folder=`*directory*

This specifies the directory in which you want to save standard mail files. If the directory name specified does not begin with a / (slash), it is presumed to be relative to `$HOME`. If `folder` is an exported shell variable, you can specify file names (in commands that call for a *filename* argument) with a / before the name; the name will be expanded so that the file is put into the `folder` directory.

To put a value in the `record` variable, use the following format:

`set record=`*filename*

This directs `mailx` to save a copy of all outgoing messages in the specified file.

The header information is saved along with the text of the message. By default, this variable is disabled.

The `outfolder` variable causes the file in which you store copies of outgoing messages (enabled by the variable `record=`) to be located in the `folder` directory. It is established by being named in a `set` command. The default is `nooutfolder`.

The `alias` and `group` commands are synonyms. In Figure 11-5, the `alias` command is used to associate a name with a single login; the `group` command is used to specify multiple names that can be called in with one pseudonym. This is a nice way to distinguish between single and group aliases, but if you want, you can treat the commands as exact equivalents. Notice, too, that aliases can be nested.

In the `.mailrc` file shown in Figure 11-5, the alias `robertsgrp` represents five users; four of them are specified by previously defined aliases and one, `mark`, is specified by a login. The fifth user, `pat`, is specified by both a login and an alias. The next group command in the example, `accounts`, uses the group `robertsgrp` plus the alias `donna`. It expands to six logins.

The `.mailrc` file in Figure 11-5 includes an `if-endif` command. The full syntax of that command is:

```
if s|r
  mail_commands
else
  mail_commands
endif
```

The `s` and `r` stand for send and receive, so you can cause some initializing commands to be executed according to whether `mailx` is entered in input mode (send) or command mode (receive). In the preceding example, the command is issued to change directory to `$HOME/mail` if reading mail. Here, the user elected to set up a subdirectory to handle incoming mail.

The environment variables shown in this section are those most commonly included in the `.mailrc` file. You can, however, specify any of them for one session only whenever you are in command mode. For a complete list of the environment variables you can set in `mailx` see the `mailx`(1) manual page in the *User's Reference Manual.*

12 Communication Tutorial

Introduction

The UNIX system offers a choice of commands that enable you to communicate with other UNIX system users. Specifically, they allow you to: send and receive messages from other users (on either your system or another UNIX system); exchange files; and form networks with other UNIX systems. Through networking, a user on one system can exchange messages and files between computers, and execute commands on remote computers.

To help you take advantage of these capabilities, this chapter will teach you how to use the following commands:

```
ct
cu
uucp
uuname
uupick
uustat
uuto
uux
```

Sending Files

The ability to send files between computers is fundamental to electronic communications. However, the act of sending a file is just the first step in the process. Here is the overall process we discuss in this section. Keep it in mind as we progress through this section:

Send Job — The command(s) to start a file (job) on its way to a remote system, or, to a specific user on the remote system (uucp, uuto).

Check Job Status — A way to monitor and trace the progress of your job requests, as well as obtain specific information associated with that job request (mail, uustat).

Retrieve Job — The way to collect a file when it successfully arrives on the remote system (uupick).

The uucp Command

Keeping the overall process in mind, let's begin with the first step -- the command to send a file to a remote system. The command uucp (short for UNIX-to-UNIX system copy) allows you to copy files between computers. It is not an interactive command. It performs its work silently, invisible to the user. Once you issue this command, you may run other processes.

The uucp command allows you to transfer files to a remote computer without knowing anything except the name of the remote computer and, possibly, the login ID of the remote user(s) to whom the file is being sent.

Syntax

uucp allows you to send:

- one file to a file or a directory
- multiple files to a directory

To deliver your file(s), uucp must know the full pathname of both the *sourcefile* and the *destinationfile*. However, this does not mean you must type out the full pathname of both files every time you use the uucp command. You can use several abbreviations once you become familiar with their formats; uucp will expand them to full pathnames.

To specify your *sourcefile* and *destinationfile,* begin by identifying the location of your *sourcefile,* relative to your own current location in the file system. If the *sourcefile* is in your current directory, you can specify it by its name alone (without a path). If the *sourcefile* is not in your current directory, you must specify its full or relative pathname.

How do you specify the *destinationfile*? Because it is on a remote system, the *destinationfile* must always be specified with a pathname that begins with the name of the remote system. After that, however, uucp gives you a choice of formats:

- *systemname*!*fullpathname*
- *systemname*!~/[*pathname*]

Here, *fullpathname* is an explicit pathname. ~/ translates to `/var/spool/uucppublic/`, uucp's public directory on the remote system. *pathname* is a sub-directory, typically having the same name as the recipient's user id.

For pre-Release 4.0 systems, uucp's public directory is `/var/spool/uucppublic/`.

Until now we have described what to do when you want to send a file from your local system to a remote system. However, it is also possible to use uucp to send a file from a remote system to your local system. In either case, you can use the formats described above to specify either *sourcefiles* or *destinationfiles.* The important distinction in choosing one of these formats is not whether a file is a *sourcefile* or a *destinationfile,* but where you are currently located in the file system relative to the files you are specifying.

For example, let's say you are login `kol` on a system called `mickey`. Your home directory is `/home/kol` and you want to send a file called `chap1` (in a directory called `text` in your home directory) to login `wsm` on a system called `minnie`. You are currently working in `/home/kol/text`, so you can specify the *sourcefile* with its relative pathname, `chap1`. You can specify the *destinationfile* like this:

- Specify the *destinationfile* with its full pathname:

  uucp chap1 minnie!/home/wsm/receive/chap1

- Specify the *destinationfile* with *~/pathname*. This expands to the recipient's subdirectory in the public directory on the remote system.

  uucp chap1 minnie!~/wsm/chap1

  (The file will go to minnie!/var/spool/uucppublic/wsm/chap1)

The same results can be obtained by omitting chap1 at the end of the previous command line.

Example

Suppose you want to send a file called minutes to a remote computer named eagle. Enter the command line shown in the following screen:

```
$ uucp -m -j minutes eagle!/home/gws/minutes<CR>
eagleN3f45
$
```

This sends the file minutes (located in your current directory on your local computer) to the remote computer eagle, and places it under the pathname /home/gws in a file named minutes. When the transfer is complete, you, the sender, are notified by mail.

The -m option ensures that you, the sender, are notified by mail as to whether or not the transfer has succeeded. The job ID (eagleN3f45) is displayed in response to the -j option.

Even if uucp does not notify you of a successful transfer soon after you send a file, do not assume that the transfer has failed. Not all systems equipped with networking software have the hardware needed to call other systems. Files being transferred from these so called passive systems must be collected periodically by active systems equipped with the required hardware (see "How It Works" for details). Therefore, if you are transferring files from a passive system, you may experience some delay. Check with your system administrator to find out whether your system is active or passive.

The previous example uses a full pathname to specify the *destinationfile*. There are two other ways to specify *destinationfile*:

- The login directory of `gws` can be specified through use of the ~ (tilde), as shown below:

  ```
  eagle!~gws/minutes
  ```

  This is interpreted as:

  ```
  eagle!/home/gws/minutes
  ```

- The `uucppublic` area is referenced by a similar use of the tilde prefix to the pathname. For example:

  ```
  eagle!~/gws/minutes
  ```

  This is interpreted as:

  ```
  /var/spool/uucppublic/gws/minutes
  ```

How It Works

This section is an overview of what happens automatically when you issue the `uucp` command. An understanding of the processes involved may help you be aware of the limitations and requirements of the command. For further details, see the *System Administrator's Guide* and the *System Administrator's Reference Manual.*

When you enter a `uucp` command, the `uucp` program creates a work file and usually a data file for the requested transfer. (`uucp` does not create a data file when you use the `-c` option.) The work file contains information required for transferring the file(s). The data file is a copy of the specified source file. After these files are created in the spool directory, the `uucico` daemon is started.

The `uucico` daemon attempts to establish a connection to the remote computer that is to receive the file(s). It first gathers the information required for establishing a link to the remote computer from the `Systems` file. This is how `uucico` knows what type of device to use in establishing the link. Then uucico searches the Devices file looking for the devices that match the requirements listed in the Systems file. After uucico finds an available device, it attempts to establish the link and log in on the remote computer.

When uucico logs in on the remote computer, it starts the uucico daemon on the remote computer. The two uucico daemons then negotiate the line protocol to be used in the file transfer(s). The local uucico daemon then transfers the file(s) that you are sending to the remote computer; the remote uucico places the file in the specified pathname(s) on the remote computer. After your local computer completes the transfer(s), the remote computer may send files that are queued for your local computer. The remote computer can be denied permission to transfer these files with an entry in the Permissions file. If this is the case, the remote computer must establish a link to your local computer to perform the transfers.

If the remote computer or the device selected to make the connection to the remote computer is unavailable, the request remains queued in the spool directory. Twice an hour, cron starts uudemon.hour. uudemon.hour, in turn, then starts the uusched daemon. When the uusched daemon starts, it searches the spool directory for the remaining work files, generates the random order in which these requests are to be processed, and then starts the transfer process (uucico) described in the preceding paragraphs.

The transfer process described generally applies to an active computer (one with calling hardware and networking software). An active computer can be set up to poll a passive computer. Because it has networking software, a passive computer can queue file transfers. However, it cannot call the remote computer because it does not have the required hardware. The Poll file (/etc/uucp/Poll) contains a list of computers that are to be polled in this manner.

The following figure summarizes the syntax and capabilities of the uucp command.

Figure 12-1: Summary of the uucp Command

Command Recap		
uucp – copies a file from one computer to another		
command	*options*	*arguments*
uucp	-j, -m, -s and others*	*sourcefile,destinationfile*
Description:	uucp performs preliminary tasks required to copy a file from one computer to another, and calls uucico, the daemon (background process) that transfers the file. The user need only issue the uucp command for a file to be copied.	
Remarks:	By default, the only directory to which you can write files is /var/spool/uucppublic. To write to directories belonging to another user, you must receive write permission from that user and from the administrator. Although there are several ways of representing pathnames as arguments, we recommend that you type full pathnames to avoid confusion.	

* See the **uucp**(1) entry in the *User's Reference Manual* for all available options and an explanation of their capabilities.

The uuto Command

The uuto command is a simplified interface to uucp. It allows you to more easily send files to the public directory (/var/spool/uucppublic/) of a remote system.

Syntax

The basic format for the uuto command is:

uuto *filename(s) system* ! *login*<CR>

where *filename* is the name of the file to be sent, *system* is the recipient's system, and *login* is the recipient's login name. It should be noted that uuto can also route files through intermediate systems on route to the final destination system, i.e., *system!login* can be expressed as *system1!system2!...!login*

If you send a file to someone on your local system, you may omit the system name and use the following format:

uuto *filename !login*<CR>

Example

Let's take an example and see how this works.

The process of sending a file by uuto is called a job. When you issue a uuto command, your job is not sent immediately. First, the file is stored in a queue (a waiting line of jobs) and assigned a job number. When the number of the job comes up, the file is transmitted to the remote system and placed in a public directory there. The recipient is notified by a mail message and can use the uupick command (discussed later in this chapter) to retrieve the file.

For the following discussions, assume this information:

`wombat`	your login name
`sys1`	the name of your local system
`marie`	the recipient's login name
`sys2`	the name of the remote system
`money`	file to be sent

Also assume that the two systems can communicate with each other. To send the file `money` to login `marie` on system `sys2`, enter the following:

```
$ uuto money sys2!marie<CR>
$
```

The prompt on the second line is a signal that the file has been sent to a job queue. The job is now out of your hands; all you can do is wait for confirmation that the job reached its destination.

How do you, the sender, know when the job has arrived? The easiest method is to alter the `uuto` command line by adding a `-m` option, as follows:

```
$ uuto -m money sys2!marie<CR>
$
```

This option sends a `mail` message back to you, the sender, when the job has reached the remote system. It is your formal notification that you have indeed successfully transferred the file to the remote system. The message may look something like this:

```
$ mail<CR>
>From uucp Fri Feb  3 11:53 EST 1989 remote from sys1
REQUEST: sys1!wombat/money --> sys2!~/receive/marie/sys1/ (marie)
(SYSTEM sys2)  copy succeeded
?
```

Figure 12-2 is a summary of the syntax and capabilities of the `uuto` command.

Figure 12-2: Summary of the `uuto` Command

Command Recap `uuto` – sends files to another login		
command	*options*	*arguments*
`uuto`	`-m` and others*	*file system!login*
Description:	`uuto` sends a specified file to the public directory of a specified system, and notifies the intended recipient (by `mail` addressed to his or her login) that the file has arrived there.	
Remarks:	You must have read permission for the file(s) you want to send; the file's parent directory must have read and execute permissions for others. The `-m` option notifies the sender by `mail` when the file has arrived at its destination.	

* See the `uuto`(1) entry in the *User's Reference Manual* for all available options and an explanation of their capabilities.

The `uustat` Command

Now that you have sent the file, you can go to the next step -- checking the job status. If you would like to determine whether the job has left your system, you can use the `uustat` command. This command keeps track of all the uucp and `uuto` jobs you submit and reports their status.

Example

For example:

```
$ uustat<CR>
sys1N2f01  02/03-16:06  S  sys2  wombat 10   money
$
```

The elements of the line of this sample status message are as follows:

- sys1N2f01 is the job number assigned to the job by your host machine.
- 02/03-16:06 is the date and time the job was queued.
- S says that this request is to send a file (R means to receive a file).
- sys2 is the destination machine where the file will be transferred.
- wombat is the login name of the person requesting the job.
- 10 is the number of bytes in the file to be transferred.
- money is the file to be transferred.

Other status messages and options for the uustat command are described in the *User's Reference Manual*.

That is all there is to sending files and checking the progress of the job. A summary of the syntax and capabilities of the uustat command appears in Figure 12-3.

Figure 12-3: Summary of the uustat Command

Command Recap uustat – checks job status of a uucp or uuto job		
command	*options*	*arguments*
uustat	-k and others*	none
Description:	uustat reports the status of all uucp and uuto jobs you have requested.	
Remarks:	The -k option, followed by a job number, allows you to cancel the specified job.	

* See the uustat(1) entry in the *User's Reference Manual* for all available options and an explanation of their capabilities.

The uupick Command

Now that you know how to send a file and check the progress of the job, let's continue the process from the viewpoint of the user who will be receiving a file. When a file sent by uuto reaches the public directory on your UNIX system, you receive a mail message. This is your formal notification that you have received a file.

Example

To continue the previous example, the owner of login marie receives the following mail message when the file money has arrived in the public directory of her system:

```
$ mail<CR>
>From uucp Fri Feb  3 16:05 EST 1989 remote from sys2
/var/spool/uucppublic/receive/wombat/sys1/money from sys1!wombat arrived
$
```

The message contains the following information:

- The first line tells you, the receiver, when the file arrived at its destination.
- The first portion of the second line (up to the word "money") gives the pathname of the public directory where the file money has been stored.
- The rest of the line (after the word "from") gives the name of the remote system, the remote sender (user), and a status of the file transfer ("arrived").

Once you have disposed of the `mail` message, you can use the `uupick` command to store the file where you want it. Type the following command after the system prompt:

```
uupick<CR>
```

The command searches the public directory for any files sent to you. If it finds any, it reports the filename(s). It then prints a ? prompt as a request for further instructions from you.

For example, if the owner of login `marie` issues the `uupick` command to retrieve the `money` file, the command will respond as follows:

```
$ uupick<CR>
from system sys1: file money ?
```

There are several responses; here are the most common responses and what they do.

The first thing you should do is move the file from the public directory and place it in your current directory. To do so, type an `m` after the question mark:

```
? m<CR>
$
```

This response moves the file into your current directory. If you want to put it in some other directory instead, follow the `m` response with the directory name:

? m *other_directory*<CR>

If other files are waiting to be moved, the next one is displayed, followed by the question mark. If not, `uupick` exits and the system returns a prompt.

If you do not want to do anything to that file now, press the RETURN key after the question mark:

```
? <CR>
```

The current file remains in the public directory until the next time you use the `uupick` command. If there are no more messages, the system returns a prompt.

If you already know that you do not want to save the file, you can delete it by typing `d` after the question mark:

```
? d<CR>
```

This response deletes the current file from the public directory and displays the next message (if there is one). If there are no additional messages about waiting files, the system returns a prompt.

Finally, to stop the `uupick` command, type a `q` after the question mark:

```
? q<CR>
```

Any unmoved or undeleted files will wait in the public directory until the next time you use the `uupick` command.

Other available responses are listed in the *User's Reference Manual.*

You now know how to send a file to a remote system, monitor the progress of the job, and retrieve the file from the public directory. Figure 12-4 summarizes the syntax and capabilities of the `uupick` command.

Figure 12-4: Summary of the `uupick` Command

Command Recap		
`uupick` – searches for files sent by `uuto` or `uucp`		
command	*options*	*arguments*
`uupick`	–ssystem	

Description:	`uupick` searches the public directory of your system for files sent by `uuto` or `uucp`. If any are found, the command displays information about the file and prompts you for a response. `uupick` invoked with the –s*system* option will search the public directory for files sent only from *system*.
Remarks:	The question mark (?) at the end of the message shows that a response is expected. A complete list of responses appears in the *User's Reference Manual*.

Networking

Networking is the process of linking computers and terminals so that users can:

- log in on a remote computer as well as a local one
- log in and work on two computers in one work session (without alternately logging off one and logging in on the other)
- exchange data between computers

The commands presented in this section help you perform these tasks. The `ct` command allows you to connect your computer to a remote terminal that is equipped with a modem. The `cu` command enables you to connect your computer to a remote computer, and the `uux` command lets you run commands on a remote system without being logged in on it.

On some computers, the presence of these commands may depend on whether or not networking software is installed. If it is not installed on your system, you will receive a message such as the following when you type a networking command:

```
ct: not found
```

Check with your system administrator to verify the availability of networking commands on your UNIX system.

Connecting a Remote Terminal: the `ct` Command

The `ct` command connects your computer to a remote terminal equipped with a modem, and allows a user at that terminal to log in. To do this, the command dials the telephone number of the modem. The modem must be able to answer the call. When `ct` detects that the call has been answered, it issues a login prompt.

This command can be useful when issued from the opposite end, that is, from the remote terminal itself. If you are using a remote terminal that is far from your computer and want to avoid long distance charges, you can use `ct` to have the computer place a call to your terminal. Simply call the computer, log in, and issue the `ct` command. The computer will hang up the current line and call your (remote) terminal back.

If ct cannot find an available dialer, it tells you that all dialers are busy and asks if it should wait until one becomes available. If you answer yes, it asks how long (in minutes) it should wait for one.

Command Line Format

To execute the ct command, use this format:

ct [*options*] *telno*<CR>

The argument *telno* is the telephone number of the remote terminal.

Sample Command Usage

Suppose you are logged in on a computer through a local terminal and you want to connect a remote terminal to your computer. The telephone number of the modem on the remote terminal is 555-3497. Enter this command line:

```
ct -h -w5 -s1200 9=5553497<CR>
```

The equal sign (=) represents a secondary dial tone.

ct will call the modem, using a dialer operating at a speed of 1200 baud. If a dialer is not available, the -w5 option will cause ct to wait for a dialer for five minutes before quitting. The -h option tells ct not to disconnect the local terminal (the terminal on which the command was issued) from the computer.

Now imagine that you want to log in on the computer from home. To avoid long distance charges, use ct to have the computer call your terminal:

```
ct -s1200 9=5553497<CR>
```

Because you did not specify the -w option, if no device is available, ct will send you the following message:

```
1 busy dialer at 1200 baud Wait for dialer?
```

If you type n (no), the ct command will exit. If you type y (yes), ct will prompt you to specify how long it should wait:

```
Time, in minutes?
```

If a dialer is available, `ct` responds with:

```
Allocated dialer at 1200 baud
```

This means that a dialer has been found. In any case, `ct` asks if you want the line connecting your remote terminal to the computer to be dropped:

```
Confirm hangup?
```

If you type `y` (yes), you are logged off and `ct` calls your remote terminal back when a dialer is available. If you type `n` (no), the `ct` command exits, leaving you logged in on the computer, and does not attempt to call you back.

Figure 12-5 summarizes the syntax and capabilities of the `ct` command.

Figure 12-5: Summary of the ct Command

Command Recap		
ct – connect computer to remote terminal		
command	*options*	*arguments*
ct	-h, -w, -s and others*	*telno*
Description:	ct connects the computer to a remote terminal and allows a user to log in from that terminal.	
Remarks:	The remote terminal must have a modem capable of answering phone calls automatically.	

* See the ct(1) entry in the *User's Reference Manual* for all available options and an explanation of their capabilities.

Calling Another UNIX System: the cu Command

The cu command connects a remote computer to your computer and allows you to be logged in on both computers simultaneously. This means that you can move back and forth between the two computers, transferring files and executing commands on both, without dropping the connection.

The method used by the cu command depends on the information you specify on the command line. You must specify the telephone number or system name of the remote computer. If you specify a telephone number, it is passed on to the automatic dial modem. If you specify a system name, cu obtains the phone number from the Systems file. If an automatic dial modem is not used to establish the connection, the line (port) associated with the direct link to the remote computer can be specified on the command line.

Once the connection is made, the remote computer prompts you to log in on it. When you have finished working on the remote terminal, log off it and terminate the connection by typing <~.>. You will still be logged in on the local computer.

The cu command is not capable of detecting or correcting errors; data may be lost or corrupted during file transfers. You can check for loss of data by using the `sum` command. Before transferring *file* from your local system, issue the `sum` command, using *file* as an argument. Repeat the command on the remote system when *file* is received. The resultant outputs should match, to indicate accurate file transmission.

Command Line Format

To execute the cu command, follow this format:

`cu` [*options*] *telno* | *systemname*<CR>

The components of the command line are:

telno — the telephone number of a remote computer

Equal signs (=) represent secondary dial tones and dashes (–) represent four-second delays.

systemname — a system name that is listed in the `Systems` file.

The cu command obtains the telephone number and baud rate from the `Systems` file and searches for a dialer. The `-s`, `-n`, and `-l` options should not be used together with *systemname*. (To see the list of computers in the `Systems` file, use the uuname command.)

Once your terminal is connected and you are logged in on the remote computer, all standard input (input from the keyboard) is sent to the remote computer, with the exception of tilde (~) commands. Figures 12-6 and 12-7 show the commands you can execute while connected to a remote computer through cu.

Figure 12-6: Command Strings for Use with cu

String	Interpretation
~.	Terminate the link.
~!	Escape to the local computer without dropping the link. To return to the remote computer, type <^d> (control-d).
~!*command*	Execute *command* on the local computer.
~$*command*	Run *command* locally and send its output to the remote system.
~%cd *path*	Change the directory on the local computer where *path* is the pathname or directory name.
~%take *from* [*to*]	Copy a file named *from* (on the remote computer) to a file named *to* (on the local computer). If *to* is omitted, the *from* argument is used in both places.
~%put *from* [*to*]	Copy a file named *from* (on the local computer) to a file named *to* (on the remote computer). If *to* is omitted, the *from* argument is used in both places.
~~...	Send the line ~... to the remote computer.
~%break	Transmit a BREAK to the remote computer (can also be specified as ~%b).

Figure 12-7: Command Strings for Use with cu (continued)

String	Interpretation
`~%ifc`	Toggles the input flow control setting. When enabled, incoming data may be flow controlled by the local terminal (can also be specified as `~%nostop`).
`~%ofc`	Toggles the output flow control setting. When enabled, outgoing data may be flow controlled by the remote host (can also be specified as `~%noostop`).
`~%debug`	Turn the `-d` debugging option on or off (can also be specified as `~%d`).
`~t`	Display the values of the terminal I/O (input/output) structure variables for your terminal (useful for debugging).
`~l`	Display the values of the termio structure variables for the remote communication line (useful for debugging).

NOTE

The use of `~%put` requires `stty` and `cat` on the remote computer. It also requires that the current erase and kill characters on the remote computer be identical to the current ones on the local computer.

The use of `~%take` requires the existence of the `echo` and `cat` commands on the remote computer. Also, `stty tabs` mode should be set on the remote computer if tabs are to be copied without expansion.

Sample Command Usage

Suppose you want to connect your computer to a remote computer called eagle. The phone number for eagle is 555–7867. Enter the following command line:

```
cu -s2400 9=5557867<CR>
```

The -s2400 option causes cu to use a 2400 baud dialer to call eagle. If the -s option is not specified, cu uses a dialer at the default speed, 1200 baud.

When eagle answers the call, cu notifies you that the connection has been made, and passes eagle's login prompt to you:

```
Connected
login:
```

Enter your login ID and password.

The take command allows you to copy files from the remote computer to the local computer. Suppose you want to make a copy of a file named proposal for your local computer. The following command copies proposal from your current directory on the remote computer and places it in your current directory on the local computer. If you do not specify a file name for the new file, it will also be called proposal.

```
~%take proposal<CR>
```

The put command allows you to do the opposite: copy files from the local computer to the remote computer. If you want to copy a file named minutes from your current directory on the local computer to the remote computer, type:

```
~%put minutes minutes.9-18<CR>
```

In this case, you specified a different name for the new file (minutes.9-18). Therefore, the copy of the minutes file that is made on the remote computer will be called minutes.9-18.

Figure 12-8 summarizes the syntax and capabilities of the cu command.

Figure 12-8: Summary of the cu Command

Command Recap cu – connects computer to remote computer		
command	*options*	*arguments*
cu	-s and others*	*telno* (or) *systemname*
Description:	cu connects your computer to a remote computer and allows you to be logged in on both simultaneously. Once you are logged in, you can move between computers to execute commands and transfer files on each without dropping the link.	

* See the cu(1) entry in the *User's Reference Manual* for all available options and an explanation of their capabilities.

Working on a Remote System: the uux Command

The command uux (short for UNIX-to-UNIX system command execution) allows you to execute UNIX system commands on remote computers. It can gather files from various computers, execute a command on a specified computer, and send the standard output to a file on a specified computer. The execution of certain commands may be restricted on the remote machine. You will be notified by mail if the command you have requested is not allowed to execute (restricted).

Command Line Format

To execute the uux command, follow this format:

uux [*options*] *commandstring*<CR>

The *commandstring* is made up of one or more arguments. All shell special characters (such as "<>|^\fP'') must be quoted either by quoting the entire *command-string* or quoting the character as a separate argument. Within the *command-string* the command and file names may contain a *systemname!* prefix. All arguments that do not contain a *systemname* are interpreted as command arguments. A file name may be either a full pathname or the name of a file under the current directory (on the local computer).

Sample Command Usage

If your computer is hardwired to a larger host computer, you can use uux to get printouts of files that reside on your computer by entering:

```
pr minutes | uux -p host!lp<CR>
```

This command line queues the file `minutes` to be printed on the area printer of the computer `host`.

See the uux(1) manual page in the *User's Reference Manual* for details. Figure 12-9 summarizes the syntax and capabilities of the uux command.

Figure 12-9: Summary of the uux Command

Command Recap uux – executes commands on a remote computer		
command	*options*	*arguments*
uux	-p, and others*	*commandstring*
Description:	uux allows you to run UNIX system commands on remote computers. It can gather files from various computers, run a command on a specified computer, and send the standard output to a file on a specified computer.	
Remarks:	By default, the uux command can only run the mail command. Check with your system administrator to find out if other commands are executable via uux.	

APPENDIX A: SUMMARY OF THE FILE SYSTEM

APPENDIX A: SUMMARY OF THE FILE SYSTEM

A Summary of the File System

The UNIX System Files

This appendix summarizes the description of the file system given in Chapter 1 and reviews the major system directories in the root directory.

File System Structure

The UNIX System files are organized in a hierarchy; their structure is often described as an inverted tree. At the top of this tree is the root directory, the source of the entire file system. It is designated by a / (slash). All other directories and files descend and branch out from root, as shown in Figure A-1.

Figure A-1: Directory Tree from root

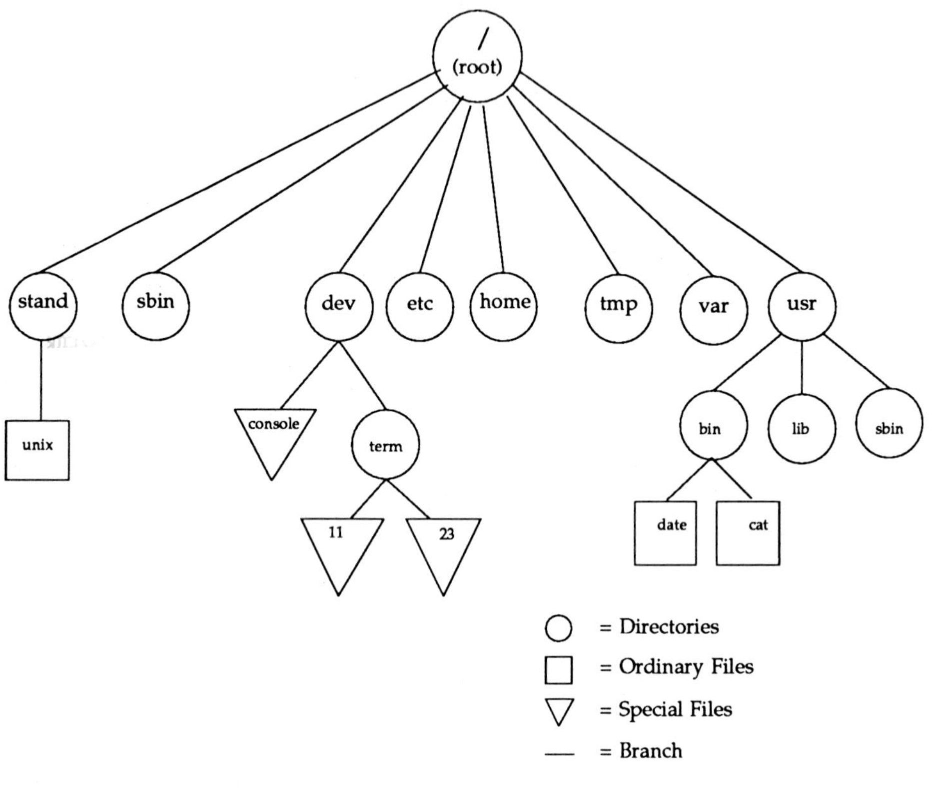

One path from root leads to your home directory. You can organize and store information in your own hierarchy of directories and files under your home directory.

Other paths lead from root to system directories that are available to all users. The system directories described in this book are common to all UNIX System V Release 4 installations and are provided and maintained by the operating system.

In addition to this standard set of directories, your UNIX system may have other system directories. To obtain a listing of the directories and files in the root directory on your UNIX system, type the following command line:

```
ls -l / <CR>
```

To move around in the file structure, you can use path names. For example, you can move to the directory `/usr/bin` (which contains UNIX system executable files) by typing the following command line:

```
cd /usr/bin <CR>
```

To list the contents of a directory, issue one of the following command lines:

```
ls <CR>          # list files and directories
ls -l <CR>       # list files and directories in long format
```

To list the contents of a directory in which you are not located, issue the `ls` command as shown in the following examples:

```
ls /usr/bin <CR>        # short listing
ls -l /usr/bin <CR>     # long listing
```

The following section provides brief descriptions of the root directory and the system directories under it, as shown in Figure A-1.

UNIX System Directories

`/`	the source of the file system (called the root directory)
`/stand`	contains programs and data files used in the booting process
`/sbin`	contains essential executables used in the booting process and in manual system recovery
`/dev`	contains special files that represent peripheral devices, such as:

`console`	console
`lp`	line printer
`term/*`	user terminal(s)
`dsk/*`	disks

`/etc`	contains machine-specific administrative configuration files and system administration databases
`/home`	the root of a subtree for user directories
`/tmp`	contains temporary files, such as the buffers created for editing a file
`/var`	the root of a subtree for varying files such as log files
`/usr`	contains other directories, including `lib` and `bin`
`/usr/bin`	contains many executable programs and utilities, including the following:

```
cat
date
login
grep
mkdir
who
```

`/usr/lib`	contains libraries for programs and languages

APPENDIX B: SUMMARY OF UNIX SYSTEM COMMANDS

B Summary of UNIX System Commands

Basic UNIX System Commands

`at` — Request that a command be run in background mode at a time you specify on the command line.

A sample format is:

```
at 8:45am Jun 09<CR>
command1<CR>
command2<CR>
<^d>
```

If you use the `at` command without the date, the command executes within twenty-four hours at the time specified.

`banner` — Display a message (in words up to ten characters long) in large letters on the standard output.

`batch` — Submit command(s) to be processed when the system load is at an acceptable level. A sample format of this command is:

```
batch<CR>
command1<CR>
command2<CR>
<^d>
```

You can use a shell script for a command in `batch`(1). This may be useful and timesaving if you have a set of commands you frequently submit using this command.

`cat` — Display the contents of a specified file at your terminal. To halt the output on an ASCII terminal temporarily, use <^s>; type <^q> to restart the output. To interrupt the output and return to the shell on an ASCII terminal, press the BREAK or DELETE key.

`cd` — Change directory from the current one to your home directory. If you include a directory name, this command changes from the current directory to the directory specified. By using a path name in place of the directory name, you can jump several levels with one command.

`cp`	Copy a specified file into a new file, leaving the original file intact.
`cut`	Cut out specified fields from each line of a file. This command can be used to cut columns from a table, for example.
`date`	Display the current date and time.
`diff`	Compare two files. The `diff`(1) command reports which lines are different and what changes should be made to the second file to make it the same as the first file.
`echo`	Display input on the standard output (the terminal), including the carriage return, and returns a prompt.
`ed`	Edit a specified file using the line editor. If there is no file by the name specified, the `ed`(1) command creates one. See Chapter 6 for detailed instructions on using the `ed`(1) editor.
`grep`	Search a specified file(s) for a specified pattern and print those lines that contain the pattern. If you name more than one file, `grep`(1) prints the file that contains the pattern.
`kill`	Terminate a background process specified by its process identification number (PID). You can obtain a PID by running the `ps`(1) command.
`lex`	Generate programs to be used in simple lexical analysis of text, perhaps as a first step in creating a compiler. See the *Programmer's Guide* for details.
`lp`	Print the contents of a specified file on a line printer, giving you a paper copy of the file.
`lpstat`	Display the status of any requests made to the line printer. Options are available for requesting more detailed information.
`ls`	List the names of all files and directories except those whose names begin with a dot (.). Options are available for listing more detailed information about the files in the directory. (See the `ls`(1) page in the *User's Reference Manual* for details.)

`mail` — Display any electronic mail you may have received at your terminal, one message at a time. Each message ends with ? prompt; `mail`(1) waits for you to request an option such as saving, forwarding, or deleting a message. To obtain a list of the available options, type ?.

When followed by a login name, `mail`(1) sends a message to the owner of that name. You can type as many lines of text as you want. Then type <^d> to end the message and send it to the recipient. Press the BREAK key to interrupt the mail session.

`mailx` — `mailx`(1) is a more sophisticated, expanded version of electronic mail.

`make` — Maintain and support large programs or documents on the basis of smaller ones. See the `make`(1) page in the *User's Reference Manual* for details.

`mkdir` — Make a new directory. The new directory becomes a subdirectory of the directory in which you issue the `mkdir` command. To create subdirectories or files in the new directory, it is convenient to move into the new directory with the `cd` command.

`mv` — Move a file to a new location in the file system. You can move a file to a new file name in the same directory or to a different directory. If you move a file to a different directory, you can use the same file name or choose a new one.

`nohup` — Place execution of a command in the background, so it will continue executing after you log off of the system. Error and output messages are placed in a file called `nohup.out`.

`pg` — Display the contents of a specified file on your terminal, a page at a time. After each page, the system pauses and waits for your instructions before proceeding.

`pr` — Display a partially formatted version of a specified file at your terminal. The `pr`(1) command shows page breaks, but does not implement any macros supplied for text formatter packages.

`ps`	Display the status and number of every process currently running. The `ps`(1) command does not show the status of jobs in the `at`(1) or `batch`(1) queues, but it includes these jobs when they are executing.
`pwd`	Display the full path name of the current working directory.
`rm`	Remove a file from the file system. You can use metacharacters with the `rm`(1) command but should use them with caution; a removed file cannot be recovered easily.
`rmdir`	Remove a directory. You cannot be in the directory you want to delete. Also, the command will not delete a directory unless it is empty. Therefore, you must remove any subdirectories and files that remain in a directory before running this command on it. (See the `-r` option of `rm`(1) in the *User's Reference Manual* for removing directories that are not empty.)

`sort` Sort a file in ASCII order and display the results on your terminal. ASCII order is as follows:

1. special characters
2. numbers before letters
3. upper case before lower case
4. alphabetical order

There are other options for sorting a file. For a complete list of `sort`(1) options, see the `sort`(1) page in the *User's Reference Manual.*

`spell`	Collect words from a specified file and check them against a spelling list. Words not on the list or not related to words on the list (with suffixes, prefixes, and so on) are displayed.
`stty`	Report the settings of certain input/output options for your terminal. When issued with the appropriate options and arguments, `stty`(1) also sets these input/output options. (See the `stty`(1) page in the *User's Reference Manual.*)
`uname`	Display the name of the UNIX system on which you are currently working.

`uucp`	Send a specified file to another UNIX system. (See the `uucp(1)` page in the *User's Reference Manual* for details.)
`uuname`	List the names of remote UNIX systems that can communicate with your UNIX system.
`uupick`	Search the public directory for files sent to you by the `uuto(1)` command. If a file is found, `uupick(1)` displays its name and the system it came from, and prompts you (with a ?) to take action.
`uustat`	Report the status of the `uuto(1)` command you issued to send files to another user.
`uuto`	Send a specified file to another user. Specify the destination in the format *system*!*login*. The *system* must be on the list of systems generated by the `uuname(1)` command.
`vi`	Edit a specified file using the `vi(1)` screen editor. If there is no file by the name you specify, `vi(1)` creates one. (See Chapter 7 for detailed information on using the `vi(1)` editor.)
`wc`	Count the number of lines, words, and characters in a specified file and display the results on your terminal.
`who`	Display the login names of the users currently logged in on your UNIX system. List the terminal address for each login and the time each user logged in.
`yacc`	Impose a structure on the input of a program. See the *Programmer's Guide* for details.

APPENDIX C: QUICK REFERENCE TO FACE

C Quick Reference to FACE

Introduction

Chapter 5 is designed to teach you how to use the FACE Interface. If you have worked through it, you are familiar with the various methods of executing a command. To refresh your memory, they are:

- Select the command from the Command Menu. You will be prompted for any additional information that is needed.
- Position the cursor on the command in the Command Menu and press (CTRL-J). The command appears on the command line, where you may type any arguments you care to include, and then press (ENTER). You will be prompted for any additional information that is needed.
- Press (CTRL-J) to access the command line, then type the command and any arguments you care to include, and press (ENTER). You will be prompted for any additional information that is needed.
- Use the function key (or its alternate keystroke) to which the command has been assigned. You will be prompted for any additional information that is needed.

When a command is shown as it would be typed on the FACE command line, the following conventions are used:

- `Constant Width typeface` shows parts of the command that you must type exactly as shown.
- *Italic typeface* shows parts of the command that are variable: you must supply the appropriate value.
- Brackets `[ ]` around an option or argument show that it is optional.
- Ellipses, . . . , show that an argument or option to the command can be used more than once.
- The prompt —> preceding each command example is used to indicate that the command is typed after you have accessed the command line by pressing (CTRL-J).

Related FACE Office tasks are grouped by category in this appendix, in the following sections:

- Commands and Command Menu Tasks
- File and Folder Commands and Tasks
- Frame Commands and Tasks
- Programs Tasks
- Miscellaneous Tasks

For each command or task covered in these sections, a summary of the steps to complete it using function keys and named keys and FACE menus is given. (Alternate keystrokes are indicated for those who don't have all named keys or working function keys.) This summary is followed by a section titled "From the Command Line," which shows how to do the same task using the command line (if practical to do so).

Commands and Command Menu Tasks

Cancel a Command

1. Press CANCEL (or CTRL-f 6).

Get Help for a Command

1. Press CMD-MENU (or CTRL-f 7).
2. Position the cursor on command.
3. Press HELP (or CTRL-f 1).
4. Use NEXTPAGE (or CTRL-f 3) if scroll icon appears in the lower right border.

From the Command Line

`-->help` *command*

View the Command Menu

1. Press CMD-MENU (or CTRL-f 7).

File and Folder Commands and Tasks

Copy a File or File Folder

1. Position the cursor on the file or folder to be copied.
2. Press CHG-KEYS (or CTRL-f 8).
3. Press COPY (or CTRL-f 2).
4. Navigate to the destination folder and press ENTER.
5. Press SELECT (or CTRL-f 8).
6. If there already is a file or folder with the same name in the destination folder, you will have to type a new name for the copy, then press ENTER.

From the Command Line

-->copy *name* [[to] *destination* [*newname*]]

where *name* is the file or folder to be copied, *destination* is the full pathname of the destination folder, and *newname* can be the same as *name* if there is no file or folder with that name in *destination*. In the absence of *newname*, the copy is called *name*.

Create a File or Folder

1. Navigate to the folder in which you want to create the new file or folder.
2. Press CHG-KEYS (or CTRL-f 8).
3. Press CREATE (or CTRL-f 6).
4. Type the name of the new file or folder, then press ENTER.
5. If you are creating a file, select `Standard file` from the Choices menu:
    1. Type information in the file using the editor invoked when you create the file.
    2. Write and quit the file using your editor commands.

6. If you are creating a folder select `File folder` from the Choices menu.
7. The new file or folder will be listed in the folder in which you created it.

From the Command Line

`-->create` [*newname*] [[`in`] *destination*]

where *newname* is the name of the new file or folder, and *destination* is the folder in which it will be created. In the absence of *newname*, you will be prompted for a name. In the absence of *destination*, *newname* will be created in the current frame. If the current frame is not a folder, *newname* will be created in the /home/login folder.

Delete a File or Folder

1. Position the cursor on the name of the file or folder you want to delete.
2. Press CHG-KEYS (or CTRL-f 8).
3. Press DELETE (or CTRL-f 4).
4. At the message line prompt telling you that FACE is preparing to delete the file or folder named, press ENTER to continue the delete procedure. If the a file folder being deleted contains other files or file folders, FACE will display a warning to that effect.

   One of the following actions will occur:

   1. The file or folder will be deleted (moved to the WASTEBASKET folder).
   2. You will be prompted to give a new name for the file or folder in WASTEBASKET, if the WASTEBASKET folder already contains a file or file folder with the same name.
   3. You will be warned that you cannot delete a folder that is currently open, or that *contains* a currently open file or folder, until you close the open file or folder.
   4. A file or folder already in the WASTEBASKET folder will be permanently removed from the computer if you execute `delete` on it.

From the Command Line

`-->delete` [*name*]

In the absence of *name*, the file or folder that the cursor is currently positioned on will be deleted.

Display the Contents of a File

1. Position the cursor on the name of the file you want to display.
2. Select `display` from the Command Menu.

From the Command Line

`-->display` [*filename*]

where *filename* is the name of a standard file in the current folder, or the full pathname of a standard file not in the current folder. In the absence of *filename*, the current file is assumed.

Display the Full Pathname of a File or Folder

1. Position the cursor on the name of the file or file folder for which you want to obtain the full pathname.
2. Press CMD-MENU or CTRL-f 7 to display the Command Menu.
3. Select `show-path`.
4. The full pathname of the file or file folder will be displayed in a frame. Press CANCEL or CTRL-f 7 to return to the previous frame.

From the Command Line

`-->show-path`

Find a Specific File or Folder

1. Navigate to the folder you want to *begin* the search in. (The `find` command only searches through folders under your current location.)
2. Select `find` from the Command Menu.
3. A Find form lists four search criteria with default values filled in:

   Name: (file or folder name)
   Type: (a valid file type)
   Owner: (owner's login ID, or leave it blank if you are the owner)
   Age: (number of days)

   1. If you want to search using the default values, press **ENTER**. The effect of using all four default values is to list all files and folders under your current location.
   2. If you want to enter different criteria to limit the search in various ways, either type a new value in one or more fields, or press **CHOICES** (or **CTRL-f** **2**) to see valid responses for the field the cursor is positioned on. Use form navigation keys and **ENTER** to select a value. You need only fill in information pertinent to the file(s) you are looking for.

4. Press **SAVE** (or **CTRL-f** **3**) to run `find` with your search criteria.

From the Command Line

-->`find` [*name*] [[`in`] *foldername*]

where *name* is the name of the file(s) or file folders to search for, and *foldername* is the folder the search will start in. If *foldername* is not specified, the search begins at the current folder (or the /home/login folder if you are not in a folder).

Move a File

1. Position the cursor on the name of the file or folder to be moved.
2. Press CHG-KEYS (or CTRL-f 8).
3. Press MOVE (or CTRL-f 3).
4. Navigate to the destination folder.
5. Press SELECT (or CTRL-f 8).

   If the destination folder already contains a file or folder with the same name you will be prompted to supply a new name for the file or folder you are moving.

From The Command Line

`-->move` [*name*] [[`to`] *destination* [*newname*]]

where *name* is the name of the file or folder you want to move, and *destination* is the folder you want to move it to. In the absence of *name* the current file or file folder is assumed. In the absence of *destination*, you will be prompted for it. In the absence of *newname* the file or file folder will be named *name*.

Organize the Appearance of Files in a Folder

1. Position the cursor on the name of the folder you want to organize.
2. Select `organize` from the Command Menu.
3. An Organize form lists three fields. To change the default values for:

Default Organization:	Press CHOICES (or CTRL-f 2 until the value you want appears in the field. The value `no` in this field means this folder will be organized according to the next two fields in this form. The value `yes` in this field means the display of this folder will revert to the defaults as set in the Preferences form.

Folder Display Format: Press [CHOICES] (or [CTRL-f] [2]). A Choices menu appears. Select the value you want.

Folder Display Order: Press [CHOICES] (or [CTRL-f] [2]). A Choices menu appears. Select the value you want.

4. Press [SAVE] (or [CTRL-f] [3]) to organize the folder.

From the Command Line

`-->organize` [*frameID*]

where *frameID* can be the full pathname of the frame or the frame identification number. In the absence of *frameID*, the active frame is assumed.

Change the Description of a File

1. Position the cursor on the file or folder you want to redescribe.
2. Select `redescribe` from the Command Menu.
3. Type the new description when prompted for it on the command line, press [ENTER].

From the Command Line

`-->redescribe` [*name* [*new description*]]

where *name* is the name of the file or folder you want to redescribe, and *new description* is a description up to 23 characters long, and can include spaces. In the absence of arguments, `redescribe` assumes the current file or folder and prompts for a description. In the absence of *new description* you will be prompted for it.

Change the Name of a File or Folder

1. Position the cursor on the name of the file or folder you want to rename.
2. Press CHG-KEYS (or CTRL-f 8), then press RENAME (or CTRL-f 5).
3. At the command line prompt, type the new name for the file or folder, then press ENTER.

From the Command Line

-->rename [*oldname*] [[to] *newname*]

In the absence of arguments the current file or file folder is assumed and you are prompted for *newname*. In the absence of *newname*, you will be prompted for it.

Change Permissions on an Existing File or Folder

1. Position the cursor on the name of the file or folder for which you want to change the permissions.
2. Press CHG-KEYS (or CTRL-f 8), then press SECURITY (or CTRL-f 7).
3. When the Security form appears, you can change the permissions for yourself, members of your group, and for all other users on your computer (if you are the owner). If you are not the owner, you can only look at the form.

   Use the navigating and editing keys for forms.
4. When you are done changing permissions:
    1. Press SAVE (or CTRL-f 3) to save the new permissions for this file or folder.

       OR
    2. Press CANCEL (or CTRL-f 6) if you change your mind and want to restore the default values.

From the Command Line

`-->security` [*name*]

In the absence of *name*, the current file or folder is assumed.

Set Permissions for New Files and Folders

1. Select `Preferences` from the Office menu.
2. Select `File permissions` from the Preferences menu.
3. When the Security form appears, you can change the permissions for yourself, members of your group, and for all other users on your computer.

   Use the navigating and editing keys for forms.
4. When you are done changing permissions on new files or file folders:
   1. Press [SAVE] (or [CTRL-f] [3]) to save the new permissions for this file or folder.

      OR
   2. Press [CANCEL] (or [CTRL-f] [6]) if you change your mind and want to restore the default values.

From the Command Line

`-->preferences`

This allows you to access the Preferences menu without having to first return to the Office menu.

Recover a Deleted File or Folder

1. Select `Wastebasket` from the Office menu.
2. Position the cursor on the file or folder in the WASTEBASKET folder that you want to recover.
3. Select `undelete` from the Command Menu to return the file or folder to the folder from which it was deleted. (Note that if you have renamed or deleted the folder from which the file or folder came, you will not be able to return it there with `undelete`.)

From the Command Line

`-->undelete` [*name*]

where *name* is the name of a file or folder if you are currently in the WASTEBASKET folder, or the full pathname of the file or folder in the WASTEBASKET folder if some other frame is current. In the absence of *name*, the current file or file folder is assumed. The `undelete` command operates on files or file folders in the WASTEBASKET folder that were put there by the `delete`, `move`, or `copy` commands.

Edit a File

1. Position the cursor on the file you want to edit, and press ENTER.
2. Edit the file using the editor that you are placed in automatically (the default editor is `vi`).
3. To save your changes, use the editor command that "writes" the contents of the file to permanent storage, then quit the file.

If you accidentally select a file and don't know how to use the `vi` editor, type `:q!` to get out of the file without changing it, and put yourself back in your FACE Office. Then see a knowledgeable `vi` user for instruction on the use of that editor.

From the Command Line

-->*filename*

where *filename* is the name of the standard file if you are currently in the same folder, or it is the full pathname of the file if you are in some other folder. *filename* will be opened for editing with `vi` by default, or with whatever editor you have named in the Preferences form (see "Setting Your Office Preferences," in Chapter 5 of this guide).

Print a File on Paper

1. Position the cursor on the file you want to print.
2. Select `print` from the Command Menu
3. Select one of the three print commands that will appear in a Print menu.

   The screen will clear, and a message will give you the id number of your printing job.
4. Press ENTER to get back to your FACE Office.

From the Command Line

-->`print` [*filename*]

where *filename* is the name of the file if you are in the same folder, or it is the full pathname of the file if you are not in the same folder. In the absence of *filename*, `print` assumes the current file.

Frame Commands and Tasks

Cancel a Frame

1. Press CANCEL (or CTRL-f 6) to cancel the current frame.

From the Command Line

`-->cancel` [*frameID* ...]

where *frameID* is the number of the frame you want to close (located to the left of the frame title). You can name up to 24 frame numbers as arguments to `cancel`. In the absence of *framenumber* the current frame is assumed.

Clean up the FACE Screen

1. Select `cleanup` from the Command Menu.

   This will close all open frames except the AT&T FACE menu and any other folders defined to be open upon logging in.

From the Command Line

`-->cleanup`

Go To a Specific Frame

1. Select `goto` from the Command Menu.
2. At the command line prompt, type the frame number, or the pathname of the frame title, of any open frame in your Office, then press ENTER.

From the Command Line

`-->goto` [*frameID*]

where *frameID* can be either the frame number or the pathname of the frame you want to go to. *frameID* cannot contain blank spaces. In the absence of *frameID*, `goto` prompts you for it.

Get Help for the Current Frame

1. Press HELP (or CTRL-f 1).

From the Command Line

```
-->help
```

Provides context-specific help on the current frame or action you are performing.

Update Information in a Frame

1. If a frame is open, select `update` from the Command Menu to show changes you have made to its contents.

From the Command Line

-->`update` [*frameID*]

where *frameID* is the full pathname of a frame or the frame identification number. In the absence of *frameID*, the current frame is assumed.

Move or Reshape a Frame

1. Navigate to the frame you want to move or reshape.
2. Select `frm-mgmt` from the Command Menu.
3. The Frame Management menu appears.
    1. Select `move` if you want to move the current frame to a new location, but retain its original shape.
    2. Select `reshape` if you want to reshape the current frame and/or move it to a new location. Note that only text and menu frames can be reshaped.

4. Use the arrow keys (or their alternate keystrokes) to move the frame to the new location, or to make it bigger or smaller.

From the Command Line

`-->frm-mgmt` *[operation]*

where *operation* can be either `list`, `move`, or `reshape`. In the absence of *operation*, you are put in the Frame Management menu. The current frame is always assumed.

The `list` operation provides a list of all the open frames and suspended files on the screen. The `move` and `reshape` operations allow you to temporarily move a frame and increase/decrease a frame's size and shape. The location and size of the frame revert to the FACE default as soon as the frame is closed, or when you log out. In the case of `reshape`, any command that causes the menu or text frame to be updated will also cause it to revert to its original shape.

Programs Tasks

Add a Personal Program

1. Create or install the executable file (application) on your computer.
2. Select `Programs Administration` from the Office menu.
3. Select `Add Programs` from the Programs Administration menu.
4. An Add Programs form will appear. Navigate to the `Program Menu Name:` field.
5. Type in the name you want the application to be listed as in the Programs menu, and press ENTER.
6. Navigate to the `Name of Command:` field.
7. Type in the full pathname of the executable file.
8. Navigate to the `Working Directory:` field.
9. Type in the full pathname of the directory (folder) where any files created by the application will be placed. (Type a dot (.) if you want them placed in whatever is the current folder when you use the service.)
10. Navigate to the `Prompt for Arguments:` field.

    Enter `yes` if you want users to be able to supply arguments to this program when it is selected. Enter `no` if you do not want them to be able to supply arguments.
11. Press SAVE (or CTRL-f 3) to save these values.

    The Programs menu will be updated to show the new service the next time you open it. If it is open now, and you want to update it immediately, navigate to it and execute the `update` command.

Modify a Personal Program

This task explains how to modify the personal program you have added to the Programs menu (changing any of the fields in the Add Program form). It is not an explanation of how to modify a shell script if the service executes one. To modify a file containing a shell script, simply edit the file, and change the script.

1. Select `Programs Administration` from the Office menu.
2. Select `Modify Programs` from the Programs Administration menu.
3. Select the program you want to modify from the the Personal Programs menu.
4. The Modify Program form appears. Modify fields in this form using the navigation and editing keys that work in forms.
5. When you are done modifying the fields, press (SAVE) (or (CTRL-f) (3))

   The Programs menu will be updated to show the new program the next time you open it. If it is open now, and you want to update it immediately, navigate to it and execute the `update` command.

Remove a Personal Service

1. Select `Programs Administration` from the Office menu.
2. Select `Remove Programs` from the Programs Administration menu.
3. Select the program you want to remove from the the Personal Programs menu.

   A Confirmation frame appears.
4. Press (CONT) (or (CTRL-f) (3)) to remove the program, or (CANCEL) (or (CTRL-f) (6)) to cancel this task.

The Programs menu will be updated to show the program has been removed the next time you open it. If it is open now, and you want to update it immediately, navigate to it and execute the `update` command.

Use a Program

1. Select `Programs` from the FACE menu.
2. Select the program you want to use from the Programs menu.

   NOTE: Other than `Mail Services`, and `Spell Checker`, which are explained in Chapter 5 of this guide, you will have to obtain instructions on the use of particular programs from your system administrator or another knowledgeable user.

From the Command Line

`-->programs`

This will open the Programs menu, from which you can select the program you want to run.

Send Mail

1. Select `Programs` from the FACE menu.
2. Select `Mail Services` from the Programs menu.
3. Select `send mail` from the Mail Services menu.
   1. You can type in the login ID(s) of the recipient(s) (or full route to another computer, i.e., *othercomputer*`!`*login*) in the `To:` field. When sending mail to more than one recipient, type a space between each login ID.
   2. Or, you can press [CHOICES] (or [CTRL-f] [2]) to see a menu of login IDs for users on your computer from which you can select the recipient's login ID. If there are fewer than four other users on your computer, your choices will appear in the field itself and you can navigate through them by continuing to press [CHOICES].
4. When you have typed, or selected, the login ID of the person you want to send mail to, press [SAVE] (or [CTRL-f] [3]) to save that value in the `To:` field.

5. The screen clears, and the UNIX System `mailx` command takes over.

You can cancel the mail by typing `~x`.

6. Type the subject of your message in the `Subject` field, or press ENTER to skip this field.
7. Type your mail message.

   See the `mailx` manual page in the *UNIX System V User's Reference Manual* for information on editing a mail message in progress.
8. Press ENTER, so you are on a new line, then press CTRL-d to send the message.
9. Press ENTER to return to FACE.

From the Command Line

`-->!mailx` *login* ...

where `!` means the command that follows is a UNIX System command, and *login* is the login ID of the recipient of this mail. Note that you can name more than one recipient on the `mailx` command line.

Read Mail

1. Select `Programs` from the Office menu.
2. Select `Mail Services` from the Programs menu.
3. Select `New Mail` from the Mail Services menu.

   The screen will clear if you have new mail waiting to be read.
4. After a list of mail header lines is printed the prompt `?` will appear.

   The `?` prompt will appear at the end of each mail message you read. You can use any one of the following responses whenever you get the `?` prompt.

1. Press ENTER to start reading the next message (or the first message if you are currently at the end of the mail headers).
2. Type *n*, where *n* is the number of a specific message, to read that message.
3. Type `s` to save the message in a file called `mbox` in `$HOME`.
4. Type `s` *filename* to save the message in a file called *filename* in `$HOME`.
5. Type `d` to delete the message you just read. Type `d` *n* to delete message number *n* (even if it is not the message you just read). Type `d` *n–n* to delete a range of messages, from *n* to *n*.
6. Type `quit` to exit from the `read mail` service.

5. Press ENTER to return to the Mail services menu.

See Chapter 9 "Electronic Mail Tutorial" in this guide, and the `mailx`(1) manual page in the *UNIX System V User's Reference Manual* for complete information on `mailx`.

From the Command Line

`-->!mailx`

where `!` means the command that follows is a UNIX System command, and `mailx` is the command that `read mail` runs when you select it from the Mail Programs menu.

Check Spelling

1. Select `Programs` from the Office menu.
2. Select `Spell Checker` from the Programs menu.
3. A form titled `Spell Checker` will be displayed, and you are prompted to enter the full pathname of the file you want to run the spelling checker on.

   Enter the full pathname of a file and press SAVE to start the spelling checker.

4. A frame titled `Spell Checker Output` will display spelling errors or inform you that none were found, whichever is the case.

Miscellaneous Tasks

Get Help for the FACE Interface

1. Press HELP (or CTRL-f 1) to get help on whatever frame you are in.
2. Press CONTENTS (or CTRL-f 8) to see a Table Of Contents menu of other topics you can get help on.

   Most of these menu items will present you with general information on FACE. However, `Commands Overview` presents a menu of FACE commands from which you can select one and receive information on its use.

Exit from FACE

1. Select `Exit FACE` from the Office menu to exit from FACE *and* log off the computer.

From the Command Line

```
-->exit
```

Refreshing the Screen

1. Select `refresh` from the Command Menu to redraw the terminal screen if stray characters appear.

   Unlike the `cleanup` command, `refresh` does not close any frames.

From the Command Line

```
-->refresh
```

Run a Shell Script

1. Position the cursor on the shell script you want to run.
2. Select `run` from the Command Menu to run the shell script.

   NOTE: If the shell script does not run, select `security` from the Command Menu and make sure that your (owner's) run/search permissions are set to `yes` for the file.
3. When the shell script ends, press ENTER to return to FACE.

From the Command Line

-->`run` [*filename*]

where *filename* is the name of the shell script you want to run. In the absence of *filename*, `run` assumes the current file.

Use an Executable File

1. Position the cursor on the Executable file you want to run and press ENTER.
2. When the Executable file ends, press ENTER to return to FACE.

From the Command Line

-->*filename*

where *filename* is the name of the Executable file you want to run.

Enter the UNIX System

1. Select `UNIX System` from the Office menu.

From the Command Line

-->`unix-system`

Exit from the UNIX System

1. At the prompt `UNIX:`, type `exit`, or press CTRL-d.
2. Press ENTER to return to FACE.

Suspend a File

You may only suspend a file if the editor you are using has some method of executing UNIX System commands, as `vi` does.

Suspending a file is useful when you want to look at other files, or do other work, but do not want to write and quit a file you are editing with `vi`.

1. Type `:!facesuspend`, and press ENTER.

   You will be returned to the FACE Interface, where you can do other work before returning to the suspended file.

Up to five files can be suspended at the same time.

Return to a Suspended Command

1. Select `frm-mgmt` from the Command Menu.
2. Select `list` from the Frame Management menu.

   The Open Frames menu lists all open frames and all suspended files.
3. Select the suspended file you want to return to.

APPENDIX D: QUICK REFERENCE TO ed COMMANDS

APPENDIX D: QUICK REFERENCE TO ed COMMANDS

D Quick Reference to ed Commands

ed Quick Reference

The general format for ed commands is:

[address1,address2]command[parameter]...<CR>

where *address1* and *address2* denote line addresses and the *parameters* show the data on which the command operates. The commands appear on your terminal as you type them. You can find complete information on using ed commands in Chapter 6, "Line Editor Tutorial."

The following is a glossary of ed commands. The commands are grouped according to function.

Commands for Getting Started

ed *filename*	Accesses the ed line editor to edit a specified file.
a	Appends text after the current line.
.	Ends the text input mode and returns to the command mode.
p	Displays the current line.
d	Deletes the current line.
<CR>	Moves down one line in the buffer.
–	Moves up one line in the buffer.
w	Writes the buffer contents to the file currently associated with the buffer.
q	Ends an editing session. If changes to the buffer are not written to a file, a warning (?) is issued. Typing q a second time ends the session without writing to a file.

Line Addressing Commands

`1, 2, 3...`	Denotes line addresses in the buffer.
`.`	Denotes address of the current line in the buffer.
`.=`	Displays the current line address.
`$`	Denotes the last line in the buffer.
`,`	Addresses the first through the last line.
`;`	Addresses the current line through the last line.
+*x*	Relative address, determined by adding *x* to the current line number.
−*x*	Relative address, determined by subtracting *x* from the current line number.
/*abc*	Searches forward in the buffer and addresses the first line after the current line that contains the pattern *abc*.
?*abc*	Searches backward in the buffer and addresses the first line before the current line that contains the pattern *abc*.
g/*abc*	Addresses all lines in the buffer that contain the pattern *abc*.
v/*abc*	Addresses all lines in the buffer that do not contain the pattern *abc*.

Display Commands

p	Displays the specified lines in the buffer.
n	Displays the specified lines preceded by their line addresses and a tab space.

Text Input Commands

`a`	Enters text after the specified line in the buffer.
`i`	Enters text before the specified line in the buffer.
`c`	Replaces text in the specified lines with new text.
`.`	When typed on a line by itself, ends the text input mode and returns to the command mode.

Delete Text

`d`	Deletes one or more lines of text (command mode).
`u`	Undoes the last command given (command mode).

Substitute Text

address1,address2`s/`*old_text*/*new_text*/*command*

Substitutes *new_text* for *old_text* within the range of lines denoted by *address1,address2* (which may be numbers, symbols, or text). The *command* may be `g`, `l`, `n`, `p`, or `gp`.

Special Pattern-Matching Characters

`.`	Matches any single character.
`*`	Matches zero or more occurrences of the preceding character.
`[...]`	Matches any character that is in the brackets.
`[^...]`	Matches any character that is not in the brackets.
`.*`	Matches zero or more occurrences of any character.
`^`	Matches the beginning of the line.
`$`	Matches the end of the line.
`\`	Takes away the meaning of the special character that follows.

`&`	Substitutes the text matched by the substitution pattern in the replacement string.
`%`	Repeats the last replacement string.

Text Movement Commands

`m`	Moves the specified lines of text after a destination line; deletes the lines at the old location.
`t`	Copies the specified lines of text and places the copied lines after a destination line.
`j`	Joins contiguous lines.
`w`	Copies (writes) the buffer contents into a file.
`r`	Reads in text from another file and appends it to the buffer.
`W`	Appends text to an existing file.

Other Useful Commands and Information

`h`	Displays a short explanation for the preceding diagnostic response (?).
`H`	Turns on the help mode, which automatically displays an explanation for each diagnostic response (?) during the editing session.
`l`	Displays nonprinting characters in the text.
`f`	Displays the current file name.
`f` *newfile*	Changes the current file name associated with the buffer to *newfile*.
`!`*command*	Allows you to escape, temporarily, to the shell to execute a shell command.
`ed.hup`	Saves the buffer in a special file called ed.hup if ed is interrupted.

E Quick Reference to vi Commands

vi Quick Reference

This appendix is a glossary of commands for the screen editor, vi. The commands are grouped according to function.

The general format of a vi command is:

[*x*][*command*]*text-object*

where *x* denotes a number and *text-object* shows the portion of text on which the command operates. The commands appear on your screen as you type them. For an introduction to the use of vi commands, see Chapter 7, "Screen Editor Tutorial."

Commands for Getting Started

Shell Commands

TERM=*code*	Puts a code name for your terminal into the variable TERM.
export TERM	Conveys the value of TERM (the terminal code) to any UNIX system program that is terminal dependent.
tput init	Initializes the terminal so that it will function properly with various UNIX system programs.

NOTE Before you can use vi, you must complete the first three steps represented by the above lines: setting the TERM variable, exporting the value of TERM, and running the tput init command.

vi *filename*	Accesses the vi screen editor so that you can edit a specified file.

Basic vi Commands

<a>	Enters text input mode and appends text after the cursor.

<ESC>	Escape; leaves text input mode and returns to command mode.
<h>	Moves the cursor one character to the left.
<j>	Moves the cursor down one line in the same column.
<k>	Moves the cursor up one line in the same column.
<l>	Moves the cursor one character to the right.
<x>	Deletes the current character.
<CR>	Carriage return; moves the cursor down to the beginning of the next line.
<ZZ>	Writes to the file those changes made to the buffer that have not already been written and quits vi.
:w	Writes to the file those changes made to the buffer.
:q	Quits vi if changes made to the buffer have been written to a file.

Commands for Positioning in the Window

Positioning by Character

<h>	Moves the cursor one character to the left.
<BACKSPACE>	Backspace; moves the cursor one character to the left.
<l>	Moves the cursor one character to the right.
<space bar>	Moves the cursor one character to the right.
<f*x*>	Moves the cursor right to the specified character *x*.
<F*x*>	Moves the cursor left to the specified character *x*.
<t*x*>	Moves the cursor right to the character just before the specified character *x*.

<Tx> Moves the cursor left to the character just after the specified character *x*.

<;> Continues the search for the character specified by the <f>, <F>, <t>, or <T> commands. The ; remembers the character specified and searches for the next occurrence of it on the current line.

<,> Continues the search for the character specified by the <f>, <F>, <t>, or <T> commands. The , remembers the character specified and searches for the previous occurrence of it on the current line.

Positioning by Line

<j> Moves the cursor down in the same column one line from its present position.

<k> Moves the cursor up in the same column one line from its present position.

<+> Moves the cursor down to the beginning of the next line.

<CR> Carriage return; moves the cursor down to the beginning of the next line.

<–> Moves the cursor up to the beginning of the next line.

Positioning by Word

<w> Moves the cursor to the right to the first character in the next word.

<b> Moves the cursor back to the first character of the previous word.

<e> Moves the cursor to the end of the current word.

Positioning by Sentence

<(>	Moves the cursor to the beginning of the sentence.
<)>	Moves the cursor to the beginning of the next sentence.

Positioning by Paragraph

<{>	Moves the cursor to the beginning of the paragraph.
<}>	Moves the cursor to the beginning of the next paragraph.

Positioning in the Window

<H>	Moves the cursor to the first line on the screen, or "home."
<M>	Moves the cursor to the middle line on the screen.
<L>	Moves the cursor to the last line on the screen.

Commands for Positioning in the File

Scrolling

<^f>	Scrolls the screen forward a full window, revealing the window of text below the current window.
<^d>	Scrolls the screen down a half window, revealing lines of text below the current window.
<^b>	Scrolls the screen back a full window, revealing the window of text above the current window.
<^u>	Scrolls the screen up a half window, revealing the lines of text above the current window.

Positioning on a Numbered Line

<G> — Moves the cursor to the beginning of the last line in the buffer.

<*n*G> — Moves the cursor to the beginning of the *n*th line of the file (*n* = line number).

Searching for a Pattern

/*pattern* — Searches forward in the buffer for the next occurrence of the pattern of text. Positions the cursor under the first character of the pattern.

?*pattern* — Searches backward in the buffer for the first occurrence of pattern of text. Positions the cursor under the first character of the pattern.

<n> — Repeats the last search command.

<N> — Repeats the search command in the opposite direction.

Commands for Inserting Text

<a> — Enters text input mode and appends text after the cursor.

<i> — Enters text input mode and inserts text before the cursor.

<o> — Enters text input mode by opening a new line immediately below the current line.

<O> — Enters text input mode by opening a new line immediately above the current line.

<ESC> — Escape; returns to command mode from text input mode (entered with any of the above commands).

Commands for Deleting Text

In Text Input Mode

<BACKSPACE>	Backspace; deletes the current character.
<^w>	Deletes the current word delimited by blanks.
<@>	Erases the current line of text.

In Command Mode

<x>	Deletes the current character.
<dw>	Deletes a word (or part of a word) from the cursor through the next space or to the next punctuation.
<dd>	Deletes the current line.
<*n*d*x*>	Deletes *n* number of text objects of type *x*, where *x* may be as a word, line, sentence, or paragraph.
<D>	Deletes the current line from the cursor to the end of the line.

Commands for Modifying Text

Characters, Words, Text Objects

<r>	Replaces the current character.
<s>	Deletes the current character and appends text until the <ESC> command is typed.
<S>	Replaces all the characters in the current line.
<~>	Changes upper case to lower case or lower case to upper case.
<cw>	Replaces the current word or the remaining characters in the current word with new text, from the cursor to the next space or punctuation.

<cc>	Replaces all the characters in the current line.
<*n*c*x*>	Replaces *n* number of text objects of type *x*, where *x* may be a word, line, sentence, or paragraph.
<C>	Replaces the remaining characters in the current line, from the cursor to the end of the line.

Cutting and Pasting Text

<p>	Places the contents of the temporary buffer (containing the output of the last delete or yank command) into the text after the cursor or below the current line.
<yy>	Yanks (extracts) a specified line of text and puts it into a temporary buffer.
<*n*y*x*>	Extracts a copy of *n* number of text objects of type *x* and puts it into a temporary buffer.
<"*l*y*x*>	Places a copy of text object *x* into a register named by a letter *l*. *x* may be a word, line, sentence, or paragraph.
<"*x*p>	Places the contents of register *x* after the cursor or below the current line.

Other Commands

Special Commands

<^g>	Gives the line number of current cursor position in the buffer and modification status of the file.
<.>	Repeats the action performed by the last command.
<u>	Undoes the effects of the last command.
<U>	Restores the current line to its state prior to present changes.

<J> — Joins the line immediately below the current line with the current line.

<^l> — Clears and redraws the current window.

Line Editor Commands

: — Tells vi that the next commands you issue will be line editor commands.

:sh — Temporarily returns to the shell to perform some shell commands without leaving vi.

<^d> — Escapes the temporary return to the shell and returns to vi so you can edit the current window.

:*n* — Goes to the *n*th line of the buffer.

:*x,z*w *filename* — Writes lines from the number *x* through the number *z* into a new file called *filename.*

:$ — Moves the cursor to the beginning of the last line in the buffer.

:.,$d — Deletes all the lines from the current line to the last line.

:r *filename* — Inserts the contents of the file *filename* under the current line of the buffer.

:s/*text*/*new_text*/ — Replaces the first instance of *text* on the current line with *new_text.*

:s/*text*/*new_text*/g — Replace every occurrence of *text* on the current line with *new_text.*

:g/*text*/s//*new_text*/g — Changes every occurrence of *text* in the buffer to *new_text.*

Commands for Quitting vi

`<ZZ>`	Writes the buffer to the file if you haven't already done so, and quits `vi`.
`:wq`	Writes the buffer to the file and quits `vi`.
`:w` *filename* `:q`	Writes the buffer to the new file *filename* and quits `vi`.
`:w!` *filename* `:q`	Overwrites the existing file *filename* with the contents of the buffer and quits `vi`.
`:q!`	Quits `vi` whether or not changes made to the buffer were written to a file. Does not incorporate changes made to the buffer since the last write (`:w`) command.
`:q`	Quits `vi` if changes made to the buffer were written to a file.

Special Options for vi

`vi` *file1 file2 file3*	Enters three files into the `vi` buffer to be edited. Those files are *file1*, *file2*, and *file3*.
`:w` `:n`	When more than one file has been called on a single `vi` command line, writes the buffer to the file you are editing and then calls the next file in the buffer (use `:n` only after `:w`).
`vi -r` *file1*	Restores the changes made to *file1* that were lost because of an interrupt in the system.
`view` *file1*	Displays *file1* in the read-only mode of `vi`. Any changes made to the buffer will not be allowed to be written to the file.

APPENDIX F: SUMMARY OF SHELL COMMAND LANGUAGE

APPENDIX F: SUMMARY OF SHELL COMMAND LANGUAGE

F Summary of Shell Command Language

Summary of Shell Command Language

This appendix is a summary of the shell command language and programming constructs discussed in Chapter 9, "Shell Tutorial." The first section reviews metacharacters, special characters, input and output redirection, variables and processes. These are arranged by topic in the order that they were discussed in the chapter. The second section contains models of the shell programming constructs.

The Vocabulary of Shell Command Language

Special Characters in the Shell

`* ? [ ]` Metacharacters; used to provide a shortcut to referencing filenames, through pattern matching.

`&` Executes commands in the background mode.

`;` Sequentially executes several commands typed on one line, each pair separated by `;`.

`\` Turns off the meaning of the immediately following special character.

`'...'` Enclosing single quotes turn off the special meaning of all characters except single quotes.

`"..."` Enclosing double quotes turn off the special meaning of all characters except $, single quotes and double quotes.

Redirecting Input and Output

`<` Redirects the contents of a file into a command.

`>` Redirects the output of a command into a new file, or replaces the contents of an existing file with the output.

`>>` Redirects the output of a command so that it is appended to the end of a file.

`|` Directs the output of one command so that it becomes the input of the next command.

`*command*` Substitutes the output of the enclosed command in place of `*command*`.

Executing and Terminating Processes

batch — Submits the following commands to be processed at a time when the system load is at an acceptable level. <^d> ends the batch command.

at — Submits the following commands to be executed at a specified time. <^d> ends the at command.

at -l — Reports which jobs are currently in the at or batch queue.

at -r — Removes the at or batch job from the queue.

ps — Reports the status of the shell processes.

kill *PID* — Terminates the shell process with the specified process ID (PID).

nohup *command list* &

Continues background processes after logging out.

Making a File Accessible to the Shell

chmod u+x *filename*

Gives the user permission to execute the file (useful for shell program files).

mv *filename* $HOME/bin/*filename*

Moves your file to the bin directory in your home directory. This bin holds executable shell programs that you want to be accessible. Make sure the PATH variable in your .profile file specifies this bin. If it does, the shell will search in $HOME/bin for your file when you try to execute it. If your PATH variable does not include your bin, the shell will not know where to find your file and your attempt to execute it will fail.

`filename` — The name of a file that contains a shell program becomes the command that you type to run that shell program.

Variables

`positional parameter` — A numbered variable used within a shell program to reference values automatically assigned by the shell from the arguments of the command line invoking the shell program.

`echo` — A command used to print the value of a variable on your terminal.

`$#` — A special parameter that contains the number of arguments with which the shell program has been executed.

`$*` — A special parameter that contains the values of all arguments with which the shell program has been executed.

`named variable` — A variable to which the user can give a name and assign values.

Variables Used in the System

`HOME` — Denotes your home directory; the default variable for the cd command.

`PATH` — Defines the path your login shell follows to find commands.

`MAIL` — Gives the name of the file containing your electronic mail.

`PS1, PS2` — Defines the primary and secondary prompt strings, respectively.

`TERM` — Defines the type of terminal.

LOGNAME	Login name of the user.
IFS	Defines the internal field separators (normally the space, the tab, and the carriage return).
TERMINFO	Allows you to request that the curses and terminfo subroutines search a specified directory tree before searching the default directory for your terminal type.
TZ	Sets and maintains the local time zone.

Shell Programming Constructs

Here Document

```
command <<!
input lines
!
```

For Loop

```
for variable<CR>
        in this list of values<CR>
do the following commands<CR>
        command 1<CR>
        command 2<CR>
            .<CR>
            .<CR>
        last command<CR>
done<CR>
```

While Loop

```
while command list<CR>
do<CR>
    command1<CR>
    command2<CR>
        .<CR>
        .<CR>
    last command<CR>
done<CR>
```

If...Then

```
if this command list is successful<CR>
then command1<CR>
    command2<CR>
        .<CR>
        .<CR>
    last command<CR>
fi<CR>
```

If...Then...Else

```
if command list<CR>
   then command list<CR>
   else command list<CR>
fi<CR>
```

Case Construction

```
case word<CR>
in<CR>
    pattern1)<CR>
        command line 1<CR>
             .<CR>
             .<CR>
        last command line<CR>
    ;;<CR>
    pattern2)<CR>
        command line 1<CR>
             .<CR>
             .<CR>
        last command line<CR>
    ;;<CR>
    pattern3)<CR>
        command line 1<CR>
             .<CR>
             .<CR>
        last command line<CR>
    ;;<CR>
esac<CR>
```

break and continue Statements

A `break` or `continue` statement forces the program to leave any loop and execute the command following the end of the loop.

APPENDIX G: SETTING UP THE TERMINAL

Setting up the Terminal

Setting the TERM Variable

AT&T supports many types of terminals for use with the UNIX system. Because some commands are terminal dependent, the system must know what type of terminal you are using whenever you log in. The system determines the characteristics of your terminal by checking the value of a variable called TERM which holds the name of a terminal. If you have put the name of your terminal into this variable, the system will be able to execute all programs in a way that is suitable for your terminal.

This method of telling the UNIX system what type of terminal you are using is called setting the terminal configuration. To set your terminal configuration, type the command lines shown on the following screen, substituting the name of your terminal for *terminal_name*.

```
$ TERM=terminal_name
$ export TERM
$ tput init
```

These lines must be executed in the order shown; otherwise, they will not work. Also, this procedure must be repeated every time you log in. Therefore, most users put these lines into a file called `.profile` that is automatically executed every time they log in. For details about the `.profile` file, see Chapter 7.

The first two lines on the screen tell the UNIX system shell what type of terminal you are using. The `tput init` command line instructs your terminal to behave in ways that the UNIX system expects a terminal of that type to behave. For example, it sets the terminal's left margin and tabs, if those capabilities exist for the terminal.

The `tput` command uses the entry corresponding to your terminal in its database to make terminal dependent capabilities and information available to the shell. Because the values of these capabilities differ for each type of terminal, you must execute the `tput init` command line every time you change the TERM variable.

For each terminal type, a set of capabilities is defined in a database. This database is usually found in either the `/usr/share/lib/terminfo` or `/usr/share/lib/terminfo` directory, depending on the system.

Every system has at least one of these directories; some may have both. Your system administrator can tell you whether your system has the `terminfo` and/or the `.COREterm` directory.

The following sections describe how you can determine what *terminal_names* are acceptable. Further information about the capabilities in the `terminfo` data-base can be found on the `terminfo(4)` manual page in the *Programmer's Reference Manual*.

Acceptable Terminal Names

The UNIX system recognizes a wide range of terminal types. Before you put a terminal name into the `TERM` variable, you must make sure that your terminal is within that range.

You must also verify that the name you put into the `TERM` variable is a recognized terminal name. There are usually at least two recognized names: the name of the manufacturer and the model number. However, there are several ways to represent these names: by varying the use of uppercase and lowercase, using abbreviations, and so on. Do not put a terminal name in the `TERM` variable until you have verified that the system recognizes it.

The `tput` command provides a quick way to make sure your terminal is supported by your system. Type:

`tput -T`*terminal_name* `longname<CR>`

If your system supports your terminal it will respond with the complete name of your terminal. Otherwise, you will get an error message.

To find an acceptable name that you can put in the `TERM` variable, find a listing for your terminal in either of two directories: `/usr/share/lib/terminfo` or `/usr/lib/.COREterm`. Each of these directories contains a collection of files with single-character names. Each file, in turn, holds a list of terminal names that all begin with the name of the file. (This name can be either a letter, such as the initial A in AT&T, or a number, such as the initial 5 in 5425.) Find the file whose name matches the first character of the name of your terminal. Then list the contents of the file and look for your terminal.

You can also check with your system administrator for a list of terminals supported by your system, and the acceptable names you can put in the TERM variable.

Example

Suppose your terminal is an AT&T Teletype Model 5425. Your login is `jim` and you are currently in your home directory. First, verify that your system supports your terminal by running the `tput` command. Next, find an acceptable name for it in the `/usr/share/lib/terminfo/A` directory. The following screen shows which commands you need to do this:

```
$ tput -T5425 longname
AT&T 4425/5425
$ cd /usr/share/lib/terminfo/A
$ ls
ATT4410
ATT4415
ATT4418
ATT4424
ATT4424-2
ATT4425
ATT4426
ATT513
ATT5410
ATT5418
ATT5420
ATT5420-2
ATT5425
ATT5620
ATT610BCT
ATTPT505
$
```

Now you are ready to put the name you found, `ATT5425`, in the `TERM` variable. Whenever you do this, you must also export `TERM` and execute `tput init`.

```
$ TERM=ATT5425
$ export TERM
$ tput init
$
```

The UNIX system now knows what type of terminal you are using and will execute commands appropriately.

Windowing

The area of the terminal screen in which you work and display files is similar to the window of a house: both are devices that frame a part of a whole (whether the world or a file) for viewing. For this reason, the working area of a terminal screen is called a window. Until now we have assumed that your terminal screen has only one window (the whole screen). However, some terminals—but not the 5425—allow you to create more than one window on your screen. Each window on a windowing terminal has its own shell and functions almost exactly like a separate terminal. To help you take advantage of this feature, the UNIX system provides a set of software tools called the Basic Windowing Utilities.

We have already discussed how you can perform several tasks simultaneously with one screen by using tools such as background mode and the `at` command. With multiple windows you have the additional capability of working interactively with more than one process at a time. You can keep track of several processes at once or look at more than one file simultaneously. If you have a windowing terminal and the Basic Windowing Utilities are installed on your UNIX system, you can use the techniques described in this section to make efficient use of your terminal.

Creating Windows

To create a window you must draw it on your screen and set up the shell associated with it. The shell is the command interpreter; it allows you to work interactively with the UNIX system. Without a shell assigned to it, a window is simply a drawing on your screen.

The `layers` command allows you to draw a window on any windowing terminal. If you execute it without any arguments, you must use the mouse to draw a window. If you give specifications for windows as arguments to the `layers` command, you can program the drawing of windows and avoid using the mouse; your windows will be drawn automatically by the `layers` command.

Drawing Windows With a Mouse

The easiest way to draw windows is with the mouse. First, enter the `layers` command.

```
layers<CR>
```

Next, press a button on your mouse; a pop-up menu of layer operations will appear on the screen. Choose the menu option for drawing windows (such as `New`), and use the mouse to draw one (see the terminal owner's manual for instructions).

To create more than one window, reinvoke the menu, make your selection, and draw with the mouse. (You cannot issue the `layers` command again.) In response, the terminal draws your window(s) on the screen and then waits for commands from the terminal.

Drawing Windows Without a Mouse

If you prefer to program the drawing of windows, you must first create a file containing the number and dimensions of the windows you want. Then run the `layers` command with the name of that file as an argument, and the `-f` option. This option tells the command to read your specifications file. The general command line format is:

`layers -f` *file*`<CR>`

The specifications file must contain a line for each window you want, in the following format:

origin_x origin_y corner_x corner_y command_list

The first four fields of the line define the coordinates of the window. The *origin_x* and *origin_y* entries specify the position on the screen of the top, left-hand corner of the window, the point at which the command starts drawing. The *corner_x* and *corner_y* entries specify the position of the lower, righthand corner.

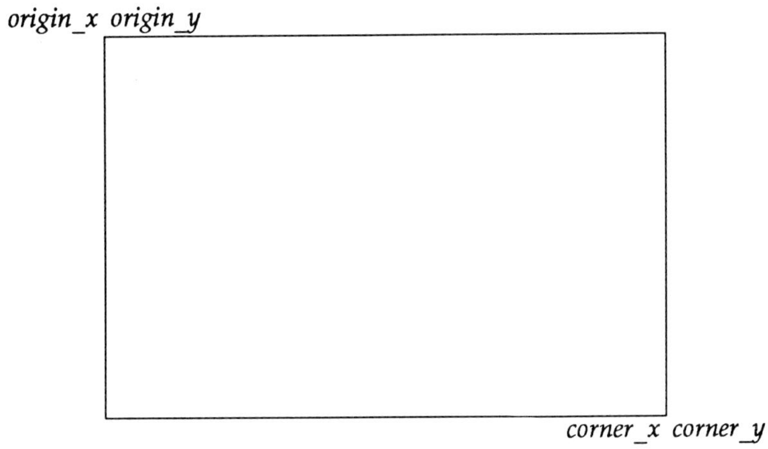

For example, to create a large rectangular window and a small one, write a specification file with the following lines:

```
0       0       650     300
650     0       792     175
```

Windows drawn to these specifications will look like this:

The fifth field of each line in your specifications file is *command_list*. Here you must enter a command that will assign a shell to the window. In this field, you can also assign a particular terminal type or an editor to the window.

To be able to assign a shell to your terminal, you must first set the shell variable. The command that allows you to assign a shell to your window is `exec` (short for execute). Enter this command with an argument specifying the type of shell you want to run in the window. To run the same type of shell that normally runs on your terminal, enter the following:

```
exec $SHELL
```

To run the standard UNIX system shell, enter

```
exec /usr/bin/sh
```

You may also want your window to provide features that are available only on a type of terminal other than the one you are using. Specify the terminal type you want and assign it to the `TERM` variable. If you include this assignment in the *commands_list* field, place it before the `exec` command. Separate all three requests (terminal type, `TERM` assignment, and `exec` command) with semi-colons, and leave spaces on both sides of each semi-colon. For example, say you want your window to provide the features of an HP 2621 terminal running the same type of shell that you normally run on your terminal. Type the *commands_list* field in your specifications file as follows:

```
hp2621 ; TERM=hp2621 ; exec ; $SHELL
```

To summarize, the specifications file must contain a line for each window that you want to create, and each line must include five fields: four coordinates for drawing the window and one command line that assigns a shell to the window. The command line may also include the assignment of a particular editor or terminal type to the window. The following example of a specifications file incorporates the previous examples of fields:

```
8      0      650    300     exec $SHELL
675    0      800    175     exec /usr/bin/sh
0      200    800    900     vi ; exec $SHELL
0      800    792    1024    hp2621 ; TERM=hp2621 ; exec $SHELL
```

When your specifications file is ready, run the `layers` command as follows:

`layers -f` *specifications_file*<CR>

The windows you have requested will be drawn on the screen, and the shells you assigned to them will be activated and ready for your commands.

Working with Layers

Once you have windows on your screens, you need to learn how to work with them: how to navigate among them, use each one as a terminal, and delete them. You can perform all these tasks by pressing different buttons on the mouse (see the owner's manual for your terminal for specific instructions).

Programmers who want to write their own programs for creating or using windows can do so with the library of functions called `libwindows`. (See the `libwindows`(3X) entry in the *Programmer's Reference Manual*.)

GLOSSARY

Glossary

address

Generally, a number that indicates the location of information in the computer's memory. In the UNIX system, the address is part of an editor command that specifies a line number or range.

append mode

A text editing mode in which the characters you type are entered as text into the text editor's buffer. In this mode you enter (append) text after the current position in the buffer. See text input mode, compare with command mode and insert mode.

argument

The element of a command line that specifies data on which a command is to operate. Arguments follow the command name and can include numbers, letters, or text strings. For instance, in the command `lp -m myfile`, `lp` is the command and `myfile` is the argument. See option.

associative array

A collection of data (an array) where individual items may be indexed (accessed) by a string, rather than by an integer as is common in most programming languages. The data item is said to be "associated" with the pair *array-name: string*, where *string* is the index.

ASCII

(pronounced "as'-kee") American Standard Code for Information Interchange, a standard for data transmission that is used in the UNIX system. ASCII assigns sets of 0s and 1s to represent 128 characters, including alphabetical characters, numerals, and standard special characters, such as #, $, %, and &.

AT&T 3B Computers

Computers manufactured by AT&T Technologies, Inc.

background

A type of program execution where you request the shell to run a command away from the interaction between you and the computer ("in the background"). While this command runs, the shell prompts you to enter other commands through the terminal. Compare with foreground.

baud rate

A measure of the speed of data transfer from a computer to a peripheral device (such as a terminal) or from one device to another. Common baud rates are 300, 1200, 4800, and 9600. As a general guide, divide a baud rate by 10 to get the approximate number of English characters transmitted each second.

buffer

A temporary storage area of the computer used by text editors to make changes to a copy of an existing file. When you edit a file, its contents are read into a buffer, where you make changes to the text. For the changes to become a part of the permanent file, you must write the buffer contents back into the file. See permanent file.

child directory

See subdirectory.

coerce

To force a data object to be treated a particular way.

command

The name of a file that contains a program that can be executed by the computer on request. Compiled programs and shell programs are forms of commands.

command file

See executable file.

command language interpreter

A program that acts as a direct interface between you and the computer. In the UNIX system, a program called the shell takes commands and translates them into a language understood by the computer.

command line

A line containing one or more commands, ended by typing a carriage return (<CR>). The line may also contain options and arguments for the commands. You type a command line to the shell to instruct the computer to perform one or more tasks.

command mode

A text editing mode in which the characters you type are interpreted as editing commands. This mode permits actions such as moving around in the buffer, deleting text, or moving lines of text. See text input mode, compare with append mode and insert mode.

concatenate

To combine two strings into one that comprises the characters of the first followed by the characters of the second.

context search

A technique for locating a specified pattern of characters (called a string) when in a text editor. Editing commands that cause a context search scan the buffer, looking for a match with the string specified in the command. See string.

control character

A nonprinting character that is entered by holding down the control key and typing a character. Control characters are often used for special purposes. For instance, when viewing a long file on your screen with the cat command, typing control-s (^s) stops the display so you can read it, and typing control-q (^q) continues the display.

current directory

The directory in which you are presently working. You have direct access to all files and subdirectories contained in your current directory. The shorthand notation for the current directory is a dot (.).

cursor

A cue printed on the terminal screen that indicates the position at which you enter or delete a character. It is usually a rectangle or a blinking underscore character.

default

An automatically assigned value or condition that exists unless you explicitly change it. For example, the shell prompt string has a default value of $ unless you change it.

delimiter

A character that logically separates words or arguments on a command line. Two frequently used delimiters in the UNIX system are the space and the tab.

diagnostic

A message printed at your terminal to indicate an error encountered while trying to execute some command or program. Generally, you need not respond directly to a diagnostic message.

directory

A type of file used to group and organize other files or directories. You cannot directly enter text or other data into a directory. (For more detail, see Appendix A, Summary of the File System.)

disk

A magnetic data storage device consisting of several round plates similar to phonograph records. Disks store large amounts of data and allow quick access to any piece of data.

electronic mail

The feature of an operating system that allows computer users to exchange written messages via the computer. The UNIX system `mail` and `mailx` commands provides electronic mail in which the addresses are the login names of users.

environment

The conditions under which you work while using the UNIX system. Your environment includes those things that personalize your login and allow you to interact in specific ways with the UNIX system and the computer. For example, your shell environment includes such things as your shell prompt string, specifics for backspace and erase characters, and commands for sending output from your terminal to the computer.

erase character

The character you type to delete the previous character you typed. The UNIX system default erase character is `#`; some users set the erase character to the `BACKSPACE` key.

escape

A means of getting into the shell from within a text editor or other program.

execute

The computer's action of running a program or command and performing the indicated operations.

executable file

A file that can be processed or executed by the computer without any further translation. When you type in the file name, the commands in the file are executed. See **shell procedure**.

file

A collection of information in the form of a stream of characters. Files may contain data, programs, or other text. You access UNIX system files by name. See **ordinary file**, **permanent file**, and **executable file**.

file name

A sequence of characters that denotes a file. (In the UNIX system, a slash character (/) cannot be used as part of a file name.)

file system

A collection of files and the structure that links them together. The UNIX file system is a hierarchical structure. (For more detail, see Appendix A, "Summary of the File System.")

filter

A command that reads the standard input, acts on it in some way, and then prints the result as standard output.

final copy

The completed, printed version of a file of text.

foreground

The normal type of command execution. When executing a command in foreground, the shell waits for one command to end before prompting you for another command. In other words, you enter something into the computer and the computer "replies" before you enter something else. Compare with **background**.

full duplex

A type of data communication in which a computer system can transmit and receive data simultaneously. Terminals and modems usually have settings for half duplex (one-way) and full duplex communication; the UNIX system uses the full-duplex setting.

full pathname

A pathname that originates at the root directory of the UNIX system and leads to a specific file or directory. Each file and directory in the UNIX system has a unique full pathname, sometimes called an absolute pathname. See pathname, compare with relative pathname.

global

A term that indicates the complete or entire file. While normal editor commands commonly act on only the first instance of a pattern in the file, global commands can perform the action on all instances in the file.

hardware

The physical machinery of a computer and any associated devices.

hidden character

One of a group of characters within the standard ASCII character set that are not printable. Characters such as backspace, escape, and <^d> are examples.

home directory

The directory in which you are located when you log in to the UNIX system; also known as your login directory.

input/output

The path by which information enters a computer system (input) and leaves the system (output). An input device that you use is the terminal keyboard and an output device is the terminal display.

insert mode

A text editing mode in which the characters you type are entered as text into the text editor's buffer. In this mode you enter (insert) text before the current position in the buffer. See text input mode, compare with append mode and command mode.

interactive

Describes an operating system (such as the UNIX system) that can handle immediate-response communication between you and the computer. In other words, you interact with the computer from moment to moment.

line editor

An editing program in which text is operated upon on a line-by-line basis within a file. Commands for creating, changing, and removing text use line addresses to determine where in the file the changes are made. Changes can be viewed after they are made by displaying the lines changed. See text editor, compare with screen editor.

login

The procedure used to gain access to the UNIX operating system.

login directory

See home directory.

login name

A string of characters used to identify a user. Your login name is different from other login names.

log off

The procedure used to exit from the UNIX operating system.

metacharacter

A subset of the set of special characters that have special meaning to the shell. The metacharacters are *, ?, and the pair [ ]. Metacharacters are used in patterns to match file names.

mode

In general, a particular type of operation (for example, an editor's append mode). In relation to the file system, a mode is an octal number used to determine who can have access to your files and what kind of access they can have. See permissions.

modem

A device that connects a terminal and a computer by way of a telephone line. A modem converts digital signals to tones and converts tones back to digital signals, allowing a terminal and a computer to exchange data over standard telephone lines.

multitasking

The ability of an operating system to execute more than one program at a time.

multiuser

The ability of an operating system to support several users on the system at the same time.

operating system

The software system on a computer under which all other software runs. The UNIX system is an operating system.

option

Special instructions that modify how a command runs. Options are a type of argument that follow a command and usually precede other arguments on the command line. By convention, an option is preceded by a minus sign (–); this distinguishes it from other arguments. You can specify more than one option for some commands given in the UNIX system. For example, in the command `ls -l -a directory`, `-l` and `-a` are options that modify the `ls` command. See argument.

ordinary file

A file, containing text or data, that is not executable. See executable file.

output

Information processed in some fashion by a computer and delivered to you by way of a printer, a terminal, or a similar device.

parameter

A special type of variable used within shell programs to access values related to the arguments on the command line or the environment in which the program is executed. See positional parameter.

parent directory

The directory immediately above a subdirectory or file in the file system organization. The shorthand notation for the parent directory is two dots (..).

parity

A method used by a computer for checking that the data received matches the data sent.

password

A code word known only to you that is called for in the login process. The computer uses the password to verify that you may indeed use the system.

pathname

A sequence of directory names separated by the slash character (/) and ending with the name of a file or directory. The pathname defines the connection path between some directory and the named file.

peripheral device

Auxiliary devices under the control of the main computer, used mostly for input, output, and storage functions. Some examples include terminals, printers, and disk drives.

permanent file

The data stored permanently in the file system structure. To change a permanent file, you can make use of a text editor, which maintains a temporary work space, or buffer, apart from the permanent files. Once changes have been made to the buffer, they must be written to the permanent file to make the changes permanent. See **buffer**.

permissions

Access modes, associated with directories and files, that permit or deny system users the ability to read, write, and/or execute the directories and files. You determine the permissions for your directories and files by changing the mode for each one with the chmod command.

pipe

A method of redirecting the output of one command to be the input of another command. It is named for the character | that redirects the output. For example, the shell command `who | wc -l` pipes output from the `who` command to the `wc` command, telling you the total number of people logged into your UNIX system.

pipeline

A series of filters separated by | (the pipe character). The output of each filter becomes the input of the next filter in the line. The last filter in the pipeline writes to its standard output, or may be redirected to a file. See **filter**.

positional parameters

Numbered variables used within a shell procedure to access the strings specified as arguments on the command line invoking the shell procedure. The name of the shell procedure is positional parameter `$0`. See **variable** and **shell procedure**.

prompt

A cue displayed at your terminal by the shell, telling you that the shell is ready to accept your next request. The prompt can be a character or a series of characters. The UNIX system default prompt is the dollar sign character (`$`).

printer

An output device that prints the data it receives from the computer on paper.

process

Generally a program that is at some stage of execution. In the UNIX system, it also refers to the execution of a computer environment, including contents of memory, register values, name of the current directory, status of files, information recorded at login time, and various other items.

program

The instructions given to a computer on how to do a specific task. Programs are user-executable software.

read-ahead capability

The ability of the UNIX system to read and interpret your input while sending output information to your terminal in response to previous input. The UNIX system separates input from output and processes each correctly.

relative pathname

The pathname to a file or directory which varies in relation to the directory in which you are currently working. See pathname, compare with full pathname.

remote system

A system other than the one on which you are working.

root

The source directory of all files and directories in the file system; designated by the slash character (/).

screen editor

An editing program in which text is operated on relative to the position of the cursor on a visual display. Commands for entering, changing, and removing text involve moving the cursor to the area to be altered and performing the necessary operation. Changes are viewed on the terminal display as they are made. See text editor, compare with line editor.

search pattern

See string.

search string

See string.

secondary prompt

A cue displayed at your terminal by the shell to tell you that the command typed in response to the primary prompt is incomplete. The UNIX system default secondary prompt is the "greater than" character (>).

shell

A UNIX system program that handles the communication between you and the computer. The shell is also known as a command language interpreter because it translates your commands into a language understandable by the computer. The shell accepts commands and causes the appropriate program to be executed. The `sh(1)` and `ksh(1)` entries in the *User's Reference Manual* describe two of the available shells.

shell procedure

An executable file that is not a compiled program. A shell procedure calls the shell to read and execute commands contained in a file. This lets you store a sequence of commands in a file for repeated use. It is also called a shell program or command file. See executable file.

silent character

See hidden character.

software

Instructions and programs that tell the computer what to do. Contrast with hardware.

source code

The uncompiled version of a program written in a language such as C or Pascal. The source code must be translated to machine language by a program known as a compiler before the computer can execute the program.

special character

A character having special meaning to the a program. Shell special characters are used for common shell functions such as file redirection, piping, background execution, and file name expansion. Shell special characters include <, >, `|`, `;`, `&`, `*`, `?`, `[`, and `]`. Editors such as `ed` and `vi` also have special characters.

special file

A file (called a device driver) used as an interface to an input/output device, such as a user terminal, a disk drive, or a line printer.

standard error

An open file that is normally connected directly to a primary output device, such as a terminal printer or screen. Error messages and other diagnostic output normally goes to this file and then to the output device. You can redirect the standard error output into another file instead of to the printer or screen; use an argument in the form 2> *file*. Error output will then go to the specified file.

standard input

An open file that is normally connected directly to the keyboard. Standard input to a command normally goes from the keyboard to this file and then into the shell. You can redirect the standard input to come from another file instead of from the keyboard; use an argument in the form < *file*. Input to the command will then come from the specified file.

standard output

An open file that is normally connected directly to a primary output device, such as a terminal printer or screen. Standard output from the computer normally goes to this file and then to the output device. You can redirect the standard output into another file instead of to the printer or screen; use an argument in the form > *file*. Output will then go to the specified file.

string

Designation for a particular group or pattern of characters, such as a word or phrase, that may contain special characters. In a text editor, a context search interprets the special characters and attempts to match the specified pattern with a string in the editor buffer.

string variable

A sequence of characters that can be the value of a shell variable. See variable.

subdirectory

A directory pointed to by a directory one level above it in the file system organization; also called a child directory.

system administrator

The person who monitors and controls the computer on which your UNIX system runs; sometimes referred to as a super-user.

terminal

An input/output device connected to a computer system, usually consisting of a keyboard with a video display or a printer. A terminal allows you to give the computer instructions and to receive information in response.

text editor

Software for creating, changing, or removing text with the aid of a computer. Most text editors have two modes--an input mode for typing in text and a command mode for moving or modifying text. Two examples are the UNIX system editors `ed` and `vi`. See line editor and screen editor.

text formatter

A program that prepares a file of text for printed output. To make use of a text formatter, your file must also contain some special commands for structuring the final copy. These special commands tell the formatter to justify margins, start new paragraphs, set up lists and tables, place figures, and so on. Two text formatters available on the UNIX system are `nroff` and `troff`.

text input mode

A text editing mode in which the characters you type are entered as text into the text editor's buffer. To execute a command, you must leave text input mode. See command mode, compare with append mode and insert mode.

timesharing

A method of operation in which several users share a common computer system seemingly simultaneously. The computer interacts with each user in sequence, but the high-speed operation makes it seem that the computer is giving each user its complete attention.

tool

A package of software programs.

tty

Historically, the abbreviation for a Teletype® terminal. Today, it is generally used to denote any user terminal.

user

Anyone who uses a computer or an operating system.

user-defined

Something determined by the user.

user-defined variable

A named variable given a value by the user. See variable.

UNIX system

A general-purpose, multiuser, interactive, time-sharing operating system developed by AT&T Bell Laboratories. The UNIX system allows limited computer resources to be shared by several users and efficiently organizes the user's interface to a computer system.

utility

Software used to carry out routine functions or to assist a programmer or system user in establishing routine tasks.

variable

A symbol whose value may change. In the shell, a variable is a symbol representing some string of characters. Variables may be used in an interactive shell as well as within a shell procedure. Within a shell procedure, positional parameters and keyword parameters are two forms of variables. (Keyword parameters are discussed in detail in the "Shell Tutorial" chapter.)

video display terminal

A terminal that uses a television-like screen (a monitor) to display information. A video display terminal can display information much faster than printing terminals.

visual editor

See screen editor.

working directory

See current directory.

INDEX

Index

G

H

I

K

L

M

N

O

P

R

V

W